INDIA FROM LATIN AMERICA

This book studies the economic history of India and traces the Indian path of development from a Latin American framework and perspective. Despite sharing many historical and geological similarities, dialogue between the young democracies of Latin America and the Indian subcontinent is still extremely scarce.

The volume builds a common research agenda for the economic development of the Global South. It offers Latin American insights and highlights novelties and commonalities the region shares with India's economic development. It pays special attention to the (geo)political, technological, financial, and institutional aspects related to the specific geographical and demographical features of the Indian subcontinent.

A step towards strengthening the dialogue on economic development in the Global South, this book will be of interest to scholars and researchers of heterodox economics, Indian economy, comparative economics, macroeconomics, political economy, economic history, development studies, Latin American studies, and South Asian studies.

Manuel Gonzalo graduated with magna cum laude in economics from UBA (Universidad de Buenos Aires), Argentina. He has a master's degree in economics and industrial development from UNGS (Universidad Nacional de General Sarmiento), Argentina and a doctoral degree in economics from UFRJ (Universidade Federal de Rio de Janeiro), Brazil. He is Adjunct Professor at the Degree on Development Economics of the UNQ (Universidad Nacional de Quilmes), Associate Professor at the school of economics of UNDEC (Universidad Nacional de Chilecito), and Co-Coordinator at the South Asia working group of CARI (Consejo Argentino para las Relaciones Internacionales). He has 20 years of experience in doing research, fieldworks, and giving classes and lectures at different universities of Argentina, Brazil, and India (UNQ, UNGS, UNDEC, UNSAM, UNTREF, UNCAUS, UTDT, FLACSO, UNDEF, ISEN, UFRJ, FIOCRUZ, JNU, etc.) mainly on comparative development, innovation and entrepreneurial systems, and industrial, STI and international cooperation policy. He was visiting researcher at the Center for Development Studies (CDS), Jawaharlal Nehru University (JNU), Kerala, India, and at the Research Network on Local Productive and Innovative Systems (Redesist), Economics Institute (IE), UFRJ, Rio de Janeiro, Brazil. He assesses Latin American governments, firms, think tanks, and international organisms in building their relationship with India, South Asia, and the Global South.

INDIA FROM LATIN AMERICA

Peripherisation, Statebuilding, and Demand-Led Growth

Manuel Gonzalo

Routledge
Taylor & Francis Group
LONDON AND NEW YORK

First published 2023
by Routledge
4 Park Square, Milton Park, Abingdon, Oxon OX14 4RN

and by Routledge
605 Third Avenue, New York, NY 10158

Routledge is an imprint of the Taylor & Francis Group, an informa business

British Library Cataloguing-in-Publication Data
A catalogue record for this book is available from the British Library

Library of Congress Cataloging-in-Publication Data
Names: Gonzalo, Manuel (Professor of economics), author.
Title: India from Latin America : peripherization, statebuilding, and demand-led growth / Manuel Gonzalo.
Description: Abingdon, Oxon ; New York, NY : Routledge, 2023. | Includes bibliographical references and index.
Identifiers: LCCN 2022022743 (print) | LCCN 2022022744 (ebook) | ISBN 9780367542023 (hardback) | ISBN 9781032367309 (paperback) | ISBN 9781003091752 (ebook)
Subjects: LCSH: Economic development—India. | Economic development—Latin America. | India—Economic policy. | Latin America—Economic policy.
Classification: LCC HC435 .G646 2023 (print) | LCC HC435 (ebook) | DDC 338.954—dc23/eng/20220525
LC record available at https://lccn.loc.gov/2022022743
LC ebook record available at https://lccn.loc.gov/2022022744

ISBN: 978-0-367-54202-3 (hbk)
ISBN: 978-1-032-36730-9 (pbk)
ISBN: 978-1-003-09175-2 (ebk)

DOI: 10.4324/9781003091752

Typeset in Sabon
by Apex CoVantage, LLC

CONTENTS

FIGURES

TABLES

FOREWORD

The understanding of the relationship between structural change and processes of economic and social transformations has been pursued for centuries. In the nineteenth century, with the Industrial Revolution in England and the deepening of colonisation by European countries, the debate on this relationship has acquired novel characteristics. In colonial countries the debate had two opposing facets. On one hand, scholars in the tradition of political economy have emphasised how the characteristics of the capitalist mode of production – elements and activities necessary to produce and reproduce real, material life – result in class conflict in capitalist societies, hence hampering the possibilities of virtuous processes of development (Karl Marx), and have discussed how internal processes of structural change could be triggered in European laggard countries (Frederic List). On the other hand, for colonised countries in the "South", a general idea supported predominantly by neoclassical economists was that "North" countries would bring "development", in a typical "white men's burden" way.

With a few exceptions, up to the end of the Second World War, these opposing visions conformed to the debate on development. Among these exceptions, the Indian School of Political Economy that emerged at the end of the nineteenth century stands out prominently. Authors such as Mahadev Govind Ranade and Dadabhai Naoroji, identified as early nationalists, frustrated by what was happening in colonial India and dissatisfied with the kind of Western economics taught at Western-style universities there, developed new approaches. Even though they utilised Western economic ideas and Western notion of development, they argued that India needed a proper local system to develop.

All this changed after the end of the Second World War in the twentieth century, when Economics of Development as a specific field within Economics emerged. The development debate in the North followed the neoclassical paradigm – market imperfections, price distortions, externalities, and so on – mingled with Keynes' seminal contributions on capital accumulation and distribution. Ragnar Nurkse, Rosentein Rodan, and Arthur Lewis were the key scholars in this approach. Even though Lewis, arguably its most important author, with his dualistic model recognised the importance of previous works of classical economists, such as Marx with his theory of primitive capitalist accumulation, they were bounded by the neoclassical paradigm.

The Latin American structuralist school that emerged in the late 1940s–early 1950s contradicted such approach and introduced a truly political economy view of development processes. One of the main characteristics of the Latin American structuralist school was the central role it gave to the importance of endogenising technology in the underdeveloped economies.

Furtado was the pioneer in dealing with this theme, which was – and still is – absent from the neoclassical work on development. His focus was on the origins and characteristics of technical progress in European industrialisation, emphasising its influence on the reproduction and transformation of capitalist society and the determination of the historical process through which the hierarchies of regions and countries are formed (Furtado, 1961). In 1954, he pointed out that the significant modifications generated by technical progress could only be captured through "a global vision of the national system" and in its relations with the "environment that controls and influences it". He insisted, therefore, that it was necessary to understand them as a whole, warning that it was not possible to capture their nature and impact by limiting the analysis to the macroeconomic or microeconomic level, and especially isolating it from its social character.

Besides exploring the importance of technical progress for the development of advanced countries and its social character, Latin American structuralism argued that its historical evolution was linked to the underdevelopment of the periphery. Furtado pointed out that underdevelopment was not a sequential or linear process. It is a specific historical process and not a stage through which economies that have already reached a higher degree of development have necessarily passed.

Hence, for the Latin American structuralist school, development in the centre generates underdevelopment in the periphery. Remarking that the evolution of the capitalist system produces, on one hand, systemic and virtuous development and, on the other, underdevelopment and subordination, the Latin American structuralist school noted that the effect of its expansion in the peripheral countries created hybrid structures, one part of which tended to behave like a capitalist system, the other part to remain within the pre-existing archaic structure, amplifying the asymmetrical development conditions. In a period when industrialisation was perceived as a shortcut to development, Furtado stressed that if a country industrialises and grows without breaking with inequality, the tendency would be its reproduction and deepening, if we insisted on copying the models of technology, life and policies of the central countries.

Such conceptual pillars together with more recent Latin American contributions on the role of the state in the economy and inter-state competition in the finance-dominated global capitalism of today, the neo-Schumpeterian broad understanding of the National Systems of Innovation (NSI), and the Keynesian-Kaleckian-Sraffian principle of effective demand are combined in an extremely innovative manner by Manuel Gonzalo to analyse the long-term historical process of transformation of the economy and society of the Indian subcontinent.

Gonzalo's book is a remarkable work arguably breaking new ground on the development debate. It discusses India's economic and social transformation in three parts: Indian peripherisation, statebuilding, and demand-led growth, each one conducted within the above-mentioned framework. It blends, in a systemic way, time (history), space (geography), and power relations, all essential to understand processes of development and structural transformation in a proper way.

In his final chapter, Gonzalo states that, with this book, he hopes to contribute towards the development of a common economics development research agenda oriented to the Global South needs, potentialities, and challenges. I am absolutely convinced that he has more than succeeded in this endeavour.

I am certain that readers interested in understanding the complex nature of long-run processes of development will enjoy reading this essential book.

Dr. José E. Cassiolato
Redesist, IE, Universidad Federal de Rio de Janeiro (UFRJ)
July 2021, Rio de Janeiro, Brazil

FOREWORD

In 2005, while in Research and Information System for Developing Countries (RIS), I got an opportunity to associate with the preparation of the First India, Brazil South Africa (IBSA) Economic Cooperation report for which I proposed the title "The Trinity of the South". IBSA partnership has been moving firmly forward as a trinity with different forums therein, including the IBSA academic forum at the instance of Sachin Chaturvedi, RIS. Indeed, there are other attempts also in this direction. Especially notable has been the publication of a set of books on Brazil, Russia, India, China, and South Africa (BRICS) by José E. Cassiolato, Rasigan Maharajh, and other colleagues at the instance of Globelics with the support of International Development Research Centre (IDRC). Yet, there is reason to believe that much more could be done to facilitate learning from each other's experience that necessitates a holistic analysis of the relevance of Latin American experience to any of the countries in the IBSA group.

It is at this juncture that this brilliant academic initiative by Manuel Gonzalo to understanding India's development experience using a Latin American lens assumes importance. The purpose of book is to articulate the long-term development path of India from a Latin American perspective within a broad canvas of the (geo)political, technological, financial, and institutional aspects related to the specific features of the Indian subcontinent. In doing so, the study offers certain novel insights and reflections based on the Latin American experience. It also contributes towards the development of a common development research agenda oriented to the needs, challenges, and the potential of the Global South. The present book, emerged out of the PhD thesis of Manuel, based on his extensive field work and interactions in India, indicates his ability to grow beyond PhD work and make use of the broad-based learning acquired to reflect on issues of wider relevance.

This eminently articulated volume with a historical perspective dating back to the days of Vasco da Gama till the contemporary times, to the best of my knowledge, is first of its kind. The process of deindustrialisation that India subjected to wherein her share in global manufacturing declined from about 25% during early 1700 to less than 2.5% at the time of independence has been subjected to much discussion by economic historians from India and abroad. Viewed from the Latin American perspective, the much-explored drain of resources and deindustrialisation of India during the colonial period have been articulated as the process of peripherisation with much wider ramification for the development process. The second part of the book analyses emergence of the Indian state and the Indian National System of Innovation (NSI), in the context of the colonial rule, and further highlights the Indian statebuilding and as it evolved over time. The evolution of the NSI between independence in 1947 and the external crises of 1989–1990 has been divided into three phases: Nehruvian phase, Indira Gandhi's first phase, and the 1980s – first led by Indira Gandhi and then by her son, Rajiv Gandhi. The third part deals with the period since liberalisation of 1991. Drawing extensively from the previous studies and based on his empirical analysis, the reader is provided with a scholarly analysis of the different dimensions of India's higher growth, underlying factors, and its implications on poverty and inequality. It highlights the role of autonomous demand based on the upper class/caste consumption, global capital inflows, and government and private investment in infrastructure, driven by energy and urbanisation pressures. Other factors like the Indian Diaspora in the US and the complementarity between Indian capabilities and the US Information and Communications Technology (ICT) outsourcing business opportunities also played their role.

His attempt at examining India's development trajectory using a Latin American lens has been highly rewarding. As the new century is touted as Asia's century and India is setting ambitious targets to emerge as the second-largest economy in the world, the experience of Latin American countries, once acclaimed as the star performers and today caught up in deindustrialisation and middle-income trap, might be of much relevance. This book tends to suggest that India's higher growth under globalisation has been fuelled by the autonomous consumption, direct government expenditure, and investment in infrastructure, which are built on the three pillars of Indian business groups, multinational firms, and the government (upper segments of the bureaucracy and the main political parties). While the gross domestic product (GDP) boomed, manufacturing lagged much behind and inequality reached unacceptable levels. India needs to ensure that the country is not caught up in premature deindustrialisation, confined to the lower middle-income trap, and the prosperity is shared. On the whole, this excellent analytical contribution offers fresh insights on India's development trajectory and is a must read for the academia, policymakers, and all those interested in understanding India's development experience from a long historical perspective.

Dr. K.J. Joseph
Director, Gulati Institute of Finance and
Taxation (GIFT)/President of Globelics
August 2021, Thiruvananthapuram, Kerala, India

FOREWORD

From my current task as Deputy Director of the Asian Affairs Committee of the Argentine Council for International Relations (CARI, Argentina), I share with Dr. Manuel Gonzalo similar tasks as a teacher and researcher in various Argentine universities, while we have also shared activities within the framework of the Latin American Association for Asian and African Studies (ALADAA), an association that brings together Latin American researchers and students who address issues related to Asia and Africa, of which I was General Secretary until recently. Our mutual interest in studying India and South Asia brought us in touch and cemented our friendship.

The book that Manuel Gonzalo presents proposes to develop a long-term narrative of the development of India, from a Latin American perspective, which includes methodological and conceptual specificities, concluding with reflections on the Indian experience from Latin America, the current and future relevance of the Indian Ocean, and the identification of potential lines of research to strengthen the dialogue among the Global South scholars.

The author's commitment, both in the research reported in the book and in the publication of the work, shows a fundamental need in the intercultural dialogic framework: the need to know the other (which, in turn, enables a return on oneself) as well as a permanent critical monitoring of this dialogue. In fact, the large number of current imaginaries about the other societies with which we interact both at the level of collective actors of all kinds and individuals requires the permanent study and monitoring of various sources of information, which allow us to undo the fallacies, stereotypes, and the myths to be able to approach the others in a less uncertain way.

In the case of India, one of the most relevant emerging actors of today, Manuel Gonzalo's proposal contributes greatly to the reflection on that country, from a Latin American perspective, which adds originality in its production inviting us to continue studying and questioning the understanding of India in its economy and its integrality, revisiting the methodological and theoretical frameworks that we use for it.

Perhaps the greatest attraction of India for authors who approach it from any perspective is that it always invites the challenge of another return to it in permanent novelty (new elements to consider, new methodological perspectives with which to approach, new categories with which to rethink it, etc.), for its diversity, trying to get closer to it more and better, returning in that dynamic, new own meanings. In this context, the task of Manuel Gonzalo, already initialised his passage in this sense, is fully accomplished and is a considerable contribution to interested readers and scholars of India, in its originality, its rich systematisation of literature and data on the subject considered, and also dialoguing with Indian and South Asian productions about it.

I hope that this book will become reference and teaching material for teachers, researchers, students, and stakeholders in India. In my case, it only remains to proudly enjoy accompanying such a challenging task and invite you to do the same.

Dr. Lía Rodríguez de la Vega
Asian Affairs Committee, Argentine Council
for International Relations (CARI)
August 2021, Buenos Aires, Argentina

FOREWORD

One of the great debates in contemporary economic history is known as "The Great Divergence": the process that, since the nineteenth century, differentiated the economic performance of a handful of Western European countries and Dominions of the former British colonisation, such as the US, from the rest of the world. The divergence ranges from living conditions, industrialisation, and military power. The trajectory of the Industrial Revolution in each territory, its temporal and geographical sequence, as well as its differentiated impacts on the global economic organisation through international trade and finance largely explain the issues raised by the debate.

Political organisations around the world were not unscathed by this transformation either. The sudden commercial, financial, and, especially, military dynamism of the Western European powers were used as tools for aggression and military interventions that ended with the establishment of colonial or semi-colonial regimes in almost all Eurasian territories. Likewise, economic forces tended to reinforce the industrial power of the West to the detriment of Eastern societies, which suffered severe processes of "deindustrialisation", or to be more precise, loss of complexity of their economic organisations.

In the Latin American context, the structuralist tradition – a theoretical conception born in the post-war period under the aegis of the Economic Commission for Latin America (ECLAC) – had thought a theoretical framework that interprets this divergence. According to Raúl Prebisch, a leading figure of structuralism, at the end of the nineteenth century, an economic structure characterised by a centre-periphery duality was consolidated. The way in which each country or region was incorporated into the international division of labour during the nineteenth century marked its long-run trajectory. Exports to the world market were the main sources of social power for the political coalitions, which intervened in the statebuilding process in Latin America. These states were organised, both in economic and political terms, following an "outward" commercial orientation. No political coalition obtained its power from local economic sources in order to drive the statebuilding process in Latin America. International trade and British finance were the main sources of taxation and funding and were also foreign sales that attracted investment, modern technologies, and immigrants.

This process had three fundamental consequences for Latin America. First, most of the wars that led to the formation of states, as well as the conflicts that followed their consolidation, were based on the dispute for control of the ports and navigable rivers through which export and import commodities circulated. Later, other disputes were related with the layout of the railway lines that redefined the accumulation spaces in each territory. Second, as productive structures oriented almost exclusively abroad were consolidated, the social and political organisation became extremely vulnerable to the ups and downs of international trade and finance, such as terms of trade falls or indebtedness cycles. These processes always were highly sensitive to fluctuations in central economies. Third, the phenomenon of structural heterogeneity, that is, the enormous differences in productivity and international insertion between exporting activities and the rest of the territories and populations, led to the formation of dual economic societies. These organisations were characterised by income inequalities, regional asymmetries, and, in certain cases, the complete disengagement of the most advantaged from the rest of the country, the so-called enclave economies.

Although the main focus of Manuel Gonzalo's text is what has happened in the Indian subcontinent since this period, the theoretical developments and questions formulated by Latin American structuralism are present in his work. Unlike Latin America, the insertion of the subcontinent into the global commercial order homogenised by the Europeans did not occur simultaneously with the formation of (at least formally) independent states but with open colonisation by the British Empire. Also unlike Latin America, the subcontinent's per capita endowment of natural resources was extremely low in order to grow on a natural resources export-led model. Simultaneously, the competition from British manufactures made cheaper by the technical revolution had devastating effects on the complexity and diversification of the subcontinent's production. In South Asia, unlike Latin America, very competitive manufacturing activities were destroyed by British competition, as well as workers with technical knowledges, jobs, exports, and commercial networks. The effects in Asia were devastating: deindustrialisation was compounded by deurbanisation and the consolidation of an economic order whose structural heterogeneity took on unimaginable scales in Latin America.

The Asian economies lacked natural resources and were incomparably more sophisticated in manufactures than the European colonies of America. By this reason, the impact of the Industrial Revolution in Asia was far more devastating. Latin America was endowed with a relative abundance of natural resources and was very poor in manufactures. This circumstance explains, at least until the end of the Second World War, the highly differentiated performances of the Latin American and Asian peripheries. The former was born peripheral, since its nation states were successful variants of the colonial period. The second was turned peripheral, by a process of forced peripherisation. Since the independence of the Indian subcontinent and the Chinese Revolution, a reverse of fortunes began between both regions. While Latin America remains mired in its peripheral "destiny", Asia tends to resume its ancestral centrality. Gonzalo's work is enriching because he offers an original look of the Indian subcontinent from the most relevant problems and theoretical characterisations of Latin America.

Dr. Eduardo Crespo
Federal University of Rio de Janeiro (UFRJ), Brazil &
National University of Moreno (UNM), Argentina
August 2021, Buenos Aires, Argentina

ACKNOWLEDGEMENTS

This book is a direct sub-product of my PhD thesis in Economics at the Institute of Economy (IE) of the Federal University of Rio de Janeiro (UFRJ), Brazil. It has been an intense, rich, and diverse transit mainly between Rio de Janeiro, India, and Buenos Aires. During this journey, different people, institutions, and spaces have been relevant.

José E. Cassiolato has been a main emotional, material, and conceptual support. Eduardo Crespo has functioned as a permanent intellectual stimulus. K.J. Joseph has been a link with India and a fundamental promoter for the publication of this book.

In Brazil, RedeSist has provided me a stimulating and affectionate working group. I would particularly like to highlight João, my travel and discussion partner; Marina, for her support at key moments; Gabi, for her spirit; Helena Lastres, for her permanent good vibes; and Fabi, Tati, and Maz, for their affection and support.

The group of Argentines from the effective demand in Rio has also been important: Gachi, Facu, Lauti, and Grajaú; Marga, Andrés, Luki, and the *asados vermelhos*; Amico, Marcela, and the *Baixo Bota*; and Javier's birthdays in Leblón.

I will remember different chats between *pingados* and *queijos quente* with my colleagues at the Teatro de Arena. I would like to highlight the moments shared with the *pata mineira*: Faustinho, Cabula, Gabi, and Chico Bento, and the *churrascos* at Rodrigo, Kaio, and Miguel's house. Also the talks with Guillerme Haluska and the lunches and outings with Sergio Páez. Thanks to Pedro Navarrete for receiving me in Brasilia and to Patrick for showing me Petrópolis.

Some professors have been formative: Mario Possas, Carlos Medeiros, and Franklin Serrano. The courses of Jaques Kerstenetzky and Luiz Carlos Prado have contributed through their approach and bibliography. Fiori, Numa, and PEPI have also contributed to develop the "inter-state competition" approach.

Maria's apartment in Paulo Barreto and Voluntarios da Patria has been the place where I lived in Brazil, wrote most of this book, and that allowed me to know the streets of Botafogo and Rio de Janeiro.

In India, K.J. Joseph has facilitated my stay at the Center for Development Studies (CDS), Kerala, and Professor Nagaraj, of the Indira Gandhi Institute of Development Research (IGIDR), has been a gateway to the Indian economic structure. I must also thank Professors Bala Subrahmanya and H.S. Krishna from the Indian Institute of Science (IIS), Bangalore, and José Thomas and Dinesh Abrol, for their support in Delhi. Among friends and colleagues on campuses I would like to highlight the moments shared with Rajesh GK, Kashif Mansoor, Chandra Shekar, Smruti Ranjan Sahoo, Anurag Anand, Papaiah Basu, Nimita Pandey, Sohan Sha, Sarfaraz Hamid, and between many other Indian faces.

Globelics has been one of my main spaces of international academic insertion in these years. It is nice to meet Olga Mikheeva, Rajesh, Nadja Nordling, Carlos Gonzalo Acevedo, Kenneth Fung, Patty Cabero, and Lourenço Faria, among other alumni. Rasigan Maharajh and Keun Lee have been two generous people.

Upon my return to Argentina, Lía Rodríguez from the Working Group on India and South Asia of the Argentine Council for International Relations (CARI), Carlos Moneta of the National University of Tres de Febrero (UNTREF), and Paloma Ochoa from ICBC Foundation have been among the first to get interested in and to support my work on India. Rubén Ascua, José Borello, and the UNRAF (Universidad Nacional de Rafaela) have also contributed to the 2019 fieldwork.

Marian, Fede, Laura, Moldo, Exe, and Tacho have been permanent companions. Marce, Chacha, and Nico are the friends who are there.

Regarding the actual format of the book, Rosaura Flynn has contributed with her aesthetic sense through the illustrations and maps. Brian and Inés Casserly have contributed to the English revision. The Institute of Industry (IDEI) at UNGS and Prodem have contributed to fund this revision. From Routledge India, Shashank Shekhar Sinha, Antara Ray Chaudhary, and Anvitaa Bajaj have worked in the book edition.

To my parents, for giving me the training and support.

To Kalanda, for being such a nice person and accompanying and helping me during this process.

The PhD would not have been done without the financial support of the National University of General Sarmiento (UNGS), the National Council for Scientific and Technological Development (CNPQ), the Ministry of Science and Technology of Brazil, the Federal University of Rio de Janeiro (UFRJ), and Coordenação de Aperfeiçoamento de Pessoal de Nível Superior (CAPES). This book could not be written without the existence of the public education in Argentina, Brazil, and India.

INTRODUCTION

The main objective of this book is to present a long-term understanding of the Indian path of economic development from a Latin American perspective, paying special attention to the (geo)political, technological, financial, and institutional aspects related to the specific geographical and demographical features of the Indian subcontinent. Even though the Indian and the Central and South American subcontinents share a common geological origin and experienced the Global North colonial penetration and colonisation, and that most of the countries of the subcontinents are young democracies that shared a Non-Alignment geopolitical posture during the Cold War and are now part of the Global South, with an increasing trade and investment flux during the twenty-first century, mutual understanding and, mainly, systemic research efforts between the economic development scholars of both subcontinents are still extremely scarce. Indeed, even though there have been a few comparative studies that include some countries of both continents,[1] until today, there have been no studies like the one presented in this book: adopting a broad view of the Indian long-term path of development with Latin American conceptual and methodological lenses (and elaborated by a Latin American author).

Consequently, this study can be particularly useful both to Latin American development economic scholars interested in the Indian and South Asian path of development and to the Asian and South Asian ones who would like to increase their understanding and knowledge of some Latin American conceptual insights and authors, mainly on development economics. As there are some structural issues and historical periods of the Indian path of development that have similarities to the Latin American ones, interesting and useful conceptual and historical cross-fertilisations between both experiences can be extracted. In more general terms, we hope that this book will help to enhance the dialogue on economic development among Global South scholars. This one is an initial and partial step, with a lot of work still to be done.

Intellectual activity cannot be divided into watertight regions. There are influences as well as theoretical streams between scholars and from traditions

DOI: 10.4324/9781003091752-1

from different parts of the world. Therefore, the Latin American "flavour" of our approach is neither isolated nor closed. The theoretical and methodological framework that will be presented is mainly based on the contributions of different Latin American authors, who have been inspired to discuss the Latin American problems and economic development issues but, at the same time, are part of different global political economy traditions. Indeed, despite this Latin American approach (and the Latin American origin of the author of this book), an important and significant challenge and research effort was done (including a six-year deep exploration of the Indian literature and an extensive fieldwork) to capture and understand the main Indian historical processes that will be presented and discussed, under their own circumstances and implications, without trying to force them into a Latin American conceptual "box". Thus, regarding the organisation of the book, Chapters 2, 3, 5, 7, and 8 are focused on the Indian historical experience, mainly based on Indian authors and documents, while Chapters 1, 4, 6, 9, and the Final Remarks explicitly aim to introduce Latin American insights, authors, and cross-fertilisation.

Our Latin American approach, further explored in Chapter 1, is based on three main conceptual/methodological roots: 1) the structuralism of the Economic Commission for Latin America and the Caribbean (ECLAC), with the specific contributions of Prebisch, Furtado, and Pinto; 2) some Latin American contributions on the role of the state in the economy and inter-state competition in global capitalism, such as the ones by Fiori and Medeiros, blended with the broad understanding of the National Systems of Innovation (NSI), based on the work of Cassiolato, Lastres, and the RedeSist (Rede de Pesquisa em Arranjos e Sistemas Produtivos e Inovativos Locais); and 3) the Brazilian conceptual path from the Keynesian-Kaleckian principle of effective demand to the Sraffian supermultiplier, with Tavares, Possas, and Serrano as main references of the University of Campinas (UNICAMP) and Federal University of Rio de Janeiro (UFRJ) schools of political economy.

We have been inspired by long-term methodological approaches. In international literature, mainly Braudel's *Mediterranean* (1949), Polanyi's *Great Transformation* (1944), Jared Diamond's *Guns, Germs and Steel* (1997), and Freeman and Louçã's (2001) *As Time Goes By: From the Industrial Revolution to the Information Revolution*. Regarding the Indian discussion, among others, we have extensively consulted the classic works of Panikkar (1953) on Asia and the Western dominance, Chaudhury's work (1985) on the Indian Ocean, and the more recent global history contributions of Nayyar (2013) and Roy (2012a). As for Latin America, the most influencing long-term narratives that inspired this book have been the ones of Furtado (1959, 1969) and Caio Prado (1942) on the Brazilian engagement with global capitalism and the books of Ferrer (1963) and Schvarzer (1996) on the Argentinean economy and industrial long-term development, respectively. In this context, in particular, we will work under the ECLAC's "historical structuralist" methodological approach (further explained in Chapter 1).

In our narrative we have used maps, quotations of other authors, and illustrations. Maps have been necessary because of the relevance given to geography in the understanding of the Indian development and to orientate the non-Indian reader in the Indian subcontinent. The use of quotations as an intertext narrative resource is used to present some key ideas and authors in their own words, highlighting the Indian scholars' contributions. Illustrations are used to give some insight, contextualise, and give a break to the reader. Regarding the research on India, it has been mainly based on a) an extensive literature (secondary sources) review; b) the use of primary sources, mainly from different Indian and international organisations, official publications, and statistics; and c) a fieldwork in India of over four months conducted in 2016, and another one of over one month in 2019, interviewing different Indian key sources such as professors, policymakers, and researchers.

Focusing on the subject and content of this book, there should not be much argument on the relevance of developing an accurate understanding of the Indian economic path of development, given India's place in contemporary global capitalism. With growth accelerating since the 1980s, in the first quarter of the twenty-first century, India's gross domestic product (GDP) has been growing at an impressive 6.5% average rate. At present, Asia is the most dynamic continent in terms of urbanisation, weaponisation, GDP growth, infrastructure development, energy needs and investment, and so on. In this context, India is experiencing a slow but constant urbanisation process with a total population of around 1.3 billion and a growing middle class. India occupies the main place in the Indian Ocean and is a central geopolitical and geoeconomical player for the US, China, and Middle East countries. India is one of the top five countries of the world in terms of military expenditure, experiencing a process of modernisation of its military capabilities. But fundamentally, the Indian continent and its people have a civilizational history.

Although not so discussed among Western scholars until the beginning of the twenty-first century, with the expansion of the Islamic world in the seventh century, the Indian Ocean was one of the most important crossroads of trade and wealth in the world (Chaudhury, 1985; Roy, 2012a). The African, the Indo-Arabic, the Hindu, the Hindonesian, and the Chinese shared the trade ports of the Indian Ocean (Chaudhury, 1985; Subrahmanyam, 1990). The Indian Ocean waters were open to trade and developed different market forms. At the beginning of the eighteenth century, Indian textiles clothed millions of Indians, Southeast Asians, fashionable men and women in Europe, American slaves and peons, Africans, and others throughout the Middle East (Riello and Roy, 2009). Even more, as shown in Nayyar

(2013), based on figures of Maddison, in 1700, India represented 24.5% of the world GDP, and in 1750, India's manufactures represented 24.5% of the total world manufactured production (Bairoch, 1982).

As highlighted by Vries (2016, p. 10):

> When it comes to manufacturing, early modern India . . . in several respects was a more likely candidate than early modern China to be the first or in any case an early industrializing country. In Great Britain's industrialization, cotton played a central role: India's cotton production was second to none in sophistication far into the eighteenth century.

However, by 1913, the Indian participation in the world's GDP had decreased to 7.5%, and its share in the worldwide manufactures dropped to 1.4% (Nayyar, 2013; Bairoch, 1982; Clingingsmith and Williamson, 2008). Two central historical processes occurred between the eighteenth century and the beginning of the twentieth century related to our objective: the Industrial Revolution and the British colonisation of the Indian subcontinent. A deep analysis of the causes and drivers of the Industrial Revolution exceeds the scope of this research, but in the first part of this book, we will present and discuss the main features of the Indian Ocean region, the Indian subcontinent (and its people), and its relationship with the European people, mainly the British.

Chapter 2 introduces the Indian Ocean production and trade relations before the British penetration into the Indian subcontinent, in order to contextualise and give a real dimension of the relevance of the Indian subcontinent as the gravitational centre of the Indian Ocean ecosystem. In Chapter 3, we will introduce the penetration and domination of the British of the Indian subcontinent since the Battle of Plassey (1757). This period appears in the recent global history literature as the one of the "great divergence" between the West and the East (Pomeranz, 2000; Parthasarathi, 2011). We will show how the Indian subcontinent was transformed from the Indian Ocean manufacture and trade centre into a global periphery of the British Crown. In Chapter 4, with a Prebischian-ECLAC center-periphery scheme as a background, but not limited by it, we will work on the idea of "peripherisation" as a broader process than the one presented by most of the literature as the "Indian deindustrialisation". This consideration will also focus on the Latin American economic development scholar mindset. Therefore, we hope that this first part of the book makes a contribution particularly to both the Indian and the Latin American scholars mainly interested in the "great divergence" debate.

In the second and third parts of the book, we will explore and discuss the Indian path of development since its independence to the present days. In a recent revisionist trend, this period is being reinterpreted by several respectable scholars, both Indian and Western, as a case of a necessary transition from a state-led, "socialist" regime to a market-driven economy in which liberalisation, attitudinal shift regarding the Indian business groups, and market development have been the main growth drivers (Bhagwati and Panagariya, 2013; Bhandari and Goswani, 2000; Delong, 2003; Rodrik and Subramanian, 2008, 2005). We will also point out some nuances on this extended view, both the one related to the "socialist-regime", showing that in fact it was a mixed economy, and the one referred to as market-driven growth, showing that the state still has a primary role in the Indian economy.

In the second part of the book, our main object of analysis is the Indian statebuilding as a broad background for the emergence and conformation of the Indian National System of Innovation (NSI) until the end of the 1980s. Consequently, in Chapter 5, we will mainly interrelate the context of the Indian state emergence and its intrinsic geopolitical and political tensions, the macroeconomic and technological challenges of a young democracy, and the main Science, Technology, and Innovation (STI) policies and NSI structuring. This mix, which gives central relevance to the role of the state, but at the same time tries to avoid the so-called methodological nationalism, is not very present in the Indian NSI literature. In Chapter 6, we reflect and discuss the achievements and debts of the Indian state and its NSI during the Cold War period, introducing some Latin American insights and comparisons. This part of the book contributes to both Indian and Latin American scholars interested in the role, drivers and limitations of statebuilding policies, particularly in the STI domain, understood under a broad NSI focusing device (Cassiolato and Lastres, 2005, 2017).

In the third and last part of the book, we will deal with the Indian Ocean geopolitical chessboard configuration since the 1990s, with the implementation of the New Economic Policy (NEP) during the emergence of the Washington Consensus order, particularly focusing on the Indian growth drivers. Our main contribution here is the presentation of a Brazilian demand-led understanding of the Indian growth acceleration, paying attention to the role of the autonomous expenditures (Serrano, 1995, 2016). Our geopolitical understanding and contextualisation allow us to present an insight on the Indian external sector and financing performances in the context of the Indian post–Cold War approximation to the Western world, particularly the economic and financial complementation and alignment with the US, given China's expansion as a global superpower, instead of an abstract idea of liberalisation and export-led growth.

In Chapter 7, we will present the main Indian political and geopolitical changes since the 1990s, predominantly related to the downfall of the USSR and the growing relevance of the US in the Indian foreign and domestic policies, the consolidation of China as a global superpower, and the emergence of the Bharatiya Janata Party (BJP) as a dominant domestic political force.

Without ignoring the role of exports, we will present a demand-led growth insight, highlighting the role of private autonomous consumption led by upper class/caste urban groups and a credit boom, public and private investment related to infrastructure (mainly in answer to the Indian urbanisation and energy needs), and several government massive public programmes and transferences. The roles of remittances, service exports, and capital flows from the US, closely related to the Indian Americans inserted in Silicon Valley and the Indian Diaspora in general terms, are highlighted as responsible for driving the Indian external restriction and consequently allowing growth acceleration.

In Chapter 8, we will detail some structural sources of growth/autonomous expenditures related to urbanisation, construction and real estate, the case of public/private investment in energy infrastructure, and the Indian external sector. We will also take a snapshot of some socio-economic indicators in order to show that the Latin American concept of "structural heterogeneity" totally fits to describe the contemporary Indian productive and social structures. In Chapter 9, we will reflect on the Indian growth process since the 1990s from a Latin American point of view, making a parallelism between the Indian growth acceleration and the Brazilian growth "miracle" of the 1960s and 1970s: Belindia's metaphor of accelerated high growth and repressed salaries under the military government. Indeed, even though the Indian democracy has never had a military coup, it still has a rigid caste system and class configuration.

We conclude with some final remarks written in the middle of the COVID-19 crisis, and we suggest some future lines of thinking and research for the strengthening of the Global South economic development dialogue. Hope you enjoy the (long-term) reading.

Note

1 Among others, the works of Evans (1995), Kohli (2004), and Pedersen (2008) are milestones for the comparative studies literature, including Namboodiripad's (1973) analysis of the Chilean coup and his attempt to draw out lessons for the Indian Left. And there are different works mainly comparing Brazil and India. For instance, two recent studies have contrasted the trajectories of Brazil and India focusing on wage-led/profit-led growth, inequality, and human development (Sirohi, 2019; Barbosa et al., 2017). However, none of these studies focus on the Indian subcontinent's long-term development path, nor do they depart from an explicit Latin American framework.

1
A LATIN AMERICAN APPROACH

Our approach is based on three main Latin American methodological/theoretical blocks.[1]

1.1 The pioneer Economic Commission for Latin America and the Caribbean's structuralist influence

Most of the Latin American development economic scholars have had an explicit or implicit influence on the Economic Commission for Latin America and the Caribbean (ECLAC). Created in 1948, Raúl Prebisch led the intellectual challenge of building both a conceptual and a policy-oriented agenda for ECLAC. Prebisch's 1950s works, *El desarrollo económico de la América Latina y algunos de sus principales problemas* (1949); the introduction of *Estudio ecónomico de América Latina* (1950), later called by Hirschman the *Manifiesto Latinoamericano*; and *Problemas teóricos y prácticos del crecimiento económico* (1951) are among the main contributions of a Latin American scholar to political economy thinking, configuring a research agenda, the early ECLAC's one, that is still inspiring and applicable (Rodríguez, 2006; Medeiros, 2020; Bielschowsky, 2016, 2020; Gurrieri, 2011).

Prebisch's main theoretical contribution, the centre-periphery structure, aims to conceptualise the Latin American insertion into global capitalism and its consequences related to the dissemination of technical change and, in more general terms, to welfare (Rodríguez, 2006; Bielschowsky, 1998, 2016, 2020; Perez Candeltey and Vernengo, 2016, Medeiros, 2020; Sztulwark, 2003; among many others). Presbich's reflections on the impact of the 1930 crisis in the Argentinian agro-export model was conducive to the formulation of the centre-periphery conceptual structure (Perez Candeltey and Vernengo, 2018; Perez Candeltey et al., 2019). The constitution of the capitalism centre is a movement that began in England with the Industrial Revolution,[2] spread all around Europe, took root in the US, and then reached Japan.[3] Simultaneously to the consolidation of these industrial centres, different countries, colonies, and territories were inserted into the system as

DOI: 10.4324/9781003091752-2

a vast and heterogeneous group of regions, mainly located in the Southern Hemisphere, called periphery.

Given the colonial and global trade links, the periphery conforms to a system in which its structural characteristics, the role of its components, and the relations between them are subordinated to the centre's needs (or we could say, demand) (Gurrieri, 2011). In Prebisch's works, this subordination has different forms and channels, but the main one is the unequal dissemination of technical progress, which basically reaches the periphery's primary sectors, oriented to produce food and primary goods to answer the centre's needs. Consequently, the limited dissemination of technical progress originates a dual economic structure, with the primary sector inserted in the global economy, producing at the "best-practice", and the low-productivity subsistence agriculture oriented to the local population needs.[4] This dual productive structure contrasts with the mostly homogenised one of the industrialised centres.

The "dual" character of the periphery reinforces the unequal absorption of technical progress, resulting in a lower growth of the average labour productivity and in the median income of the periphery.[5] The different salary paths between centre and periphery are the main cause behind the deterioration in the terms of trade, both by the greater bargaining power of the Unions at the centre and the superabundance of labour in the periphery. In Prebisch's (1951, p. 29) words:

> As a result of the protection of primary production in the great industrial centres, the proportion of the population gainfully employed in these activities has not decreased to the extent it might otherwise have done, and consequently the increase of the population gainfully employed in industry, services and other activities has not been as great as it might otherwise have been. Likewise, in the periphery there would not be such a pressing need for labour to obtain employment in secondary and tertiary occupations when it is unavailable in primary activities. The protective tendencies of the industrial centres merely accentuate the compulsory migration of the peripheral population from primary into secondary production and services, since ultimately this displacement is caused by the extension of technical progress.

Centre and periphery are part of the same interconnected capitalist system. The existence of a centre implies the existence of a periphery (and, in some sense, development implies underdevelopment[6]). Thus, the centre-periphery scheme was a direct blow to the international trade theory based on the principle of comparative advantages and a main antecedent to the different types of unbalanced, unequal exchange and dependentist theories (Vernengo, 2006). But most important to our ends, Prebisch's approach emphasises the relevance of the regional insertion into global capitalism as decisive for the productive structure and the income level.

Under Prebisch's institutional and theoretical umbrella, Celso Furtado further developed ECLAC's methodological approach historicising the Latin American structuralism, in what was later called the "historical-structuralist" method[7] (Bielschowsky, 2016). As discussed in Boianovsky (2015), a young Furtado was influenced by the École des Annales, particularly by Pirenne's works privileging structural (rather than eventful) history and stressing the method of comparative history through long-time periods and large geographical areas. Indeed, the main referent of the Annales school, Braudel, interpreted structures as stable long-term phenomena featuring "obstacles" (geographical, biological, etc.) which constrain changes.

Referring to his interaction with Braudel during the two decades he lived in Paris, Furtado says that Braudel's notion of *longue durée* may be applied to the study of external dependence as the determining long-term feature of Brazilian economic history (Boianovsky, 2015). In fact, it was through the long-term approach to economic development/underdevelopment that Furtado focused on the recurring nature of the external sector bottleneck for the Latin American economies, signalling a line of work that would later be continued by several Latin American authors contributing to the external restriction (US dollar scarcity) and its implications in terms of inflation, distributive conflict, and so on.

In his two main contributions related to the implementation of the "historical-structuralism", *Formação econômica do Brasil* (1959), the book that resulted from his PhD thesis, and *A economia latino-americana* (1969), Furtado took on the intellectual challenge of fusing history and economic theory. The long-term approach allowed him to expose repeated patterns of not-strictly-economic, semi-autonomous processes, such as settlement, urbanisation, migration, natural resources allocation, and so on, which configurate the conceptual structures (economic parameters) of the Latin American pattern of development. Thus, the "non-economic" features turn out to be of paramount relevance for the economic structural configuration (Boianovsky, 2015).

Referring to "historical-structuralism", Bielschowsky (2016, p. 11) says:

> In other social science disciplines, such as linguistics and anthropology, where "structuralism" originates, this concept typically corresponded to a synchronous or an ahistorical methodological toolkit. In the Commission's economic analysis (ECLAC), however, structuralism is essentially an approach that is guided by the search for diachronic, historical and comparative relations, which is better suited to the "inductive" method than to a "positive heuristic". This lays the essential foundations for the theoretical construction of ECLAC historical comparative analysis: the underdeveloped

> structures of the Latin American periphery constrain, rather than determine, specific behaviours of paths that are unknown a priori. For that reason, they deserve and demand studies and analyses in which universal-type economic theory can only be used with reservations, to be able to incorporate those historical and regional specifics.

Departing from the dual model developed by Prebisch and Furtado, Anibal Pinto introduced the concept of "structural heterogeneity" (Pinto, 1970). The broad idea of structural heterogeneity refers to the coexistence of productive practices and social relations that belong to different periods and paths of development in a region coexisting within the limits of a country (Pinto and Di Filippo, 1982). Consequently, structural heterogeneity is expressed both in the production forms and in the social relations inherited from the colonial times, including the successive transformations driven by the different "techno-economic paradigms", as we would call it nowadays. Therefore, three main dimensions could be highlighted regarding the structural heterogeneity: the productive one, the social relations one, and the political one.

Compared to Prebisch's pioneer dual model, Pinto's (1970) structural heterogeneity gives a more accurate account of the Latin American industrialisation process:

> In view of the changes wrought by industrialization, the productive structure of Latin America can usefully be divided into three broad strata, for certain analytical purposes to be mentioned below. Firstly, there is a "primitive" stratum, in which productivity and per capita income levels are probably similar (and sometimes below) those that prevailed in the colonial economy, and, in some cases, the pre-Colombian economy. At the other extreme, there is a "modern pole", consisting of export, industrial and service activities that function with productivity levels similar to the averages of the developed economies; and, lastly, there is the "intermediate" stratum which, to some extent, corresponds more closely to the average productivity of the national system. Note the multisector nature of each of the strata, and how this framework differs from the more common urban-rural dichotomy.

Despite the "homogenisation" intention of the industrialisation efforts through the development of the modern sector, Pinto states that the results have been the coexistence of the main "sectors" in the same national economy, with different productivity levels, scarce connections between them, and geographically fragmented. This means that, despite the intentions of generating an endogenous dynamic, the industrialisation process contributed to generate an "internal periphery" in the urban centres (Pinto, 1972). Since Pinto's contribution, the structural heterogeneity approach has been widely used to characterise the Latin American diversity in terms of productive and social structures (Rodríguez, 2006; Mancini and Lavarello, 2013; Sztulwark, 2003).

1.2 Latin American contributions on inter-state global competition and the broad understanding of the National Systems of Innovation (NSI)

In contemporary international literature, the relevance of the state has been mainly approached in the research line related to the developmental or, more recently, the entrepreneurial state (Mazzucato, 2013; Skocpol, 1985; Wade, 1990; Amsdem, 2001; Reinert, 1999; Chang, 2005; etc.). For the Indian context, the discussion about the goals and limitations of the developmental state is presented in a political economic framework in Kohli (2007a, 2007b, 2004), Chibber (2003), and Bagchi (2003).

However, some of these approaches suffer from the so-called methodological nationalism[8] in trying to explain the state drivers mainly by domestic factors, or by dividing the analyses between internal and external causes, with the limit of the state as the division line. In a less monolithically way, Mann (1986, 1993, 2012a, 2012b) asserts that society is formed around different but interconnected networks of economic, political, military, and ideological powers. Although the state is the main national epicentre of political power, the structuring and functioning of the other networks are governed by broader global, regional, and local trends and social dynamics. Consequently, there is neither a linear nor a unique relationship to explain why and how the state operates between these networks of power.

In Latin America, the ECLAC pioneers (Prebisch, Furtado, and Pinto) identified the state as a key actor of the industrialisation process. In fact, they were engaged with the Latin American policymakers in the articulation of different policies and the planning of techniques for development. However, they did not have a systematic discussion and theorisation about the drivers, actors, and forces that would propel the state to assume a developmental role in Latin America. Perhaps because of their close relation to the policymakers, or by the Cold War context, it was implicitly presumed that the state would have a developmental role. In some sense, the first cohort of Latin American structuralists implicitly had an instrumentalist, pragmatic, policy-oriented conception of the state (Fiori, 2020).

With the difficulties and limitations of the advanced phase of the industrialisation by import substitution in Latin America during the 1960s and 1970s, related to the expansion of the imports of capital goods and the increasing dependence on multinational corporations, the debt crisis of the

1980s, the downfall of the USSR, and the consolidation of the Washington Consensus since the 1990s, the Latin American political economic mindset about the state suffered different historical, conceptual, and ideological setbacks (Medeiros, 2011; Vernengo, 2020). In turn, the market/state failure and rent-seeking frameworks consolidated almost worldwide to set the role of the state and its main limitations.

The 2000s economic and political context demanded new efforts to review the role of the state in Latin America. The return to power of some "centre-left" parties, the growing role of industrial and innovation policies, and the improvement in terms of trade gave space to the emergence of different research agendas in Latin America. Adopting a realistic geopolitical view Fiori (1999, 2007, 2020) uses a long-term Braudelian approach to explain the systematic pressures that boost interstate competition and policy efforts. Broadly, in Fiori, capitalism implies the systemic inter-state competition and pressure to build monetary, technological, and/or, mainly, military power. This constant, expansive, and never-ending competition between states fuels both wars and private competition.

Medeiros (2013, 2011, 2003) digs deeper into the institutional configuration of the states, giving account both of their geopolitical and class embeddedness. Conceptually mixing classical political economy, Latin American structuralism, and a Gramscian perspective, Medeiros (2011, p. 44) asserts:

> [F]irst, modern explanations about developmental states and the role of institutions neglect the different challenges and circumstances created by initial conditions and how different economic and social structures influence institutions (a bias opposed to ECLAC's classical structuralism that neglected the autonomous role of institutions). The major challenge to explain development strategies is to articulate the two dimensions. Secondly, it assumes the proposition according to which the international environment is not identical for developing nations and is influenced by the hegemonic state's economic and political action, creating different development opportunities for them. Finally, it considers that the state (and its developmental historical variant) cannot be viewed as an agent above interests, apart from social classes and relations with other states, but rather, as a central institution where the dominant class, or some of its sectors, leads a coalition of power and builds a hegemonic project compatible with a particular accumulation strategy. Moreover, the compatibility between the growth strategy of the dominant fractions of capital and the nation development cannot be assumed and it is precisely the tension between them that explains the evolution and crisis of development strategies as hegemonic projects.

Regarding these Latin American contributions about state behaviour in the context of the different geopolitical, class, and institutional configurations, José Eduardo Cassiolato, Helena Lastres, and the RedeSist[9] researchers formulated a research agenda on the broad understanding of the NSI conceptual focusing device oriented to discuss the relationship between innovation and development in developing countries (Cassiolato, 2008; Cassiolato et al., 2013; Scerri and Lastres, 2013; Cassiolato and Gonzalo, 2015).

In general terms, the NSI conceptual approach is based mainly on two streams of literature: the works of Serra (1613) and List (1841) on the relevance of domestic market and knowledge for the development of a country and Schumpeter's emphasis on innovation and economic change. In its contemporary formulation, the NSI emerged as a focusing device from the 1980s Organisation for Economic Co-operation and Development's (OECD) expert group on science, technology, and competitiveness, impelled mainly by Lundvall, Freeman, and Chesnais (Sharif, 2006). Freeman's (1982) work on technological infrastructure and international competitiveness reintroduced List's (1841) ideas supporting a historic and context-specific approach to the competitiveness discussion, stressing on the "non-price factors" of trade dynamic (Lundvall, 2015). In Lundvall's (1985) work on the Danish user-producer relations and interactions, he used the concept of "innovation systems", and in Freeman's (1987) work on Japan's institutional and policy set up to support competitiveness, he used the NSI expression. After Freeman's (1987) work, the NSI approach received quite a lot of attention, mainly because both academics and policymakers were trying to understand the extraordinary Japanese competitive performance. The subsequent publications of Lundvall (1992) and Nelson (1993) were part of the initial works on NSI.

Lundvall et al. (2009) explicitly avoid the methodological nationalism, emphasising the systemic understanding of the NSI, defining it as an open, evolving, and complex system that encompasses relationships within and between organisations, institutions, and socio-economic structures, which determine the rate and direction of innovation and competence-building emanating from processes of science-based and experienced-based learning. Broadly, two main perspectives on NSI have been adopted since then: the narrow and the broad ones (Lundvall et al., 2009; Cassiolato and Lastres, 2005). The narrow one mainly assimilates innovation in science and technology, analysing the relationships between the science and technology actors and institutions, with a special emphasis on R&D (Niosi et al., 1993).

The broad Latin American NSI perspective adopted in this book is in the conceptual line of the RedeSist research agenda, and it is rooted in the historical approach to the NSI and technical change adopted in Freeman (1995)[10] and Freeman and Louçã (2001). Departing from the linear model of innovation, and understanding innovation as a systemic, contextual, and cumulative process, the broad Latin American approach gives space to different dimensions that affect innovation and capability building such as geopolitics, social institutions, macroeconomic performance, financial systems, demand, infrastructure, market conditions, and so on (Cassiolato and Lastres, 2005, 2017, 1999; Cassiolato et al., 2008). In doing so, the broad understanding dialogues with the works of Fiori and Medeiros, related to the inter-state competition. It also allows a dialogue with demand-led growth contributions, based on public and private autonomous expenditure and the limitations imposed by the external restrictions (instead of the hybridisation with an endogenous growth model). In other words, Cassiolato (2008, p. 10) states:

> The broad perspective includes different, connecting subsystems that are influenced by various contexts: geopolitical, cultural, social, political, economic, local and so on. First there is a production and innovation sub-system which contemplates the structure of economic activities, their sectoral distribution, degree of informality and spatial and size distribution, the level and quality of employment, the type and quality of innovative effort. Second there is a sub-system of capacity-building, research & technological services which considers education (basic, technical, undergraduate and postgraduate), R&D, training and capacity-building, S&T information, metrology, consulting, intellectual property. Third, there is a policy, representation and financing sub-system, which takes into account explicit policies (S&T&I, industrial, sectoral) and implicit policies (macroeconomic, investment, trade, etc.), regulation (sectoral, foreign trade, intellectual property, environment, innovation), promotion, financing and representation. Finally, there is the role of demand, which most of the times is surprisingly absent in most analyses of innovation systems. This dimension includes a pattern of income distribution, structure of consumption, social organisation and social demand (basic infrastructure, health, education).

At the same time, the broad conception of the NSI incorporates the 1970s contributions of the Latin American School on Science, Technology and Society.[11] In particular, the RedeSist approach highlights Herrera's (1973) groundbreaking discussion on the articulation between the scientific and R&D efforts of the Latin American countries and the needs of their productive structures and societies. Herrera pointed out that, more than how much to invest in R&D, a fundamental problem has been the orientation and indigenisation of the R&D efforts, their connection with the concrete problems of the Latin American societies, and the interaction between the Latin American Science, Technology, and Innovation (STI) institutions. Indeed, Herrera's contribution is a precedent to the neo-Schumpeterian conceptualisations of systems of innovation, criticising the linear model of innovation (Cassiolato and Lastres, 2005).

Herrera introduced three useful categories for our ends. The "explicit scientific policy", that is, the official policy, which is expressed in the laws, regulations, and statutes of the government offices, ministries, and in the planning documents, is commonly known as the official scientific policy of a country. However, it is the second category, the "implicit policy", that determines the role and relevance of science and technology in a society. The "implicit policy" is much harder to perceive and understand because it has no formal documents or structure, but it reveals the effective demand for science and technology of the "national project", the third category, in force in a society. The "national project" is defined as the set of objectives and the model of country aspired by the social sectors that have, directly or indirectly, the economic and political control of the society. This implies the concrete existence of an elite with enough power to articulate and implement their concrete objectives.

As Global South countries inherit the colonial global insertion and underdeveloped relations, in terms of institutional setting incompleteness, weak infrastructure development, scarce interactions between the actors, the role of transnational actors tending to lock in indigenous technological efforts, and so on, they demand a broad NSI approach (Cassiolato, 2008; Lastres and Cassiolato, 2017).[12]

1.3 A Brazilian path from the Keynesian-Kaleckian principle of effective demand to the Sraffian supermultiplier: the role of autonomous expenditures

The principle of effective demand was popularly introduced by Keynes (1936) and, in an even more explicit way, by Kalecki (1933, 1968, 1971). In general terms, effective demand theories state that demand determines output and capacity, adjusting through the process of some kind of accelerator and/or multiplier mechanism (Garegnani, 1962; Lavoie, 1992; Serrano, 1995, 2016; Serrano and Freitas, 2017; Possas, 1987; Crespo, 2016). But there are different versions and perceptions of the principle of effective demand. In the Kaleckian version, in the long run, investment generates savings through variations in the level of GDP. The link between investment and demand are the variations in the degree of capacity utilisation or the creation of new capacity.

In Brazil, the Latin American country where the Keynesian-Kaleckian framework is more deeply rooted, we identify three main authors and momentums related to the demand-led growth thinking: Maria da Conceição Tavares since the 1970s, Mario Possas since the 1980s, and Franklin Serrano since the 1990s. All three of them are institutionally related to the Universidade Federal de Campinas' (UNICAMP) and the Universidade Federal de Rio de Janeiro's (UFRJ) schools of political economy.

A primary and groundbreaking contribution of Maria da Conceição Tavares to the Latin American political economy thinking was the introduction of the Kaleckian framework into the Brazilian analysis, institutionally based at UNICAMP (Tavares and Serra, 1971; Tavares, 1973, 1976, 1978; Serrano, 2001; Bastos and D'Avila, 2007; Vernengo, 2006; among others). In their debate with Furtado (1966), Tavares and Serra (1971), from an effective demand perspective, argued that investment in the Brazilian high growth "miracle" of the 1960s and 1970s would be accelerated by the upper classes' "autonomous expenditures" and the state's direct expenditure in infrastructure. The political arrangement articulated behind the Brazilian miracle, "the triple alliance", included the multinational corporations and the financial capital, the Brazilian upper bourgeoisie, and the state, which were in the hands of the military (Evans, 1979, 1982; Rodríguez, 2006; Bastos and D'Avila, 2007; Serrano, 2001; Vernengo, 2006).

Departing from Tavares, the work of Possas has been another substantial contribution, particularly in Possas and Baltar (1983), regarding the formalisation and integration between trend and cycle in a Kaleckian growth model, and in Possas (1987), trying to integrate the macro Keynesian-Kaleckian framework of micro-Schumpeterian elements such as market structures, the type of competition, and the companies' behaviours as sources of "autonomous investments". In Possas (1987), the final output was a theoretical division between the cycle, which would be governed by the effective demand principle, and the trend, which would be governed by the structural change expenditures and innovation efforts. However, although much broader and micro-founded that most of the Kaleckian models, Possas (1987) does not "resolve" the paradox of investment: its double character both as supply and demand creator. In fact, in Possas (1987), there would not be a problem with the double character of investment because there is no "gravitation force": the degree of capacity utilisation function as the adjustment variable of the mismatches between demand and investment.

Since the 1990s, the UNICAMP's authors have mainly focused on the financial and technological aspects of Brazilian capitalism as the main limitation to autonomous investment. The absence of long-term financing, the high interest rate, or the particularly high Brazilian entrepreneurs' liquidity preferences are underlined as the main problems to the increase of autonomous investment (Tavares, 1999; Cardoso de Mello and Novais, 1998; Bastos and D'Avila, 2007; among others).

However, although these issues are of main relevance, raising questions about who is going to invest, in which sectors, and with which techniques, they do not fully explain the aggregate long-term investment behaviour. If in the long term the investment is autonomous, and we accept that commodities are exchanged by their production costs, there would be neither adjustments nor reactions to the mismatches between capacity and effective demand. However, in a fully induced-investment theory, even in the long run, entrepreneurs can be Schumpeterian, they can replace one another through innovation, but the aggregate investment must adjust to demand, implying a trend to a normal degree of capacity utilisation for the whole economy in the long run (Serrano and Freitas, 2017; Garegnani and Palumbo, 1998; Cesaratto et al., 2013; Ciccone, 1995).

That said, it is useful to clearly define autonomous expenditure, a main concept for Serrano's (1995, p. 15) "Sraffian supermultiplier"[13]:

> The types of expenditure that should be considered autonomous according to our criteria include: the consumption of capitalists; the discretionary consumption of richer workers that have some accumulated wealth and access to credit; residential "investment" by households; firms' discretionary expenditures (that are sometimes classified as "investment" and sometimes as "intermediate consumption" in official statistics) that do not include the purchase of produced means of production such as consultancy services, research & development, publicity, executive jets, etc . . .; government expenditures (both consumption and investment); and total exports.

In Serrano's (1995) "Sraffian supermultiplier", investment is completely induced by autonomous expenditures, which are the main long-term growth drivers.[14] Determining the level and dynamics of the autonomous expenditures turns out to be the main issue for understanding long-term growth.[15] However, it is almost impossible to develop any "endogenous" general theory to explain autonomous expenditures, as stated in Serrano (1995, p. 42):

> The levels and growth rates of the autonomous expenditures depend crucially on factors as diverse as: the nature of the financial system and the conditions of consumer credit, the pace of technological change and the process of competition with regard to product innovation and product differentiation strategies of the firms, the relation between managers and owners, government expenditure (and taxation) policy and, in the case of an open economy, the international competitiveness of the domestic firms (and the country's exchange rate policy). The virtual impossibility of deriving formally a general "endogenous" trend for the autonomous components of demand seems to have led the vast majority of multiplier-accelerator theorists to ignore the role of this component of aggregate demand in the explanation of the long-run trends of capital accumulation.

In this book, we will make an effort in order to build a narrative paying central attention to some of these autonomous expenditure drivers, predominantly related to the geopolitical/military, demographical, technological, financial, and institutional aspects, which have had an influence in the long-term Indian economic growth.

Notes

1 The selection of the authors and conceptual elements is partial, determined by the author. There are several Latin American authors who were not included in this framework. Indeed, it was not the intention of this work to make an exhaustive revision of the Latin American contributions to development economics but to state the main conceptual background on which our research on India was done.
2 Pérez (2001, 2010) is another relevant Latin American scholar who later contributed to understand the emergence and development of the different techno-economic paradigms in close relation with the emergence of a regional or global centre, such as England and Europe, the US, and Asia.
3 Interestingly, some Latin American authors later discussed Prebisch's understanding on the centre's growth drivers. For instance, Pérez Candeltey and Vernengo (2016) state that Prebisch adopted a dynamic perspective on growth in the centre, in which forced savings precede investments as a key element of the cycle. Serrano (2016) follows the same line of thought, signalling that Prebisch approach is a supply side one, without breaking with Say's law. As for Crespo (2016), he maintains that in Prebisch's centre-periphery scheme, the centre acts as a source of effective demand for the periphery, in the form of exports. In this sense, Prebisch, as Kaldor (1978), would adopt a demand-export-led approach to growth in the periphery.
4 Industrial development is seen by Prebisch, in line with Kaldor, as the main way of technological diffusion.
5 Different Latin American authors later worked on the idea of a dual economy (in international terms, Lewis model is quite similar). In particular, Rangel (2012) deeply worked and expanded the dual model to analyse the Brazilian economy.
6 For Furtado (1971, p. 115), development and underdevelopment relations are at the same time historically and synchronically configured: "Underdevelopment is, then, a discrete historical process through which economies that have already achieved a high level of development have not necessarily passed".
7 In a similar fashion to Furtado, Caio Prado's *Formação do Brasil contemporâneo* (1942) has had a deep influence in this book. Caio Prado's long-term materialist approach to Brazilian history, a seminal work for the Brazilian economic history and thinking, is helpful to think any colonial type of insertion into global capitalism. For Caio Prado, given the absence of feudalism, the Brazilian global insertion was capitalist since its origins, "since the colonial moment". The sense of colonisation, in Caio Prado, answered to the Portuguese capitalist global trade enterprise. Indeed, Caio Prado, "the first Brazilian marxist", was one of the authors who most clearly emphasised the relevance of the colonial moment as a global and capitalist one (Ricupero, 1999).
8 For a discussion on the problems of the methodological nationalism, see Gore (1996), Medeiros (2010, 2011), and Crespo and Muñiz (2017).
9 For a deeper understanding of the RedeSist research agenda and works, see www.redesist.ie.ufrj.br.
10 See Lastres and Cassiolato (2017) for an exploration of the commonalities between Furtado and Freeman in relation to economic development and the role of technical change.

11 Broadly, the Latin American School on Science, Technology and Society was composed by scholars such as Jorge Sábato and Oscar Varsavksy, from Argentina; José Leite Lopes, from Brazil; Miguel Wionczek, from Mexico; Francisco Sagasti, from Peru; Máximo Halty Carrere, from Uruguay; and Marcel Roche, from Venezuela (Herrera, 2015; Kreimer et al., 2004; Vidal and Marí, 2002; among others).

12 Different scholars have been working and adapting the NSI approach for the developing countries' challenges, mainly around the Globelics community. To mention only some of them, in the Latin American context, we can highlight the work of the Lalics community with prominent scholars such as Cassiolato, Lastres, Arocena, Sutz, Yoguel, Dutrenit, Szapiro, and so on. In the Asian context, the works of Indialics and Cicalics are also important with K.J. Joseph, Dinesh Abrol, and Keun Lee as some main scholars among many others.

13 The term "supermultiplier" was introduced, with different implications, by Hicks (1950).

14 The details of the Sraffian supermultiplier stylised model can be seen in Serrano and Freitas (2017). Here we will only say that the output will be determined by the variations of the autonomous expenditures, mediated by the given technical-capital-to-capacity-output ratio, the normal degree of capacity utilisation, the rate of depreciation, and the aggregate marginal propensity of a country to save.

15 In international literature, the recent works of Deleidi and Mazzucato (2019), from a neo-Schumpeterian perspective, and of Nah and Lavoie (2016), from a neo-Kaleckian one, converge to the same conceptual line.

Part I

PERIPHERISATION

2

THE INDIAN OCEAN ECOSYSTEM

Mathematicians have divided chronological events into four categories: the stationary, the long-term, the cyclical, and the random. For the countries of the Indian Ocean, the stationary component of time is seen in the unchanging nature of the sea, its area and its depth, salinity and temperature, all of which contributed to the quality of marine life and man's capacity to take a harvest from the sea.

Chaudhury (1985, p. 21)[1]

[T]he discovery of America and that of a passage to the East Indies by the Cape of Good Hope, are the two greatest and most important events recorded in the history of mankind.

Adam Smith, quoted by Findlay and O'Rourke (2007, p. 143)

India as a land of Desire formed an essential element in general history. From the most ancient times downwards, all nations have directed their wishes and longings to gaining access to the treasures of this land of marvels, the most costly which the earth presents, treasures of nature -pearls, diamonds, perfumes, rose essences, lions, elephants, etc. – as also treasures of wisdom. The way by which these treasures have passed to the West has at all times been a matter of world-historical importance bound up with the fate of nations.

Hegel, quoted by Panikkar (1953, p. 21)

One of the central arguments of this study has been that such specific developments in the triangular nexus between state, producing economy and external commerce are intimately related, on the one hand, to an internal and autochthonous groundswell, and, on the other, to opportunities provided by the very process of interaction with other economies.

Subrahmanyam (1990, p. 370)

DOI: 10.4324/9781003091752-4

The main objective of this chapter is to give a broad picture of the dynamics of the Indian Ocean economic, productive, and social relations until the British initial penetration in the subcontinent.

2.1 The Indian Ocean "from the rise of Islam" to da Gama (seventh century–1498)[2]

The emergence of the Tang dynasty in China in 618 and Muhammad's journey to Mecca in 622 were the starting years of an increasing trade flux that connected the different cultures, productive systems, and ideas of the two geographical divisions of the Indian Ocean, the western and the eastern, that met at the volcanic mountains of Java.[3] In this section, a big picture of the dynamics of the Indian Ocean ecosystem, "from the rise of Islam" to the arrival of Vasco da Gama at Calicut in 1498, will be presented.

2.1.1 Monsoons, trade ports, and emporia trade

The influence of climate synchronised the agricultural and productive dynamic of the Indian subcontinent. The monsoon[5] winds, which originated in the Equator and carried rain clouds into the Himalayan barrier, functioned as a cyclical component of time, aligning the dynamic of the ecosystem to a main variable: the water supply. The food habits and demand for commodities arising from the pattern of agriculture gave rise to the contours of both trade and social relations. In food terms, broadly, Asia could be divided into two main blocs: the wheat and the rice ones. The amount of rainfall of the monsoons determined the geographical limits between wheat and rice growing. Rice was a valuable trading commodity because it could be kept for several years, improving in taste, even. On the contrary, wheat was susceptible to insect attacks and was seldom transported by sea for any long distance. Famines also depended on the "good" or "bad" winds of the monsoons.

The sailing season was fixed by the timing of the monsoons too. The monsoon winds reduced travel times providing favourable wind currents. Storms at sea had critical effects for the population: if the Red Sea fleet of the Surat merchants failed to arrive, the financial and liquidity crisis affected all the community. The Indian Ocean is composed of six separate seas, each of them with its own timetable for correct departures and arrivals and linked to a regional economy, with the seasonal pattern of the wind system determining the time profile of the trip and the rain precipitations. The distance time was usually fixed, although it depended on the weather conditions. Each sea had its own particularities and its particular expert sailors. For instance, the Red Sea and the Persian Gulf, due to their unusual shape, presented their own navigational problems, with its specific community of sailors. To sail in the southern Indian Ocean out of season represented extreme danger deriving from storms and hurricanes.

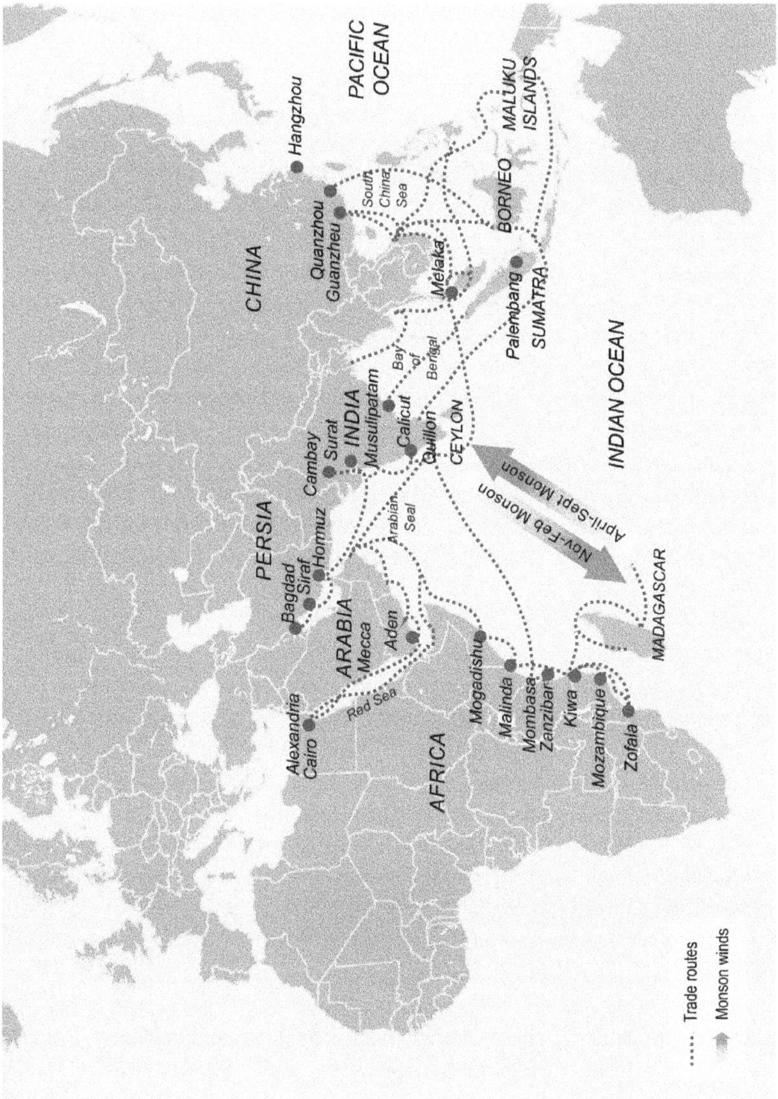

Figure 2.1 Indian Ocean trade routes and monsoon winds, 650–1498.[4]

Source: Elaborated by Rosaura Flynn.

Although there were ports in the Indian Ocean that possessed open seafronts, most of them were located at some distance from the open sea, at the estuaries of a river. This was because they were better protected against winds, waves, and pirates. The main rivers of the Indian Ocean are the Euphrates-Tigris, the Indus, the Ganges, the Chao, the Mekong, the Hsi Kiang, and the Yangtze Kiang. As the movement of goods by land, whether by pack animals or in wheeled vehicles, was complicated, the rivers were used to bridge the distance between seaports and landlocked cities. When navigation of the deltas and the upper reaches of the rivers became obsolete, new and better-suited ports and towns emerged. Few port-towns produced export goods in quantity, so most of them had to be brought from a distance to the places of shipment. Every major seaport, including Hormuz, Aden, Cambay, Surat, and Malacca, were crowded with sailors offering their services.

Emporia cities arose to handle the trade (Chaudhury, 1985; Subrahmanyam, 1990). The Indian Ocean and the Mediterranean Sea were held together by the urban connection between Malacca, Calicut, Cambay, Aden, Cairo, Alexandria, and Venice. The flow of goods and men on an east-west axis would not have been possible without the existence of these cities. The functional role of caravan cities such as Aleppo and Baghdad was not dissimilar. Malacca was a strategic strait, where the monsoon winds shifted. It linked the eastern and middle circuits, being a convenient place for traders to wait for the next journey. The economic and strategic importance of Malacca was not lost on either the Chinese in the early 1400s or, a century later, the Portuguese.

Asia's medieval trade was based mainly on four products: silk, porcelain, sandalwood, and black pepper. They were exchanged for incense, horses, ivory, cotton textiles, and metal goods. Spices, silks, cotton textiles, porcelain and glass, jewellery, and finely cut precious stones reflected the strengths of social conventions in regional markets. The Middle East was a large area of mass consumption, which imported goods from other parts of Asia like food, aromatic and medicinal plants, and manufactured goods. Slave trade was a profitable business too. It was carried out by the Arabs, Persians, and Indians. The slave trade was primarily composed of young girls used for domestic work and harems and men for hard labour.

For the Indian subcontinent, Subrahmanyam (1990) groups three main types of trade: coastal, overland, and overseas. The coastal trade went from Bengal in the east to Konkan and Gujarat in the west. It was conducted by smaller ships depending on the monsoon winds and the agriculture surplus. This was a more stable trade with regions that were not self-sufficient in foodgrains to support a growing population. Overland trade was mainly determined by the regional distribution of areas of production and mass consumption of particular goods. The overland trade could be divided, on the one hand, by trade using the inland waterways and, on the other hand, the trade on pack bullocks and other means of land-bound packers. River trade was limited for the most part to the southern Indian continent and comparable in dimensions to the great Gangetic or Indus systems in the north.

Overseas trade, until the arrival of the Portuguese, had different characteristics (Subrahmanyam, 1990). For instance, in South India, in the coast of Malabar, the main ports were Calicut, Kollam (Quilon), and Cannanore. Trade was oriented in two main directions: towards the Red Sea, the Persian Gulf, and the ports of Gujarat, on the one hand, and to Malacca and the eastern Bay of Bengal, on the other. Commerce with Africa was also done from Calicut. In the Coromandel Coast, the main high-sea trade was concentrated in the port of Pulicat. Pulicat's high-sea links extended in two directions: to southern Burma and to Malacca and the south-east. Besides, from other minor intermediate ports of the Coromandel Coast, textiles trade was done with Ceylon, Bengal, and South Asia.

2.1.2 Cosmopolitan empires, shipbuilding, and gunpowder

Apart from the emergence of Surat, in the early seventh century, and Masulipatnam, in Coromandel, none of the ports of the Indian Ocean had close links to an inland empire. As highlighted by Roy (2012a), whereas the littoral was the centre of commercial activity, most settlements, especially the larger ones, were formed inland. Land tax pulled the capital to the interior, but commerce pulled the trading centres to the coast. For instance, the Samudri king ruled a small state from Calicut, Cambay had its own king, and so on. As a consequence, the "commercial" operators in these ports needed to adapt to pan-regional economic or political tendencies rather than try to control and shape these forces.

The Indian Ocean was an area of social and cultural diversity rooted in four main different communities: the Indo-Arabic, the Hindu, the Indonesian, and the Chinese. Sea trade, supplemented by the Central Asian caravan routes, created a sense of unity (Chaudhury, 1985). Ethiopians traded gold and ivory; Malays, pepper and nutmeg; and Yemenis, frankincense and myrrh. Along with this string of emporia, merchants spoke a babel of different languages as part of the long process that brought goods from one end of the Indian Ocean to the other. The idea of a common geographical space defined by the exchange of ideas and material objects was quite strong, not only in the minds of merchants but also in those of political rulers and ordinary people.

Distinct communities of merchant-sailors operated the ships forming the main component of the Indian port towns. In Cambay, they were the Gujarati Muslims; in Malabar, the Mapilla Muslims; in Coromandel, the Chulia merchants and the Telugu Chettis; and in eastern India, the Oriyas and Bengalis. Some of these were mainly merchants, while others were shipowners and merchants. Mercantile enterprise was linked to a local shipbuilding tradition. Among them, the Gujarati experienced a significant expansion in the scale of their business in the fifteenth century due to the suspension of direct Arab-Chinese trade. Taking advantage of the business opportunity, they settled in Malacca and Aden and built close ties between West Asia and Cambay.

In this context, the Indian Ocean had some periods of community predominance (Marks, 2007). From 650 to 1000, the period of "the rise of Islam" (Chaudhury, 1985), Arab traders and sailors carried goods and ideas all the way from the Islamic Near East to Southeast Asia and China. They spread their language and the Islamic religion throughout the region, from East Africa to Indonesia. For instance, in the ninth century, thousands of Arabs, Persians, and Jews took residence in the southern China city of Guangzhou, and a mosque was built there. Muslim traders were well received at the port of Canton, and they were allowed to conduct their commercial and communal affairs through their traditional Islamic institutions.

A second period began around 1000 until 1500, when the Chinese merchants saw the profits to be made in the trade and, with or without the support of their government, sailed into the Indian Ocean to compete with the Arabs. After that, although Arab traders were still important, they were not the only ones plying the waters of the Indian Ocean. In the western zone, Arab traders were the most active, although Indian merchants also participated. The central circuit from Ceylon to the Bay of Bengal and to Southeast Asia was dominated by Indian merchants, although the Arabs and other Muslims were very active there too. At the same time, the Indian merchants were not a homogenous group. For instance, the Jain traders of Gujarat, with ascetical values, could not eat with, drink with, or marry the Chettiars of the Coromandel Coast. Finally, in the east, the Chinese dominated the South China Sea circuit from China to Indonesia and the Strait of Malacca.

Regarding the Islamic hegemony, Subrahmanyam (2012, p. 31) suggests that at the ports and trade connections, the level of cosmopolitanism of this whole period was impressive:

> It has at times been assumed that the commercial expansion of these centuries was part of a phase of "Arab dominance" of Indian Ocean trade. But this is surely too simplistic, for other Asian merchant groups participated in this trade on a large scale as well. These included Gujarati . . . and Bohras, Tamil, and Telugu Chettis, Mappila and Maraikkayar Muslims from southern India, Chinese from Fujian and other provinces of the southeast in the Celestial Empire, and the Iranian tujjar.

The shipbuilding was not homogeneous either. Each community had its own style and technology, in close relation with the seas and geography where they were located. The Chinese boats, with their flat bottoms and the shallow draft of the typical junk, were ideal for sailing in shoal and estuarial waters, but in open sea, the junk was in danger. The Indo-Arab ship, with its keeled hull and the big lateen sail, gave the sailors a degree of control which was lacking in the Chinese junk. The Arab sailors had experience in the Mediterranean Sea. The Indonesians, meanwhile, had their own shipbuilding style, with a great reputation. And the Africans also built their own traditional boats, the "dhows".

Trade was conducted largely without the need to resort to force of arms. African dhows, Chinese junks, and Indian and Arab merchant ships all sailed without naval convoys from their native lands. However, the strength of the navies of the Indian Ocean varied (Lewis, 1973). For instance, Arabs developed capabilities in the Mediterranean Sea and had a period of sea war strength during the tenth and eleventh centuries (Lewis and Runyan, 1985). The Indonesians possessed fast-moving war vessels, and their reputation as sea fighters was well known. On the contrary, the Indian subcontinent remained rather vulnerable to enemy attacks (Chaudhury, 1985). Besides, according to Chaudhury (1985), Asian trade ports were not always capable of defending their merchants against pirates. None of the great ports of trade, Aden, Hormuz, Calicut, or Malacca, were walled or fortified.

Margariti (2008), based on anthropological evidence, asserts that there were pirate groups operating in the Persian Gulf and the Red Sea. In fact, it was not that the local players did not know about violence at the sea; Gujarat pirates and Malaysian sea fighters were described as active members of this ecosystem. However, before the arrival of the Portuguese, there had been no organised attempt by any inland political power to control the sea routes and the long-distance trade of Asia. The Indian Ocean and its different seas were not dominated by any empire, and there were no systematic efforts from the inland powers to control the sea. The Chinese empire, although its junks were as large and powerful as sixteenth-century European ships, was busy maintaining its political and economic power on terra firma and never considered overseas colonial ventures. At the same time, Indian lack of interest in sea power remains enigmatic. The large territorial kingdoms of India, with their cities far from the sea, showed no interest in maritime mastery. In this line, Marks (2007) maintains that from 650 to 1500, trade in the Indian Ocean seemed to have been self-regulating. In the Indian Ocean trading emporium, there was some kind of law of reciprocity. Rulers and princes refrained from interfering in the commercial affairs of merchants from abroad, and these guaranteed good behaviour.

Regarding financing, Chaudhury (1985) affirms that this is one of the least known issues of the period. Bills of exchange were quite developed to finance commerce from one port to another. Merchants had a big role in financing long trips. There existed a fine line between family, private, and commercial property. Family wealth was one of the main forms of private capital accumulation, although merchants also channelled some noblemen's wealth into the trade business. Anyway, there was nothing similar to stock options or state financing commerce in a systematic way.

2.1.3 India "clothing"[6] the Indian Ocean ecosystem

The Indian subcontinent population in the 1600s was of little more than 100 million people (Subrahmanyam, 1990). This represented almost one-fifth of the world population and one-third of the Asian population of the time. Indian textiles not only clothed 100 million Indian people, but they were perhaps also the most global among the various goods entering long-distance trade between 1500 and 1800. In 1500, cotton textiles were the centre of the manufacturing life of the Indian subcontinent and the foundation of a wide-ranging trade that spread from India via land and sea.

Different types of textiles, mainly cotton textiles, were traded by Indian merchants in exchange for a variety of commodities, mainly spices, foodstuff, and luxuries. Quality was judged by the fineness of the yarn, the number of threads to the inch, and by the less palpable criteria of artistic excellence. South India had very developed cotton regions; a major concentration of producers was located in the Coromandel plain, and other smaller ones were in inland regions such as Coimbatore, Mysore, and Andhra (Subrahmanyam, 1990). There was some kind of symbiotic relationship between the dominance of the coast in textile production and the production of cotton in the dry interior. In the coast, Surat (Gujarat) provided high-grade silk and mixed fabrics, Coromandel (Madras) was traditionally the leading producer of inexpensive cotton textiles, and, later, Bengal specialised in luxury cotton, silk, and mixed fabrics. It was a regional specialisation with a well-articulated system of exchange with the Indian Ocean.

Other towns like Patna, Benares, Lahore, Multan, Allahabad, and other particular regions were reputed for specific varieties (Raychaudhuri, 1982a). Exports came mainly from four regions: the Indus Plain including Punjab and Sind; Gujarat and the west coast; the Coromandel Coast, both south and north; and Bengal. In addition to fabric and clothing, the range of products included sailcloth, cotton carpets, bedcovers, pillowcases, handkerchiefs, mattresses, embroidered quilts, bed-hangings, tents, and so on. Cotton yarn production was an independent manufacturing activity and a second occupation in weavers' families. Yarn was produced by a subsistence-oriented system in peasant households. Broach, Balasore, and Kasimbazar are mentioned as major sources of yarn supply.

The Indian textiles were regularly sold in Bandar Abbas by Indian merchants and then transported by land and sea to Persia, Baghdad, and Basra, where they changed hands and reached Constantinople via Syria (Riello and Roy, 2009). The caravan trade carried Indian textiles to Ethiopia, especially cheap striped textiles, along with silver and gold. East Africa exchanged primary products for Asian manufactured goods, cottons, other fine textiles, Islamic earthenware, glass, and Chinese porcelain. Considerable quantities of Asian textiles also arrived in Congo as luxury cloths. In Africa, Indian cloth functioned as currency. Southeast Asia was another key market. In this case, Gujarati merchants dominated the trade with Malacca from the port of Cambay.

The Indian Ocean was a huge, sophisticated, and articulated market for Indian textiles. Indeed, when the Europeans arrived in the Indian Ocean region, they were marvelled over the Indian textiles. As quoted in Riello and Roy (2009, p. 1), John Huyghen van Linschoten noted in his *The Voyage of John Huyghen van Linschoten to the East Indies* (1598):

> [G]reat traffique into Bengala, Pegu, Sian, and Malacca, and also to India . . . there is excellent faire linnen of Cotton made in Negapatan, Saint Thomas, and Masulepatan, of all colours, and woven with diverse sorts of loome workes and figures, verie fine and cunningly wrought, which is much worne in India, and better esteemed then silke, for that is higher prised than silke, because of the finenes and cunning workmanship.

It was a proto-industrial production. Cotton was spun and woven in artisans' homes with material financed by merchants, who then collected the thread and cloth for dyeing and printing before being brought to the market. To meet both domestic and foreign demand, Indians developed a whole manufacturing system, from growing the cotton to elaborating it. Prakash (2009) pointed out that the three key elements in this system were the weavers' need of finance, their limited access to the market, and their need to avoid the risks associated to forecast the demand behaviour. This contract system was a variant of the standard European putting-out system. However, unlike the European case, the Indian weaver bought his own raw material and exercised formal control over his output. Of course, the merchant who had given the advance had first claim on the output, and debt obligations often rendered the artisans subject to coercive control by the merchants.

The unquestioned domination of Indian textiles in the Indian Ocean trade should be understood in terms of the subcontinent's capacity to deliver to the market a wide range of goods at highly competitive prices. The "competitive advantages" of the Indian textiles were based on the development of multiple shafts and pedals, which allowed weavers to count on the availability of relative inexpensive dyes such as indigo, and skilled and cheap labour engaged in all the stages of the textile production, from cotton growing to spinning, printing, weaving, and so on (Machado, 2009). This resulted in an extremely efficient industry with which no other region could compete in

Figure 2.2 Gujarat-made bedcover. Eighteenth century. Cotton with silk.
Source: MET Museum – Public Domain. www.metmuseum.org/art/collection/search/229248

terms of price and quality until the development of industrial production in Europe. In this respect, Baber (1996, p. 62) states:

> Indian dyeing techniques and procedures for rendering them permanent, together with the preparation of a very wide range of vegetable dyes, relied on quite sophisticated methods, which continued to be superior to other techniques until the invention and manufacture of artificial dyes in Germany. Depending on specific

regional conditions, a number of innovations, such as the harnessing of water power for operating the cotton gin and the use of crank handles attached to the spinning wheels, were introduced.

2.2 The Europeans in the Indian Ocean: creatures from a different ecosystem (1498–1757)

2.2.1 Genesis of the all-sea route to India

With the emergence of the Italian city states and the commercial rivalry between Genoa and Venice, the Christian Mediterranean became a space of open naval conflicts. The Venetian confrontations with the Muslim fleets fused together the interests of the merchants and the state. This Italian path was reproduced later in Seville, Lisbon, Amsterdam, and London. The "gunpowder trade" was transplanted to the Indian Ocean by the beginning of the sixteenth century (Chaudhury, 1985).

The Portuguese[7] venture into the Indian Ocean had, at the same time, religious and mercantilist motivations. The Cape of Good Hope route implied the overcoming of the transport-technology barrier to the growth of Euro-Asian trade (Prakash, 2008). The volume of trade was no longer limited by the capacity constraint imposed by the availability of pack animals and riverboats in the Middle East. For about a century, until challenged by the monopoly given by the Pope to the Dutch and the English in the 1590s, the only merchant group engaged in trade between Europe and Asia along the all-water route were the Portuguese.

European and, more specifically, Mediterranean shipbuilding enjoyed some crucial improvements during the fifteenth century. As explained in Findlay and O'Rourke (2007), a first decisive innovation was the adoption of the Arab triangular fore-and-aft lateen sail. It was much more flexible to the direction of the wind than the old Roman square-rigged sails. A second major influence came from north-western Europe, whose cogs had retained the square rig but improved on its design in relation to the Roman original. These ships were reintroduced to the Mediterranean after the Crusades, becoming the standard form of transport for large cargoes.

Vasco da Gama's road to India was a laborious effort that included centuries of naval expertise and capabilities, strong financing, and political decision-making. Portugal took advantage of the accumulation of knowledge that came from the competition between Genoa and Venice, during the thirteenth and fourteenth centuries, for the trade hegemony in the Mediterranean. Sagres became what we would call today an "R&D lab", bringing together mathematicians, cartographers, Moorish prisoners who had different knowledge of the Indic and African seas, and so on. This was later institutionalised as the Naval Academy of Sagres, which provided cutting-edge naval knowledge for Portuguese sailors. Henry "The Navigator" was the man who led this enterprise. Henry's figure synthesised the religious and mercantilist spirit of the adventure: in his "private" sphere, he was a trader in sugar and slaves and a patron of corsair ventures; in his "public" life, he was Master of the Order of Christ and creator of the Portuguese Crown patronage of missions (Subrahmanyam, 2012; Panikkar, 1953).

Financing was not a minor factor for the sustainability of the conquest. The resources of the Order of Christ, inherited from the Order of the Knights Templar, were used mainly to finance the marine explorations. Besides, the princes of Antwerp also provided resources to the Indian enterprise (Panikkar, 1953, p. 35):

> Armada followed armada in unending succession under trained captains and the Portuguese chiefs in the Indian waters knew that men and ships were on the way bringing succour to them. Even in the most difficult circumstances, they could, therefore, hold out with the firm conviction that help was not far away . . . the Portuguese Government had the financial backing of the great merchant princes of Antwerp who, realizing the revolutionary change in trade that the Portuguese discoveries involved, had hastened to annex the benefits. The Weslers, for example, had invested in the Portuguese voyages of 1505, and the Lisbon Government had found it necessary as early as 1503 to open a depot for spices in Antwerp. To this system of continuous reinforcements . . . must be attributed the success that attended the navies of Portugal on the Eastern seas.

Da Gama's expedition to India also implied a sailing challenge. According to Kaplan (2010a), da Gama reacquainted Europeans with the monsoon wind system. Arab navigators in what is today Kenya helped him do that. Calicut, located at the south of the Indian subcontinent, at the contemporary Indian state of Kerala, was ideally situated to take advantage of the monsoon winds from the Red Sea to the Indian coast and back to the Arabian shores. This had implications in terms of both agriculture and sailing: Calicut was one of the Indian main producers of tropical spices, and it was in a mainstream road of the Indian Ocean sea trade.

The sea gunpowder was one of the main novelties of the Portuguese ships in the Arabian Sea. To Panikkar (1953), the arrival of the *San Gabriel* vessel in the Indian Ocean introduced a revolutionary factor: the cannon carrying ship. The weaponry of the Portuguese ships was totally unexpected and new in the Indian seas and gave an immediate and decisive advantage to the Portuguese. The only non-European power which had developed gunnery on the sea was the Ottoman Empire, and when the Portuguese arrived in Calicut, the Turks had no navy in the Indian Ocean. At this point, most of the authors, such as Chaudhury (1985), Panikkar (1953), and Findlay and O´Rourke (2007), agree. The Portuguese cannons were a distinctive competitive advantage for the initial Portuguese presence at the trade ports. For instance, the Malaysian struggles with the Portuguese are remembered as great sea confrontations. Scenes in the Indian Ocean related in *The Voyage of François Pyrard of Laval to the East Indies, the Maldives, the Moluccas and Brazil* quoted by Subrahmanyam (1990, p. 259) had this epic tenure:

> The War between them is very cruel and merciless, for the Malabars are so courageous that they never surrender, and prefer death. I have seen them, when in battle with the Portuguese, on perceiving that they were the weaker side and could not avoid being taken, all come to one side of their galliot, and go down with their booty, galliot and all, and sometimes even wait till some Portuguese had boarded their vessel, so that they should perish with them.

The Muslim quasi-monopoly over the spice trade and the influence that they had over the Zamorin of Calicut were not expected by da Gama in his first trip of 1489. After a formal exchange of compliments, da Gama returned back to Portugal. The second expedition was of a much bigger scale: 33 ships, 1,500 men, and a powerful armada commanded by Pedro Cabral. This expedition was the first violent act of the Portuguese in the Indian Ocean. For our ends, we can add that a series of naval confrontations took place in the ports of South India between 1489 and 1510. This tension also involved the sultan of Cairo and the sultan of Gujarat, who had commercial interests in the area. Although the Portuguese had superiority in terms of gunpowder, Calicut's zamorin in joint military efforts with the sultan of Egypt and other local powers prevented the Portuguese conquest over Calicut. However, the Portuguese enjoyed a monopoly in the sea trade route between Europe and the Indian Ocean that lasted for more than century, from 1489 to 1600, when Northern European companies were created.

2.2.2 A Goa-centred network

The "Portuguese India" was not a geographically well-defined space but a complex maritime network of territories, establishments, goods, people, and administrative interests in Asia and East Africa (Subrahmanyam and Thomaz, 1991). It was centred in Goa, but with port presence in Calicut, Ceylon (Sri Lanka), Malacca, Macao, and even Nagasaki. In its initial period, this network was built through military power, but later, it was mainly developed by negotiations and balancing of power with different local merchants and rulers. Regarding the Portuguese territorial presence and the local connections, Panikkar (1953, p. 39) says:

> Goa was no doubt occupied and converted into a great base, but this was with the help of Tulaji, the Hindu chief of the area, who joined with the Portuguese in order to weaken the Adil Shahi

> Sultan's authority in the neighborhood . . . Goa was at an extremity of Adil Shai's extensive dominions and its conquest and fortification by the Portuguese were matters of great importance to the Hindu Empire of Vijayanagar in its campaigns against Islam. The Vijayanagar Emperors were quick to realize that Goa provided them an outlet to the sea, through which they could get not only arms and equipment, but the horses which they needed so much for their cavalry. Actually, therefore, the conquest of Goa was not the establishment of the Portuguese as a land power in India, but the creation of a suitable place for naval operations in the Indian Ocean.

Albuquerque, perhaps the most important captain in Portuguese naval history in the Indian Ocean, managed to temporarily conquer, with Chinese support, the port of Malacca, which was controlled by the sultans of Malaya. After Malacca, the Portuguese reached Japan, where they "founded" Nagasaki in 1571. Nagasaki would have given the possibility of controlling the flow of commerce with the Pacific Ocean, but it never occurred. As is noted by Panikkar (1953, p. 41):

> With the conquest of Malacca, Albuquerque completed the structure of European maritime Empire in Asia. He had set out to build up a commercial Empire based on an unchallengeable position in the Indian Ocean. The major ports on the coast of Africa were already under Portuguese domination, but before his time there was in India only a small foothold in Cochin, and no strong points anywhere from which Portuguese naval authority could be enforced. By the annexation of Socotra, by political influence at Ormuz and by holding Malacca, he established a system of control which remained unshaken as long as Portuguese naval power remained powerful enough in Europe.

As can be seen in the next map, a Portuguese proto "string of pearls" was built in the Indian Ocean. With the Portuguese trying to maintain the Indian route in secret, in 1504, a decree forbade the insertion of any details about the route after the Congo in any map.

All in all, the Indian subcontinent was never under a real threat of Portuguese territorial dominance.[8] No strong Asian power of the time, whether in India, the Middle East, or China, considered the Portuguese to be a serious threat to the existing balance of power (Prakash, 2008). No Asian ruler saw the need to build a navy such as the Japanese built after Commodore Perry's visit to Japan in 1853. In fact, to Panikkar (1953), the big achievement of the Portuguese during the first period of their supremacy was to prevent the Arabian traders to participate in the spice trade.

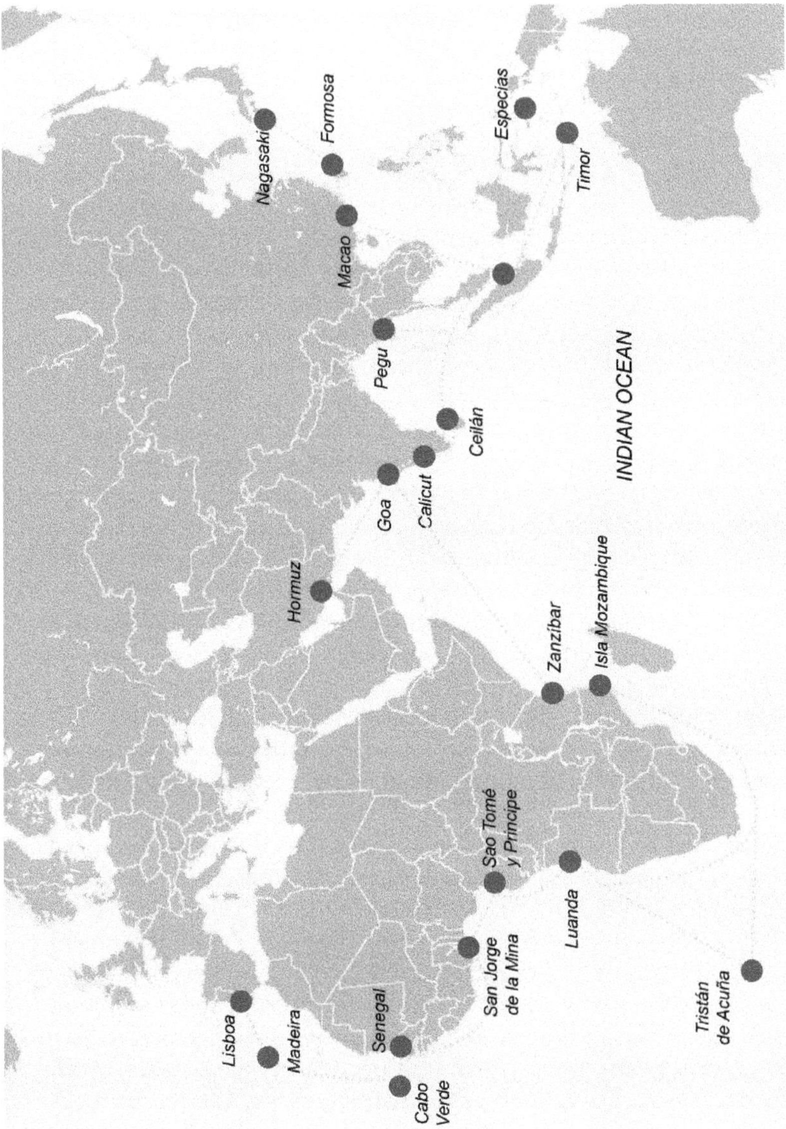

Figure 2.3 The Portuguese proto "String of Pearls", 1580.

Source: Elaborated by Rosaura Flynn.

Regarding the general framework of the Asian trade, for Chaudhury (2008), the aspirations and the activities of the Estado da Índia represented an institutional innovation: a complete state monopoly of an important commercial product was not unknown, but it was a rare phenomenon. For Indian merchants and political rulers, it was a relatively novel experience to encounter an imperial scheme that was being directed from a power centre which was situated many thousands of miles overseas, in another continent. Pepper and spices were the main commodities on which the Portuguese founded their imperial ambitions.

The main trade item was spices, mainly pepper, though some other goods were also procured. The procurement of pepper in India was arranged by the Portuguese, while the trading in Europe was through contract sales based until the middle of the century in Antwerp and thereafter at Lisbon. According to Prakash (2008), partly because of the absence of a strong mercantile tradition among the Portuguese, not comparable in any sense to that of the north-western Europeans, and partly because the Crown had provided the main financing and the infrastructural support to the efforts, the overseas enterprise in Asia was dominated from the very beginning by the Portuguese Crown.

The cargoes sent from Lisbon in exchange for pepper included precious metals; non-precious metals such as copper, lead, tin, and mercury; and other goods such as coral, wines, olive oil, and so on. However, metals dominated the exports, and copper was the most important. According to Chaudhury, it was not until the third decade of the sixteenth century that silver from the mines of Mexico and Peru began to reach the Iberian Peninsula in large quantities and re-exported to the Indian Ocean region. Indian textiles were used primarily to buy Indonesian spices and drugs and Chinese porcelain and silk. Slave trade was also used into intra-Ocean transactions.[9]

For Prakash (2008), the attempt to monopolise the spice trade was unambiguous. It called for a total exclusion of Asian shipping from the Persian Gulf and the Red Sea and the regulation of the rest of the Asian trade. The "institutional platform" used to implement this policy was the "cartaz", that all Asian ships were obliged to carry. The document obliged all Asian ships to call at a Portuguese-controlled port and, following the establishment of the Portuguese customs houses there, to pay customs duties. Enemies of the Portuguese were not allowed, and banned goods such as spices were not to be carried. There is some evidence that an equivalent of the "cartaz" existed in the Asian seas before the arrival of the Portuguese, but the scale on which this restrictive measure was used by the Portuguese was unprecedented.

The Portuguese were able to enforce such requirement only during the first years, essentially because of the near absence of effective naval gunpower capabilities in the Indian and most other Asian port cities of the time. After some decades, the Portuguese capabilities of "enforcement" of the all sea route were challenged. The Estado da Índia lacked the resources in men and ships to sustain an effective blockade of the Red Sea for a century (Prakash, 2008). The only area in which the Portuguese were reasonably successful was in preventing ships from Malabar going to the Red Sea, but shipping from Kanara (Karnataka) and the Bay of Bengal continued to carry Indian pepper to the Red Sea from the late 1530s onwards, mainly through the agency of the Gujarati sailors and traders. For Chaudhury (2008), the "cartaz" system was partially ineffective due to corruption and administrative laxity.

A variety of interest groups were involved in the Portuguese network (Prakash, 2008). In Lisbon, in addition to the Crown, merchant guilds, financiers, and bankers of various European nationalities were essential constituents of the operation, and also main links with the European ecosystem. These guilds played an important role in the procurement and the transportation of the return cargo from Asia. Within Asia, the Portuguese presence had different facets. In the first place was the official presence in the form of the Estado da Índia, which was supposed to take care of the commercial interests of the Crown. But the employees of the Estado, from the Viceroy down, simultaneously engaged extensively in trade in their private capacity under a variety of arrangements. Finally, private Portuguese traders, the Casado traders, operated neither under the protection of the Estado da Índia nor outside of it.

The Portuguese also had different phases of interaction and articulation with regional players in order to control trade. Subrahmanyam (1990, p. 258) relates:

> [T]he Portuguese rapidly entered into conflictual relations with the Samudri Raja and the Pardesi merchants of Calicut, and encouraged Cochin to develop itself as a rival to Calicut. In the early phase, the Portuguese even used as agents in the procurement of commodities for the cargoes of Europe-bound carracks Mappila merchants such as Cherian and Mamali Marakkar. Once again, conflict and partnerships with local networks.

Gujarat, Bengal, Masulipatnam, and many other ports of the Indian Ocean were not under the control of the Portuguese. In the second half of the sixteenth century, there were different political disputes in South India, mainly between the Bahmani kingdom's successor, the Golconda Sultanate, the Gajapati, and the Empire of Vijayanagar (Subrahmanyam, 1990). In short, these disputes resulted in the decline of Pulicat as a high-sea port and the rise of Masulipatnam, which reached its climax in the 1600s. In fact, the regulations governing the Goa customs house mentioned the textiles from Masulipatnam and the duties to be charged on them. Furthermore, the growth of the Bay of Bengal as a trading system, which involved different ports, was another spot that was outside the sphere of control of the

Portuguese. Persian merchants were dominant in the Bengal coast and in its surrounding ports; both the South Indian fragmentation of power and the emergence of Bengal as a central commercial hub are important in the process to understand port settlements of the Northern European companies during the sixteenth century.

2.2.3 From the Iberian people to the North European people

The growth of Protestantism in Europe indirectly impacted the Indian Ocean ecosystem (Panikkar, 1953). For the Protestant nations, the Papal grant of a monopoly to Portugal had no validity. But what was changing since the end of the sixteenth century was the balance of power in Europe. Elizabeth, the English Queen, was challenging Phillip II's monopoly in the Spanish Main. At the same time, the spice epicentre had been shifting from Lisbon to the ports of the Netherlands at the end of the sixteenth century. The demand for spices was greater in the northern regions of Europe, and the trade was also being controlled by the northern traders.

To Chaudhury (1978), the commercial and financial supremacy of Amsterdam during this period was beyond anyone's doubts. The Dutch emerged by 1650 as the leaders in global commerce in virtually all of the seas and oceans in the world (Findlay and O´Rourke, 2007). The foundation of Dutch commercial prosperity rested on a worldwide carrying trade and a massive concentration of marketing and stapling functions in Amsterdam. The biggest profits were made by the Dutch through their ability to import and redistribute a wide variety of goods throughout the markets of Europe and Asia. Much of the Mediterranean and the Baltic trade was carried out with Dutch ships. Besides, the Dutch were the masters of the European bullion trade. The bankers of Amsterdam could issue bills of exchange on Cadiz and Lisbon, in quantities which the London of William III found hard to rival (De Vries, 1973).

In 1592, the leading Dutch merchants decided to establish a company for trading with India. The first Dutch fleet sailed in 1595. Of the 259 men who left, only 80 returned, but it was a success in commercial terms. The United East India Company (Dutch Verenigde Oostindische Compagnie, VOC) was formally created in 1602. It had not only the monopoly of trade but also wide sovereign powers to sign alliances, conquer territories, build forts, and so on. Dutch shipping consisted of large armed vessels of 500–1,000 tons, which led them to become a formidable power (Israel, 1989). The contest for the control of trade in the Atlantic and in Indonesia between the Dutch and the Spanish was fierce and only occasionally contained by diplomatic efforts (Roy, 2012b).

The decline of the Portuguese network in the Indian Ocean was a warfare process and not a punctual event. A first deal was signed between the Dutch and the Zamorin of Malabar, one of the main enemies of the Portuguese

(Panikkar, 1953). The Dutch's first attempt to displace them occurred in the islands of Indonesia, where the Portuguese were not solidly established. A major victory was achieved in the Battle of Swally, in 1612, but the Dutch settlement in Indonesia was only fully achieved in 1619, when they conquered and occupied Jakarta. Later, in 1641, the Dutch conquered Malacca[10] and, in 1654, occupied the port of Ceylon. After Ceylon, the Portuguese network downfall was swift. Cochin was occupied in 1660, and other small trading ports fell one by one to the Dutch.

In 1599, the Dutch raised the price of pepper from 3 to 8 pounds, and the British merchants decided to join in the Eastern trade. In December 1600, the British East India Company (BEIC) received from Queen Elizabeth the monopoly to trade in the East and was allowed to carry bullion from England to finance its trade. Spices were the primary objective. The first vessel reached Sumatra in 1602, but there was no demand for British products. So the Company's agents thought that they could finance the pepper imports through Asian intra-trade: they realised that there was a great demand for Indian textiles in Bantam and Moluccas. This way they could finance the pepper imports with these "carry-trade" profits. The Dutch-consolidated power in Indonesia was the main factor that led the English to concentrate on the Indian coasts. The first British trading post was established in Surat, in 1612. However, the Civil War in England affected the Company's situation. As a consequence, during the first half of the seventeenth century, the East India Company only embarked on a diplomatic policy of extending their trading posts along India. They settled in Masulipatnam in 1641, and they obtained the permission of the Empire of Vijayanagar to build a fort in Madras on the same year.

England emerged from the Civil War with a strong navy and an aggressive middle class willing to challenge the Dutch commercial hegemony. According to Findlay and O´Rourke (2007), it was the newly enhanced power of Parliament acting in the collective interest of the national mercantile class, rather than the "grace and favour" of a monarch, that was responsible for the British mercantilist policies. All in all, it was the Restoration that gave a great impulse to the BEIC (Panikkar, 1953; Bandyopadhyay, 2004).

In the Indian Ocean, the BEIC moved its headquarters from Surat, where they were supervised by South Indian rulers, to Bombay, which Charles II had received from the Portuguese Crown in 1661, as dowry for his bride, and was handed over to the BEIC in 1668 for an annual rent of 10 pounds[11] (Bandyopadhyay, 2004). A better defence system could be built in Bombay.

Sir Josiah Child[12] was appointed to lead the BEIC with a forward policy. Indeed, he "declared war" on the Mughal Empire. As a consequence, the BEIC settlements in Bengal were occupied and mostly destroyed. The Company was forced to behave in the future. However, after these events, thanks to the indulgence of Emperor Aurangzeb, the BEIC was allowed to fortify in a fishing village in Calcutta (1690). The Company did not attempt any other forcible interventions until the 1750s.

In Europe, the first Anglo-Dutch war in 1642 launched a mercantilist war competition that included the second and the third Anglo-Dutch war and continued until the Napoleonic Wars started in 1803. In the Indian Ocean, in order to keep up with the other European powers, Henry IV, from France, also founded a French East Indian Company in 1601. Despite several voyages, it was not until Colbert that the company received a push. Colbert's original idea was to establish a French authority in Ceylon. A fleet was sent in 1670, but the Dutch prevented the French from settling, and the main French achievement was the foundation of Pondicherry, at the south-east coast of the Indian subcontinent.

Regarding the territorial big picture of the Indian Ocean at the end of the seventeenth century, Panikkar (1953, p. 51) says:

> [T]he power of the Portuguese had been eliminated effectively from the Indian Ocean and from the Pacific, though their establishments at Goa, Macao, and Timor were left undisturbed. The Dutch controlled the coastal tracts of Ceylon and had a few trading establishments on peninsular India, of which the most important were Cochin and Negapatam. They occupied Malacca and controlled the trade of Malaya. In Indonesia, they had built up an Empire based on commercial monopoly and with China and Japan, they carried on a profitable trade. The British, excluded from the Indonesian islands, had concentrated on India where they had built up an extensive trading organization. Last, of all, the French had entered the Orient and staked their claims at Pondicherry.

According to Roy (2012b, p. 121), the BEIC appearance altered the balance of power in the Indian Ocean ecosystem:

> Although technically a joint-stock firm, the company did not represent a unitary command-and-control structure. Its overseas trading enterprise was possible because of the peculiar nature of the principal-agent relations that it entailed, combining modern joint-stock operation with a pre-modern form of partnership between risk-taking peripatetic sailors and soldiers, and risk-averse sedentary town merchants. These two classes of people did share a common interest in the profits of Asian trade, but they were not friends otherwise. A decisive change of balance in the partnership could see the sailors-cum-soldiers try to establish a sphere of the political authority thereby defying the wishes of their principals, the capitalists. Colonization was an outcome of the unstable partnership that formed the basis of these enterprises.

Regarding the intracompany competition at the Indian Ocean, Subrahmanyam (1990, p. 282) says:

> The use of violence was an intrinsic part of the market strategy of the Dutch Company from as early as 1615 or 1620 . . . but that process of expanding into markets was often at the cost of other European rivals. Moreover, the barriers to entry by which these partial or complete monopolies operated, once created, were backed by live ammunition.

Indeed, the North European companies were a typical creature of the European ecosystem, particularly in geopolitical terms, in a period of emergence of the Northern powers. Although they were private companies, "the first joint-options companies in the world", they competed in both military and diplomatic terms backed by their states' navies and financed by other European powers to control the lucrative trade networks, which connected Europe with the Indian Ocean. However, different principal-agency issues and imperial competition relations affected the "objective function" of the companies, both in the European and the Indian Ocean ecosystems.

2.2.4 Bombay, Madras, and Calcutta: the "gates" of India

Still in the sixteenth and early seventeenth centuries, the Indo-European trade was closely dependent on Asian traders (Roy, 2012a; Subrahmanyam, 1990). They controlled many aspects of Indo-European business, except for the final sale and shipment by sea, functioning not only as agents for the Europeans inside India but also as main actors in overland trade. All forms of caravan trade and fluvial trade were dominated by the Indians. The Europeans had no option but to operate within the given organisational structure, including accommodation by bankers and money changers, partnerships with local merchants, the services of artisans, and so on (Prakash, 2008). Indeed, although the Portuguese had the "hegemony" over the pepper trade during the sixteenth century, the Indian maritime trading communities were still really only involved in the coastal trade.

However, Indian maritime trade experienced a rearrangement during the seventeenth century (Dasgupta, 1967, 2008). With the emergence of the English and Dutch companies, the western Asia trade was re-emphasised at the expense of the south-east, which had marked Indian trade in the previous century. In this shift, the final breakdown of Portuguese restrictions liberated maritime trade in the Indian Ocean. This, plus the growing demand in Europe, caused a period of prosperity in the local merchant communities. In the first half of the seventeenth century, the BEIC used its naval forces to serve as escorts for Indian ships carrying valuable cargoes to the Red Sea, the Persian Gulf, and pilgrims to Mecca (Findlay and O'Rourke, 2007). As said, carrying-trade and naval protection were the main initial businesses of the BEIC.

Different processes of knowledge exchange and dissemination occurred during this period. Roy (2012a) stresses that during the seventeenth century, Indian practices were far behind the European ones in sailing: instruments such as the telescope and compass were unknown to Indian sailors. The Indian ships were heavier and were constructed with little iron, which made them unsuitable for long voyages. In the period between 1620 and 1670, the ships increasingly exhibited "European" traits such as multiple decks, heavier armament, and so on (Prakash, 1990). In the case of the telescope, which was widely used by the European sailors, there is no evidence of its use by Indians, either for navigational or for astronomical observations, during the seventeenth century. However, different European methods and techniques, such as the iron nailing, were quickly adopted by the Indian people, as stated by Qaisar (1982):

> It is remarkable that the Indians lost no time in adopting the new technique. They sensed the danger and readily adopted the alien technique of iron nailing. It was no accident, then, that an Arab merchant in 1507 built a galleon in the Portuguese style in Gujarat. When Goa was conquered by Albuquerque in 1509, a good deal of pitch, oakum, cordage, and nails were discovered in storehouses. Even earlier (1501), Cabral was given to understand that the ships on the south-west coast were made with iron nails. Varthema, writing about Calicut in the first decade of the sixteenth century, observed the use of "an immense quantity of iron nails" in Indian ships.

Furthermore, during the seventeenth century, the Dutch and the English East India companies, as well as private English traders, became important buyers of ships constructed at Narsapur Peta and other Indian shipbuilding centres such as Hugli in Bengal.[13] Many of these ships were built on the basis of European designs and in some cases under European supervision.

In the second half of the seventeenth century, the BEIC finally settled in at the three port-cities that would configure its future penetration into the Indian subcontinent, relocating the trade dynamics of the subcontinent (Panikkar, 1953, Roy, 2012a). Although the acquisition of Madras (1640), Bombay (1661), and Calcutta (1690) came to the English separately, it included a process of threats or warfare with local states. According to Roy (2012a), each of these territories emerged not only as a little colony with its own laws and administration but also as a commercial centre, a port, and a destination for migrant Indian artisans and merchants. Each one started small, with a small European population and a port without a harbour. The fort and its walls enclosed the factory and the European population; the villages formed a kind of suburb from which supplies of goods and workers came from. But they grew rapidly: Madras reached a population of over 300,000 by 1700, while Calcutta and Bombay had 100,000 and 70,000, respectively, by the middle of the eighteenth century (Roy, 2012a). Gradually, in Bombay, Calcutta, and Madras, the English were becoming landlords.

This geographical change was highlighted by Roy (2012a, p. 121):

> Another sphere in which the Europeans made a significant change, urbanisation, again invites us to the institutional and knowledge outcomes of the contact. Trade historians see the emergence and meteoric rise of Bombay, Madras, and Calcutta merely a diversion of trade from the established centres such as Surat, Masulipatnam, or Hooghly. In fact, these three cities represented a different business culture in coastal India. For one thing, Madras and Bombay broke the geographically conditioned dependence of port cities on internal navigation and Mughal roads. Even more than Surat, these were ocean-bound ports. For another, Surat and Masulipatnam were cities that did not belong to merchants; in those cities, the merchants did not make laws, in Bombay they did. The three cities were, institutionally speaking, worlds apart from the Indian littoral spaces.

2.2.5 India "clothing" Europe

In parallel with the displacement of the principal seaports, a second profound change occurred during the seventeenth century with the Euro-Asian trade: Indian textiles boomed in Europe. In short, the European nations arrived in Asian waters in search of spices, but with the total exclusion of the British from Indonesia and the growth of trade with the ports of China, the interest of the BEIC shifted to textiles, calico, muslin, silks, and so on. The strict prohibition on the import of French linens and silk into Britain at the end of the seventeenth century was a main first push for Indian cotton textiles. Indian cotton textiles helped to create a new middle-class and bourgeois notion of fashion in Europe (Riello and Roy, 2009). They became popular because of their cheapness, colourfulness, durability, and washable quality, competing with and replacing wool clothing.[14] For Chaudhury (2008), the imported textiles could be classified under five groups: plain white cotton, plain dyed cotton, striped and check cotton, chintz and embroidered cloth, and silk piece-goods, including fabrics containing a mix of cotton and silk yarn. India's textiles had been traded beyond its shores long before the European arrival, but the volume of transactions taking place from the sixteenth century on appears as a completely new phenomenon. According to Findlay and O'Rourke (2007), in 1750, textiles were between 60% and 80% of the BEIC's imports to England.

It is important to notice that the Indian trading posts were not "demand" posts for the British goods. It was the New World that was fuelling Asian trade, strengthening the European consumer boom (Roy, 2012a). Virginia tobacco in the middle of the seventeenth century and Caribbean sugar in the eighteenth century were the most important American goods. Indian textiles were used as means of payment in Africa for slaves. For a brief period in the seventeenth century, Persian horses went to India to balance the trade. But it was silver from the Americas that greatly contributed to the making of Asian trade. The Spanish conquest had made silver cheaper in Europe than in Asia. These events, together with the almost inexhaustible demand for silver from India, made it possible to continue the purchases of Asian goods until the mid-eighteenth century.

This lack of demand for Western goods during the seventeenth century gradually turned into a serious problem in England and France. Although the growth of wealth helped to maintain the demand, the East India trade was looked at with disapproval and was subjected to strong criticism, and the popularity of Indian textiles became a great political issue (Panikkar, 1953). Thus, in 1677, the British Parliament banned all but woollen goods for winter use. The Navigation Acts, which restricted the use of foreign ships for trade between every country except England, and the Calico Acts, which gradually banned the import of textiles into England, should be understood as an emergent of this protectionist displeasure and the beginning of a period of protection to English national industries.

Notes

1 The author assumes responsibility or liability for any issues arising out of the use of all chapter epigraphs in this book

2 This section is mainly based on the masterpiece of Professor Chaudhury (1985) *Trade and Civilization in the Indian Ocean: An Economic History from the Rise of Islam to 1750*. Chaudhury's book is, in some sense, an Indian version of Braudel's (1949) work on Mediterranean.

3 To see the characteristics of the volcano's areas of Java, see Herzog's (2016) *Into the Inferno*.

4 Maps used in this book are for representational purposes only. The international boundaries, coastlines, denominations, and other information shown in the maps in this work do not necessarily imply any judgement concerning the legal status of any territory or the endorsement or acceptance of such information.

5 The monsoon, as a seasonal wind, reverses direction twice a year. The Indian subcontinent heats up since June, creating a low-pressure system that draws cool moist air from the south-west. This produces a wind that blows through the summer months and brings the rains to sustain India's agriculture. In the autumn, the cycle reverses. This allowed merchants from the West to make a round-trip journey to India within a single year. The same cycle occurred from the Bay of Bengal to India's east to the islands of Southeast Asia.

6 This expression is taken from the title of the book of Riello and Roy (2009).

7 It is relevant to point out that Portuguese were not the first European people in reaching the Indian subcontinent; the ancient Greeks and Romans were the first. They have even found Roman coins in West Bengal, up the Hooghly River near present-day Kolkata (Kaplan, 2010b). For a quick analysis of the Portuguese experience regarding the type of relations that characterised the emergence of an inter-state and capitalist system, see Fiori (2014).
8 For a detailed view of the genesis and functioning of the Estado da Índia, see Subrahmanyam (2012).
9 It is important to remember that the Portuguese were sugar producers in America, so they were mainly involved in slave trade. Over 5 million slaves were traded by the Portuguese between 1519 and 1867 as part of the transatlantic commerce (Findlay and O'Rourke, 2007). In the same period, the British transatlantic slave trade registered 3 million people, the French 1.5 million, and Dutch and Spanish half a million each.
10 In 1642, the Dutch also drove the Portuguese out of the Gold Coast in Africa, the main source of Portuguese slave trade. At the same time, this opened this rich slaving area to other Europeans, mainly the English.
11 Bombay had been given to Charles II through the Treaty of Whitehall, which involved a mutual defence pact between the Portuguese and the British Crown against the aggression of the Dutch.
12 Child was a relevant figure not only because of his personality but also because he wrote a mercantilist classic, *A New Discourse of Trade*.
13 See more on technology transfer, indigenisation, and knowledge flows in Qaisar (1982), Baber (1996), and Subrahmanyam (1988), among others.
14 See Beckert (2014) for an in-depth global analysis of the cotton industry and Lemire (2009) and Berg (2009) for an analysis of the European consumers and of cotton as a fashion and luxury good.

3

THE INDIAN SUBCONTINENT PERIPHERISATION

It is a little awkward to use the name India for the entire territory of three independent states. But India in the larger sense, comprising Pakistan, India, and Bangladesh together, is still a valid geographical expression. The region containing the three countries is separated from the land-mass of the rest of Asia by the highest mountain ranges in the world. From the Himalayas, lower ranges run down, on flanks, west and east, in practically uninterrupted series, down to the sea. The sub-continent enclosed by these ranges and the sea, approximately between latitudes 8° N and 37° N and longitudes 61° E and 97° 30' E, contains two broad physical divisions, the Indo-Gangetic plains and the peninsula.

Habib (1982, p. 1)

It would have required supernatural vision for an observer in 1750 to foretell that in the course of fifty years a European nation would have conquered a third of India and would be preparing to contest with the Marathas for a position of paramountcy over the rest; for after 250 years the position of European nations in India was substantially the same as it had been after Albuquerque in 1515.

Panikkar (1953, p. 71)

As we examine this protracted process in detail, it becomes clear that both pressures from the periphery and impetus from the metropole constantly interacted with each other, and search for revenue, quest for trading privileges and the imperatives of military exigencies all took the driving seat in turn to accelerate the process of territorial conquest and erect in India the most magnificent Empire that Britain ever had.

Bandyopadhyay (2004, p. 42)

Whatever the relative magnitude of European commerce in India, it was undoubtedly a factor, though not the only factor – in the changing direction and composition of India's foreign trade. A major feature of the changes in the map of India's foreign trade in the first half of the eighteenth century was the

DOI: 10.4324/9781003091752-5

> decline of Gujarat and the corresponding increase in the importance of Bengal.
>
> Raychaudhuri (1983, p. 25)

> It is tempting to give the different railway patterns shorthand labels, such as "advanced" for the rail networks and "colonial" or "underdeveloped" for short lines running inland from a harbour. To do so, however, would be doubly misleading, for colonialism took many forms, and the relationships between railways and the rest of the society are exceedingly complex. India, which emerged from colonial rule with a "developed" rail network and an "underdeveloped" economy, is a case in point.
>
> Headrick (1988, p. 51)

This chapter will mainly address the Indian subcontinent's path since the British "victory" in Plassey in 1757 until the First World War. This period will be characterised as a process of peripherisation of the Indian subcontinent by the British rule.

3.1 The Indian subcontinent's geography and demography circa 1600

The Indian subcontinent is a triangle that is suspended from the land mass of Central Asia. Geologically, the Indian subcontinent rifted from Gondwana and merged with the Eurasian plate around 55 million years ago. Bounded in the north by the Himalayas, the land is accessible from that direction only through a number of north-west-facing passes. The Arabian Sea forms the western boundary, and the Bay of Bengal the eastern one.

The subcontinent can be roughly divided into three geographic areas. The northern region extends from the north-west lands watered by the Indus River to the north-eastern region watered by the Ganges River. The third main river of the northern area is the Brahmaputra. The Himalayas are the source of all three. Rajasthan and the Punjab hills are in this northern region too. The central area is called the Deccan and includes hill and forest zones as well as the arid Deccan Plateau. The southern region is separated from the rest of the land by the Nilgiri Hills. The climate is mainly tropical, with rainfall for much of the subcontinent dependent on the monsoon winds. The plains of the northern regions are fed by mountain snows, being less dependent on the monsoon winds than the peninsular India in the south. All through human history, the North Indian rivers have been some of the main "feeders" of the world.

South India is the portion of the peninsula that is to the south of an imaginary line from about 13° North, on the Malabar Coast of the Arabian Sea, to about latitude 18° North on the Coromandel Coast of the Bay of Bengal. From the fifth century on, a civilisation developed in the Tamil plain that profoundly influenced people over a great portion of the southern peninsula. From an early time, the sea offered the South Indians opportunities for both trade and piracy.

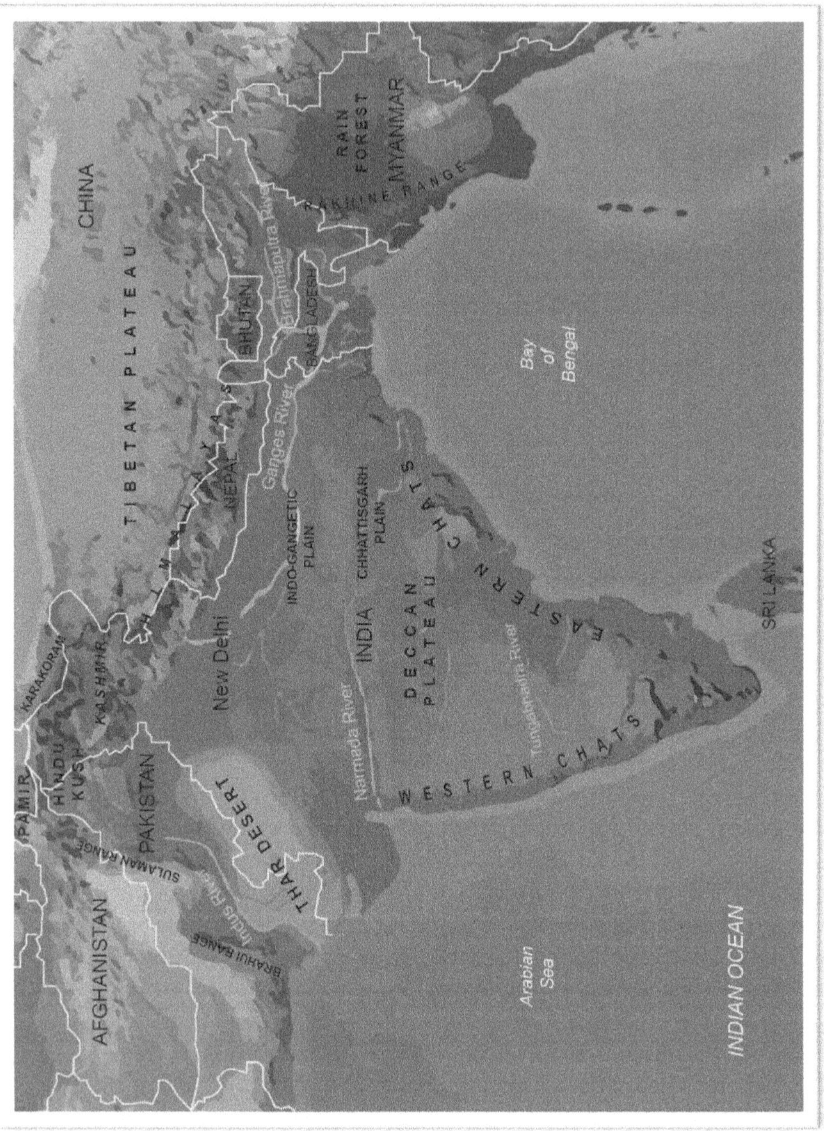

Figure 3.1 The Indian subcontinent in South Asia

Moreland's estimation of around 100 million people living in the Indian subcontinent around 1600, although there are different methodological discussions, is widely accepted (Habib, 1982). Other estimates also discussed in Habib (1982) suggest that there were 140 million people. Only 15% of this population was urban population. More than two-thirds of them lived in the northern area, near the Indus and the Ganges Rivers. In fact, the Mughal Empire was mainly located in this area.

3.2 The Mughal Empire's downfall[1]

The British penetration in the Indian subcontinent cannot be understood without considering the Mughal Empire's downfall. The Mughal Empire was founded in 1526 by Zahiruddin Babur and reached its climax with Emperor Akbar in the second half of the sixteenth century (Sharma, 2019). Babur, descended from the Turco-Mongol conqueror Timur, on his father's side, and from Genghis Khan on his mother's side, came from Central Asia, establishing in Kabul and pushing southward through the Khyber Pass, occupying much of northern India after his victory at Panipat in 1526. The last great ruler was Aurangzeb, who governed from 1658 to 1707.

In general terms, the Mughal Empire and the Qing or the Ottoman Empires were all based on military strength and sedentary agriculture, usually described as "gunpowder Empires" (Metcalf and Metcalf, 2013). Under the emperor, the most important element in the structure of power was the military aristocracy. In fact, the Mughal military strength was based on the use of horsemen, an Arab-root warfare technology (Rothermund, 1988). The military aristocracy was divided into various ethno-religious groups: Turkish (called Turanis); Persian-speaking groups from Iran, Afghanistan, and Iraq (called Iranis); the Indian Muslims; and the Hindus (mainly the Rajputs and Marathas).

The effectiveness of their relation with the emperor depended on the constant expansion of resources, which explains the permanent drive towards the territorial conquest of Mughal India. Roy (2012a) points out that Islam supplied a cooperative principle among communities that colonised open land on the frontiers, cleared forests, and supplied soldiers. Particularly in the north of the Indian subcontinent, the need to expand territorially was mainly based on the need to add new land to tax and finance military expenditure. As showed in the classic work of Habib (1963), *The Agrarian System of Mughal India*, the Mughal land-revenue system rested on the agreement that the peasant was left with provisions for his subsistence, while the surplus was taken by the empire in the form of land revenue.

All in all, an empire which imposed itself from the top, and its increasing economic pressures, was perhaps never fully accepted by the rural society (Bandyopadhyay, 2004). Peasant unrest was a recurring theme, but fear of the Mughal army prevented the problem from escalating most of the times. Furthermore, the local landlords or zamindars had a key role (Raychaudhuri, 1982b). They were the ones who mediated in the relation between the military aristocracy and the peasants. There was a big heterogeneity among the zamindars. Some of them, for instance, the Rajputs, had considerable political influence and power in the Mughal Empire. At the same time, the alignment of the zamindars with the Mughal was partial. Although Akbar had tried to gain the zamindars as allies, after the end of Aurangzeb's period in 1707, the zamindars support began to flounder due to the increasing pressure over the land revenue.

Despite being invaders, the Mughals were quite open, both in religious and ethnic terms. The unifying ideology was the loyalty to the emperor. Although they had a Persian liturgy, they did not try to impose a Muslim sectarian identity. In fact, there were not any forced conversions to Islam. In this line, during the Akbar period, when the Mughal cultural life experienced its peak, there was quite an open court, including Brahmans, yogis, Jains, Jesuits, Muslims, and so on (Sharma, 2019; Metcalf and Metcalf, 2013). For instance, the Mughal painting and architecture, Persian rooted, but transformed by the Indian context and knowledge, are main references of the Mughal period. Among the Mughals' architectural heritage you can find Agra Fort, Fatehpur Sikri, Red Fort, Humayun's Tomb, Lahore Fort, and the Taj Mahal. Different health care systems such as Ayurveda, with Sanskrit origins, and the Arab Yunani Tibb, cohabited and reinforced each other. Raychaudhuri says (1982b, p. 181):

> Poets, scholars, artists, musicians, calligraphists, physicians and the like were all beneficiaries of imperial or aristocratic munificence. Together, they constituted a fair proportion of the middle class . . . the peasant's surplus was very usefully at work here, helping to create and continue significant cultural forms, the rich tapestry of Indo-Mughal civilization.

Regarding the use and spread of technology, Raychaudhuri (1982a, 1982b) is really critical, pointing out the extreme simplicity of instruments and techniques during the Mughal period. He highlights that they did not know the use of coal, had no proper cast iron, and were unfamiliar with the techniques of deep mining, and their chemical industry was primitive. He adds that there was no inclination to replace copiers with the printing press and that the shortcomings in fuel resources, metallurgy, and chemical industries blocked any prospect of wide-ranging technological development. In this respect, Habib (1995a) is less critical, although he highlights the lack of development of mining engineering as a critical factor for energy and industrial development. The delay in introducing and diffusing metal, particularly iron, to replace other materials was also an important element. In general terms, the labour-based techniques seemed to prevail. However, artisans were quite specialised.

The maximum expansion of the Mughal Empire was reached in 1707 with Aurangzeb. Aurangzeb is considered a more conservative emperor, particularly in religious terms. He changed Mughals' tradition of religious tolerance, established by Akbar, to a more intolerant policy. But mainly, he initiated

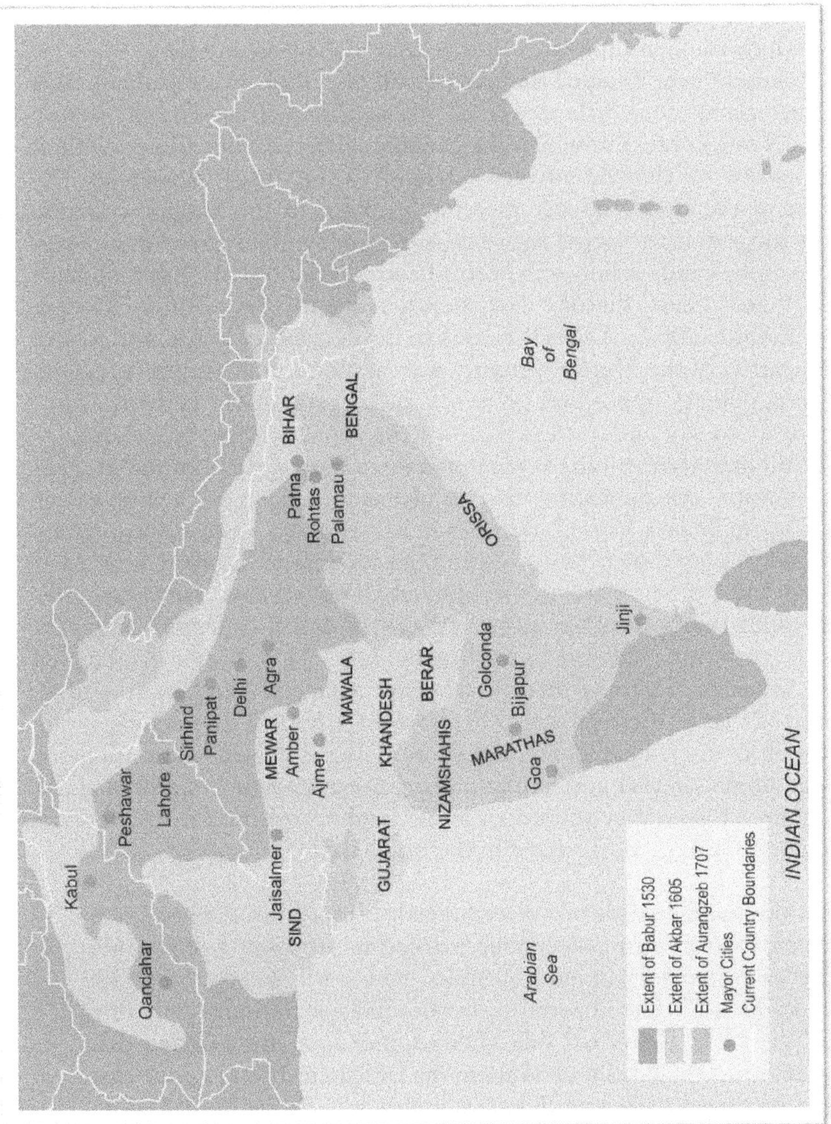

Figure 3.2 Mughal Empire, 1530–1707.

Source: Elaborated by Rosaura Flynn.

expansionist campaigns in western India against the two autonomous forts of Bijapur and Golconda and against the Marathas in the south. Instead of allowing the Deccan sultanates to remain as buffer states against the threat of the Marathas, Aurangzeb chose to take them on and confront the Marathas directly. This geopolitical error can be traced to his fanatical Sunni orthodoxy, which could not tolerate the Shia faith of the Deccan rulers.

The causes of the Mughal decline are still discussed. Some scholars such as Clingingsmith and Williamson (2008) suggest that the Persian victory happened in a context in which the Mughals suffered from an agricultural crisis, caused by climatic adversity, related to the "bad" monsoons. The increase of the crops and rice prices contributed to the Mughal collapse. Others focus directly on the figure of Aurangzeb and his expansionist policy. We understand, in line with Metcalf and Metcalf (2013), Raychaudhuri (1982a), and others, that the "Imperial overstretch", as called by Findlay and O'Rourke (2007), is closely related to the dynamic of power and wealth accumulation of the Mughal Empire. A limitation in the resources, caused by a long military opposition or territorial overexpansion, perhaps aggravated by a drought and a stressed ecosystem, could explain the collapse.

Metcalf and Metcalf (2013) identified three fracture lines of the Mughal fragmentation: the zamindars, the peripheral princes, and the state governors. The zamindars, as said, were landlords who also acted as local rulers. They had increased their power during the seventeenth century, and many of them had become part of the Mughal ruling scheme. However, after Aurangzeb's death, all over north and central India, different zamindars arose as a constant challenge to the Mughal rule. The princes were accepted by the Mughals as part of their networks of alliances. The Rajputs can be considered one of these groups. They also were part of an uprising in the eighteenth century. Finally, the governors were designated by the emperor as local administrators and had attained a good amount of autonomy. As independent rulers, they started to refuse sending revenues to Delhi. Raychaudhuri (1983, p. 3), referring to the Mughals' fragmentation, says:

> By the middle years of the eighteenth century the Empire lay in ruins, its once vast possessions reduced to "roughly a rectangular wedge of territory about 250 miles from north to south and 100 miles broad". The imperial governors did not formally deny their allegiance to Delhi, but one after another they had asserted their autonomy: the Nizam-ul-Mulk in the Deccan in 1724 . . ., the eastern provinces of Bengal, Bihar, and Orissa in about 1740; Gujarat and Sind in 1750, Oudh in 1754. Independent Pathan dynasties ruled in Farrukhabad and Rohilkhand within striking distance of the capital. The Rajput alliance destroyed by Aurangzeb's wars was never completely restored. In the far south, the former Hindu kingdom of Mysore was to grow powerful under the adventurer Haidar

> Ali. The southernmost parts were divided up into a number of small principalities.

It is in this context of fragmentation during the first half of the eighteenth century that different uprisings occurred all around India. In Hyderabad, for instance, there was the Nizam uprising in 1723 that defeated Mubariz Khan, the local Mughal administrator. The re-emergence of the Marathas, in the central part of the subcontinent, the Sikhs in Punjab, Jats and Afghan kingdoms in the north, and the Mysore and Tipu Sultan in the South were part of the uprising process. Finally, the context was propitious for the British East India Company's (BEIC) advance, as Dalrymple (2015) says:

> The rapid rise of the East India Company was made possible by the catastrophically rapid decline of the Mughals during the 18th century. As late as 1739, when Clive was only 14 years old, the Mughals still ruled a vast Empire that stretched from Kabul to Madras. But in that year, the Persian adventurer Nadir Shah descended the Khyber Pass with 150,000 of his cavalry and defeated a Mughal army . . . Three months later, Nadir Shah returned to Persia carrying the pick of the treasures the Mughal Empire had amassed in its 200 years of conquest: a caravan of riches that included Shah Jahan's magnificent peacock throne, the Koh-i-Noor, the largest diamond in the world, as well as its "sister", the Darya Nur, and "700 elephants, 4,000 camels and 12,000 horses carrying wagons all laden with gold, silver and precious stones", worth an estimated £87.5m in the currency of the time.

3.3 From Plassey (1757) to the end of the BEIC monopoly (1813): territorial penetration, fiscal militarism, and textile exports

3.3.1 Plassey, the local opportunity in a broad conquest mission

The BEIC penetration in India can be understood as a process driven by factors both in the Indian Ocean ecosystem level and in Europe (Bandyopadhyay, 2004; Hejeebu, 2015, etc.). The BEIC officials responded to the specific Indian Ocean "opportunities" in a general framework of expansion that was stimulated from Britain, even with internal political conflicts and subject to the specific political situations.

In Europe, the eighteenth-century changes pushed Portugal and the Dutch to the back: only France and England remained in the contest in the Indic (Panikkar, 1953). According to Findlay and O'Rourke (2007), the main characteristic of the eighteenth century was the almost constant war between Britain and France. Although much of the fighting was in the European mainland, they were also worldwide in scope and extent, including North America, the West Indies, and the Indian subcontinent. In Britain, military spending as a percentage of total expenditure averaged about 70% in the Nine and Seven Years' Wars with the French. As a percentage of national income, it rose from 9% in 1710 to 14% in 1760 (Findlay and O'Rourke, 2007).

In the Indian subcontinent, the directors of the Companies understood the devastation that the Anglo-French War would impose on the Indian trade. The French Company was consolidated in Pondicherry in the southeast. Indeed, the trade between France and India flourished between 1728 and 1740, increasing almost tenfold (still half of the British trade) (Findlay and O'Rourke, 2007). The French was the last European company in arriving in the Indian subcontinent, but they were the first in conceiving the project of territorial penetration. They realised that in the middle of the eighteenth century, the Indian subcontinent was vulnerable to be taken over by any leading European power. This would be at a low price for a small but well-trained army of native troops, led by European officers using modern artillery and armaments and supplemented by diplomacy to deepen the local fragmentation.

On the other hand, with episodic military support from the British government, the BEIC directors worked to find a way to avert a liquidity crisis at home. Bengal represented 60% of English imports from Asia in the mid-eighteenth century (Bandyopadhyay, 2004). In 1690, Aurangzeb had granted the BEIC the right to duty-free trade in Bengal. In 1696, they were granted the landowner rights in three villages: Kolkata, Sutanuti, and Gobindapur. However, after the death of Aurangzeb in 1707, the situation became unstable again for the BEIC. Although in 1717 the new emperor, Farrukhsiyar, assured the BEIC duty-free trade and allowed them to rent 38 villages around Calcutta, the new autonomous ruler of Bengal, Murshid Quli Khan, refused to extend the duty-free permission. The conflict between the BEIC and the Bengal nawab[2] had started.

The French victories in South India made the English feel insecure about a possible alliance between them and the nawab of Bengal. In 1755, the BEIC started revamping its fortification in Calcutta without permission, giving protection to fugitives from the nawab's court too. In 1756, Siraj-ud-Daulah became the nawab. He stopped the British duty-free treatment and took over the English factory of Kasimbazar. According to Bandyopadhyay (2004, p. 43), the crisis made Robert Clive, the BEIC director who arrived from Madras, decide on a coup d'état:

> The confident servants of the Company in Calcutta were not prepared to tolerate a young tyrannical nawab threatening to destroy their trading privileges . . . There was already a disaffected faction

> at the nawab's court, consisting of merchants, bankers, financiers and powerful zamindars, like the Jagat Seth brothers . . . who felt threatened by the assertion of independence by a young nawab enthusiastically trying to reorder the balance of power in his court. There was also a natural communion of interests between the Indian mercantile community and the European traders, as many of the Indian merchants were operating in collaboration with the English Company and private traders.

The Battle of Plassey was part of a clash of interests that ended with the decision to replace Siraj with Mir Jafar, his military commander. The local partnership was a key element for the British penetration in Bengal. Thus, in June 1757, Siraj was defeated by Clive with the largest contingent of the nawab army remaining inactive. The new nawab of Bengal, Mir Jafar, became a puppet in the hands of the English (Bandyopadhyay, 2004). As stated by Dalrymple (2015), within a few years, 250 company clerks backed by the military force of 20,000 locally recruited Indian soldiers became the effective rulers of Bengal.

3.3.2 Territorial penetration and fiscal militarism

After Plassey, private trade, both from the Company's officials and private merchants, boomed. Bullion imports from Britain stopped, and bullion was exported from Bengal to China and other ports of India to finance British imports. In a few decades, Bengal's export of raw cotton to China became central to the BEIC entire system for remitting money from India to Britain through Canton and its expanding tea trade with London. This solved one of the Company's primary annual objectives, which was the regular provision of substantial liquid funds. Large quantities of tea were exported from Canton to Britain, Europe, and the Atlantic world. Raw cotton and illegal shipments of opium from Bengal would help the BEIC generate funds. Thus, the control of Bengal trade and taxes allowed the BEIC to endogenously finance its military expansion reducing its dependency on British investors and the Crown (Chaudhury, 1983).

In the Indian subcontinent, at the end of the eighteenth century, the BEIC faced three main local powers: 1) the Maratha Empire, covering the western and central parts of India; 2) the Nizam of Hyderabad, in the Deccan Plateau; and 3) the Tipu Sultan, who ruled over Mysore, in the south. The Marathas had established a powerful empire centrally controlled from Poona (Dalrymple, 2015). However, a new period of furious territorial expansion of the BEIC started after Plassey, as stressed by Dalrymple (2015):

> (The BEIC) using its rapidly growing security force – its army had grown to 260,000 men by 1803 – it swiftly subdued and seized an

> entire subcontinent. Astonishingly, this took less than half a century. The first serious territorial conquests began in Bengal in 1756; 47 years later, the company's reach extended as far north as the Mughal capital of Delhi, and almost all of India south of that city was by then effectively ruled.

The main battles and expansion agreements with local powers were the Battle of Buxar (1764); the final victory over the Tipu Sultan (1799); the Treaty of Bassein (1802), by which they took over Poona and consequently Delhi (1803); and the victory over the Marathas, by which they dominated central and south India (1817). Buxar was the first big battle where the British realised that their army, with a unitary European command and discipline and well-paid sepoys,[3] could defeat the Indian forces with relative ease. In Buxar, they defeated the alliance of three local leaders, and as a result of the BEIC victory, the Treaty of Allahabad was signed, by which the BEIC received the right to collect revenue (Dewani) from Bengal, Bihar, and Orissa. In return, the Company would pay an annual tribute of £260,000.

Figure 3.3 Shah 'Alam conveying the grant of the *Dewani* to Lord Clive.

Source: Drawn by Rosaura Flynn based on "Shah 'Alam conveying the grant of the Dewani to Lord Clive, August 1765", oil painting, Benjamin West, c. 1818. British Museum.

In the South, the Tipu Sultan from Mysore was the main opponent to the BEIC. There were four periods of confrontation: 1767–1769, 1780–1784, 1790–1792, and 1799. These wars also involved the Marathas, the biggest power in extension after the Mughal downfall, who fought in some battles for the British and in some for the Tipu Sultan and the French who supported Tipu from Pondicherry. The English finally took possession of Mysore in 1800.

With the Marathas, the BEIC disputed three wars between 1817 and 1819. The British did not completely defeat them, but they gained much of their territories. The expansion to the North involved disputes that ended with a treaty obtaining Awadh. The other adversaries in the North were the Sikh from Punjab. The English took advantage of internal disputes and declared the war in 1845. It ended with a humiliating treaty in 1846, resulting in the annexation of Jalandhar Doab; Kashmir was given to Raja Gulab Singh Dogra of Jammu, an English ally, and Dalip Singh retained his throne but was to be guided by an English resident. The final annexation of Punjab occurred in 1849.

The expansion to the South included the disputes with the French forces. The first war occurred in 1740 in Madras, but the end of hostilities in Europe after the Treaty of Aix-La-Chapelle left the Indian conflict in standby. The Second Carnatic War was fought in 1752, in the context of successive disputes between the local power, the French, and the British-supporting opposition candidates. The BEIC won, occupied Arcot, and placed Muhammad Ali in charge of the Carnatic. The Third Carnatic War happened in the outbreak of the Seven Years' War. In 1761, Pondicherry capitulated, and the last French forts in Carnatic fell that same year. As said, all these wars included alliances with local powers, such as the Tipu of Mysore or the Carnatic Nawab.

The British were much better financed than the French in the Indian Ocean: Bengal's trade volume was four times larger than Pondicherry's. With this broad "fiscal base", the English could pay for the sepoy army, which was basically a mercenary army (Metcalf and Metcalf, 2013). The British expansion cannot be understood without this relationship between fiscal militarism and the sepoy army. The ratio between Indians and British in the army was around 10 to 1. In a similar vein as in the Mughal Empire, the British fiscal militarism obliged the BEIC to expand in search of new territories in order to obtain more resources. Since the eighteenth century, it was not only by trade that the BEIC was financed, but gradually, land revenue also started to be a new source of income.

The military-territorial expansion of the BEIC can be observed in the next maps.

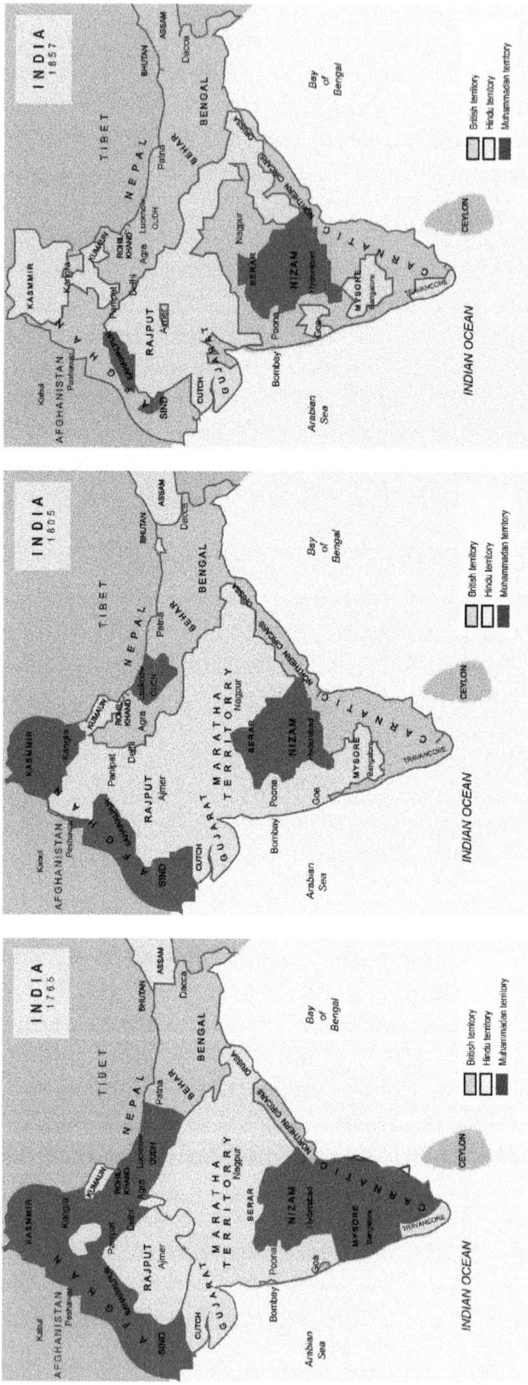

Figure 3.4 Expansion of the BEIC in the Indian subcontinent: 1765, 1805, 1857.

Source: Elaborated by Rosaura Flynn.

The tradition of recruiting peasant armies had been developing in North India since the sixteenth century, confirming a "military labour market" (Kolff, 1990). With the irruption of the BEIC, the sepoys were trained and disciplined according to European military standards and commanded by European officers. According to Bandyopadhyay (2004), the sepoy numbers grew from 82,000 in 1794, to 154,000 in 1824, to 214,000 in 1856. In the first period, the recruitment process was focused mainly on upper-caste Brahman and Rajput peasants from Awadh and Bihar. Then the selection was broadened to include lower castes. Gurkha soldiers were recruited since 1815 from Nepal. Their martial tradition and European training made the Gurkhas the most trusted soldiers of the British army.

We could not say that the Indian subcontinent was not accustomed to war (Hoffman, 2015). In fact, the downfall of the Mughal Empire gave place to different internal warfare competitions during the eighteenth century. So, what explains the BEIC extraordinary penetration in the Indian subcontinent? According to Qaisar (1982), the Mughals quickly accepted the European pistols and muskets, importing gunsmiths and artillerymen to manufacture their weapons, although Indian gunpower was inferior to the European one, and it was increasingly imported. Rothermund (1988, p. 17) says:

> [A]ll weapons the company used were well known to Indian rulers . . . Better organisation and discipline were the only secrets of the company's success . . . The daring cavalry dashed ahead, the artillery was left behind and often fired only some desultory shots in order to show its presence . . . The straggling infantry, ill-trained and ill-equipped, was often more of a nuisance than of use in the decisive battle. Moreover, Indian rulers and generals were not good at financing wars: they might win a battle, but then proved to be unable to pay their troops . . . they (the BEIC) did not invest much in cavalry and artillery, but rather relied on a well-trained infantry, which was regularly paid and drilled and could mow down the Indian cavalry by shooting with machine-like precision. The military feudal man on horseback was a valiant fighter, but he was an individualist at heart who looked for his counterpart on the other side with whom he could engage in a duel worthy of a warrior.

Although his words are quite impressive (and could also have a European bias), he gives some interesting clues about the BEIC superiority: 1) military organisation, 2) financing, and 3) cavalry versus infantry. Metcalf and Metcalf (2013) also stress the importance of military organisation as the BEIC competitive advantage.[4] It can be inferred that the military training and organisation of the BEIC officials, complemented with the numerous and well-paid sepoys, were more effective on the battlefield. Regarding financing, we have already highlighted that it was crucial at sea war, and most of the authors underline that it was also important for land war. First, as explained, Bengal's fiscal militarism was a key advantage. Thus, the BEIC had much less fixed costs than the local powers, and this was an advantage (Hoffman, 2015). The BEIC did not have to maintain a court, an empire, or any other bureaucratic structure apart from the sepoy army. This model was very flexible, it grew when it had to fight, but it did not create a noble structure, at least in the first period. Furthermore, the financing from Britain also helped, as said by Dalrymple (2015):

> [P]erhaps most crucial (reason for the BEIC triumph) was the support that the East India Company enjoyed from the British parliament. The relationship between them grew steadily more symbiotic throughout the 18th century. Returned nabobs like Clive used their wealth to buy both MPs and parliamentary seats – the famous Rotten Boroughs. In turn, parliament backed the company with state power: the ships and soldiers that were needed when the French and British East India Companies trained their guns on each other.

Dalrymple (2015) also highlighted the importance of the financing by the Bank of England:

> On 15 July 1772, the directors of the East India Company applied to the Bank of England for a loan of £400,000. A fortnight later, they returned, asking for an additional £300,000. The bank raised only £200,000. By August, the directors were whispering to the government that they would actually need an unprecedented sum of a further £1m . . . the East India Company really was too big to fail. So it was that in 1773, the world's first aggressive multinational corporation was saved by history's first mega-bailout – the first example of a nation-state extracting, as its price for saving a failing corporation, the right to regulate and severely rein it in.

Third, as we have seen, Mughals' style of war was horsemen-based, a typical style of war for plunder or pillage. But the British war technology was different; it was based in well-trained infantry. In this clash of styles, the British "software" succeeded. Besides, the system of local alliances, designed mainly by Clive, also played an important role both for the expansion and for the conservation of the territories. This network of alliances was developed in Arcot, Awadh, and Hyderabad (Metcalf and Metcalf, 2013). The BEIC offered protection from external powers to the different nawabs, but the latter's troops had to be available to the British. In doing so, both forces reduced fixed costs of war, and, for the British, these alliances functioned as "buffer states" inside the Indian subcontinent.

3.3.3 Deindustrialisation?

Between 1780 and 1790, there was still a sharp trade surplus in favour of India in relation to its commerce with Europe (Chaudhury, 1983). Average annual imports from India reached £7,331,569 against £2,393,610 in exports. Around one-third of Europe's imports from India were directly controlled by the BEIC. But English private traders licensed by BEIC, with around 6% of the market; clandestine trade under the British flag, with 27%; and other imperial companies, which totalised 38%, were also quite involved in Europe's imports. It is interesting to note that these companies also worked for the BEIC, trading in the rest of Europe as subcontractors and functioning as a way to channel remittances of the BEIC directors and officials.

If we analyse the exports from Bengal between 1795 and 1805, as in Table 3.2, we can see that piece goods, raw silk, opium, and cotton have a continuous growth rate. In the case of piece goods, the most industrialised, the peak is reached in 1802, doubling the amount of 1795. It has to be noted that these exports, since the second half of the eighteenth century, were growingly re-exported to other European countries from Britain (the import substitution process was also having a place in Britain!); however, as stated by Chaudhury (1983, p. 806):

> [T]he far more important characteristic of the half a century following the revolution of 1757 was the fact that Indian trade still

Table 3.1 Trade between India and Europe, estimated annual average, 1780–1790

	Imports to India		*Exports from India*	
	(£)	*(%)*	*(£)*	*(%)*
Foreign companies:				
Dutch, French, Danish, Portuguese	992,64	41.5	2,757,763	37.6
Clandestine trade:				
English trade under foreign flags	615,3	25.7	2,000,000	27.3
English private trade:				
Licensed by the East India Company	439,6	18.4	403,565	5.5
East India Company	346,07	14.4	1,962,095	26.8
Privilege goods shipped on the Company's ships			208,146	2.8
Total	**2.393.610**	**100.0**	**7,331,569**	**100.0**

Source: Chaudhury (1983)

> continued to flow along the traditional channels and its composition was based on an exchange of fine textiles, foodstuffs, and other raw materials for precious metals and certain manufactured products.

Until the beginning of the nineteenth century, India was not only surplussing Europe in its trading balance but also, among its exports, piece goods were growing. In fact, the BEIC directors were much more focused in sending remittances to Britain[5] than in the import substitution process and the industrial interests that were growing in England. Consequently, the Indian subcontinent's share in the world manufacturing output went from 24.5% to 19.7%, between 1750 and 1800 (Bairoch, 1982). India was starting its relative decline in the global manufacture output. A much broader process, the Industrial Revolution, was taking place.

3.4 1813–1850s: structural change

Kaldor (1978) defines deindustrialisation as a continuous declining share of a country in the global trade of manufactures, with a deterioration in its balance of trade in manufacturing (Ray, 2016). Since Marx (1853), there have been several methodological, interpretative, and empirical debates about Indian deindustrialisation.[6] For Clingingsmith and Williamson (2008), India deindustrialised between 1750 and 1860, with two sub-periods, between 1750 and 1810 and between 1810 and 1860. They maintain that in the first period, the rise in grain prices deteriorated Indian competitiveness, while in the second period, the effects of the Industrial Revolution were the main drivers of the deindustrialisation process.

According to Bairoch's (1982) numbers, the Indian relative participation in the world manufacturing output went from 24.5% in 1750 to 19.7% in 1800, to 17.6% in 1830, and to 2.8% in 1880. So the sharper drop in the relative participation was between 1800 and 1880. In a more long-term analysis, Clingingsmith and Williamson (2008), based on Bagchi (1976), show that the industry-dependent population in the Gangetic Bihar, one of the most populated areas of the Indian subcontinent, went from 28.5% or 21.6% in 1809–1813 (depending on the methodology applied) to 8.5% in 1901. If we take the spinners' and the weavers' participation in the total occupation of the Gangetic Bihar, it went from 12.6% to 1.3% between 1809–1813 and 1901 (Bagchi, 1976).

It seems quite clear that most of the Indian deindustrialisation process occurred in the first half of the nineteenth century. In line with Chaudhury (1983), we understand that the end of the BEIC monopoly on Indian trade implicitly symbolised the victory of the lobby of the British textiles and private merchants and traders, which, after a period of internal protection, passed to demand free commerce in their trade with the colonies.

Table 3.2 Exports from Bengal to Europe between 1795 and 1805, in rupees

	Piece Goods	*Indigo*	*Sugar*	*Raw Silk*	*Grain*	*Opium*	*Cotton*	*Treasure*	*Sundry Articles*	*Imports Re-exported*
1795–1796	9,483,284	6,251,424	820,186	581,183	911,365	1,308,360	147,211	–	549,062	398,056
1796–1797	7,426,752	3,233,797	1,157,715	340,975	887,630	1,331,255	138,870	–	355,018	485,185
1797–1798	5,748,617	5,459,844	846,752	612,253	557,401	1,077,961	107,711	–	391,172	279,018
1798–1799	5,774,057	2,379,629	1,401,646	667,300	879,713	1,255,579	427,053	–	637,467	452,484
Total 4 years	**28,432,710**	**17,324,694**	**4,226,299**	**2,201,711**	**3,236,109**	**4,973,155**	**820,845**	**–**	**1,932,719**	**1,614,743**
1799–1800	12,001,199	3,553,949	2,389,691	1,433,751	1,249,274	2,880,593	–	–	942,599	1,135,383
1800–1811	14,167,106	3,988,293	1,000,099	1,051,957	1,421,940	3,452,432	–	–	1,040,059	1,893,006
1801–1802	16,591,309	3,848,139	1,201,798	1,365,882	2,259,618	2,751,515	–	231,406	1,117,435	1,967,068
1802–1803	18,594,676	2,973,754	1,081,544	1,638,467	2,544,676	3,943,951	–	1,567,039	1,879,165	2,152,171
1803–1804	16,169,478	4,469,930	1,071,366	1,910,398	3,267,196	4,188,225	2,313,185	251,008	918,685	1,132,854
Total 5 years	**77,523,678**	**18,834,065**	**6,744,498**	**7,400,455**	**10,742,704**	**17,217,116**	**2,313,185**	**2,049,453**	**5,897,943**	**8,280,542**
1804–1805	11,085,509	6,477,041	1,820,446	3,382,000	2,889,913	6,412,283	1,941,507	129,516	–	968,497
1805–1806	12,849,670	5,221,609	3,324,168	3,086,491	2,460,716	5,866,888	3,044,544	–	–	710,405

Source: Chaudhury (2008)

Table 3.3 World manufacturing output, 1750–1939 (in %)

Year	*India*	*China*	*Rest of the Periphery*	*Developed Core*
1750	24.5	32.8	15.7	27.0
1800	19.7	33.3	14.7	32.3
1830	17.6	29.8	13.3	39.5
1880	2.8	12.5	5.6	79.1
1913	1.4	3.6	2.5	92.5
1938	2.4	3.1	1.7	92.8

Source: Clingingsmith and Williamson (2008)

Table 3.4 Population dependent on industry in the Gangetic Bihar (in %)

	1809–1813	*1901*
Assumption A*	28.5	8.5
Assumption B**	21.6	8.5

Source: Clingingsmith and Williamson (2008) based on Bagchi (1976)

* Each spinner supports only himself or herself.
** Each spinner also supports another person.

Table 3.5 Indian exports from Bengal by commodity, 1811–1851 (in %)

Year	*Indigo*	*Piece Goods*	*Raw Silk*	*Raw Cotton*	*Opium*	*Sugar*	*Total*
1811–1812	18.5	33.0	8.3	4.9	23.8	1.5	90.0
1814–1815	20.0	14.3	13.3	8.0	N.A	3.0	58.6
1828–1829	27.0	11.0	10.0	15.0	17.0	4.0	84.0
1834–1835	15.0	7.0	8.0	21.0	25.0	2.0	78.0
1839–1840	26.0	5.0	7.0	20.0	10.0	7.0	75.0
1850–1851	10.9	3.8	3.8	19.1	30.1	10.0	77.6

Source: Chaudhury (1983)

If we analyse the Indian trade in Bengal, the main Indian port, as it is shown next, there was a dramatic decrease in the piece goods export participation between 1811–1812 and 1814–1815 (after the end of the BEIC monopoly): from 33% to 14.3%. Moreover, in 1850, the piece goods participation fell to 3.7%. The structural change in the Indian export composition was almost done! In parallel, the raw cotton exports went from over 5% to 20%, from 1811–1812 to 1834–1835. Sugar and opium participation also gradually grew during this period. For the whole period, indigo,[7] raw silk, opium,[8] and cotton accounted together for around 60% of the total exports. The rise of the opium trade was mainly directed to China and indigo to Britain and Europe.

Table 3.6 British cotton textile exports to the Indian market, 1831–1835 to 1880–1881

	Indian Consumption of Cotton Textiles (m lb)	*Share Taken by British Exports (%)*
1831–1835	375	3.9
1856–1860	455	35.3
1880–1881	600	58.4

Source: Ellison (1968)

At the same time, the British cotton textile exports penetration in the Indian market gradually increased from 3.9% in 1831–1835 to 58.4% in 1880–1881 (Ellison, 1968). Thus, the exports of cotton goods from the UK to India increased from 0.8 million yards in 1815 to 45 million yards in 1839 (Habib, 1982).

3.4.1 Which were the main causes of this sharp Indian deindustrialisation?

The Indian deindustrialisation should be understood as part of a much broader and global process that was the British Industrial Revolution. To explain the Industrial Revolution exceeds our purpose; however, we understand it as a global-scale process, which not only included India (although it was the "Jewel in the crown"). This process included a mix of agricultural, transport and energy revolutions, exponential increase in commerce with the colonies, and growing technical changes, all backed and stimulated by the evolution of the European war states, mainly materialised in the development of the naval industry. These and other causes generated the British emergence.[9]

That said, regarding the causes of the Indian deindustrialisation, this process was driven by a mix of local and global processes, price and no price mechanisms, technological and institutional drivers, and violent and non-violent means. Some liberal authors tend to explain the deindustrialisation process as a result of the market forces.[10] For instance, Roy (2012a) mainly attributes the deindustrialisation to Britain's productivity gains in textile manufacture and to the world transport revolution. Clingingsmith and Williamson (2008) agree on these factors, adding that improvements in British productivity, first in cottage production and then in factory goods, led to declining world textile prices, making production in India increasingly uneconomic.

In our view, these "market forces" are mainly technical achievements of British industry, in a particular geopolitical context. This brought on the introduction of novel sources of energy, with notable improvements in machinery designs, leading to a substantial reduction of unitary costs of production, which were translated to international terms of trade. As shown next, the productivity of labour in spinning 1980s yarn in England sharply increased in the last three decades of the eighteenth century, going from 2,000 operative hours to process 100 lb of cotton to 135 operative hours. Due to this improvement, England increased its share in the international market, essentially in the market for cotton textiles. The total amount of British cotton goods exports jumped between 1794–1796 and 1804–1806, from 15.6% of total British exports to 42.3% (Findlay and O'Rourke, 2007). Also, in the first half of the nineteenth century, the British terms of trade dropped around 40% (Clingingsmith and Williamson, 2008).

Thus, the process that ended with the British textile Industrial Revolution could be interpreted as an import substitution process promoted by the British local textile manufacturers against the Indian textile imports. Since the eighteenth century, the Navigation Acts, which restricted the use of foreign ships for trade between every country except England, and the Calico Acts, which gradually taxed or banned the import of textiles from India, were an emergent of this period of protection to English national industries, mainly textiles. Indian patterns and designs had quickly become fashionable, forcing domestic textile producers to react both by lobbying for protection and imitating through printing on wool, linen, and calico. However, no attempt by English producers to imitate Indian labour-intensive production methods was economically viable at British wage rates, as shown in Table 3.8; the comparison of weekly earning of cotton workers between Britain and

Table 3.7 Best-practice labour productivity in spinning 1980s yarn in England, 1780–1825 (operative hours to process 100 lb of cotton)

Year	*Technology*	*Operative Hours to Process 100 lb of Cotton*
1780	Crompton's mule	2.000
1790	100 spindle mule	1.000
1795	Power-assisted mule	300
1825	Roberts' automatic mule	135

Source: Broadberry and Gupta (2005)

Table 3.8 Weekly earnings of cotton operatives in Britain and India, circa 1680–1820 (s/d)

Year	*Lancashire*	*India*	*Lancashire as % of India*
1680	6s/0d	1s/6d	400
1770	9s/0d	1s/6s	600
1790	13s/3d	2s/0d	663
1820	10s/4d	2s/0d	517

Source: Broadberry and Gupta (2005)

India was always superior to 4 to 1 (Broadberry and Gupta, 2005). Energy-intensive techniques were emerging.

In addition, it is a historical fact that there were non-market forces such as explicit violence and institutional development that expressed imperialistic forces (Dutt, 1901; Naoroji, 1901; Wallerstein, 1986; Roy, 2000; between others). For instance, analysing the internal causes of the sharp change in the external trade composition, Chaudhury (1983, p. 843) says:

> [T]he loss of the export market was preceded by a long period of political instability and the attempt by the East India Company to control the activities of weavers, all of which must have contributed to partial dislocation of the industry. However, the first half of the nineteenth century contains many accounts of the severe suffering of unemployed spinners and weavers in Bengal, and there were differences of opinion whether agricultural occupation could provide alternative employment . . .. After Plassey, the BEIC merchants gradually imposed their authority to coerce weavers.

Both institutional and financing controls were part of the deindustrialisation process. In 1765, the Bengal spinners were obliged to sell their goods only to the BEIC. The Agency Houses also started operating in this period, controlling the financing of the spinners and gradually increasing their control over the productive process and the commercial flow. The Agency Houses were mainly managed by ex-servants of the BEIC. They controlled trade and financing of cotton, indigo, and sugar, and the corresponding houses in London collected remittances and supplied them with funds. By the 1820s, they also acquired an interest in shipping, extending their commercial interest to Malacca, Java, China, Manila, Mauritius, and so on (Bhagwati and Desai, 1970). No doubt, these "institutional arrangements" were concrete imperialist institutions that contributed to change the trade pattern.

Tariff policy was another instrument used to promote British-manufactured goods. Chaudhury (1983, p. 865) states:

> In Bengal, the rates of duties on exports and imports were fixed at 5 to 10 percent in 1810, and next year the principle of favouring British trade and shipping was introduced by doubling the rates of duty on goods carried by foreign ships. Subsequently, the duty on British imports was reduced to 2,5% percent and metal goods exempted altogether. The decline in the share of continental countries in India's trade after 1814 . . . was almost certainly due to these high preferential duties, and foreign vessels were now excluded from the coastal trade of India through a regulation which stipulated that they should proceed from British Indian ports direct to their own

countries. The regulations in force in Bombay and Madras during this period were similar to those in Bengal on the point of giving preference to British goods.

The Charter Act of 1813 deprived the BEIC of its monopoly trade between Britain and India, although its monopolistic trade with China was left untouched. In 1832, there was a parliamentary inquiry on the BEIC performance in India. This inquiry gave an account of the English winds of reform regarding the BEIC. In 1833, a Charter Act was passed renewing the BEIC role for another 20 years but abolishing the BEIC monopoly of tea trade with China. The BEIC possessions in India were to be held in trust for the British Crown, and there was an advance in the institutionalisation of India as a formal colony of the Crown. The Charter of 1853 renewed the Charter of 1833 but not for 20 years. The BEIC days of territorial expansion over the Indian subcontinent were ending. After the Indian Mutiny of 1857,[11] which among other things expressed the institutional and functional incapacity of the BEIC to govern a whole subcontinent, the British Crown directly assumed control of the Indian subcontinent. The so-called imperialism of free trade was taking over the power (Gallagher and Robinson, 1953).

Figure 3.5 Suppression of the Indian Mutiny by the English.[12]

Source: Drawn by Rosaura Flynn based on "Suppression of the Indian Revolt by the English" by Vasily Vereshchagin, 1884. Wikimedia Commons – https://commons.wikimedia.org/wiki/File:Vereshchagin-Blowing_from_Guns_in_British_India.jpg.

3.5 1850s–1914: railways, agriculture (famines), and "wealth drain"

The Indian Mutiny of 1857 marked the downfall of the BEIC and the formalisation of the Indian Raj. From that moment, the Indian subcontinent was formally assumed as a colony of the British Crown. Next, we will focus mainly on three main interrelated aspects: 1) the railways' development, 2) the agriculture development and its relationship with famines, and 3) the "wealth drain". After the territorial penetration, with the formalisation of the British control, these three processes consolidated the peripherisation process started since Plassey.

3.5.1 Railways

The railway system was, by large, the main investment (and material contribution) made by the British in India. Its development started in 1853, and, by 1910, it was the fourth-largest railway system in the world (Hurd, 1983). The Indian rail network was the costliest construction project undertaken by any colonial power in any colony. Of the £271 million of British capital exported to India before 1911, around £200 million were invested in railways (Tomlinson, 1979). Given its relevance, there are many works that analyse its development. We will focus mainly on the works that focus on understanding its functionality to the Raj, the net contribution to the Indian economy, and its relation to the peripherisation process.

Prior to the railway construction, transport across the Indian subcontinent was costly and difficult. The main and cheaper way of transport was the river shipping concentrated on the Indus and Ganges valleys and the coastal regions (Roy, 2012a; Hurd, 1983). The pressure for the railways' development was instilled in Britain by the merchants and industrialists since around the 1840s and, in India, due to the importance of the railway in military terms.

The railways project received the support of the cotton manufacturers of Lancashire and Glasgow and their members of Parliament, because the British cotton industry had been hurt by the American "cotton famine" of 1861. But they were not the only interested party; there were other influential lobbies such as the London East India houses, the P&O line, the city bankers, the *Times*, the *Economist*, railway journals, and many hardware manufacturers (Headrick, 1988).

In India, the Raj Viceroy viewed the railways as an instrument for military control of the population and for defending the borders (Hurd, 1983). In fact, large sums of money were expended to develop lines to strategic points on the borders. Anyway, after the Indian Mutiny of 1857, and with the consolidation of the textile industry in England, the railway construction became an imperial priority. According to Hurd (1983, p. 739), the construction of rail network lines was quite rapid:

> In 1860 there were 1,349 kilometres, but by 1870 there were 7,678 kilometres, by 1890, 25,495 kilometres, by 1920–1, 56,980 kilometres, and by 1946–7, 65,217 kilometres. The first lines were built inland from the major ports of Bombay (1853), Calcutta (1854), and Madras (1856). By 1867, of India's twenty largest cities . . . nineteen were on railway lines, and by 1947 all but a few districts in remote regions were served by railways. The density of rail lines grew from 35 route kilometres per 10,000 square kilometres in 1880 to 159 in 1946–7. Assuming that the sphere of the trading area extended for 32 kilometres on either side of the track, by 1946–7, 78 percent of India's total area fell within the range of the railway system.

As we can see in Figure 3.6, the main internal railways' routes were meant to connect the three presidency city-ports, Calcutta, Madras, and Bombay, and to reach Punjab, one of the main agriculture areas and the northern borders.

Until the 1870s, private British companies built the railways. The initial cost was quite expensive, both because of the engineering works related to overcoming rivers and mountains and because of the overprice charged by some companies. They were given a guaranteed 5% dividend, covered by the Indian government (tax on the Indian people). The companies were given free land with 99 years' leases. At any time before that, even a few months before the expiry of the lease, the companies could return the lines to the government and claim full compensation for all the capital. Indeed, this type of "Private Public Partnerships (PPP)" was described by some authors as an instance of private enterprise at public risk (Bandyopadhyay, 2004).

In 1870, the Indian government began building new lines at a rapid pace too. Despite their lower initial cost, the state lines lost money because the companies had already taken up the most profitable routes between the major cities, while the government's lines were built into border areas or in regions affected with famines. Since the 1880s, most private lines started giving profits of over 5%. However, altogether, the government's guarantee payments to the railway companies in their first 40 years of operation reached £50 billion (Headrick, 1988).

Railway construction integrated land and sea, making a reduction in the carriage costs of low-valued high-bulk commodities possible. Then, steamships connected coastal trade with international trade. The railways network favoured the connection between internal markets and the ports but provided no interconnection between the internal city markets. The preferential freight charges were less for bulk manufactured goods travelling from

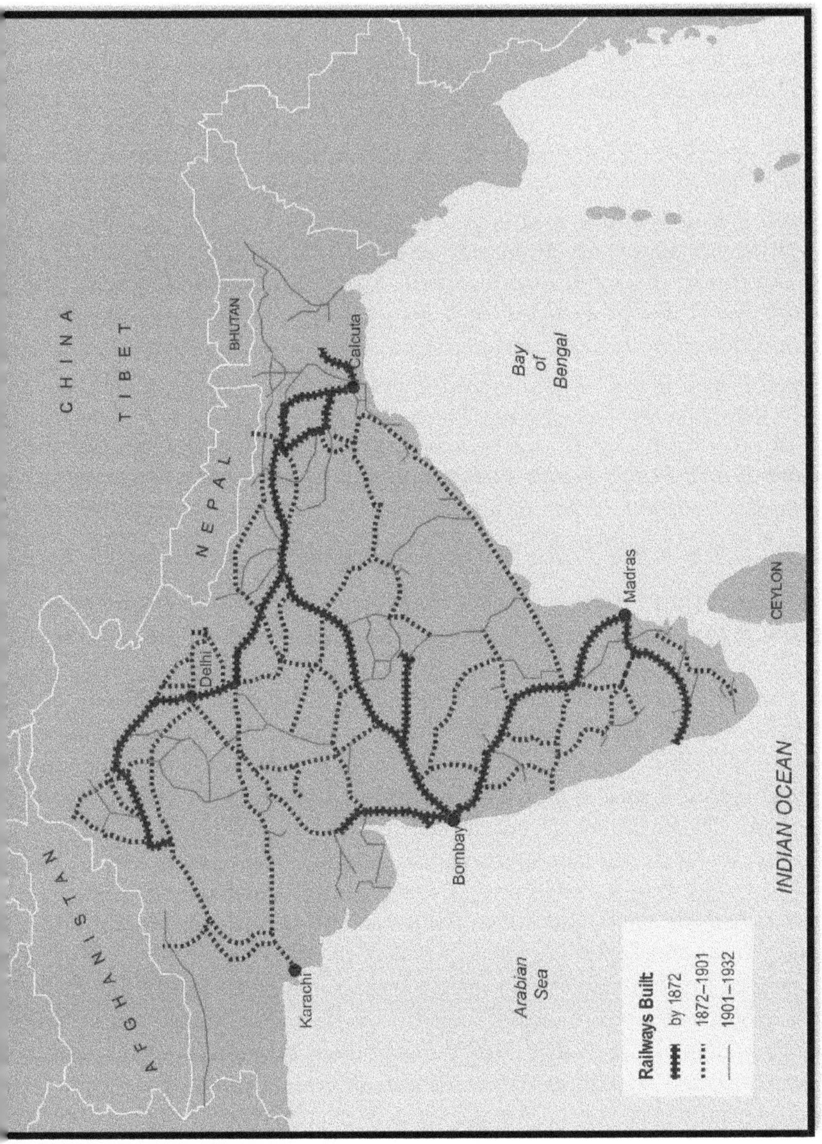

Figure 3.6 Major Indian railways lines, 1872–1932.

Source: Elaborated by Rosaura Flynn.

the ports to the interior than raw materials from the interior to the ports (Bandyopadhyay, 2004). Thus, the total tonnage capacity of ships entering the three major ports of the subcontinent, as said, Bombay, Calcutta, and Madras, was less than 100.000 in 1800, increasing to 1.2 million in 1844 and reaching 4.2 million in 1900. The railways were a necessary complement to agriculture development oriented to external markets. In this sense, Hurd (1983, p. 745) says:

> The reduction of shipping costs, therefore, must be counted as a major factor in changing India's position in international trade. Railways helped Indian agricultural commodities to become competitive internationally and made possible an enormous expansion in the export of products such as wheat, rice, jute, leather, oilseeds, and cotton. Before railways, only a very small proportion of agricultural output normally was exported, but after railways, substantial amounts of both food and non-food crops began to be shipped overseas – as much as 13 percent of the wheat produced and an even greater percentage of non-food crops . . . Before railways, the sub-continent exported no wheat at all, but by 1886 India was supplying 23 percent of Britain's imports of wheat. In real terms, the value of exports increased 230 percent from 1862.

The relationship between famines and the railway development is controversial. Some authors maintain that they contributed to the reduction of famines, but many others believe the contrary. According to Headrick (1988), the Famine Commission recommended in 1880 that 5,000 miles of railway line were urgently needed and that the Indian railway system should expand to 20,000 miles to reach the major famine zones. However, the government finally set up a minimal programme of famine railroads. According to Sen (1980), railways contributed to famines because they allowed foodgrains to leave drought-stricken areas during times of famine. In the same line, according to Sweeney (2011), the protective railways built in the 1880s and the 1890s did not mitigate the effects of the 1896 and 1901 famines.

In terms of local linkages and indigenous technological development, the benefits were even lower. Most of the management, equipment, and skilled labour came from Britain. Rails, points, fishplates, machinery, locomotives, and even sleepers were almost all built outside India. There was very little technology transfer in low-tech areas such as platelaying. In fact, the multiplier effects of the railway construction boom benefited Britain directly: in the 1880s, 22% of the British locomotive production went to India. The Raj did little to stimulate the development of heavy industry or management skills within the country. For instance, until the 1920s, the mechanical engineers on the Indian railways were all Europeans; Indians were not welcomed into the profession (Headrick, 1988). The Government of India urged companies to "buy British" (Hurd, 1983).

Even though there was no state demand until the interwar period, Indian people's "catch-up" was quick, as highlighted by Hurd (1983, p. 749):

> Indian railway workshops had proved capable of manufacturing competitively-priced locomotives as early as 1865 when a locomotive was made at the Byculla works in Bombay. Yet, between 1865 and 1941 Indian workshops produced only 700 locomotives, while British firms exported some 12,000 to India. The importance to the British locomotive industry of the Indian market is indicated by the fact that of the total output of a group of British locomotive firms, fully 22 percent was shipped to India. India's loss from the purchase policies of the railways was not limited to her lack of progress in developing heavy industry. She also failed to reap the benefits of the spread effects to industry which would have occurred. Instead, the spread effects stimulated the British economy.

The Indian people welcomed the railways. The British thought that they were not prepared for them, but they grew crowded from the very beginning. Another positive consequence of the railways was the postal system. Before the mid-nineteenth century, the postal systems run by the individual presidencies and Indian states were expensive and unreliable. Thus, in increasing the speed and safety of the mail, no reform was as effective as the spread of railways.

Roy (2012a) maintains that the railway development was positive because it integrated the local inland markets with the world market. However, to Headrick (1988, p. 56):

> India had one of the world's top rail networks, at least from 1890 on. Yet among nations with large rail networks, India remains a special case for two reasons: it was the only colony among sovereign states; and it was the only one of them that failed to industrialise during the railway boom . . . a different kind of imperialism, one that would have built a railway network beneficial to India rather than to Britain. This is the most difficult of all scenarios to imagine.

The railways were the most important material contribution of the Raj to the Indian subcontinent: it developed an infrastructure that could not have been developed by indigenous efforts. In an indirect way, the railways contributed to the integration of the Indian territory. However, the main purpose and use of the railway network were to reinforce the Indian subcontinent insertion as a peripheral space of the British Crown. No major technology transfers, no major public purchase oriented to local suppliers, and no major local linkages were there. If in the first half of the twentieth century, India lost her role as a regional centre of textile production and exports, the second half consolidated her integration to the world economy as an agriculture commodity exporter. The consequences in terms of the welfare of the Indian population were not the main aim of the British.

3.5.2 Agriculture, irrigation, and famines

The industrial and transport revolutions, mainly through the steamship technology, the opening of the Suez Canal in 1869, and the development of the railways in India, were a main thrust to the increase in the trade flux between the Indian subcontinent and Europe. Indeed, the opening of the Suez Canal cut the distance between Britain and Bombay from 10,667 miles to 6,224 miles and between Britain and Calcutta from 11,900 miles to 8,083 miles (Findlay and O'Rourke, 2007). The steamship technology reduced fuel requirements, and it added the possibility to pick up coal at Gibraltar, Malta, Port Said, and Aden.

The reduction in the costs of transport both increased the volume of trade and consolidated the structural change in the Indian exports composition from a textile supplier to an agriculture commodity supplier. According to Chaudhury (1983), between 1814 and 1850, four commodities accounted for around 60% of Indian exports: indigo, raw silk, opium, and cotton. However, for the second half of the century, as shown in Table 3.9, raw cotton, foodgrains, seeds, raw jute, and tea explained around half of the Indian exports. To Habib (1995b), this period represented a real shift in Indian agriculture to the production of raw material for England, a shift in relative acreage from foodgrains to non-food crops, and a rise within the acreage committed to foodgrains of the portion devoted to crops for export.

Raw cotton went from a participation of 19.1% of Indian exports in 1850–1851 to a peak of 35.2% in 1870–1871. Foodgrains went from 4.1% to its peak of 19.5% between 1850–1851 and 1890–1891. Seeds evolution is similar, from 1.9% to 12% between 1850–1851 and 1910–1911. The American Civil War in 1860 and the possibility of interruptions to Lancashire's cotton supplies explain the Indian raw cotton impetus during the 1860s. In the case of foodgrains, Burma's rice and Indian wheat were the main products. The most important market for Indian wheat was Britain, taking almost 20% of its total imports from India at the end of the nineteenth century (Chaudhury, 1983).

As a consequence of the increase in the world trade, foodgrains demanded container bags. This explains the growth of raw jute and manufactured jute goods exports. Jute, after cotton, grew to be the second main industry of India during this period. Regarding tea development, from England's point of view, this is the case of import substitution from a non-colonial area

Table 3.9 Exports from India: commodity composition, % of selected items in total export value, 1850–1851 to 1935–1936

Year	*Raw Cotton*	*Cotton Goods*	*Indigo*	*Food Grains*	*Raw Jute*	*Manufactured Jute Goods*	*Hides and Skins*	*Opium*	*Seeds*	*Sugar*	*Tea*
1850–1851	19.1	3.7	10.9	4.1	1.1	0.9	1.8	30.1	1.9	10.0	0.2
1860–1861	22.3	2.4	5.7	10.2	1.2	1.1	2.0	30.9	5.4	3.1	0.5
1870–1871	35.2	2.5	5.8	8.1	4.7	0.6	3.7	19.5	6.4	–	2.1
1880–1881	17.8	4.2	4.8	17.1	5.2	1.5	5.0	18.2	8.6	–	4.2
1890–1891	16.5	9.5	3.1	19.5	7.6	2.5	4.7	9.2	9.3	–	5.5
1900–1901	9.4	6.4	2.0	13.1	10.1	7.3	10.7	8.8	8.3	–	9.0
1910–1911	17.2	6.0	0.2	18.4	7.4	8.1	6.2	6.1	12.0	–	5.9
1920–1921	17.4	7.6	–	10.7	6.8	22.1	3.5	–	7.0	–	5.1
1930–1931	21.0	1.6	–	13.5	5.8	14.5	5.3	–	8.1	–	10.7
1935–1936	21.0	1.3	–	–	8.5	14.5	–	–	–	–	12.3

Source: Chaudhury (1983)

such as China to a colonial land such as India. The tea industry was almost entirely developed with British capital and enterprises (Chaudhury, 1983).

Agriculture was the main source of revenue both for the Mughals and for the British. The land tax extraction during the British period experienced different forms. First, the Permanent Settlement introduced a fixed tax, vested the land ownership right in the zamindars, and reduced the peasant status to tenants. The coercion was mainly impelled by the British and the zamindars on the peasants. After that, the British realised that with the Permanent Settlement, the zamindars were benefiting more than the Raj, so they implemented the Ryotwari Settlement during the first half of the nineteenth century. Peasants were vested with the property right, but they were also taxed, and they had to directly pay the Raj officials. Finally, the Mahalwari Settlement was introduced, trying to maximise the revenue of each land, by different tax rates, but it worked only partially because of its implementation difficulties.

Bandyopadhyay (2004) says that a common feature of the three systems was the over-assessment, as the primary aim of the British was to maximise revenue income. In general terms, the results were mounting debt and dispossession, in the case of the peasants, and increasing land sales (concentration of the land property), in the case of the zamindars. The levels of coercion, between the British and the upper classes and castes, and peasant resistance differed according to the different regions and years.

Agriculture was closely related to irrigation development. But irrigation did not concentrate the same resources as the railways of the Raj. The British works in irrigation were limited, except for the construction of some irrigation canals in the north related to the Indus and the Ganges, mainly directed to the agriculture area of Punjab, and other canals in the presidency cities of Bombay, Bengal, and Madras (Bandyopadhyay, 2004). Although between 1900 and 1933 the area under irrigation almost doubled, it was mainly an improvement in absolute terms. When the British left India in 1947, only a quarter of the total cropped area was under public irrigation. Public irrigation facilities remained inadequate, creating few areas of relative prosperity. Canals were feasible in regions such as the plains of the Ganges or the Indus, where rivers supplied large volumes of water, but they were few in the rivers of the Deccan Plateau, where water scarcity limited the possibilities of fertiliser application. Roy (2012a) and Habib (1995a) identify the lack of investments in irrigation as the main cause of the Indian agriculture low productivity improvement during the Raj.

Irrigation for the famine areas was not a profitable business, for the private and the public works depended on the availability of resources. The famine of 1876–1878, which mainly affected Madras and Mysore, demonstrated the need for famine finance to be made a permanent part of government estimates. A Famine Commission was created to study the history of famines and the possibilities of its prevention in the 1880s. In 1900, an Irrigation Commission was created to link irrigation to drought areas. However, as with the famine railway routes, having in mind that during the First World War, the British investment inflows to India almost stopped, it is not difficult to infer that both commissions created in the late Raj, and with not many resources and priority, did little for famine prevention.

The Raj period was characterised by some authors as a process of "commercialisation" of the Indian agriculture (Ghose, 1982; Habib, 1995a, 1995b). According to Habib (1995a, p. 331):

> While the conditions of the poorer peasantry and rural proletariat become more and more critical, the extending production of commercial crops laid the basis for extensive landlord and rich-peasant agriculture. In 1891 the smaller proprietors cultivated 54% of the cultivated area in the Punjab; in 1900, only 45% . . . This was the basis of the formal conversion of the zamindar into the modern Indian landlord. The long series of tenancy acts, beginning with the Bengal Rent Act of 1859, merely extended recognition to his new position, and to the subsidence of the bulk of the Indian peasantry into mere tenantry-at-will.

The "commercialisation" of agriculture implied the advance in the development of market relations in agriculture production. With the railway development, some irrigation, and the telegraph, the British connected different crops and seed areas of the Indian subcontinent to produce for the British needs and to supply European countries. The market development in agriculture tended to favour differentiation within the peasantry and concentration of land in the new landlord class (ex-zamindars). This was considered a sign of progress towards capitalist agriculture. However, the initiatives had severe consequences both in terms of output and for the peasants' living conditions.

Regarding the output, agricultural yields were largely static in colonial India, and between 1920 and 1947, the production of food crops lagged behind the rate of population growth. In terms of welfare, the worst consequences materialised mainly in the famines of 1876–1878, with 3.5 million deaths and 36 million affected; 1896–1897, with around 5 million deaths and almost 100 million affected; and 1943, with 1.5 million deaths, mainly in Bengal (Visara and Visara, 1983).[13]

The main problem of the commercialisation process in relation to famines was that the development of crops and seed markets, without any buffer intervention of the state (or any collective institution or mechanism to back up the market functioning in terms of foodgrain stocks), instead of reducing famines, added a new famine cause.[14] The main reason is that it was not only the food supply but also its distribution that determined the incidence of famines. Thus, an increase in the international price of the crops or a local shortage of crops in the connected markets could end in a general increase in the prices that led to famine, especially, in a context of debt and low (or even no) peasant income. On the other hand, not all the people starved to death during a famine; in fact, many were able to make extraordinary economic gains during them. In this line, Ghose (1982, p. 378) remarked:

> First, the mayor famines and scarcities occurred during a period when India was a food-surplus country and was, in fact, exporting large quantities of foodgrains. Exports of foodgrains were taking place even in years when thousands, or perhaps millions, were dying of starvation. At this aggregate level at least, it seems clear that these famines were not precipitated by absolute shortages of food caused by uncontrollable vagaries of nature. In fact, there were never simultaneous crop fails all over India or even in a whole province. Second . . . India's agrarian economy could be characterized as a non-monetized exchange economy. For a significantly large proportion of the population, food supply depended on "employment entitlements". This fact makes it easy to understand why localized crop failures produced disastrous famines.

Ghose (1982) characterised the famines between 1860 and 1910 in four aspects: a) none of the famines was caused by an absolute food shortage; b) those who suffered starvation deaths were mainly landless labourers, small artisans, and petty traders; c) foodgrains were actually being exported in substantial quantities during famine periods even in the worst affected areas (e.g., 1877, 1896–1897, and 1899–1900 were years of severe famines, although net exports of foodgrains continued); and d) crop failures precipitated famines not because they created an absolute shortage of food but because they created a collapse in the income of the lower castes and classes.

The statement of the Famine Commission (1880, p. 29) quoted by Ghose (1982, p. 380) is really illustrative of this "new market-path to famines":

> The first effect of a drought is to diminish greatly, and at last to stop, all field labour, and to throw out of employment the great mass of people who live on the wages of such labour. A similar effect is produced next to the artisans, the small shop-keepers, and traders, first in villages and country towns, and later on in the larger towns also, by depriving them of their profits, which are mainly dependent on dealings with the least wealthy classes; and, lastly, all classes become less able to give charitable help to public beggars, and to support their dependents. Much of the agricultural classes as possess a proprietary interest in the land, or a valuable right of occupancy in it, do not as a rule require to be protected against starvation in time of famine unless the calamity is unusually severe and prolonged, as they generally are provided with stocks of food or money, or have credit with moneylenders. But those who, owning only a small plot of land, eke out by its profits their wages as

labourers, and rack-rented tenants-at-will living almost from hand-to-mouth, are only a little way removed from the class of field-labourers; they possess no credit, and on them pressure soon begin.

It is not necessary to say that the commercialisation process, meaning the market process development, implied day-by-day coercion over the peasants. It seems accurate to point out that some peasants went to money crops because they were more profitable and not because of coercion mechanisms, but coercion was oriented to produce land ownership transfers and tax collection of over-indebted and starving low classes and castes (Davis, 2001). Some of these situations ended in revolts, such as the Indigo Rebellion of 1859–1860. This coercion also functioned as a stimulus for the emergence of the Indian National Movement.

To sum up, the agriculture development during the second half of the nineteenth century restructured the Indian agricultural relations and land possession, in order to channel part of the Indian agriculture production to foreign markets, stimulating capital and land accumulation in some segments of the new-old landlord class. The adverse consequences were severe for Indian people: the aggregate production of food crops lagged behind population growth; investment in irrigation was insufficient and concentrated at the external-markets-oriented areas; and the impact of famines was not reduced, but on the contrary, it was amplified.

Figure 3.7 Famine genocide in Madras, India, under British colonial rule.

Source: Drawn by Rosaura Flynn based on Wikimedia Commons. https://commons.wikimedia.org/wiki/File:1876_1877_1878_1879_Famine_Genocide_in_India_Madras_under_British_colonial_rule_2.jpg.

3.5.3 *The "wealth drain"*

The "drain" theory was mainly introduced and developed by the moderate nationalist intellectual Dadabhai Naoroji, in his *Poverty and Un-British Rule in India*, and it was further developed by the nationalist historian Romesh Chunder Dutt in *The Economic History of India* and by William Digby in *Prosperous British India*. Conceptually, the "wealth drain" implied a transfer of resources from India to England without the former getting back any equivalent economic, commercial, or material return (Patnaik, 2017; Chandra, 2016).[15] Describing the "drain of wealth" theory, Chaudhury (1983, p. 869) says:

> An unusual characteristic of India's foreign trade throughout the period of this survey (1757–1947) was the existence of a large export surplus, which was not offset by either a rise in her foreign-exchange reserves or an increase in overseas lending. In fact, the permanently favourable balance of trade, after including movements of treasure, was accompanied by a net import of capital after 1850. The key to the puzzle lies in the invisible items in her balance of payments and the unilateral transfer of funds that she had to make to Britain as part of the political charges debited to her external account.

For Patnaik (2017, p. 278), the concept of drain implies that:

> a substantial part (up to one-third) of the total tax and other revenues raised within the colony was not spent in the normal way within the country, but set aside for sterling expenditure by Britain on its own account abroad. But how did the transformation of rupees in the Indian budget into sterling with Britain take place? By using that part of revenues to reimburse colonized producers of export goods (the very same producers who had paid in the taxes in the first place!), while the financial gold and foreign exchange (forex) earned through their global net commodity exports were appropriated by the metropolis for its own use.

There are different estimations and calculations of the total amount of the drain. Naoroji (1901) estimated it in around 5 and 7 million pounds per year between 1835 and 1859 and between 17 and 27 million per year for 1860–1872. Cuenca Esteban (2001) maintains that it was much more limited, affirming that the net financial transfers from India to Britain reached a peak of 1 million pounds per year in the period 1784–1792, then declined to about 0.5 million pounds yearly in the period 1808–1815, and became slightly negative during 1816–1820. Both these numbers are still discussed,

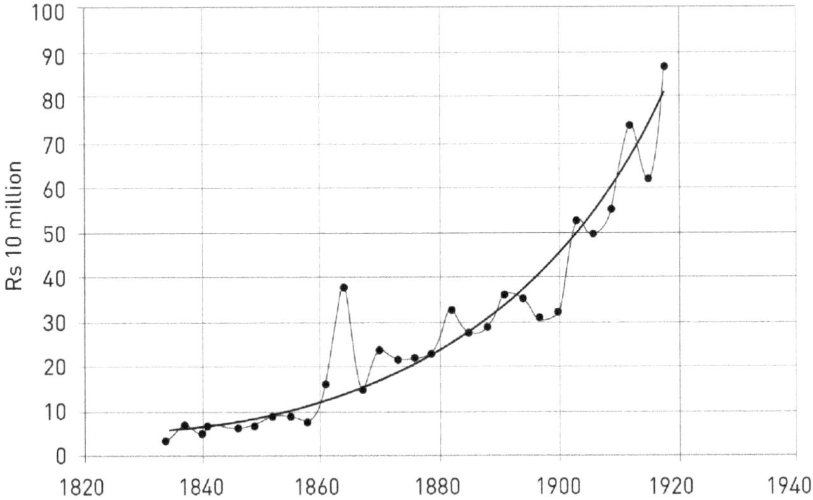

Figure 3.8 Merchandise exports surplus, India, 1833–1919.

Source: Based on Patnaik (2017).

not only because of the quality of the statistics but also because of the way of calculating and defining the "drain". This type of conceptual debate opens the door to different streams of "unequal exchange" perspectives. Here, we will only focus on introducing some elements of the so-called drain wealth, mainly related to the Indian balance of payments.

After the Charter Act of 1813, the BEIC was required to pay a nominal payment of 500,000 pounds out of the public revenues raised in India to the stockholders of the BEIC. According to Chaudhury (1983), these payments varied from 1.5 to 3 million pounds before 1850. During most part of the nineteenth century, India had negative balances in regard to most other service items and short-term capital movements, due to 1) payments of government's external obligations, 2) transfer of private savings, and 3) profits of European firms and invisible service charges such as freight on shipping, insurance, and banking commissions. All these debit items were financed through exports surplus on merchandise account, mainly textiles and raw cotton, and since the 1850s, with the railway development, through capital imports.

The exports to China were the main channel for indirect remittances to Britain. It was Britain's heavy adverse balance of trade with China, mainly based on tea, which prevented bullion moving from India to England. This pattern was maintained over most of the nineteenth century (Chaudhury, 1983). The balance of payments in favour of Britain was estimated at

25 million in 1880, covering more than a third of Britain trade deficit with the US and Europe. Re-export of tropical products to Europe was another source of profit for Britain, enabling it to purchase strategic materials from the other European countries. In this aspect, Patnaik (2017, p. 285) says:

> Compared to the demand for Britain's own goods, the demand for tropical goods by Northern populations was higher and more income-elastic. Re-exports boosted the purchasing power of Britain's domestic exports by as much as 55 percent during the period 1765 to 1821. Four-fifths of goods re-exported by Britain were from tropical regions, and the re-exports went mainly to Continental Europe. Re-exports from the Netherlands actually exceeded exports of its own domestically produced goods in the eighteenth century. The metropolis enjoyed a double benefit – not only did it get prized tropical goods free for its own use, but it got them free to exchange for temperate land products in which it was deficient.

According to De Cecco (1975), at the end of the nineteenth century, this mechanism of payment became a fundamental tool for the maintenance of an international monetary system based in the Pound Sterling Gold Standard. Chaudhury (1983, p. 877) concludes his analysis on the Indian balance of payment with these words:

> In the long-run, it was not so much the capital payments as the absence of active measures for economic development which was probably most responsible for the continuing poverty in India. The highly favourable conditions which characterized Indian exports in the second half of the nineteenth century could have been turned to India's long-term advantage had there been systematic plans for economic modernization. But the opportunity was lost because Indian foreign trade was a dependent factor in an imperial system, which had different objectives than the transformation of the domestic economy.

The export and balance of payment pattern that configured the well-known "wealth drain" theory were the main features of the behaviour of the Indian economy during the British rule. This pattern constituted an important aspect of the Indian peripherisation process, and it was also relevant to Britain, as a way to balance its trade deficit with China, Europe, and the US, and to maintain the Gold Standard. We have already explored the Indian exports' structural changes during the British rule, from textiles to raw agricultural commodities, and its implications in terms of employment and famines. This structural change is at the core of the explanation of the Indian exports dynamics and was the result of the insertion of India into the world system under the British tutelage.

Notes

1 This section is mainly based on Bandyopadhyay (2004), Raychaudhuri (1982a, 1982b), and Metcalf and Metcalf (2013). For a deeper understanding of the Mughal period, see Habib (1963, 1995b), and Richards (1993); The Mughal Empire's main characteristics will be presented because it was the most extended empire in the Indian subcontinent from the sixteenth century to the eighteenth century. However, it is important to have in mind that in central India, Maharashtra, and the Deccan and in South India, the Vijayanagara authority was an important regional power too.

2 A nawab was a native local governor, during the time of the Mughal Empire.

3 A sepoy, from *sipahi*, was an Indian infantryman employed by the armies of the BEIC.

4 Regarding military technology, it is useful to consider Hoffman's (2015, p. 7) words with respect to the broad understanding of military technology:

> The technology here encompasses a lot . . . it has to embrace everything that made victory more likely, from weapons to training and administration. Leaving part of the technology out in order to focus on the weapons alone would be a bit like trying to analyse the impact of computers by considering only the hardware and ignoring software and the Internet. As with computers, all the various parts of the gunpowder technology played a role in the European conquest.

5 According to estimations made by Cuenca Esteban (2001) between 1784 and 1792, the BEIC net financial transfers from India to Britain reached a peak of £1,014,000 annually. Indian textiles were an important money-good to repatriate wealth accumulated in India to England.

6 For Marx (1853), the agriculture of India was dependent on the government works of infrastructure, mainly in irrigation (Ray, 2016). The export-oriented textiles were the main manufactured products. In such an economy, the decline of manufactures would cause a collapse in whole society. It was in this context when Marx saw the British trade policies as the main cause of Indian downfall: "England began with driving the Indian cottons from the European market, it then introduced twist into Hindustan, and in the end inundated the very mother country of cotton with cottons" (Marx, 1853).

7 Indigo's exports growth is mainly explained by the development of the textile industry machinery in Britain and Europe and the consequent increase in the demand for printing cloth.

8 Opium was mainly exported from Calcutta and Bombay to Canton (China). The total volume of exports went from around 5.000 chests in 1800 to almost 25.000 in the 1830s.

9 See Hobsbawm (1999), Findlay and O'Rourke (2007), and Freeman and Louçã (2001), among many others.

10 Among others, this explanation was sustained by Morris (1963), Rothermund (1988), and, more recently, Williamson (2008).

11 The Indian Mutiny is also called the Sepoy Mutiny or the First War of Independence. It was an unsuccessful rebellion, which began in 1857 by Indian troops (the sepoys) serving the BEIC and spread to Delhi, Agra, Kanpur, and Lucknow.

12 This painting was allegedly bought by the British Crown and possibly destroyed. It anachronistically depicts the events of 1857, the Indian Mutiny, with soldiers wearing uniforms of the late nineteenth century.

13 Another huge famine was the one of Bengal in 1770, with around 10 million dead and 30 million affected people.

14 I follow here conceptual analysis stated by Sen (1977), developed and stylised in Ghose (1982), and detailed in an impressive way in Davis (2001). These approaches had an inspiration in Polanyi (1944), in the sense that the development of the market without any collective backup and controls can have severe negative impacts on the society as a whole.

15 At the same time, the drain theory was a simple but powerful conceptual instrument for the Indian national leaders to blow on the Raj.

4

FROM REGIONAL CENTRE TO GLOBAL PERIPHERY

In short, and in essence, all the great events of this era, which was rightly called "era of discoveries", are articulated in a set that is a chapter in the history of European trade. All that happened were the incidents of the immense commercial company to which the countries of Europe were dedicated since the 15th century, and which will widen their horizon across the ocean.

Caio Prado (1942, p. 19)

In Latin America, reality is undermining the outdated schema of the international division of labour, which achieved great importance in the nineteenth century and, as a theoretical concept, continued to exert considerable influence until very recently.

Under that schema, the specific task that fell to Latin America, as part of the periphery of the world economic system, was that of producing food and raw materials for the great industrial centres.

Prebisch (1949, p. 1)

The third line of expansion of the European industrial economy was towards already inhabited regions, some of which were densely populated, whose old economic systems were of various, but invariably pre-capitalistic types. The contacts between the vigorous capitalistic economies and these regions of long-standing habitation did not occur in a uniform manner. In some cases, interest was limited to the opening up of lines of trade. In others there prevailed right from the start a desire to encourage the production of raw materials for which demand was increasing in the industrial centres. The effect of the impact of capitalist expansion on the archaic structure varied from region to region, being conditioned by local circumstances, the type of capitalistic penetration, and the intensity of the penetration. The result, however, was almost always to create hybrid structures, part tending to behave as a capitalistic

DOI: 10.4324/9781003091752-6

> system, part perpetuating the features of the previously existing system. The phenomenon of underdevelopment today is precisely a matter of this type of dualistic economy.
>
> Furtado (1971, p. 115)

> Any understanding of the Commission (ECLAC)'s contribution to the history of economic ideas must start by recognizing that it represents a specific body of analysis, applicable to historical conditions that are specific to the Latin American periphery. Possibly for that reason, there are few references to ECLAC thought in the main compendia of the history of economic theory. At best these are limited to the thesis of deteriorating terms of trade and the structuralist theory of inflation. The absence of other references often results in ignorance of the explanatory power of that body of analysis, which stems from a fertile blend between an essentially historical and inductive method on the one hand, and a specific abstract-theoretical reference – the structuralist theory of Latin American peripheral development – on the other.
>
> Bielschowsky (2016, p. 8)

Latin American economic development scholars are trained to think from a peripheral perspective. In fact, since the contributions of Prebisch and the founding fathers of the Economic Commission for Latin America (ECLAC), Latin America's most relevant contributions to development economics and economic theory have been mainly focused on the consequences of the external sector constraints: the relevance of terms of trade, the structural inflation dynamic and "import" inflation, the challenge of achieving industrial competitiveness, and so on. In this context, the Indian subcontinent reconfiguration from the centre of the Indian Ocean ecosystem to a global periphery of the British Crown is a useful historical experience for Latin American economic development scholars (and for any economic development scholar) to analyse the development path of a continent that was once the regional centre of one of the most populated and industrialised regions of the world, a position that was never occupied by Latin America, and then was turned into a global periphery such as Latin America was. Indeed, Furtado highlighted in *La Economía Latino-Americana* (2007) that a main difference between America's colonial experience and the Indian one is that the Indian subcontinent had a very developed textile industry.

The Indian Ocean subcontinent was, even until the eighteenth century, the centre of the Indian Ocean ecosystem: the main textile producer of the world and the second-most important manufacturer producer, after China. In numbers, in 1700, the Indian subcontinent represented 24.5% of the world's gross domestic product (GDP), and in 1750, Indian manufactures represented 24.5% of the total world-manufactured production (Nayyar,

2013; Bairoch, 1982). The Indian subcontinent industry dressed more than 100 million Indians, with its products being traded on the different coasts of the Indian Ocean and reaching both Europe and China by the combined sea-land route. Hindu, Indonesian, Persian, Armenian, Arab, Jew, and African people, as well as South Indian princes and kingdoms, were part of this ecosystem. Trade and markets were quite widespread, either inland or as port-trade and overseas trade. There was quite a developed mathematical, geographical, sailing, and shipbuilding technical and productive knowledge. Different entrepreneurial communities existed. The inland surplus was regulated by the monsoon winds and rains. In fact, the monsoon was the main regulator of this ecosystem.

There was nothing like a nation trying to monopolise neither the Indian Ocean region nor any systemic pressure for "preparing for sea war" until the Portuguese arrival, as was the case of South and Central America regarding the Spanish and Portuguese conquistadors. There were pirates but not as a systemic and state-backed action. In the same way as the Incas or Aztecs in the Americas, the Indian subcontinent inland powers were mainly land-oriented empires. Therefore, this lack of naval warlike impetus had some institutional and knowledge implications. This meant that the fields of knowledge development were different. In contrast, the Europeans invested in knowledge and systemic efforts in developing larger and stronger ships and sea gunpower. As Panikkar (1953) says, da Gama's arrival implied the beginning of the dominance of a maritime European power over the land masses of Asia. A parallel could be traced with respect to the Spanish arrival to America (Diamond, 1997).

In cultural terms, in the Indian Ocean ecosystem described in the previous chapters, as well as in the Americas, there was not any strong "national feeling". There were different regional and religious communities and networks of power, but it was only a communal or regional feeling of belonging that prevailed. Indeed, the close relation between nation and the protectionist framework seems to be quite European in nature, seeming exotic to the pre-modern Indian Ocean ecosystem. Furthermore, in this encounter of agents of different ecosystems, market forms and trade were not a main difference. The Indian Ocean waters looked much more cosmopolitan, tolerant, and open to trade than the Mediterranean ones.

In Europe, both the Crowns and the merchants had developed different instruments for financing the overseas expansion. The Dutch were perhaps the most advanced in the development of these types of instruments, but the relevance of funding can be found both in the Portuguese and in the other European companies. The stock option and monopoly structure of the Northern companies also contributed in achieving a larger scale of operations and allowed to invest more resources in military capabilities and trading infrastructure. The relationship between the British East India Company

(BEIC) and the Crown, the Parliament, and the Bank of England, in terms of funding, was also a relevant and distinctive aspect.

The Northern companies deepened the Atlantic connection with much more naval and gunpower strength, articulating the Indian textiles, the European demand, and the bullion that came from the Americas. The European demand was a welcome factor for some local players of the Indian ecosystem, such as the merchants and the port rulers. In fact, from the end of the seventeenth century and during the eighteenth century, the Indian textile exports reached their climax, making the most of the Indian Ocean, the European demand, and America's bullion. It is also important to highlight the relevance of trade triangulations for the European population. As the Indian subcontinent was not a source of effective demand for many European goods, the European companies "sold" their custody services and obtained a rent from their military-logistic monopolies to finance the imports to Europe.

The urban dynamics is another key aspect to understand the British penetration. In the Indian Ocean, each port had its own profile of merchants, shipbuilders, and entrepreneurs related to some specific communities. The Europeans tried, both by diplomatic and by violent means,[1] to make alliances with different port rulers, with the emergence or decline of a port-city implying the emergence or decline of a new set of relations. In Goa, the Portuguese gradually became rulers. But Bombay and Madras were not main ports during the sixteenth century, and although Bengal already was an important port, it was not ruled by any European power. The British were excluded from the Indonesian ports by the Dutch, the Malabar Coast was under the Portuguese influence, mainly around Goa and the Coromandel Coast, and the French were in Pondicherry. Thus, both in a planned and an emergent way, the British developed what would later be known as the presidency cities as their "gates" to India, which was a triumph of the ocean trade flux over the inland powers.

The relationship between the BEIC and the British Crown is quite controversial. Although it was driven by the directors' and officials' "thirst for profit", which was represented in the figure of Clive, the BEIC penetration into the Indian subcontinent cannot be explained as an individual willing process. The BEIC acted quite independently during the Seven Years' War because the Crown was mainly directing its resources towards the war in Europe. This moved the BEIC to look for new sources of financing and business. However, the BEIC penetration occurred in a general framework of imperial expansion. One of the more visible aspects where the British Crown support can be perceived was in the financing provided by the Bank of England to the BEIC, with a large number of British Members of Parliament owning stock options of the company.

At the same time, there was not a total alignment between the BEIC and the Crown. For instance, during the period that went from Plassey to the beginning of the nineteenth century, the BEIC was not aligned with the textile lobby that was growing in Britain, institutionally represented by the successive Calico Acts. The BEIC continued importing textiles to Europe because there was demand and it was good business. It was in the first half of the nineteenth century that, driven by the Industrial Revolution, the textile interests triumphed and forced the BEIC to operate in line with them. The BEIC primary function was under dispute among different groups both in Britain and in the Indian subcontinent, but this dispute occurred in a general frame of market and territorial expansion.

Regarding the territorial penetration and rule, both the British and the Mughals were in some sense "external" actors that managed to rule over the vast territory of the Indian subcontinent (mainly the North) for over two centuries, each sharing some common aspects: a) they mainly based their fiscal revenue on land taxes, b) they had to make alliances (and create divisions) within the different regional groups/castes to control the local population, c) these alliances were mainly, but not only, with the zamindars and the landowners, and d) they based their expansion on fiscal militarism. The Indian subcontinent as a territory that was governed by external actors, although it exceeds the objective of this work, is an important element of continuity to understand the British penetration and the absence of any "nationalistic" feeling until the emergence of the independence movement.

For instance, for a Hindu Bengal merchant, there was not much difference in being ruled by the Muslim military elite or by a British one. In fact, they would prefer a British ruler who did not get involved in their religious preferences and even let them expand their business, closely related to the external trade. Of course, both the Mughal and the British controlled the subcontinent by coercive means. However, the British expansion in a subcontinent of around 250 million people would not have been possible without local alliances. In fact, if we strictly analyse the Battle of Plassey, the first major event for the British penetration, it was more a diplomatic than a military victory. The alliances with the local merchants, zamindars, and financiers, synthesised in the figure of the Jagat Seth brothers, were the main factor to explain this first "opportunity" capitalised by the BEIC. After Plassey, fiscal militarism, the financing of war, and the soft technology used to do war were the main elements to explain the rapid territorial penetration.

If the second half of the eighteenth century represented the British penetration in the Indian subcontinent, the first half of the nineteenth century was a period of structural change in the Indian subcontinent's export profile and productive structure. In around 50 years, the Indian participation in the world manufacturing output fell from 20% to 3%, and the piece goods exports went from more than 33% of the total exports to 3.7%. Both the effects of the more global process of the Industrial Revolution and the British rule of the Indian subcontinent are related to this process. The energy and technological shift of the Industrial Revolution meant, in terms of Pérez (2001, 2010), the emergence of a new techno-economic paradigm, which made the Indian textiles proto-industry non-competitive. This process was clearly reinforced by institutional, financial, and explicit violent mechanisms oriented to "downgrade" the Indian subcontinent. Among the institutional mechanisms, the Navigation Acts, the Calico Acts, the trade tariff, the weaver's obligation to sell to the BEIC, and the Agency Houses had a main role.

In the contemporary great divergence debate, the discussion has been mainly focused on the Indian deindustrialisation process. However, in the previous two chapters, we tried to show a broader process, which included the urban, institutional, logistic, and external insertion resetting of the Indian subcontinent. During the Raj, this broader process was completed in three main infrastructural dimensions. First, the railways development, which, as said, was the main material contribution of the British to India, implied the development of a whole infrastructure both with military and commercial purposes. Paradoxically, if Prebisch understood that the diffusion of technical progress did not fully reach the periphery, the railways development represented the full introduction of a technological paradigm into the Indian subcontinent. However, the design and structure of this techno-economic paradigm were in line with the British imperial objectives, oriented to military control and to insert the Indian agriculture production into the global market. Most of the results, in terms of potential technological transfers and autonomous expenditures, were capitalised by the British firms through exports or contracts with the Raj. In fact, the Indian railway development is a main antecedent to the Private Public Partnerships (PPPs), where the British private firms were assured a minimum profit by contract.

Second, the agriculture development tended to maximise the tax collection, reforming the Indian agriculture profile and developing market relations. The consequences, both in terms of output and social welfare, were severe for the Indian people. As both the Mughals and the British used land taxation as a main financing source, zamindars were fundamental to the British capacity of collecting taxes from the peasants. The agriculture "commercialisation" process driven by the British, through peasant indebtedness, meant a process of land concentration in the zamindars' hands. This long-term productive and social group, although evolved, has gravitated in the Indian economic and social structure until nowadays, being a main obstacle, for instance, to the land reform pushed by Nehru after independence. Similarly, in Latin America, this agrarian large landowner structure has been also present in different regions as a main political actor, blocking different industrial and redistributive attempts. This is a key difference between the Indian and Latin American experience of development and the Chinese, Japanese, or Korean one, where the land reform was implemented through coercive methods.

Third, the wealth drain of the Indian subcontinent territory to supply the British financial needs was a main aspect and was a pillar to maintain the Pound Sterling Gold Standard. Trade triangulation, re-export of tropical goods, and direction of the financial flows were key contributions of the Indian subcontinent to the British imperial configuration. The British logistic control and the Indian subcontinent urban reconfiguration were fundamental elements in the triangulation dynamics. Besides, it is important to visualise the relevance of the invisible service charges (freight on shipping, insurance, and banking commissions). The British logistic control of the sea and the development of its financial system explain the main part of the "drain", with the home charges as the main visible account of the Indian colonial position. At this point, the Indian moderate nationalist intellectuals such as Naoroji and Dutt made some important contributions in the characterisation of the "Indian wealth drain". This line of thinking could be complemented with the Prebisch centre-periphery scheme and the later structuralists and dependence scholars' contributions related to unequal exchange, particularly regarding the role of interests and services payments.

In this sense, it is interesting to observe how the European powers gradually structured the global trade network determining the peripheral role of the Southern Hemisphere in line with their financial and trade needs. As it is well documented, Latin American insertion into this global trade network was mainly based on mineral exports. These minerals went first to Europe but were then re-oriented in the form of bullion to Asia, to pay for the Chinese tea and porcelain and the Indian textiles. The Indian subcontinent peripherisation process reverted this bullion flow. In fact, through trade triangulation, deindustrialisation, and wealth drain, the British managed to balance their trade deficit with Asia in such a structural way that this reverted flow gradually gained relevance in order to sustain the Pound Sterling Gold Standard.

In sum, the Indian peripherisation process implied the development of a set of coercive and non-coercive (price and no-price) relationships between the British and the Indian subcontinent based on a) the logistics and trade control coordinated by British actors, such as the BEIC; b) the territorial penetration and urban restructuration of the Indian subcontinent; c) the structural change (in the export profile and in the internal sector composition) of the Indian economy; and d) the institutional, infrastructural, financial, and autonomous state expenditure subordination of the Indian subcontinent to the British needs and demands. This subordination included the railways' development without a "catch-up" process, the deepening in the primarisation of the export profile, the reconfiguration of the agriculture production and the development of market relations in the Indian agriculture, and the consolidation of a capital account profile that assured a wealth drain to Britain through carrying trade. This process transformed a subcontinent that was, up to that moment, the Indian Ocean regional centre, into a global periphery of the British Crown.

Some liberal analysts understand this process as an export-led growth model. However, there was not much growth, and the social consequences were a disaster for the Indian people. With a completely different demographic structure than Latin America, the Indian peripherisation process implied millions of deaths due to hunger because of the price and non-price mechanisms of reconfiguration of the Indian production and its global insertion. Certainly, the main novelties that the European people introduced in the Indian Ocean ecosystem were not their cosmopolitanism or their market customs but the naval and military technologies and the financing mechanisms associated to the European war capitalism. At this last point, the Indian and Latin American colonial processes were similar.

The Indian peripherisation is a good case to discuss with the Latin American liberal scholars who remember with some nostalgia the "belle epoque" related to the primary commodity cycles, be it minerals, coffee, milk, meat, rubber, and so forth. A liberal approach to global capitalism insertion could be reasonable for a small country with abundant resources, but for a subcontinental region with hundreds of millions of people like the Indian (or, e.g., Brazilian) one, it was a disaster in terms of economic development and social welfare.

Note

1 It is interesting to quote the words of Charles Boone (1718), the English governor of Bombay, as a synthesis of the way in which violence, trade, and alliances were developed in the Indian Ocean: "If no naval force no trade, if no fear no friendship" (quoted by Chaudhury, 1985, p. 3).

Part II

STATEBUILDING

5

EMERGENCE, CONSOLIDATION, AND CHALLENGES OF THE INDIAN STATE AND ITS NATIONAL SYSTEM OF INNOVATION

> National or independence movements against colonial powers have taken roots in various other Latin American and African countries. However, the specificity of the Indian case is that intellectual struggle against colonial science policies led to the creation of a local and national basis in science institutions that worked towards the formation of an Indian science community which became an integral part of the political struggle as well . . . even before independence in 1947, the struggle against colonialism and colonial science led to a number of conceptual frameworks and views as the of science and technology in nation-building, self-reliance in science and technology, and above all, the importance of modern science and technology institutions in the development of a country.
>
> Krishna (2013, p. 142)

> The upshot of the discussion is to suggest the need for a technology policy which is more closely rooted in the socio-economic priorities which are still widely acknowledged as valid. Furthermore, they have to be judged against a long-term perspective . . . We have also noted the great importance of land-saving innovations for India, given its agroclimatic conditions and deteriorating ecological conditions. These considerations do not preclude the introduction of high technology into Indian industry if this improves the functioning of key infrastructural items such as power, transport, and communications, as any reduction in capital-output ratios in these sectors can lead to substantial saving of capital for the economy as a whole.
>
> Chakravarty (1987, p. 68)

> [W]e would re-emphasize two things: i) the inefficiencies in planning which we have highlighted in this volume were probably inevitable: there is no escape from "learning by doing" and it is pertinent to remember that few, if any, critics, and

DOI: 10.4324/9781003091752-8

> least of all the laissez-faire advocates, grasped the full dimensions of the planning and developmental problems faced by India around 1950; and ii) none of the improvements in the planning of trade, industrialization and related economic policies which we have advocated in this volume are incompatible with the basic objectives of a socialist society which stresses distributive justice, equality and the eradication of material poverty.
>
> Bhagwati and Desai (1970, p. 500)

> Whether we talk of Keynesian demand management, or of socialist planning, or of social democratic welfare, or of Third World State intervention and planning, the point of reference in every case is the "national economy". The basic premise of all these different conceptions of interventionism is that the national economy constitutes the "control area" of the State, within which, subject to whatever political economy constraints it may face, the State can act in order to achieve objectives more or less in conformity with its intentions. True, the national economy is linked to the larger international economy, but this link, it is supposed, can be adjusted through instruments such as trade policy or exchange rate policy.
>
> Patnaik (1998, p. 184)

The main objective of the chapter is to contextualise the emergence of the Indian state with a focus on the National System of Innovation (NSI) and its different configurations since the Indian independence to the 1980s, during the so-called planning period, or, in other words, during the Cold War. This chapter has two main sections. The first one will deal with the conditions of emergence of the Indian state and its NSI, mainly analysing the last period of the colonial rule, particularly after the First World War. The next one will work on the characterisation of the statebuilding and the NSI evolution between independence in 1947 and the external crises of 1989–1990, dividing it into three sub-phases: Nehru's government, between 1947 and 1964; Indira Gandhi's first phase, between 1966 and 1977; and the 1980s, first led by Indira Gandhi and then by her son, Rajiv Gandhi.

5.1 Emerging processes during the late colonial time: wars drive, national movement, and social heterogeneities (1914–1947)

In this section a brief characterisation will be given of the last phase of the colonial rule during the first half of the twentieth century, mainly the interwar period, highlighting some emergent economic and political processes and actors that configured the development of the post-independence Indian statebuilding, particularly regarding the political economic framework, the role of the state, and the science and technology's (S&T) explicit and implicit policies.[1]

With a population of almost 400 million people in the 1940s, India was one of the poorest territories in the world (Bardhan, 1984; Nagaraj, 2013a; Patnaik, 1998; Joseph et al., 2008; Habib, 1982). About 85% of the population lived in rural areas; 70% worked in agriculture, mainly subsistence agriculture; illiteracy reached 80%; child mortality was extremely high; life expectancy was of 30 years old; and malaria, together with various other infections, killed millions of people per year (Kapila, 2014, 2003). The average growth rate of the economy during the first half of the nineteenth century was lower than 2%, with a growth rate of the gross domestic product (GDP) per capita lower than 0.5% (Joseph et al., 2008; Kumar, 1982).

The initiatives linked to scientific development during the colonial period were mostly related to railroads, geology, trigonometry, botanical gardens, and questionnaires and information processed in jobs linked to the administrative and exploratory functions developed by the British in India. According to Krishna (1997, 2013), there was a centre-periphery type of division between Britain and the British Raj, where the role of the Indian establishment was oriented to research and a basic processing of information, with low degrees of development. In fact, the first three modern Indian universities, in Calcutta, Bombay, and Madras, the "presidency cities", all of them created in 1857, had as their main goal to train administrative and technical staff for the administration of the colony, offering this way few science courses.

5.1.1 The wars drive

As we have seen in the previous chapters, the Indian subcontinent entrepreneurial capabilities were there before the arrival of the British. However, the British reset its structure. Particularly in the second half of the nineteenth century, with the development of the railways, there was an extended involvement of British capital and enterprises, mainly motorised by the managing agencies. Since the end of the nineteenth century, the Indian capital was gradually moving into areas not developed by British capital, such as sugar, paper, cement, iron, and steel. The Bengal National Chamber of Commerce was founded in 1887 and the Indian Merchants' Chamber of Bombay in 1907. Parsis and Marwaris, in particular, were some of the communities that emerged and consolidated as entrepreneurs around a narrow industrial base (Bhagwati and Desai, 1970).

The First World War, by positioning India as a strategic base for the Allies and with limited trade possibilities, was a main drive for a proto-import-substitution process that contributed to the development of both the Indian capitalist and the urban working classes. Benefited by a reduction in the British imports and the war demand, several industries expanded significantly.

Steel was the main one. But there were others, such as cotton textiles, jute, coal-mining, leather, soap, shipbuilding, wool, etc.

Tata Iron and Steel Company (TISCO), which later evolved into what today is one of the main Indian "national champions", was clearly benefited during the First World War. Dorabji Tata came from a Parsi[2] family of Bombay that had made its fortune as a cotton manufacturer. Since the 1880s, without enough funding and demand from the government, Tata was trying to develop the steel and iron industry in India. As detailed in Headrick (1988), Dorabji Tata made a great effort in order to develop the steel industry in the country: he studied the British, German, and American iron and steel industrial development experiences and even travelled to these countries. The Tata family also made different investments in research of an optimal combination of iron, coal, flux, and water in India. But TISCO's "primitive accumulation" as steel producers came with the First World War (Headrick, 1988, p. 291):

> For TISCO, World War I was a godsend. India was cut off from Germany and Belgium, and British supplies became scarce. Steel imports fell by 84 percent from 1,040,000 tons in 1913–14 to 165,000 tons in 1917–18. Imports of railway supplies fell by 93 percent. Meanwhile, the demand for steel soared as the war effort put an increasing strain on the railways and the military called for ever more munitions. Its stores' policy in abeyance, the Indian government now purchased all of TISCO's output. As the Indian Industrial Commission of 1916–18 explained: "In consequence of the increased difficulties of obtaining from Europe stores for war and essential purposes, the necessity of stimulating the local manufacture of munitions became a matter of vital importance".

As stressed by Seth (1986), it was the First World War that began to give India the characteristics of a mixed economy. Wartime forced the British to set certain industries under state ownership and protect Indian industries. An Indian Industrial Commission was appointed for this purpose, with ten members, including four Indians and headed by T. H. Holland, who had served as director of the Geological Survey of India. Although the government did not follow its recommendations, the Commission's report situated the state as the main actor in the industrialisation drive.

In Britain, the opinions on the relative importance of, and control over, India began to change with the Great Depression. The British felt that they had little control over the Indian monetary and fiscal policies. Protective tariffs had already been imposed, and wartime procurement policies led to an evaporation of India's sterling debt, replaced by Britain's rupee debt to India. India's relevance to imperial defence was also under scrutiny:

the Indian Army needed modernisation and the Government of India did not have the budget. In 1939, it was decided that the British government would pay for it, including the cost of the Indian Army fighting outside India. As the Second World War broke out, the Indian Army had to be deployed in the Southeast Asian front, and as it became increasingly difficult to transfer cash during wartime, Britain's debt with India boomed to almost one-fifth of Britain's gross national product (GNP) (Bandyopadhyay, 2004).

The Second World War put India in a main geopolitical position again. According to Cohen (2001), the British transformed India into a major arms producer and a base for military operations to China, Southeast Asia, and the Persian Gulf. They conducted an active diplomacy with the Indian neighbours and accepted significant American military assistance. In relation to this, Bharat Karnad, researcher of the Centre for Policy Research and a national security expert, says (Rekhade, 2017):

> During the Second World War, India was called the Arsenal of the East. The entire allied armies' Middle East command under Montgomery and the Southeast Asian command under Mountbatten were provisioned by India. It was not Europe. Europe was fighting its own battle. It didn't have the resources. We were doing it. We made everything from guns to lorries to aircraft. We put together Lancaster bombers in Bangalore.

The war was initially beneficial to various groups of Indians: it increased the income of industrialists, merchants, and rich peasants. Employment increased by 103% during the war, but industrial production only 20% between 1939 and 1946, due to the inelasticity of supply, given the absence of a machinery and capital goods industry and the import difficulties during the war (Bhagwati and Desai, 1970). Cement, paper, iron, steel, and sugar industries received another big boost with the war. However, by 1942, the main problem was the scarcity crisis resulting from a shortfall in the supply of rice, with the Bengal famine resulting in more than 1.5 million deaths. The British power seemed stressed; while the higher food prices hit the poor, the rich suffered the profit tax, the forcible collection of war funds, and coercive sale to the British.

5.1.2 Indian National Movement, Congress Party, and Hindu Science

The Indian independence process significantly influenced the NSI conformation and main features. This process cannot be understood without visualising the central role played by the so-called Indian National Movement led by the Indian National Congress Party, founded in 1885 (hereafter, the Congress). The anti-colonial and nationalistic thinking and movement was a long-term, gradual, and heterogeneous process that had been growing since the second half of the nineteenth century (Chandra et al., 1988; Chandra, 2008, 2016). However, until the end of the nineteenth century, as it was mainly made up by liberal professionals and upper-caste intellectuals, mostly connected with the conservative landlords' interests; the Congress did what Bandyopadhyay (2004) defines as moderate politics. In fact, between 1892 and 1909, nearly 90% of the delegates who attended the Congress sessions were Hindus, only 6.5% were Muslims, and among the Hindus, nearly 40% were Brahmans while the rest were upper-caste Hindus (Bandyopadhyay, 2004).

Regarding the National Movement, before Gandhi's gravitation in the Indian political scene, Bandyopadhyay (2004, p. 284) comments:

> Nationalist movement in India before the arrival of Mohandas Karamchand Gandhi (soon to be known as Mahatma (great soul) Gandhi) from South Africa in 1915 has been described by Brown (1972) as "politics of studied limitations" and by Kumar (1971) as "a movement representing the classes" as opposed to the masses. What these descriptions essentially imply is that nationalist politics until this time was participated only by a limited group of Western-educated professionals, whose new skills had enabled them to take advantage of the opportunities offered by the Raj in the form of administrative positions, seats in the district boards or legislative councils. They belonged mainly to certain specific castes and communities, certain linguistic and economic groups, living primarily in the three presidency towns of Calcutta, Bombay, and Madras.

Although the evolution of Indian nationalism was not a linear result of Western influences, the role of Western education was quite important: designed to colonise the mind of the Indian intelligentsia, the latter selectively appropriated that knowledge to build their critique of colonialism. In fact, there was a mixed behaviour in the intelligentsia: critically absorbing the British education and with access to knowledge possibilities, pointing out some specific issues to the government, and demanding for more space in the Raj bureaucratic structure. The objective of Congress moderate politics was a full political freedom that would come gradually, where India would be given the same self-governing rights as Canada and Australia. However, after a period of illusion on the enlightenment and modernisation potentialities of the Raj rule, the upper-caste intellectuals gradually adopted a more critical attitude towards the British.

In intellectual terms, the moderate nationalists fulfil a key intellectual role in developing a political economy critical of the British Raj. The work of Dadabhai Naoroji on "wealth drain" was a potent conceptual and political approach to criticise what we characterised as the centre-periphery relationship between Britain and the Indian subcontinent (Chandra, 2016). The Indian nationalist economists who were part of the moderates, such as Naoroji, Ranade, and Dutt, were mainly focused on the effects that the British rule was having on India, with poverty as the main point. With similarities to list, not being anti-capitalists, they discussed the importance of industrialisation, the relevance of the state in industrialisation, and different criticisms to the "export-led" model that the British had developed in India.

Referring to the moderates' framework, Habib (2017) says:

> The founding fathers of the Indian National Congress . . . the "moderates", saw the country's future as one of "constitutional development" under the stewardship of England, the development paralleling a reform of the traditional society with its numerous iniquitous customs. They mostly aspired to economic progress on the lines of modern countries, with Japan increasingly taken as the model. Yet, for the reason that the moderates desired India's industrial development, they rejected free trade, the great shibboleth of a modern political economy, and instead demanded protection. Swadeshi, therefore, came more easily to their lips than Swaraj. They wished Britain to loosen the tentacles of tribute which strangled the domestic market; and one way to do so was to reduce the salary and pension drain to Britain by "Indianising" the civil services and the army officer corps. One can see now that they looked forward to a future for India as a classical bourgeois country; but there was one mitigating feature: they had a genuine sympathy for the poor, and wished, like Naoroji and Dutt, to protect the small peasant and the factory worker. It was here that the theoretical foundation was laid for the later mobilisation of the ordinary people under Gandhi and the Left.

At the same time, at the end of the nineteenth century, a more Hindu-rooted stream of thought emerged, dissatisfied with what they considered the Western-influenced moderates and the slow constitutional development articulated by moderate leaders (Habib, 2017). An idea of Hindu Science was part of this path of both ideological and scientific research of a Hindu identity, rooted in religion, that looked to connect the different scientific, medical, and technical achievements of the Indian people to a Hindu-Vedic past origin (in opposition to the hybrid framework of the moderates). Thus, the architecture of archaic Hindu Science composed an undivided origin and legitimised it in an original unity and purity.[3] Prakash (1999, p. 99) explains:

> The idea of Hindu science had originated in the Orientalist research of the late eighteenth century. But a century later, the seeds sown by the Orientalists had come to bear different fruits. No longer did it satisfy only the hunger for the knowledge of the East: Hindu science now nourished the idea of a modern Indian nation. Helped by its status as the product of academic research, the notion of Hindu science won influence beyond the circle of religious reformers. References to Hindu medicine, mathematics, astronomy, and chemistry became ubiquitous in the elite culture. Journals and pamphlets returned to the past to search for the scientific contributions of the Hindus, identifying India with Hinduism and seeking Hinduism's transcendent value in its science.

At the same time, along the first half of the twentieth century, due to the demands and lobby efforts of the Indian elite, a series of institutional structures in S&T were created (Krishna, 1997). These first efforts to shape an S&T policy oriented to the national needs were linked to the relationship and partnership between the Indian scientific elite majored in England and the local political Congress elite, including Gandhi, Nehru, Patel, and others. Within the Indian scientific community emerged M. N. Saha, who worked with stellar physics; J. C. Bose, who discovered radio waves' propagation in 1905, and C. V. Raman, who discovered the so-called Raman effect. Most of them were grouped in the Indian Association for the Cultivation of Science in Kolkata and the Indian Institute of Science in Bengaluru, of which Raman was the first Indian director from 1933 to 1948. According to Krishna (2013, p. 141):

> [T]he specificity of the Indian case is that the intellectual struggle against colonial science policies led to the creation of a local and national base in science institutions that worked towards the formation of an Indian science community which became an integral part of the political struggle as well (Krishna, 1997). Thus even before independence in 1947, the struggle against colonialism and colonial science led to a number of conceptual frameworks and views such as the role of science and technology in nation-building, self-reliance in science and technology, and above all, the importance of modern science and technology institutions in the development of the country. All these views and frameworks on science policy for development,

> which were the result of the pre-independence struggle, came to play a central part in the state policies which made science and technology important factors for development led by Jawaharlal Nehru.

The National Planning Committee formed in 1939, led by Nehru, already emphasised the importance of indigenous science efforts. For Nehru, science would have a prominent place in giving an answer to the Indian people needs, as can be inferred from his message to the Indian Science Congress in January 1938 (quoted in Prakash, 1999, p. 196):

> Though I have long been a slave driven in the chariot of Indian politics, with little leisure for other thoughts, my mind has often wandered to the days when as a student I haunted the laboratories of that home of science, Cambridge. And though the circumstances made me part company with science, my thoughts turned to it with longing. In later years, through devious processes, I arrived again at science, when I realized that science was not only a pleasant diversion and abstraction, but was the very texture of life, without which our modern world would vanish away. Politics led me to economics and this led me inevitably to science and the scientific approach to all our problems and to life itself. It was science alone that could solve these problems of hunger and poverty, of insanitation and illiteracy, of superstition and deadening custom and tradition, of vast resources turning to waste, of a rich country inhabited by starving people.

The end of the First World War marked a turning point in different aspects (Chandra et al., 1987). First, the war caused disgust in the Indian people and showed that the expectations of self-governing were too naive, positioning the need to deepen the political struggle. Second, Gandhi emerged at the centre of the post-war political scene with different strategies, looking to transform the Congress into a mass movement, including, among others, the Swadeshi, the non-cooperation, and the Quit India non-violent resistant strategies. Third, the Russian Revolution of 1917 had a great impact on the Indian independence aspirations, causing a radicalisation of the Congress economic framework, embodied in Nehru's figure, and in the political organisational landscape in general, including the founding of the Communist Party of India (CPI) in 1925 and the Congress Socialist Party (CSP) in 1934. And fourth, the war industrial stimulus affirmed in the Indian intelligentsia and the Indian political economy thinking the need and importance of state intervention and purchase power in order to propel the industrialisation process.

Figure 5.1 Nehru, Gandhi, and Sardar Vallabhbhai Patel, All India Congress Committee meeting.

Source: Drawn by Rosaura Flynn based on Wikimedia Commons – https://commons.wikimedia.org/wiki/File:Nehru,_Gandhi_and_Patel_AICC_1946.jpg.

5.1.3 Social heterogeneities at partition

Even though the National Movement and the Congress were the mainstream trends of the anti-colonial movement, they were not monolithic, and they did not integrate all the dissenting Indian groups. For instance, Chandra et al. (1987) maintain that the Indian capitalist class developed a long-term contradiction with imperialism while retaining a relationship of short-term dependence and accommodation with it. Mukherjee (1986) claims that capitalists preferred a nationalist movement with acceptable limits, not guided by left-wing radicals and sponsored right-wingers. For Bandyopadhyay (2004), the relationship between the Indian capitalists and the Congress remained strategic, issue-based, and pragmatic, coinciding with many aspects of the Congress programme. For Chibber (2003), the Bombay Plan, the main industrialisation programme developed by the capitalists, was a move that tried to avoid the radicalisation of the Quit India movement.

Each of these explanations has its valid points, but the main aspect regarding the independence movement is that the capitalist class did not politically lead the National Movement or the Congress Party. Gandhi, Nehru, and the different Congress political leaders were not immediate representatives of the capitalist class, having relative autonomy in developing a programme that, although including some main capitalist interests, such as avoiding a full-communist independence movement, encompassed a broader agenda that included different groups' and castes' interests, all glued by a growing anti-colonial feeling. It is important to highlight that the Congress, although integrating different working-class organisations that were growing mainly in the urban areas, was not an anti-capitalist party, as highlighted by Bandyopadhyay (2004, p. 378):

> Gandhi disapproved this autonomous labour militancy . . . "We seek not to destroy capital or capitalists" he reasoned, "but to regulate the relationships between capital and labour" (quoted in Ray, 1984, p. 284). The same argument resonated in Jawaharlal Nehru's statement in 1929 . . . he reminded everybody that Congress was not "a labour organization", but "a large body comprising all manner of people" (quoted in Chandavarkar, 1994, p. 414). Although the Congress Socialists showed greater sympathy for labour, the compulsion to remain an umbrella organization representing the working classes prevented Congress from integrating the working classes more closely into its movement.

In fact, its main heterogeneity was not related to class categories. Although Gandhi and Nehru were active militants in favour of a secular and unified independent India in order to include Muslims and other minorities, the Indian subcontinent's regional, religious, communal, and caste heterogeneity was too varied to be contained under the Congress' political umbrella. In religious terms, the main minority group that contested the Congress' authority and representation were the Muslims. Broadly, Muslim leaders, such as Ahmed Khan, understood the nation as a federation of communities, with different kinds of political rights. Being an ex-ruling class, Muslims considered that they should have a special place in the future Indian nation. In this context, Muslims formed the All Indian Muslim League in 1906 with its main base in Bengal, in order to politically demand protection and space as a minority group, through the creation of a separate electorate. The dispute between Congress and the Muslim League had different momentums. Gandhi supported the Khilafat movement to defend the Ottoman Caliphate at the end of the First World War, looking for a Hindu-Muslim unity. However, this union ended with the abolition of the Caliphate, and the Hindu-Muslim relationship never reached that understanding again.

Regarding the dispute about the meaning of the Indian nation between the Hindu culture and the Muslim separatism, Habib (2017) points out:

> Since the "nation" (the country as a political community) is a product of modern history, it can be argued that national consciousness developed in India only as a consequence of the development of modern means of communication, especially railways, and the creation thereby of a unified market, along with the growth of the press and the spread of modern education. But these very factors heightened the consciousness of other identities as well, such as those of religion, caste, and region. While nationalist historians like Tara Chand and Mohammad Habib laboured to prove that compositeness was the bedrock on which the Indian civilisation had been built, a point stressed too in Jawaharlal Nehru's The Discovery of India, others, like R.C. Majumdar and I.H. Qureshi, saw two mutually exclusive streams running in Indian history ever since the appearance of Islam. If Muslim separatism openly espoused the two-nation theory after the Lahore Resolution of the Muslim League (1940), Hindu "nationalism" also implicitly accepted the same theory by virtually excluding Muslims from India's cultural past and from her political future (thus the slogan, "Hindi, Hindu, Hindustan").

Figure 5.2 Muslim League leaders, 1946.

Source: Drawn by Rosaura Flynn based on Wikimedia Commons – https://commons.wikimedia.org/wiki/File:Muslim_League_leaders.jpg.

The non-Brahman castes and the untouchable groups (the Dalits) also expressed their dissent with Congress.[4] At the beginning of the twentieth century, there was an emergence of non-Brahman and Dalit political organisations, demanding a better place in the Hindu-colonial hierarchy. Among many other groups, we can mention the Pulayas of Kerala, the Chamars of Punjab, the Balmikis of Delhi, and the Namasudras of Bengal. B. R. Ambedkar, the main Dalit leader, had a principal role during this period (including the foundation of the Independent Labour Party in 1936, which won the Bombay elections in 1937) and even after independence, taking a leading part in the framing of the Indian Constitution.

According to Bandyopadhyay (2004, p. 352), the emergence of Dalit movements pointed out the Hindu political preponderance:

> Although many of these movements did not last long, their implications were quite subversive for Hindi society, as not only did they unite Dalits around the message of a commonly shared brotherhood, they also indicated their defiance of the Hindu notions of hierarchy and untouchability. This tendency to repudiate Hindu theology as a disempowering and subordinating ideology for the Dalits came to an explosive high point when in December 1927 Dr. Ambedkar in a public ceremony burnt a copy of Manusmriti, the most authentic discursive text authorizing untouchability. In 1934 he wrote to temple satyagrahis at Nasik about the futility of temple entry or seeking redress for their grievances within a Hindu religious solution. What he suggested instead was a "complete overhauling of Hindu society and Hindu theology", and advised the Dalits to "concentrate their energy and resources on politics and education".
>
> (Zelliot, 1988)

Apart from the Muslims, the Dalits, and the non-Brahman movements, the social and religious heterogeneity also included different regional communities with their own features – for instance, Sikhs, mainly in the Punjab area, and Tamils, in the south. Some of these people were politically organised as the princely states, cohabitating in the British Raj, such as the princes of Hyderabad, Mysore, and Travancore in the South or the Jammu, Kashmir, and Sikkim princes in the Himalayas. Different regional tribes, peasants, and women of different castes' sub-clusters completed the scenario. In fact, it was the presence of peasants and women that gave tenacity to the Civil Disobedience Movement of 1930–1934.

Regarding the complex meaning of "the Nation" in this context, Bandyopadhyay (2004, p. 190) reflects:

> [T]he "nation" itself is a ground of dispute and debate, a site for competing imaginings of different ideological and political interests. India was a plural society and therefore Indian nationalism was bound to have many voices, as different classes, groups, communities, and regions interpreted their "nation" in various, sometimes even contradictory, ways. Indian had many identities, like class identity, caste identity, religious identity and so on; at different historical conjunctures different identities were articulated and intersected with each other. As the colonial state sought to reinforce and substantialise these fissures, the Indian nationalists tried to publicize an alternative discourse of integration. Jawaharlal Nehru talked about "the old Indian ideal of a synthesis of different elements and their fusion into a common nationality". Such a romantic assumption of fusion was, however, to avoid the hard realities of conflict and contradiction.

The last colonial "contradiction" emerged during the partition of the subcontinent and ended with the creation of India and Pakistan in 1947. Roughly, the partition implied the division mainly of Punjab, Kashmir, and Bengal, in territories that would be part of Pakistan, a mostly Muslim state, or India, mostly Hindu. The division process of these territories, with the British army in retreat, led to a spiral of religious violence among Muslims, Hindus, and Sikhs, which involved between 10 and 12 million people trying to cross borders and between 200,000 and 1 million deaths (Chandra et al., 1987; Godbole, 2006; etc.). The emergence of India's National System of Innovation (NSI) occurred in a country with balkanisation risks, a dual productive structure, and some of the worst socio-economic indicators in the world.

5.2 The Indian NSI configuration during planning (1947–1989)

In this section, we will analyse the period between 1947 and 1989, from the Indian independence to the external crises of 1989–1990. We will divide it into three sub-periods: the Nehru's government, between 1947 and 1964; the first Indira Gandhi's period, between 1966 and 1977; and the 1980s of Indira Gandhi and Rajiv Gandhi.

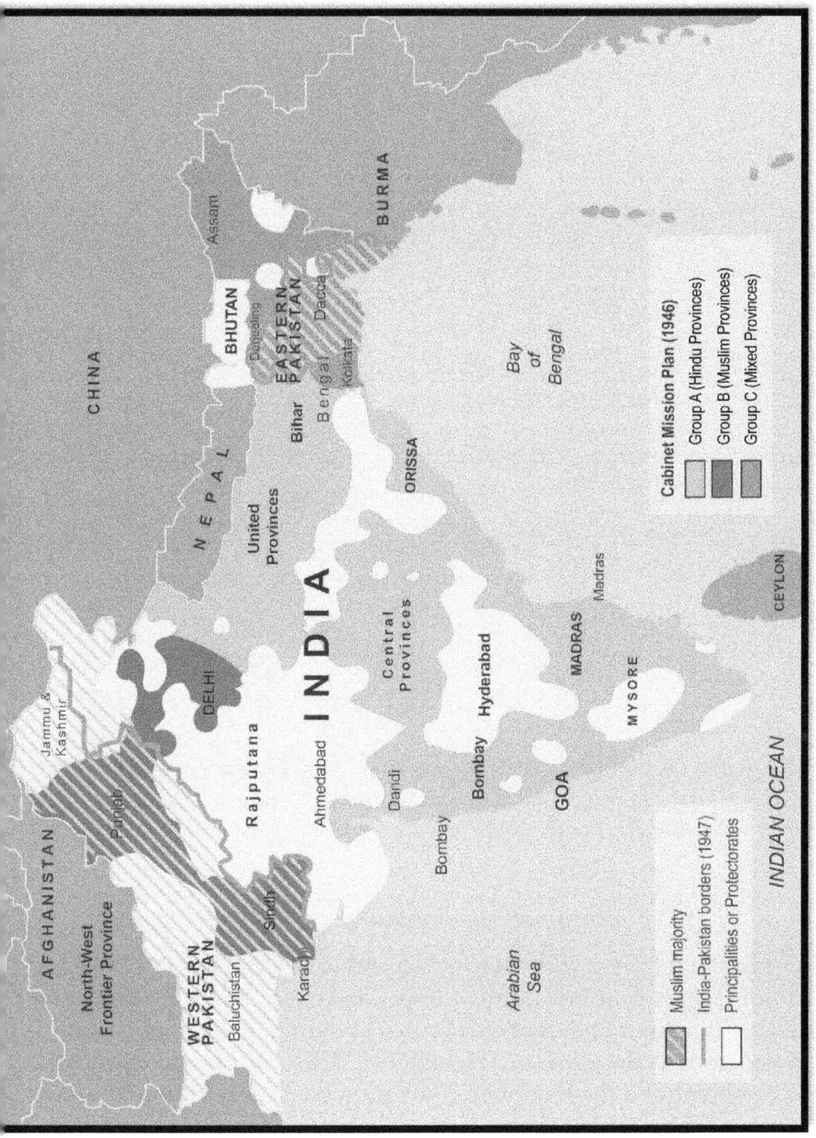

Figure 5.3 The Indian partition, 1947.

Source: Elaborated by Rosaura Flynn.

Figure 5.4 Indira Gandhi, Jawaharlal Nehru, Rajiv Gandhi, and Sanjay Gandhi.

Source: Drawn by Rosaura Flynn based on Wikimedia Commons – https://commons.wikimedia.org/wiki/File:Indira_Gandhi,_Jawaharlal_Nehru,_Rajiv_Gandhi_and_Sanjay_Gandhi.jpg.

5.2.1 Nehruvian statebuilding (1947–1964)

Nehru's historical "Tryst with Destiny" speech of 15 August 1947 marked the birth of independent India, full of hopes and expectations for the future as well as with urgent and concrete doubts about the social and geopolitical consequences of the partition. Habib (2017) describes the Independence Day's atmosphere and the economic consequences of the partition in a good manner:

> The jubilation at independence was tempered, even silenced, by the largest forced migration of the last century involving some 12 million people, and by popular reaction to the brutal massacres that

> accompanied them – massacres ultimately stayed only by Gandhiji's two fasts at Calcutta and Delhi and his martyrdom (January 30, 1948). The partitioned land, already ravaged by two centuries of colonial exploitation, now had its industrial structure thoroughly disrupted. Raw jute and cotton fields were placed on one side of the border, jute and cotton mills on the other; an extensive market for Indian coal was also lost. The adverse effects on the textile manufacture, the biggest sector in India's modern industry at the time, tended to pull back the general level of India's industrial production. The inherited British-built administrative machinery and the tendency to compromise with the established land-controlling interests led to much peasant dissatisfaction, of which the Telangana rebellion (1947–51) was the most powerful expression.

The main political issue in India in 1947 was to maintain the new Indian democracy unified and to begin with the building of a national state that, although with the inevitable inheritance of the colonial period, could give an answer to the illusions and demands raised during the colonial rule. Jawaharlal Nehru identified two main enemies of the new Indian nation, communalism and poverty, and had two themes for his election campaign, history and stability (Bandyopadhyay, 2004). The Congress, the main political inheritor of the legacy of the freedom struggle, would be the main political party in post-independent India. Nehru was both an emergent and a key player of the National Movement and the Congress Party, and, no doubt, after Mahatma Gandhi's assassination on 30 January 1948, he would have the main political role in the post-independence Indian political scenario and, consequently, in the building of the initial blocks of the Indian NSI.

5.2.1.1 Nehru, the Indian scientific elite, and Non-Alignment

Jawaharlal Nehru was the first Indian prime minister for a period of 17 years, since 1947 until his death in 1964. Nehru was born into a Kashmir Brahman family and was the son of Motilal Nehru, two times president of the Congress. He graduated with an honours degree in natural science at Trinity College and then he studied law at Inner Temple, London. He combined a liberal and secular approach to politics with a socialist/state-led approach to the economy. In fact, he admired the USSR and considered that planning and industrialisation were the main means to development.[5] Arnold (2013, p. 361) characterises this period as a phase of "Nehruvian science":

> A concept of Nehruvian science (NS) has value only if it adds analytical depth, and not mere descriptive gloss, to the understanding of the history of science in modern India and if it allows the historian to stand outside both the nationalist representation of science

> and the colonial vision of science that preceded it. There are evident dangers, in focusing exclusively on Jawaharlal Nehru (1889–1964), of exaggerating the contribution of one individual or of shrinking the temporality of postcolonialism to fit the compass of a single life. Nehru was not a practicing scientist, nor (despite his undergraduate education at Cambridge) did he possess scientific training. And yet he was one of the principal architects of modern India and, through his enduring commitment to science, a leading figure in the formation of India's science policy and practice. His personal engagement with science helps explain how, within the time frame of the late colonial and early postcolonial periods, science received such public validation; but equally it helps us to contest negative representations of science in the non-West as a form of stubborn "localism," as a kind of ethnographic aside to the "real" (i.e., Western) history of science. Nehru was one of the principal authors of postcolonial subjectivity, not least in relation to science.

Thus, the post-war Indian science institutions were structured under the leadership of Nehru, who had a close alliance with the scientific Hindu elite. For instance, S. S. Bhatnagar oversaw industrial research; Homi Bhabha, the atomic energy establishment; P. C. Mahalanobis, the Planning Commission; and D. S. Kothari, the defence establishment. Although the Hindu elite and upper middle class/castes were already incorporated to the state bureaucratic structure since the colonial period, the expansion of the state role and institutional setting after independence gave a main drive to the Hindu bureaucracy that later consolidated as a key player in the Indian policymaking and political economy (Bardhan, 1984; Patnaik, 1998; etc.). Krishna (2013, p. 143) details Nehru's articulation with the scientific community and the importance of the state in developing science institutions:

> While Nehru obtained the party's legitimation for assigning an important role of state mediation and governance of science and technology development, the government led by him after 1947 further legitimized the role of the state as it accepted the recommendations of the A. V. Hill Committee Report submitted in 1944. According to this report and the model of science advocated, all science and technology institutions and science agencies including national laboratories were to be placed under the overall control of a government body or ministry. Nehru created the Ministry of Scientific Research and Cultural Affairs in 1948 and took on the portfolio himself. The building of S&T infrastructure with new universities, science agencies and national laboratories came under the control of this ministry. Towards establishing infrastructure and building institutions in S&T, Nehru deemed it very important

to bring scientific elite and science leadership closer to the government. He used his annual full-day attendance at the Indian Science Congress every year after 1947 to strengthen his association with the scientific elite and science community.

To sum up, the period between 1947 and 1964 showed an impressive growth of the state's organisational density (Rao, 2008; Joseph and Abrol, 2009; etc.). Some of the main science agencies created and expanded were the Council of Scientific and Industrial Research (CSIR), with a network of 38 national laboratories in physical, biological, mechanical, and chemical sciences; the Department of Atomic Energy (DAE); the Defence Research and Development Organisation (DRDO), etc. (Krishna, 2013). With 30 universities in the late 1940s, 95 new universities were established, including specialised institutions such as five Indian Institutes of Technology (IITs). According to Patel (1993), this number of institutions for S&T had no rival in the third world and even among several developed countries. Table 5.1 shows the impressive increase in funding and manpower of the main Indian S&T institutions.

Some important efforts made by the Indian NSI during this period were configured by Nehru's positioning regarding the Indian geopolitical context. For instance, both nuclear and space capabilities gave their initial steps in the 1950s and early 1960s. As to nuclear capabilities, in the early days of the Cold War, India remained focused on technological advancement rather than on developing a nuclear arsenal (Ogden, 2011). Nuclear cooperation between India and many other governments such as Canada, the US, the UK, and France was developed. These cooperative efforts resulted in the building of the APSARA in 1956, the first light water research reactor of its kind in

Table 5.1 Growth of major S&T institutions in terms of funding and manpower in India

Scientific Agency	*R&D Budget (U$S PPP)*			*S&T Manpower*		
	1958–1959	*1965–1966*	*% increase*	*1958–1959*	*1965–1966*	*% increase*
DAE	16.3	42.1	258%	1,067	7,441	697%
CSIR	10.7	29.7	278%	3,512	9,515	271%
DRDO	3.1	20.4	658%	1,500	7,003	467%
ICAR	7.8	13.4	172%	1,500	8,400	560%
ICMR	1.07	2.2	206%	1,001	1,585	158%
Subtotal	38.97	107.8	277%	8,580	33,944	396%

Source: Own elaboration based on Krishna (2013)

Note: DAE: Department of Atomic Energy; CSIR: Council of Scientific and Industrial Research; DRDO: Defence Research and Development Organisation; ICAR: India Council of Agriculture Research and ICMR: Indian Council of Medical Research.

Asia, and in the development of the CIRUS heavy water research reactor, in 1960. In 1962, India began producing its own heavy water, and in 1965, plutonium was separated for the first time. In this sense, although Nehru had a public anti-military and pro-disarmament discourse and explicit policy, according to Karnad (2015), Nehru's implicit policy had a main role on the initial settings of the Indian nuclear arms power:

> For instance, of the two major things he set in motion, one was the nuclear weapons programme. He had said that India had missed out on the gunpowder revolution and was therefore enslaved. He had said that no matter what happens we were not going to miss out on the nuclear revolution. This is what is so brilliant about his disarmament cry . . . but this man (Nehru) had vision. He may have talked disarmament, but all the time as the minister for atomic energy, he encouraged, financed and ensured that Homi Bhabha set in motion what he called the Janus-faced nuclear energy programme.
>
> Do you know who Janus is? It's the god in the Greek pantheon with two faces looking in opposite directions. Janus. Civilian-military. Remarkable! When India didn't have money in the 1950s, he took money from the military and the Ministry of Defense, which is why in the 1950s the defence budget went down, just to fund the nuclear programme. He said if you have nuclear weapons, you have security. That was the point he was making. And we had reached our nuclear weapons threshold before China in March of 1964. He died in May 1964.

Related to space, with international cooperation in the peaceful uses booming on the agenda of the UN, and with the NASA making proposals for cooperation, the Indian policymakers began to think about the relevance of space research with applications in agriculture, education, industry, and other scientific areas (Reddy, 2011). In 1954, the DAE was created. In 1962, the DAE set up the Indian National Committee for Space Research (INCOSPAR), and in the second half of the 1960s, the basic infrastructure necessary for a broad-based space programme was put in place. The objectives of the programme were related to the use of orbiting satellites for communications, meteorological observation and forecasting, and remote sensing of natural and renewable earth resources.

Wilson (2003) points out that the indigenisation of aircraft capabilities was another important effort made by the Indian NSI. According to Karnad (2017):

> The other thing that Nehru did, where arms were concerned, was instead of importing combat aircraft, which is what we have been doing, he imported the best combat aircraft designer in the world

> at that time in the 1950s. He got Dr. Kurt Tank, who designed the Focke-Wulf warplanes for Nazi Germany. Can you imagine this? He imported the greatest designer of aircraft. He was commissioned to design the aircraft in 1957. By 1961, the first prototype was flying in the Bangalore skies. The first supersonic jet aircraft to be made outside of Europe and the United States in the world flew over Bangalore. In 1961 . . . Dr. Tank had designed the HF-24 Marut. That was the great combat aircraft that flew to Bangalore. It is parked in the HAL (Hindustan Aeronautics Limited) museum. It was then said to be the finest airplane in the world.

Nehru dominated the Indian foreign and security policy landscape with his Non-Alignment posture, which was a classic "balance of power" policy in the early Cold War world (Pant, 2011). Nehru (1963, p. 455) himself defined Non-Alignment as a "policy of friendship towards all nations, uncompromised by adherence to any military pacts". He understood that the newly formed, postcolonial countries of Asia and Africa had nothing to win in joining the military blocs of the big powers, positioning India as the leader of the newly independent Afro-Asian nations, demanding Dutch withdrawal from Indonesia, and supporting freedom struggles in Indochina, Malaysia, and different African countries. However, Non-Alignment was not a policy of no-relations with the blocs led by the US and the USSR. India remained a member of the Commonwealth, received US economic aid, and cultivated a friendly relationship with the Russians.

The US had been the major aid donor to India during the three First Five-Year Plans (Bhagwati and Desai, 1970). Its share on total aid use was over 70% in the First Plan, 55% in the Second, and 58% in the Third. A major shift in favour of commodity assistance is seen in the Third Plan, reaching almost half of the US aid, under the US Agricultural Development and Assistance Act of 1954, mainly concentrated on wheat. The World Bank and the International Development Association also played a role, contributing with around 12% of the external aid received. However, with the US nuclear power challenged by the USSR, the Chinese Revolution in 1949, and the outbreak of the Korean War in 1950, India began to diverge from its initial US alignment (Habib, 2017). Beginning with abstentions at the UN, India pursued a policy of Non-Alignment, which enabled it to act, for instance, as one of the peacemakers in Korea in 1952–1953. But the freezing in the relationship with the US came particularly after 1954, when the US formed a strategic anti-communist alliance with Pakistan (Scott, 2011).

Although rather cool in the beginning, a close friendship was gradually developed with the USSR. Indo-Soviet relationship was reinforced with Jawaharlal Nehru's visit to the USSR in June 1955 and the Nikita Khrushchev and Nikolai Bulganin visit to India in December 1955 (Sachdeva, 2011a). Congress was asserting its planning strategy and a "socialistic pattern of society", and Nehru was playing a leading role in the Bandung Conference. The USSR was using aid, trade, and diplomacy in developing countries in order to limit Western influence, boosting the Indo-Soviet relations in metallurgy, defence, energy, and trade sectors. From 1955 on, the USSR gave full support to India regarding Kashmir in the UN, and in 1960, India and Russia signed their first agreement for military supplies, with India receiving aircraft, helicopters, and engineering equipment for the Border Roads Organisation to construct roads in the areas disputed with China (Chandra et al., 2008). The Soviet bloc aid grew from almost 0% in the First Five-Year Plan to 6% in the Second and 12% in the Third, mainly used in the heavy industrial sector, including power, coal, drugs, steel, and oil (Bhagwati and Desai, 1970). A difference between the Soviet aid and the US one was that the Soviet grants went almost exclusively to the public sector, in order to reinforce the planning scheme and the public enterprises' capabilities, in contrast to the mixed nature (private and public) in the use of the Western aid.

With China, India tried to maintain cordial relation, being one of the first nations in recognising the People's Republic of China in December 1949. But the relationship suffered when India offered asylum to the Dalai Lama, with the Chinese seeing it as a strategy to undermine their hold over Tibet. Nehru, under pressure by the opposition and the press, and overestimating the strength of the Indian Army, made an aggressive move, resulting in a disastrous military engagement with China in October–November 1962. This resulted in a military humiliation for India, with China easily defeating the ill-equipped Indian Army and ending the conflict through a unilateral declaration of ceasefire (Bandyopadhyay, 2004). This defeat was a military keystone for the Indian defence sector, bringing to light the inevitable geopolitical and territorial competition with China and pushing the public debate about upgrading military capabilities and developing nuclear weapons (Pant, 2011; Chaulia, 2011; Cohen, 2001; etc).

5.2.1.2 Economic policy and planning[6]

Nehru (1963) argued in an article published in *Foreign Affairs* magazine that India should achieve socialism "without adhering to any doctrinaire definition of the word". Broadly, this meant planning through the democratic process for land reforms, industrialisation, and development of infrastructure facilities such as power plants, transport projects, irrigation, and so on. Besides, although Nehru's ideas had a strong influence, there were different views among the national movements about the policies for development. As explained by Abrol (2014) and Patnaik (1998), there were three main approaches: the "Nehruvian", the "Gandhian", and the "left" one. The "Nehruvian" orientation subscribed to a state-led industrialisation process, based on large public enterprises and heavy industry, public financed irrigation, and so on. The "Gandhian" framework was mainly based on the decentralisation of economic activity and the decisions left to the local villages, indigenous knowledge development, self-government, peasant promotion, and so on. The "left" orientation was based on minimising the dependence on big business and foreign firms, a mix of large state enterprises with cooperatives, land reform and radical redistribution of the assets, and so on.

The predominance of Nehru's vision led to the evolution of a developmental state, intervention in the economy, planning and guiding its growth (Chatterjee, 1997; Chakravarty, 1987). However, there was a mix of different policies based on the other views, such as the protection to the cottage industry; a Gandhian rooted policy; and a partial land reform, mainly in Calcutta, Kerala, and Tamil Nadu, where the Communist Party had a strong influence. In some sense, the three approaches cohabited in the broad economic policy framework of the period (Nagaraj, 2013a, p. 192):[7]

> This was a period of state-led import substituting industrializing to acquire quickly domestic capability to produce capital and intermediate goods, following the Mahalanobis model – named after the distinguished statistician who formulated the strategy for the second five-year plan. Assuming limited prospects for export growth to finance import requirement, the "heavy" industrialization strategy sought to maximize long-term economic growth, though it implied a slower growth of output and employment in the near term. However, to meet the employment goal – the most pressing need in the labor surplus economy – the model advocated fiscal and physical controls to promote cottage industries for the production of consumer goods, a policy that had considerable appeal among the Gandhians. The development strategy was predicated on land reforms and public investment in irrigation and flood control to augment food production and agricultural raw materials for meeting the growing demand from the industrial sector.

After independence, there was broad agreement on the need for planning. Indeed, the question was not "to plan or not to plan" but rather how planning should be implemented (Patnaik, 1998; Chaudhury, 1998; etc.). In the international scene, the Great Depression had eliminated any faith in free market, Keynesianism argued in favour of state intervention, and the Soviet Union was experiencing rates of growth that were unprecedented in human history. Within India, it was understood that *laissez-faire* was the modus operandi of economic imperialism. As stressed by Bagchi (1972), India had perhaps been the most/largest "free trade-free market" regime in the world, ending in underdevelopment, economic domination, and famines. Thus, according to Patnaik (1998, p. 165), during the 1960s, there was a common idea among the Left economists and policymakers that capitalist development needed exogenous stimuli:

> Such a stimulus can be provided in the context of an underdeveloped country that has a weak industrial base, not by exports, which are mainly of primary products with low income and price elasticities of demand internationally; nor even by import substitution which, though necessary initially, provides only a transient stimulus, but by state expenditure, which of course has to be directed towards plugging gaps in the production structure, i.e. towards heavy and capital goods production. State capitalism, in other words, is necessary not just for an anti-imperialist economic strategy, but for the development of capitalism in any case. Public investment, since it "crowds in" rather "crowds out" private investment, is necessary for sustaining capitalist growth itself.

Although the relevance of exogenous stimuli, Chakravarty (1987) highlights that the Indian planners subscribed to a supply-side view of the planning. Following Lewis's opinion, most of the Indian developmental economists agreed that the central issue for development was to understand how a country that saves 5% of its income could pass to 20%. It was viewed as a problem of primary accumulation of capital rather than a Keynesian underemployment equilibrium, and this should be solved with an accelerated growth strategy. Thus, there were three main possibilities to direct public investment: infrastructure, agriculture, and industrial development. Planners explored the three possibilities.

The Five-Year Plans were the main policymaking instrument. The process of elaborating the plans, although closely screened by Nehru, was integrated by different researchers, university professors, policymakers, economists, and technicians, resulting in rather interesting discussions and arguments around the issue of planning (Byres, 1998). Basically, the First Five-Year Plan (1951–1956) stressed on infrastructure and agriculture, spending around 30% of the public-sector outlay on irrigation and power; 27% on transport and communication; 21% on agriculture, land rehabilitation, and community developments; and only 5% on industry and minerals (Chaudhury, 1998). With many irrigation projects developed and good monsoons during these years, it resulted in high crop yields and increasing external reserves.

It was in the Second Five-Year Plan (1956–1961), Mahalanobis' one, that the public expenditure in industry jumped from 4% of the public outlay to 20%, mainly on basic industries such as iron, steel, coal, fertilisers, heavy engineering, and heavy electrical equipment.[8] The plan assumed stagnant exports, while the main trading activity was to import capital goods. Systematic model-building for the purpose of developing a strategy began with

Table 5.2 Growth rates in Indian manufacturing, 1951–1952 to 1969–1970

Industry Group	*1951–1952 to 1959–1960 (%)*	*1960–1961 to 1969–1970 (%)*
Textiles	2.98	0.70
Rubber, petroleum, and plastic products	17.54	10.40
Chemical products	7.90	8.39
Basic metal and alloys	6.52	7.01
Non-electrical machinery	21.02	17.00
Electrical machinery	17.64	14.01
Transport equipment	14.83	7.66

Source: Own elaboration based on Chandra et al. (2008)

the Second Five-Year Plan (Seth, 1986), and if in the First Plan, planners used a two-sector model, with the availability of inter-industry modelling techniques, they gradually evolved into a multisectoral approach.

The balance of payment stress of 1958 resulted in the introduction of foreign exchange budgeting in the Third Five-Year Plan (1961–1966), re-emphasising agriculture, particularly wheat production, fertilisers, and import substitution (Panagariya, 2008). Besides, the Third Plan for the first time dedicated a chapter to the problem of regional imbalances (Seth, 1986). However, the war with China in 1962 caused a redistribution of the resources in order to increase the defence budget, and Nehru's death in 1964 and the draught of 1964–1966 had an impact on the implementation of the Third Five-Year Plan. All in all, the growth rates in the Indian manufacturing sector between 1951/1952 and 1969/1970 show figures between 17% and 21% for rubber, petroleum and plastic products, non-electrical machinery, and electrical machinery for the period encompassing the First and the Second Plans.

5.2.1.3 Mixed economy

The Industrial Policy Resolution of 1948 stated that the Indian economy was a mixed economy. The government provided stimuli, directions, and also direct participation in the production, while the market, subject to regulations, also operated in determining supply, demand, and prices. To Khanna (2015), the state-owned enterprises were to make India self-reliant, promote import substitution, develop the backward regions, and prevent concentration of economic power in private monopolies. Indeed, India went from 5 Central Government Enterprises in 1951 to 47 in 1961 (Kapila, 2003).

The Industries (Development and Regulation) Act of 1951 empowered the state with the industrial licensing regime, which was used to stimulate and regulate the private-sector participation in the different sectors and regions.

The Industrial Policy Resolution of 1956 listed almost 20 industries which were of exclusive responsibility of the state: arms and ammunitions; atomic energy; iron and steel; heavy castings and forgings of iron and steel; heavy machinery required for iron and steel production; machine tool manufacturing; heavy electrical industries; coal; mineral oils; mining of iron ore and other minerals such as copper, lead, and zinc; aircraft; air transport; railway transport; shipbuilding; telephone, telegraph, and wireless equipment; and generation and distribution of electricity. There were some industries where the state would create new enterprises and the private sector would supplement the state efforts: aluminium and other non-ferrous metals not listed before, chemical industry, antibiotics and other essential drugs, fertilisers, synthetic rubber, carbonisation of coal, chemical pulp, and road and sea transport. The private sector could operate freely in the other sectors, and some exceptions were made in the former ones.

Between 1962 and 1966, in accumulated investment terms, the following 12 firms totalised more than 80% of the total investment of the state-owned enterprises: 1) Hindustan Steel, with around 45%; 2) Neyveli Lignite Corporation; 3) Heavy Engineering Corporation; 4) National Coal Development Corporation; 5) Oil and Natural Gas Commission; 6) Fertilizer Corporation of India; 7) Heavy Electrical India; 8) Indian Refineries; 9) Air India; 10) Shipping Corporation of India; 11) Indian Oil Corporation; 12) Bharat Heavy Electricals (Bhagwati and Desai, 1970). In sector-wise terms, between 1963 and 1966, steel concentrated around 43% of the cumulated investment in public-sector projects, engineering about 17%, chemicals 10%, petroleum 10%, and mining and minerals 8%.

Despite this increase in the number of the state-owned-enterprises, the private sector continued operating and even growing. The dominance of the traditional entrepreneurial communities over the Indian manufacturing market continued: the Marwari entrepreneurial community, Gujarati industrialists, Punjabis, and Parsis (Hazari, 1966). In fact, despite the restrictions, the private sector controlled by family groups was never eliminated, and, on the contrary, public investment functioned as a crowding-in mechanism (Bandyopadhyay, 2004). The top 28 industrial firms concentrated around 20% of the total industrial applications between 1959 and 1966 and around 60% of the fixed investment of the private sector, with four top houses, Birlas, J.K., Tata's, and Shri Ram, concentrating 20% of the private investment (Bhagwati and Desai, 1970).

At the same time, the government stimulated the incorporation of new professional groups such as engineers and scientists, with some kind of entrepreneurial policy, with good results in Gujarat and Punjab. Besides, a Gandhian rooted policy was implemented, mainly consisting in the reservation of the handicraft market, some small-scale final goods production, and some textile production for small enterprises and entrepreneurs, mainly in rural areas, that still operated in a putting-out system (Tyabji, 1989). In fact, these types of sectors and agricultural activities still employ most of the Indian people today.

Bhagwati and Desai (1970) say that although in 1945 the National Planning Committee had elaborated a critical resolution about the role of foreign capital, the First Industrial Policy Resolution of 1948 gave space to private foreign investment in specific circumstances. Furthermore, in 1949, Nehru announced a liberal policy towards foreign direct investment (FDI). Indeed, Abrol (2013) defines it as a period of a cautious welcome and liberal attitude towards FDI, with a concurrent technological capability building in the public sector. There were no significant restrictions on remittances of profits and dividends, although the largest ownership was preferred to be in Indian, mainly public, hands. The two main forms of private foreign operations during this period were the equity investment and the pure technical cooperation. FDI investments were centred on petroleum and manufacturing, metal products, capital goods, and chemicals (Bhagwati and Desai, 1970). Minority foreign equity participation and turnkey contracts between multinational firms and the state-owned enterprises were used to promote technological transfer (Mani, 1992).

The creation of different public development finance institutions had an important role in financing the private sector during this period, constituting the financial arm of the Indian NSI (Nayyar, 2015; Bhagwati and Desai, 1970). The main four institutions created were the Industrial Finance Corporation of India (IFCI), the National Industrial Development Corporation (NIDC), the Industrial Credit and Investment Corporation of India (ICICI), and the Refinance Corporation for Industry Private, Ltd (RCIP). The IFCI was established in 1948 to provide long-term credit for medium and large industrial enterprises. Its contribution to long-term financing was estimated in a range of 12% of the long-term industrial financing and 5% of the estimated gross fixed investment during the period 1950–1958 (Bhagwati and Desai, 1970). The NIDC started with the Second Five-Year Plan mainly for credits for the modernisation of the jute and cotton textile industries. The ICICI was established in 1955 as a private institution but with funding of the government and the World Bank, to promote industries in the private sector, assisting them in their foreign exchange needs. It operated in several sectors such as paper, engineering, sugar, plastics, chemicals, automobiles, shipping, and so on. The RCIP was established in 1958 mainly to provide refinancing to commercial banks and to medium and large firms for production purposes.

5.2.1.4 Population, infrastructure, and agriculture

Great attention was placed on improving health, mainly through the control of many infectious and parasitic diseases and through the availability of vaccines. The main achievement was the decrease of the death rates in all the country, resulting in a significant increase in the rate of population growth to 2% for the period between 1951–1961 and around 2.2% for the next three decades until 1991 (Kapila, 2014). Thus, India's population was 361 million in 1951, 439 million in 1961, and 548 million in 1971 (Kapila, 2003). This increase in the population growth rate had an unplanned impact on the food needs and the per capita GDP growth objectives.

Family planning received vital importance during the 1940s too. The need to import food, the Bhore Committee Report that highlighted the issue of family planning, and the 1951 Census that registered a significant increase in the population, all took Nehru to announce a national family planning programme. The First Five-Year Plan referred specifically to a programme of family limitation and population control. India was the first country in the world to adopt an official national population policy in support of family planning. The results of the programme seem to be mixed (Kapila, 2014). On the one hand, many Indians had reservations about the promotion and use of modern contraception methods. The resources allocated to the project were not very generous, and there was not much experience (in the world) in this type of programme. On the other hand, there were significant achievements in larger towns. For instance, Madras began applying a vasectomy campaign with success and was then followed by Kerala, Mysore, and Maharashtra. In the Third Plan, the relevance of voluntary sterilisation was reinforced. Sterilisation camps were used to promote vasectomies, and there was a shift in the approach to family planning: from a clinic-based approach to a community extension strategy.

The infrastructure and social services between 1950/1951 and 1965/1966 show a steady increase, and, as can be seen in Table 5.3, the education system expanded considerably (Bhagwati and Desai, 1970). The number of schools grew from 231,000 in 1950/1951 to 505,000 in 1965/1966. Technical education, engineering, and technology admission capacity increased significantly. The number of hospitals almost tripled, the registered nurses rose from 15,000 to 45,000, and the number of doctors also experienced a significant growth. There was a substantial growth in town and village electrification and in the installed capacity.

Agriculture has been a main challenge for Indian development.[9] Broadly speaking, India inherited a mixed agrarian structure that was almost stagnant in the first half of the twentieth century, with a significant gravitation both of landlordism and zamindars' intermediation. Land reform was promoted in the understanding that it was positive in terms of both equity and productivity. Chandra et al. (2008) point out four main aspects of Nehru's period regarding land reform and agriculture policy: 1) abolition of intermediaries (zamindars, jagirdars, etc.); 2) tenancy reforms to reduce rents and confer ownership rights to tenants; 3) limit on size of landholding with the excess over this ceiling to be taken over by the state

Table 5.3 Growth in infrastructure and social services, 1950–1951 to 1965–1966

Activity	*Unit*	*1950–1951 (%)*	*1965–1966 (%)*	*% 1950–1951 vs. 1965–1966*
Schools	Thousands	231.0	505.0	11.9
Students enrolment				
Primary stage	Millions	19.2	51.5	168.9
Middle stage	Millions	3.1	11.0	252.6
Secondary stage	Millions	1.2	5.2	329.5
Technical education (engineering and technology) admission capacity				
Degree level	Thousands	4.1	24.7	502.4
Diploma level	Thousands	5.9	49.9	745.8
Medical facilities				
Hospital beds	Thousands	113.0	300.0	165.5
Doctors	Thousands	56.0	86.0	53.6
Nurses	Thousands	15.0	45.0	200.0
Electricity: installed capacity	Million kW.	2.3	10.2	393.5
Electricity: town and villages electrified	Thousands	3.7	52.3	1313.5
Railways: freight carried	Million tons	93.0	205.0	120.4
Surfaced roads	Thousands km.	156.0	284.0	82.0

Source: Own elaboration based on Bhagwati and Desai (1970)

and redistributed among small farmers and the landless; and 4) cooperativisation programmes.

India tried to introduce land reform under a democratic regime, without using compulsory methods such as in the USSR, China, Japan, or Korea, with landlords and zamindars consolidated as upper-caste groups in the Indian social structure. With most of the Indian peasants having small plots of land, there was an important debate on land reform, with the fear that the agriculture production of the country would be reduced being promoted by different sectors, mainly in favour of a greater concentration and mechanisation. The judicialisation of land reform, driven by the zamindars, delayed the process, making the central and the state governments dependant on the courts' decisions. There existed significant institutional challenges in the implementation of the land reform, such as the measurement of the land holdings. In 1954, the Planning Commission proposed a land census that failed because the state governments did not support it. For instance, Hyderabad conducted a well-designed survey, but Uttar Pradesh refused, and Kashmir did not participate even in the debate over land reform (Kapila, 2014). As the Constitution of 1949 left the adoption and implementation of land and tenancy reforms to the state governments, the advances were heterogeneous.

The idea that conceptually backed the abolition of intermediaries was that if the ownership of land was clearly identified with the management of land, this would be more productive. Tenancy reforms had three main objectives: to guarantee the security of tenure to tenants who had cultivated a piece of land continuously for six years, to reduce rent payments, and to give the right to the tenants to acquire the cultivated land in better conditions than the market price. Many efforts were made regarding the imposition of ceilings on the size of landholdings. However, with huge pressure from upper castes related to land interests, it was impossible to build a strong consensus in the Indian society about this issue, and this was reflected in the extreme difficulty in implementing this programme with even a reasonable degree of success.

Overall, there seems to be a consensus in various literature that the objective that succeeded the most in the implementation phase was the zamindar elimination, but advances in the other objectives, such as tenant reforms and ceilings, were limited (Bardhan, 1984; Appu, 1995; Vaidyanathan, 1994; Kapila, 2014; Rao and Storm, 1998; Ray, 2014; among many others). The judicialisation of the process and the administrative delays were the main bottlenecks. Regional disparity in terms of bargain power was a fact. For instance, in Kerala and Bengal, governed by the Communist Party, reforms progressed significantly, but in Uttar Pradesh, Bihar, and Madras, the zamindars could still retain lands under personal cultivation, reinforcing them as landlords.

Cooperative farming was the main official policy in this scheme of agrarian reorganisation (Kapila, 2003). Early planners hoped that cooperative arrangement at the community level and motivated workers helped by trained workers of the Community Development Programme (1952) would help to implement rural development projects and contribute with critical institutional changes, such as the land reform, organisation of cooperatives, and so on (Chandra et al., 1987). However, the cooperative movement didn't reach its main goal either. According to Chandra et al. (2008), two main types of cooperatives were formed: 1) cooperatives formed by traditional and influential families looking to evade land reforms and get access to state financing and 2) state-led cooperatives formed as pilot projects, but these had access to the worst land, previously uncultivated, without access to irrigation, and so on.

All in all, state role in agriculture development was not insignificant. Irrigation investment was 16.3% of the total outlay in the First Plan and 9% in the Second and Third Plans (Panagariya, 2008). Irrigation was also linked to electric power, stimulated through the building of several mega hydroelectric power projects. Various extension efforts were made, and the availability of chemical fertilisers increased from 73,000 tons in 1950/1951 to 780,000 tons in 1965/1966 (Chandra et al., 2008).

Some estimations state that agriculture output growth for this period was between 2.5% and 3% (to Rao and Storm (1998), the agricultural output growth was 2.7%, around seven times higher than during the first half of the century and slightly superior to the population growth). Around half of this growth was explained by increases in the yields per acre and the other half by increasing cropped area. This growth was unevenly concentrated, mainly based on the north-western states (Vaidyanathan, 1994), a characteristic that would continue and even was reinforced in later periods. At the same time, the import of foodgrains continued increasing, from 12 million tons in the First Plan to 20 million in the Second and 32 million in the Third. The war with China, in 1962, and Pakistan, in 1965, and the drought of 1965–1967 underlined the need to take new steps in the Indian agriculture, introducing high-yield variety seeds, with the land reform achieving only a limited and heterogeneous advance.

5.2.2. Shocks, radicalisation and technological efforts with Indira Gandhi (1966–1977)

Indira Gandhi, Nehru's daughter, was Indian prime minister on two occasions, between 1966 and 1977 and between 1980 and 1984, when she was assassinated. In this section, we will deal with her first ten years as prime minister. If Nehru's period was one of quite a general consensus in related literature, Indira's is perhaps the most controversial one. No doubt, several "shocks", such as the wars with Pakistan of 1965 and 1971, the droughts of 1964–1966, and the oil peak of 1973, impacted India, causing different economic and political internal stresses. A lower growth rate than during Nehru's years, different and substantial technological efforts, and the consolidation of a strong leadership under Indira's figure that included the declaration of the Emergency in 1975 were some of the main features of this period.

5.2.2.1 Shocks, political stress, and radicalisation

After Nehru's death, his succession occurred under the direction of the Congress leaders' group called the Syndicate (Chandra et al., 2008). Lal Bahadur Shastri, an old member of the Congress Party, was elected as prime minister and offered Indira Gandhi the Ministry of Information and Broadcasting. The war with China in 1962 led to an increase in the defence expenditure, which went from 2% of India's GDP in 1960/1961 to 4% in 1963/1964 (Ghosh, 1998). The military confrontation with Pakistan in September 1965, linked to the conflict in the Kashmir Valley, added geopolitical tension with both the US and the UK, which suspended all food and arms aid to both countries, while China accused India as the aggressor.

The drought of 1964–1966 significantly reduced the buffer food stocks and worsened the balance of payments situation (Panagariya, 2008; Ghosh, 1998). As stated by Panagariya (2008, p. 47):

> External shocks included two consecutive drought years during 1965–67; a war with Pakistan in 1965 that came on the heels of a war with China in 1962; another war with Pakistan in 1971, which was preceded by a huge influx of refugees and culminated in the creation of Bangladesh; two further consecutive droughts in 1971–72 and 72–73; and the oil price shock in October 1973, which contributed to a nearly 40% deterioration in India´s terms of trade over 1972–76. The decline in the growth rate in agriculture is to be attributed largely to droughts that more than offset the positive contribution of the Green Revolution.

As the food situation was critical, food rationing was introduced in seven states, the Food Corporation of India (1965) was created, and the initial steps to the implementation of the Green Revolution were given. After 19 months as prime minister, Shastri suffered a heart attack and died. Indira Gandhi, young and heiress of Nehru's political aura, emerged as an interesting figure to the Syndicate members. Indira took over in 1966 with India suffering a severe drought, famine growing in some states, and a "Plan holidays" for two years implemented to redirect resources to import seeds. During the first four years of the Third Five-Year Plan, India imported 25.4 million tons of foodgrain, but during 1965–1966 and 1966–1967, India had to import another 19 million tons (Panagariya, 2008). Around 15 million tons of wheat were imported from the US, under the PL 480 aid programme, with President Lyndon B. Johnson maintaining India on a "ship-to-mouth" existence, by subjecting these shipments to constant threats of suspension. As the US shipments were the only escape from famine for India, he intruded into domestic policy issues, playing a critical role in forcing the devaluation of the rupee in June 1966, the introduction of a number of changes in the industrial control system, and the initial set-up of the Green Revolution.

However, the 1966 devaluation failed to have any significant effect on the export performance, and the balance of payments was sustained mainly through external aid (Ghosh, 1998). What is more, the devaluation accelerated domestic inflation rates and generated an increasing feeling of anger among Indians, as they realised that Johnson was negotiating with the hunger of the Indian people and influencing in the Indian sovereignty.

In the domestic front, the critical economic situation at the end of the 1960s; the internal disputes between Indira, the Syndicate, and other regional and local Congress political leaders, and the political dislike of the big landlords and farmers regarding state participation in agriculture through food trade commercialisation ended with a defeat of the Congress in the 1967 Lok Sabha (parliamentary) election. This same year, there was a split in the Communist Party of India, and with it a new group surfaced, which became known as the Naxalite movement. Inspired by the Chinese Cultural Revolution and criticising parliamentarism, they looked for a more radical path to communism.

Congress parliamentary majority was drastically reduced, giving place to a period of coalition governments at the regional level with growing hostilities that ended with the split of Congress in 1969 (Chandra et al., 2008). This split gave space to a radicalisation in Indira's policymaking framework, which was initially postulated in 1967, through the Ten-Point Programme, including the nationalisation of banks and insurance companies, state involvement in import and export trade, ceilings on urban property, further regulations over monopolies and economic power concentration, public distribution of foodgrains, promotion of rural housing, and abolition on princely privileges. Indira won the 1971 elections, and with the military victory over Pakistan on the same year, she achieved her political momentum, ratifying a state-led, self-sufficient, and pro-poor policy agenda. As explained by Chandra et al. (2008):

> In August 1972, general insurance was nationalized and five months later the coal industry. The ceiling was imposed on urban land ownership. The MRTP Act to check the concentration of industrial enterprises in a few hands had already been passed in 1969 and an MRTP Commission appointed in 1971 to implement the Act . . . Legislation to reduce ceilings on agricultural landholdings and distribute surplus land to the landless and marginal farmers was also passed in several states. The central government initiated a programme of cheap foodgrain distribution to the economically vulnerable sections of society and a cash scheme for creating employment in rural areas. It also made it compulsory for nationalized banks to open branches in underbanked areas such as small towns, rural clusters and the poorer parts of the cities and to make credit available to small industries, farmers, road transporters and self-employed persons.

The internal political tensions and polarisation increased, with different uprising movements in Gujarat and Bihar. In 1975, Indira declared the state of Internal Emergency.[10] The Emergency and different political rough measures, such as taking political prisoners, press censorship, and forced sterilisation programmes, led Indira to call elections in 1977. The opposition front led by the Janata Party won, and for the first time, India had a non-Congress prime minister.

5.2.2.2 Green Revolution (and bank nationalisation)

The strong increase in population growth after independence and the low but steady rise in income per capita introduced pressure on Indian agriculture during the early 1960s (Chandra et al., 2008; Rao and Storm, 1998). The droughts of 1965/1966 and 1966/1967 installed the urgent need to improve agriculture production, placing food self-sufficiency as top objectives of the economic and foreign policy, giving place to the implementation of the so-called Green Revolution.[11]

The New Agricultural Strategy (NAS) implied a switch from an institutional-based approach, applied until the mid-1960s, which consisted basically in the implementation of land reforms and public investment in agriculture infrastructure, mainly irrigation, to a technology-based approach founded on the introduction of the high-yielding varieties (HYV), minor irrigation works, and chemical fertilisers and pesticides in determined deliberately concentrated regions and crops (mainly wheat) (Rao and Storm, 1998).

Chakravarty (1987) highlights the main aspects of the new approach, supported by the US: 1) a shift from major to minor irrigation works, which implied a shift from public financed large irrigation projects to small tube wells and energised pump sets; 2) adequate provision of credit to those considered to be credit-worthy, which meant the large farmers; 3) an increase in the rate of fertiliser and energy (electricity and diesel) consumption; and 4) the development of fertiliser-sensitive varieties of grains. According to Kapila (2003, p. 228), the seed-fertiliser-water package needed better agricultural practices for the effective use of the technology:

> First, the plan requires the fertilizer-water input at particular stages of growth to give the best yields. Secondly, as fertilizers can be absorbed by weeds as well as by the plant, effective weeding is required to prevent waste of expensive fertilizer. Thirdly, while the HYV seeds give higher yields, they are more prone to damage from excessive watering. For example, shorter-stemmed dwarf varieties are more reliable to be flooded. They thus require more effective water control and better drainage. The need is for controlled and adequate water supplies. Fourthly, being relatively new and non-acclimatized strains, they are more prone to local pests and diseases than established indigenous varieties and therefore, require a supply of germicides and pesticides.

In 1965, C. Subramaniam, Nehru's former minister of steel, mines, and industry, was appointed as minister of food and agriculture by Shastri and sustained by Indira Gandhi. At an institutional level, the Agricultural Prices Commission (APC), the FCI, and the National Dairy Development Board (NDDB) were created in 1965. The APC established minimum support prices in order to ensure remunerative prices for farmers; the FCI distributed foodgrains throughout the country and maintained buffer stock foodgrains, becoming a major player in the procurement and distribution of grains; and the NDDB promoted milk production by small producers (Panagariya, 2008).

The Rockefeller Foundation was trying to introduce the HYV from the *Centro Internacional de Mejoramiento de Maiz y Trigo* (CIMMT) of Mexico in India with the support of the Ford Foundation. The new seeds could yield more than double of the existing levels. However, the implementation of the new policy faced strong opposition from the cabinet, the public, and the Parliament (mainly from the Left), but with the support first of Shastri and then of Indira, Subramaniam went ahead with public demonstrations of the HYV potential and finally managed to implement a pilot experiment. In 1966, India imported 18,000 tons of Mexican seed that were added to the 5,000 tons of seed that already existed in India, which had been multiplied from the 250 tons imported in 1965 (Panagariya, 2008). They were distributed in Punjab, Haryana, and western Uttar Pradesh where the irrigation of Nehru's period had been concentrated. The results were decisive: in 1967/1968, India produced 17 million tons of wheat, compared with the previous record high of 12 million tons.

Several complementary investments and institutional efforts were involved in this first phase of the Green Revolution. The spread of the HYV seeds was supported by public investments in fertilisers, canal water, power, irrigation, and credit (Kapila, 2014; Bardhan, 1984; Rao and Storm, 1998, etc.). Although below other East Asia countries, including China, as can be seen in Table 5.4, there was an impressive expansion in the use of chemical fertilisers. Nutrients per unit of the cropped area increased from less than 1 kg per hectare in the early 1950s to about 5 kg in the early 1960s and to 32 kg at the beginning of the 1980s. The gross irrigated area increased from 22% in the early 1950s to 38% at the beginning of the 1960s and to 50% at the beginning of the 1980s. Electricity consumption in Indian agriculture went from 833 million kWh in 1960/1961 to 4,470 in 1970/1971 and to 14,489 in 1980/1981.

Public investment, which represented around 30% of the total agriculture gross fixed investment, and "crowded in" private investments, led to a boom, mainly in farm assets. The sale of electric and diesel pumpsets increased from 421,000 to 2.4 million between 1960/1961 and 1970/1971, tube wells increased from 90,000 to 460,000, and tractors from 31,000

Table 5.4 Use and capital formation in Indian agriculture, 1950–1951 to 1980–1981

	Unit	*1950–1951*	*1960–1961*	*1970–1971*	*1980–1981*
Fixed inputs					
Tractors	No./1.000 ha of	0.1	0.2	0.9	2.7
Electrical pumps	gross cultivate	1.0	16.8	52.0	59.8
Diesel pumps	area	2.7	19.1	50.1	56.0
Gross fixed capital formation	Rs crore	–	1777	2884	4864
Public	Rs crore	–	589	789	1892
	%		33%	27%	39%
Private	Rs crore	–	1188	2095	2972
	%		67%	73%	61%
Chemical fertilisers	kg/hectare	–	1,9	13,1	31,8
Electricity	Million kW.	203	833	4.470	14.489
Net irrigated area	Million hectares	20.9	24.7	31.1	38.7
Canals	%	39.8	42.1	41.3	39.5
Tanks	%	17.3	18.5	13.2	8.2
Tube wells	%	28.7	29.6	38.2	45.7
Gross irrigated area	Million hectares	22.6	28.0	38.2	49.8
Area under HYV seeds	% of gross cultivated area	0.0	0.0	9.3	24.9

Source: Own elaboration based on Rao and Storm (1998)

to 140,000 (Chandra et al., 2008). Regarding public-private complementation, Kapila (2003, p. 231) states:

> [A]part from the introduction of HYVs of seeds for wheat and rice, public investment in agriculture was stepped up significantly. The new technology raised the profitability of investment for farmers . . . in agriculture, there is a high complementary between public and private investment. As a result, the annual gross capital formation in agriculture, public and private combined, at constant prices, rose much faster than in the pre-green revolution period. This is reflected in the accelerated increase in gross irrigated area. From less than one million hectares per annum during the pre-green revolution period, it increased to about 2.5 million hectares per annum during the seventies. However, owing to the land constraint, the growth of the net sown area slowed down considerably. This explains why despite the accelerated increase in capital formation and the introduction of new technologies, the growth rate of agricultural output was no higher than in the pre-green revolution period.

In 1969, Indira decided to nationalise all banks whose nationwide deposits exceeded 500 million rupees, adding 14 banks and 54% of bank branches into the public-sector property, reaching a total of 84% of the bank branches in the public sector (Panagariya, 2008). A main objective of nationalisation was to channel resources into agriculture and rural areas. This objective was amply achieved: bank branches jumped to 35% in 1972 from 22% in 1969, population per branch was reduced from 64,000 in 1969 to 29,000 in 1976 and 19,000 in 1981, rural credit expanded from 2% in 1969 to 6% in 1976 and 11% in 1981, and rural bank deposits increased from 3% in 1969 to 9% in 1976 and 13% in 1981 (Panagariya, 2008). Besides, in 1972, the General Insurance Business (Nationalisation) Act created the General Insurance Corporation (GIC) as a holding company, mainly oriented to provide insurance to poor farmers and rural area population (Nayyar, 2015).

During the 1970s, the drought of 1972/1973 produced a drop in the foodgrain production of 7%, forcing again the imports from the US and making the government take over the wholesale trade in wheat, but this move showed no positive results and was abandoned (Kapila, 2014). As the oil peak of 1973 increased fertiliser prices, in 1977, a retention price scheme was introduced for urea, the main fertiliser, in order to uncouple local prices from international market price movements. As power consumption increased substantially during the 1970s, energy subsidies significantly increased. Another main trend of the 1970s was the extension of HYV technology from wheat to rice, favoured by the growth of tube wells and expanding the Green Revolution to new areas.

As for the results, between 1967/1968 and 1970/1971, foodgrain production rose by 35% (Chandra et al., 2008). Between 1964/1965 and 1971/1972, aggregate food production increased from 89 to 112 million tons, a 10% per capita increase. Net food imports decreased from 10.3 million tons in 1966 to 3.6 million tons in 1970. India achieved self-sufficiency in food matters with buffer stocks of 30 million tons and managing to export significant amounts of food at the beginning of the 1970s. According to Rao and Storm's (1998) figures showed next, the foodgrains' output growth between 1967/1968 and 1981/1982 of 2.21% was less than the 2.93% growth of the pre–Green Revolution period, because of the decrease in the cultivated area: yield growth rate in foodgrains between 1967/1968 and 1981/1982 was 1.85, but the growth in the area used was 0.37. These numbers give an account of a technology-intensive agricultural output growth rather than a land-intensive one. Besides, output growth was particularly high in wheat, achieving a 5.21% increase between 1967/1968 and 1981/1982, more than 2pp superior than all the other foodgrains such as rice, maize, and so on.

Table 5.5 Indian agricultural growth, 1891–1991, % per annum

	Pre-independence Period			*Pre–Green Revolution Period*			*Early Green Revolution Period*			*Late Green Revolution Period*		
	(1891–1946)			*(1949–1950 to 1964–1965)*			*(1967–1968 to 1981–1982)*			*(1981–1982 to 1991–1992)*		
	Area	*Yield*	*Output*	*Area*	*Yield*	*Output*	*Area*	*Yield*	*Output*	*Area*	*Yield*	*Output*
Foodgrains	0.31	–0.18	0.11	1.41	1.43	2.93	0.37	1.85	2.21	–0.26	3.19	2.92
Rice				1.33	2.13	3.49	0.69	1.45	2.16	0.62	3.25	3.87
Wheat				2.68	1.27	3.99	2.60	2.55	5.21	0.28	3.06	3.33
Jowar				0.99	1.50	2.50	–0.84	3.50	2.61	–1.96	1.83	–0.10
Maize				2.66	1.18	3.87	0.10	0.49	0.58	0,11	2.46	2.62
Non-Foodgrains	0.42	0.86	1.31	2.52	0.93	3.54	1.06	1.34	2.41	1.71	2.55	4.30
All crops	0.40	0.01	0.37	1.61	1.30	3.13	0.54	1.74	2.29	0.49	2.93	3.42

Source: Own elaboration based on Rao and Storm (1998)

Regarding the Indian research institutions, the Indian Council of Agricultural Research (ICAR) and the Punjab Agricultural University played a relevant role in the indigenisation of the HYV seeds. An intense process of import substitution on chemical fertilisers was done, going from a ratio of imports of 59.8 in 1969/1970 to 41.5 in 1979/1980 (Chakravarty, 1987). According to Long (1988, p. 404), India performed well in indigenising the HYV varieties:

> A major test for India's research effort in agriculture came when the new and potentially highly productive strains of short-stem wheat and rice began to be distributed by the international agencies that had developed them. India's agricultural research system met this suddenly developed opportunity splendidly. It moved rapidly to examine the utility of these new strains for India and undertook to develop modified strains of the "green revolution" varieties to fit India´s climates needs. The Indian government did its part by importing and later producing locally the necessary fertilizers . . . Other problems and other opportunities remain but it is clear that India´s agricultural research activities are solidly based and well supported. Given the climate-specific character of agriculture, the decentralized character of state-operated R&D is surely desirable.

The Green Revolution brought desired and undesired consequences and was not without its critics. Some main consequences explained by Chakravarty (1987) were 1) an increase in the purchase of goods which deepened the agro-industrial dependence, which created the need to ensure a continuous flow from industry to agriculture; 2) a drastic increase in the monetisation of Indian agriculture; 3) a downward rigidity in agriculture prices caused by the price support policy, which made the price determination part of a wider political process; 4) a greater sensitivity in agriculture to world market price fluctuations, particularly oil prices, due to the higher use of energy and oil-based fertilisers; and 5) an increase in agriculture mechanisation. The Green Revolution increased output, giving more than proportionate benefits to the farmers located in the structurally better-endowed regions such as Punjab and West Bengal.

Regarding concentration aspects, Rao and Storm (1998) pointed out that, as the Green Revolution was consolidated around the best agriculture- and infrastructure-endowed regions, in a strategy of concentrating growth region-wise, class-wise, and crop-wise, the "building on the best" capitalist development in the favoured regions was the direct outcome. Environmental consequences such as erosion, deforestation, an increase in flooding and drainage problems, and related mismanagement and unregulated expansion, mainly in poor areas, are highlighted by different authors such as Rao and Storm (1998), Kapila (2014), Chandra et al. (2008), and Shiva (1991).

In our view, the Green Revolution needs to be understood as a significant institutional effort made by the Indian NSI under a stressful agriculture and food security context, dependent on nature and explicitly concentrated. The whole process succeeded in increasing agricultural productivity and output but, at the same time, reinforced regional and income inequalities. Tenants who did not have the security of tenure and small peasants without access to credit were the main losers, given the increase in the agricultural capital/output ratio. However, overall, as food crops prices dropped, there was a general improvement in the poor's living conditions. The role of the state and the Indian NSI was central in the whole process, through direct public investment in infrastructure, crowding in private investment, building buffering stocks, giving credit, minimum prices, and so on. The indigenisation of the HYV technology was another significant effort and achievement.

5.2.2.3 *The big science triad: nuclear, space, and defence*

As can be seen in Figure 5.5, in nine years, between 1962 and 1971, the Indian subcontinent confrontations and military events included a major military Indian defeat against China in 1962; two military Indo-Pakistani confrontations, in 1965 and 1971; and China going nuclear, with its test in 1964. These events necessarily impacted the Indian NSI profile, deepening the nuclear, space, and defence debates; strategies; capabilities; and R&D expenditure (Joseph et al., 2008).

After the military defeat of 1962 against China, defence capability's upgrading and modernisation, including the development of nuclear weapons, increasingly occupied the minds of Indian strategists, policymakers, and public debate. Even though it received US military aid after 1962, as mentioned earlier, in 1965, the US and the UK stopped all military assistance. This, added to Johnson's "ship-to-mouth" approach to the Indian agrarian crisis, drove Indira to freeze India's relationship with the US and deepen its association with the USSR. China's nuclear test of 1964 and the Indo-Pakistan war of 1965 added pressure on the nuclear issue.

According to Cohen (2001), there were three lobby groups involved in the Indian nuclear debate in the second half of the 1960s: the "nuclear abolitionists", based on Gandhian non-violence philosophy and Nehru's anti-militarism; the "nuclear hawks", willing to support a nuclear strategy; and the "contingent hawks", who did not see India going nuclear soon, unless a threat appeared with China or any other country. During the 1960s, the "option" strategy sustained by this third group was adopted. However, after the military confrontation with Pakistan in 1971, the global and regional context forced the nuclear weaponisation option and the deepening of its relationship with the USSR, as put by Ogden (2011, p. 293):

> This deterioration was typified by the US tilt to Pakistan in the 1971 war (during which the USA sent ships into the Bay of Bengal),

Figure 5.5 Main Indian military confrontations and events between 1962 and 1999.

Source: Elaborated by Rosaura Flynn.

> by deepening China-Pakistan ties and, most critically, by the US-China rapprochement under Richard Nixon and Mao Tse Tung from 1972. These relations effectively created a China-Pakistan-USA united front against India and were strengthened by China´s regional nuclear monopoly. Such factors combined with a variety of domestic pressures, and India's Prime minister Indira Gandhi . . . decided to carry out a nuclear test to demonstrate India's capability. With a sufficiently developed nuclear programme at hand and under the codename "Smiling Buddha", India undertook her first nuclear test on 18 May 1974 – a test described as a Peaceful Nuclear Explosion.
>
> (PNE)

In this context of military pressure, the Indian space institutions grew and became more complex (Joseph et al., 2008). In 1972, the Space Commission was created to take charge of space policymaking, under the newly created Department of Space (DOS). The DOS was under direct control of Prime Minister Indira Gandhi and was linked to the Indian Space Research Organisation (ISRO), which was set up in 1969. The DOS/ISRO conducted experimental missions in the field of satellite technology, vehicle launch, and space applications. ISRO gained experience in running a satellite-based instructional television system, with support from the NASA, through the Satellite Instructional Television Experiment (SITE). The DOS also entered into the Satellite Telecommunications Experiment Project, using Franco-German communications satellite Symphonie. A station that later became the base of the Indian National Remote Sensing Agency (INRSA) was built in Hyderabad to receive data from the US Landsat.

ISRO then built its first satellites, the Bhaskara-I and the Bhaskara-II, and one experimental communication satellite, the APPLE (Ariane Passenger Payload Experiment). Furthermore, in 1973, ISRO developed the four-stage launch vehicle SLV-3, and during the 1970s, different experimental launches occurred. After a first failure, the second launch in 1980 placed a small scientific satellite of 40 kg into Earth orbit, positioning India as a member of the select group of spacefaring countries.

After the Nixon-Mao rapprochement of 1972, the USSR tried to counterbalance China's power in Asia, increasing cooperation with India. Naval and space technical assistance, MiG-21 fighter planes, tanks, ships, and other weapons and diplomatic support at the UN Security Council were obtained from the USSR. In particular, the Soviet support to the Indian space programme during the 1970s was significant, as explained by Reddy (2011, p. 315):

> In building Indian capabilities in satellite technology, the URSS played a vital role. Both the Aryabhata and the Bhaskara satellites

> were developed by joint teams of Indian-Soviet scientists and engineers. An important feature of these experimental satellite projects was that they were not modeled after the early generation satellites of the space powers, but represented state-of-the-art technology. The APPLE satellite, up-to-date in some of its features, incorporated the three-axis stabilization technology that was mastered by the USA and Europe only in the mid-1970s.

At the end of the 1970s, India consolidated the science-driven profile of its NSI based on nuclear, space, and defence blocks. According to Long (1988), the DRDO, the DAE, and the DOS concentrated over 50% of the Indian R&D expenditure at the beginning of the 1980s.

5.2.2.4 Nationalisations, indigenous development and science, and technology policy

As said before, the external shocks and the economic stress led to a radicalisation in Indira's policymaking framework, particularly during the 1970s. Nationalisations were undertaken in different sectors. Among the main regulations, we can mention the Monopolies and Restrictive Trade Practices (MRTP) Act (1969), the Industrial Licensing Policy of 1970, the Foreign Exchange Regulation Act (FERA) of 1973, and the introduction of small-scale enterprises reservation in 1967. Related to Science, Technology, and Innovation (STI) explicit policies, the Patent Act of 1970, the computer industry initial steps, the first Science and Technology Plan (STP) of 1973, and the R&D fiscal stimulus scheme should be highlighted.

The industrial nationalisations were mainly introduced in the coal, steel, textile, engineering, chemical, and oil sectors (Khanna, 2015; Kabra, 1989; Kaul, 1991; etc.). Between 1970 and 1978, the main nationalisations were the Indo-Burma Petroleum Corporation; the Indian Copper Corporation; almost 1,000 coking coal mines; several steel companies such as the Steel Containers, the Indian Oil Blending, Esso, and Burma-Shell from the oil-refining sector; more than 100 textile mills; Hindustan Tractors; Britannia Engineering; and so on (Kabra, 1989).

As a result of the reports of different commissions and committees such as the Hazari and Dutt Committees and the Monopolies Enquiry Commission, in 1969, the Monopolies and Restrictive Trade Practices (MRTP) Act was passed to regulate big businesses (Panagariya, 2008). The Act allowed the government to approve investment activity only if it would not lead to further concentration, although there were exceptions depending on the public interest in some projects and sectors. The Industrial Licensing Policy of 1970 reinforced the government's control over industry through the license system, consolidated as the main policy instrument. Previously, the small-scale industries reservation policy had been introduced in 1967. The list of products began with 47 items and expanded to 177 in 1974 and 504 items in 1978, including clothing, shoes, leather products, toys, furniture, simple electrical appliances, and so on (Panagariya, 2008).

Direct import control was consolidated in the form of a list of restrictions on importable products. Thus, the ratio of imports to GDP dropped to 3.5% in 1972/1973, including oil and petroleum products, with an average for the period between 1970 and 1980 of 5.75% (Panagariya, 2008). Similarly to the Latin American experience, although import substitution policies reduced imports of products, they increased the demand for imported capital goods and equipment.

Furthermore, the crisis of 1965–1967 drew the government's attention to foreign exchange outflows resultant from remittances of dividends, profits, and royalties. In line with the recommendations of the Mudaliar Committee on Foreign Collaboration (1966), first; in 1968, with the creation of the Foreign Investment Board (FIB); and then, in 1973, with the Foreign Exchange Regulation Act (FERA), a restrictive FDI policy was implemented (Abrol, 2013). The FIB was set up to deal with FDI of less than 20 million rupees and within the 40% equity limit, allowing only bigger shares in priority areas (Joseph and Kakarlapudi, 2014). A maximum of royalty payments was fixed, normally 5% of the sales. Foreign firms were compelled to engage Indian public- and private-sector firms as consultants, and foreign collaborations were restricted (Mani, 1992). As a result, the number of cases involving foreign equity participation declined from 165 in 1961 to 27 in 1971. IBM and Coca-Cola closed operations in India during this period.

Regarding the technology policy, a Patent Act was enacted in 1970, which reduced the terms of patents from 16 to 14 years, and for drug and food, to 7 years. Reverse engineering was the way India developed much of its technological capabilities in the pharmaceutical industry, which became in time one of India's main industrial sectors. Referring to the Patent Act, Joseph et al. (2008, p. 46) say:

> [T]he Indian Patent Act (1970) played a major role in promoting indigenous technology by way of learning by doing. The Patent Act was one of the cornerstones of India's indigenous technology development initiative. Comprehensive and extensive, the Act was aimed at protecting the nascent domestic industry and was a role model for many developing countries. In the case of food, pharmaceuticals, pesticides and other agrochemical products, the term of patents was shortened to five years from the date of sealing the patent or seven years from the date of filing whichever was earlier. The act had many interesting features, like the adaptation of process instead of product patenting, reduction in the number of years of patent protection, powerful compulsory licensing provisions, enabling state intervention in pricing of patent products and so on.

> The mechanism of process patenting proved very effective for the development of pharmaceuticals, light engineering, industrial components and even chemical process equipment industry.

The computer industry also received a great stimulus during this period (Rajamaram, 2012). After the military defeat with China in 1962, the Government of India realised that electronics and communications were important for defence issues and constituted a committee in 1963 to prepare a plan for its development. One of the main recommendations was to establish a Department of Electronics (DoE) to promote an electronics and computer industry and to constitute an Electronics Commission (EC) with wide financial and executive powers. The DoE and the EC were created in 1970. The war with Pakistan and the first Indian nuclear test, which resulted in embargos on electronics and computer imports from the US, indirectly gave a boost to the government initiatives related to local production.

The Electronics Corporation of India Ltd. (ECIL) was financed to design, develop, and produce computers using components made in India. The ECIL produced computers called TDC 312 and TDC 316, similar to the PDP series computers made by the Digital Equipment Corporation of the US. An important contribution of the ECIL was to provide computers for the Air Defence Ground Environment System (ADGES) of the Indian Air Force (Rajamaram, 2012). These systems were deployed along India's borders to detect intrusion by non-friendly aircrafts. Each system used three TDC 316 computers connected to eight display units co-developed by ECIL and the Tata Electric Company with fairly complex interface electronics. To Rajamaram (2012, p. 25), ECIL contribution, although not successful in the commercialisation of computers, was relevant for the industry consolidation:

> ECIL demonstrated that computers could be manufactured in India with local components, imported ICs, and peripherals. It, however, worked more like a cottage industry as the volume of production was small. ECIL's sales effort was poor and hence it could not sell its machines easily. Most of the ECIL machines were bought by the Atomic Energy Establishments, government departments and Universities which obtained grants from the government and were constrained to buy the ECIL machines. Only 4 machines were sold to the private sector. ECIL machines were overpriced and did not have sufficient software. However, the contribution of the ECIL was in the training of over a thousand engineers in designing systems and developing systems software. Many of them later joined the private manufacturers and software companies to lead groups there.

With the aim of promoting indigenous development and consolidating S&T planning, on the institutional level, the creation of the National

Commission of Science (NCST) of the Department of Science and Technology (DST) in 1972 (Krishna, 2013) stands out. In 1973, the first STP was formulated for the 1974–1979 period. The STP was elaborated by the NCST and not by the Indian Planning Commission, in order to coordinate the potential fragmented technological and research efforts (Sikka, 2008). The STP organised the R&D efforts in 24 sectors: family welfare and health, natural resources, fuel and power, heavy engineering, chemical industries, machine tools, mining, steel and metallurgical industries, transportation, meteorology, consumer industries, housing and urbanisation and construction technology, marine resources, education, research and extension, special materials, utilisation and recycling of wastes, village industries, information, employment of S&T manpower, instruments, small-scale industries, refrigeration and air conditioning, environmental quality, and pollution control.

There was a marked increase in the investment in the S&T sector. By the end of Fifth Five-Year Plan (1974–1978), an amount of Rs. 13,800 million was invested, quadruplicating the investment in S&T as compared to the Rs. 3,730 million spent in the Fourth Five–Year Plan (1969–1974) (Joseph et al., 2008). The outlay for R&D during the last year of the Plan (1978–1979) increased to 0.84% of the GDP. Besides, in 1974, the government had implemented a scheme that recognised the in-house R&D units of industrial firms, which were given easier access to imported equipment, raw materials, and tax concessions (Joseph and Abrol, 2009). The number of these registered units increased from 106 in 1973 to over 900 by the early 1980s (Joseph and Kakarlapudi, 2014).

5.2.2.5 Food and fuel

Rural poverty declined from 64% in 1967 to 56% in 1973 (Kapila, 2014). However, Indian poverty was a main issue. In the 1960s, a working group led by Pitambar Pant was created to study how to raise the minimum standard of living. Pant broadly stated that some degree of inequality was an essential part of the structure of incentives in any growing economy, but that 20% of the population would not be benefited by the growth process and would have to be taken care of by transfer payments.

The Fifth Five-Year Plan (1974–1978) was the first to postulate poverty alleviation (Garibi Hatao or "get rid of poverty") and employment as the main objective. The Minimum Needs Programme (MNP) was introduced in the first year of the Plan with the objective of providing certain basic minimum needs. Many institutional pro-poor initiatives were implemented, such as the Karimnagar project, initiated in Andhra Pradesh in 1972, with the aim of taking S&T to the people in rural areas (Abrol, 2010, 2014). The initiative consisted of the identification of a number of proven technologies, which could help in the socio-economic development of the participating

Table 5.6 Rates of growth in electricity capacity and generation, 1950–1985, % per annum

Period	*Capacity*	*Generation*
1950–1951 to 1959–1960	8.31	11.34
1960–1961 to 1969–1970	12.64	12.07
1970–1971 to 1979–1980	7.83	7.33
1980–1981 to 1984–1985	9.36	8.74

Source: Own elaboration based on Chakravarty (1987)

community, such as the implementation of technologies for rural water supply, road construction, and field-test R&D.

Infrastructural bottlenecks were the main causes of industrial slowdown from the mid-1960s. Power generation capacity grew slower during the 1970s than in the 1960s. State expenditure oriented to energy during the 1970s reached a plateau at around 18%. But energy bottlenecks were related not only to the planning exercise but also to implementation problems (Chakravarty, 1987). Failures to coordinate the coal, power, and transport sectors explain part of the shortages. Estimation errors in the power demand of the informal sector can also be pointed out, as well as the interregional diversities and the growth in the inter-industrial linkages. The Electricity Supply Act was amended in 1975, enabling the central government to deepen its role as central coordinator in power generation and transmission. Both issues, food and fuel, would still be present as a main challenge to the Indian economy until nowadays.

5.2.3 Internal liberalisation, government expenditure, and self-reliance redefined during the 1980s

The 1980s are a relevant period for India, because GDP growth accelerated and both internal liberalisation and state expenditure increased. Some works identify the 1980s as the beginning of the Indian "fast growth regime" (Nell, 2012; Delong, 2003). The annual average growth reached 5.9%, and the annual average growth per capita reached 3.8%, from an average of 3.7% and 1.5%, respectively, for the period between 1950 and 1980. During the 1980s, exports were given more emphases. Energy, biotech, and supercomputers were especially promoted and supported, and technology missions were introduced as the main policy instrument in order to give an answer to specific problems such as water, immunisation, oilseeds, telecommunications, literacy, and so on (Joseph et al., 2008; Krishna, 2013, etc.).

In historical terms, briefly, after Indira Gandhi's defeat in 1977, as defined by Chandra et al. (2008), the "Janata Interregnum" lasted for only three years, pushing for some liberalisation initiatives in the economic sphere.

Although without reaching political support and economic results, they lost in 1979 against Indira Gandhi. After the internal political stress caused by the declaration of the Emergency during the 1970s, Indira's second tenure as prime minister was more restrained and ended abruptly with her assassination in 1984 by her two Sikh bodyguards, in reprisal for her orders to the Indian Army to enter the Golden Temple in Punjab in the so-called Operation Blue Star.[12] Rajiv Gandhi, Indira's younger son, took over after Indira's death. He had a modern style, with a more pro-business and pro-technology bias, moving forward in the liberalisation process, promoting exports and taking some relevant initiatives for promoting technology development.

5.2.3.1 Liberalisation, government expenditure and transferences, and balance of payments constraint

The second international oil price peak of 1979 deteriorated India's terms of trade by around 30%, coinciding with the worst harvest in post-independence history, with foodgrain output declining by 13% in 1979/1980 (Ghosh, 1998). Inflation accelerated, and India suffered an industrial recession. In this context, in the first year of her second tenure as prime minister, showing a much more centrist political approach, Indira's government negotiated a loan from the Extended Fund Facility of the International Monetary Fund (IMF). The conditions involved specifying ceilings on net bank credit to the government and total domestic credit, limits to money supply (M3), and a prohibition on any further import restrictions. In addition, the government issued a "statement of economic policies" worked out in consultation with the IMF, proposing an increase in public investment for domestic oil production and infrastructure and several commitments towards economic liberalisation (Ghosh, 1998).

The voices in favour of liberalisation of the economy were increasing in the Indian domestic debate: Chinese pro-market reforms and the Japanese, Korean, and Taiwanese experiences were seen as useful references of successful transitions to export-oriented models (Panagariya, 2008; Bardhan, 1984; Lall, 1982). Besides, excessive controls, mismanagement in several state-owned enterprises, and rent-seeking were pointed out as relevant issues, not only by liberal economists but also by heterodox ones (Chakravarty, 1987; Bardhan, 1984; Ghosh, 1998). Both at state level and in the Congress Party organisation, popular participation had declined since independence days in favour of co-opted political operators and an ossified bureaucracy, resulting in the privatisation of public resources and the weakening of the state's role as a welfare-seeker (Bardhan, 1984). The still high poverty indicators were also used as a criticism of the state role and a failure of Indian "socialism". In this context, Bardhan (1984) identifies three main consolidated classes with bargain powers in the 1970s and 1980s: big businesses, rich farmers, and professionals in the public sector.

After the IMF loan, the expected liberalisation did not materialise immediately, but a number of committees were set up by the government in order to propose measures for delicensing and decontrol of domestic economic activity and imports (Panagariya, 2008). Planning as a main instrument for the Indian economy started losing force during the 1980s (Ghosh, 1998). In the Industrial Policy Statement of 1980 and the Technology Policy Statement of 1983, the schemes for capacity expansion and licensing exception were more generous and wide, imposing fewer restrictions in terms of new investment, machinery imports, and foreign exchange for the local business community (Joseph et al., 2008). For instance, 30 industries and 82 pharmaceutical products were delicensed in 1985, price and distribution controls on cement and aluminium were abolished, firms that reached 80% capacity utilisation in any of the preceding five years were assured authorisation to expand capacity, and so on.

Some first steps to trade liberalisation were introduced in 1978–1979, based on the recommendations of the P.C. Alexander Committee. It mainly recommended that products not manufactured domestically be freed from licensing and to simplify the lists of conditions for the product to "banned", "restricted", and "open general licensing" (OGL) categories. This OGL list of products increased constantly during the 1980s (Panagariya, 2008). However, several items remained the exclusive import monopoly of the state through canalising agencies. Crude oil and petroleum products were imported by the Indian Oil Corporation; iron, steel, non-ferrous metals, and fertilisers through the Minerals and Metals Trading Corporation; cereals through the FCI; and so on.

Strong export incentives were introduced with Rajiv Gandhi in the second half of the 1980s (Panagariya, 2008; Delong, 2003). Different schemes were promoted: import processes were facilitated when they had an export-related counterpart, a duty-free import regime for exporters was introduced, reduction on business income tax for exports profits, duty-free capital imports for exporters, faster processing of exports credits, permission to retain 5%–10% of foreign exchange for export promotion, and so on. The export processing zones (EPZ) and all export-oriented units (EOU), first introduced in the 1960s and 1970s, were reinforced with the opening of four more zones in Noida, Madras, Cochin, and Falta (Aggarwal, 2015).

Government expenditure went from 25% of GDP in 1979–1980 to 30% in 1988–1989, and transfer payments went from 3.9% to 10.5% in the same period. The average government expenditure and payment transfers over GDP between 1970–1971 and 1979–1980 were 21.7% and 2.7%, respectively, but in the next ten years, between 1980–1981 and 1989–1990, they rose to 28.86% and 9.41%, respectively. There was a 35% increase in the average government expenditure from the 1970s to the 1980s and a 350% increase in transfer payments. Rural employment and self-employment programmes that aimed to reduce poverty had a main role in the increase of the transfer payments (Chakravarty, 1987).[13] State participation in the economy reached a peak at the end of the 1980s, employing 19 million people, 60% of them in state-owned enterprises (Nagaraj, 2006). In 1990, India reached a maximum of 255 state-owned enterprises (Kapila, 2003). In the Sixth (1980–1984) and Seventh Five-Year Plans (1985–1989), average investment reached 22%, half public and half private. Crowding-in effects of the public investment and the investment accelerator were there, as Rakshit (2009, p. 77) points out:

> The demand-led growth during the decade raised capacity utilization and profitability and hence investment demand by private producers. Similar and more pronounced perhaps was the impact of large public sector investment in infrastructure. A measure like broad banding provided greater flexibility to private producers and additional incentives for capacity expansion. Despite the growing aggregate demand, investment and operational costs did not rise; in fact, they declined in some instances, due to the liberalization of imports of capital goods, components, parts and raw materials. Thus the overall economic environment turned relatively congenial for private investors.

The fiscal deficit grew during the 1980s, with an average for the decade of 8% and a peak of 9.9% in 1986. Interest payment went from 2.2% of GDP in 1979–1980 to 4.2% in 1989–1990, and as a percentage of the total government expenditure, it rose from 8.8% to 15.3% for the same period. In this respect, Rakshit (2009, p. 73) analyses:

> [T]he growing significance of interest payments over the decade is indicated by the fact that between 1980–1 and 1989–90 these outgoes as ratios of the government's total and revenue expenditure rose from 7.8% and 11.1% percent to 14.2 and 18.1 percent, respectively . . . one reason for the rising interest payments was the jump in primary deficit. No less important, however, was the reliance on relatively high-cost borrowing instruments for financing the fiscal deficit . . . after 1981–2 there was a sharp fall in the share of net RBI credit along with a steep rise in that of small saving in gross fiscal deficit. Small saving instruments like NSCs and PPF carried a 12 percent interest rate along with substantial benefits by way of tax concessions so that they involved a borrowing cost to the government of around 20 percent . . . the increase . . . constituted a switch from a zero cost to an extremely high-cost mode of meeting the fiscal deficit and hence one of the major reasons for the sharp, cumulative rise in the deficit during the decade.

Table 5.7 Indian fiscal and external sector indicators, 1970–1989

Fiscal Year	*Government Expenditure*	*Transfer Payments*	*Fiscal Deficit*	*Interest Payments*		*Imports*	*Exports*	*Trade Deficit*	*Current Account Deficit*
				% of GDP	*% of Total Expenditure*				
1970–1971	18.2	1.9	4.3	1.6	9.0	4.5	3.6	–0.9	–1.0
1971–1972	20.2	2.0	5.0	1.7	8.4	4.6	3.7	–0.9	–1.0
1972–1973	20.5	1.9	4.9	1.6	7.8	4.4	4.2	–0.2	–0.6
1973–1974	18.5	1.8	4.1	1.5	8.3	4.7	4.1	–0.6	1.7
1974–1975	19.2	2.5	3.9	1.5	7.9	6.2	4.8	–1.4	–1.2
1975–1976	22.0	2.8	4.4	1.4	6.4	7.0	5.9	–1.1	–0.2
1976–1977	23.3	3.4	5.1	2.0	8.4	6.8	6.7	–0.1	1.0
1977–1978	22.0	3.1	4.6	1.7	7.8	6.5	6.4	–0.1	1.1
1978–1979	23.8	3.6	5.4	2.0	8.3	7.8	6.2	–1.6	–0.2
1979–1980	25.0	3.9	6.1	2.2	8.8	8.9	6.5	–2.4	–0.5
1980–1981	26.4	8.1	7.5	2.1	7.8	9.8	6.2	–3.6	–1.5
1981–1982	26.4	7.3	6.3	2.2	8.5	9.4	6.1	–3.3	–1.7
1982–1983	27.7	8.0	5.9	2.5	8.9	9.4	6.3	–3.1	–1.7
1983–1984	27.3	8.2	7.3	2.5	9.2	8.8	6.2	–2.6	–1.5
1984–1985	29.2	9.4	9.0	2.8	9.6	8.7	6.5	–2.2	–1.2
1985–1986	28.3	9.9	8.0	3.1	11.0	8.5	5.6	–2.9	–2.1
1986–1987	32.3	10.7	9.9	3.4	1.6	8.2	5.6	–2.6	–1.9
1987–1988	31.1	10.5	9.2	3.7	11.8	8.4	5.9	–2.5	–1.8
1988–1989	30.0	10.5	8.5	3.9	13.0	9.2	6.3	–2.9	–2.7
1989–1990	29.9	11.5	8.9	4.2	14.0	9.6	7.3	–2.3	–2.3

Source: Own elaboration based on Rakshit (2009)

Table 5.8 Indian external sustainability indicators

	1980	*1987*	*1988*	*1989*	*1990*
Total debt stock as % of GDP	11.9	21.9	20.8	26.4	27.1
Total debt stock as % of exports of goods and services	136.0	287.0	280.0	308.0	313.0
Interest on exports %	4.2	14.0	13.4	17.1	18.2
Debt servicing to exports %	9.3	29.4	28.6	29.6	30.1
International reserves as % of imports of goods and services (in months)	7.9	5.3	3.7	4.4	1.9

Source: Own elaboration based on Rakshit (2009)

Both imports and exports grew as GDP percentage during the 1980s. There was a declining trend of the trade deficit as a ratio of GDP, going from 3.3% in 1981 to 2.3% in 1989–1990. Exports represented an average of 5.21% of GDP between 1970–1971 and 1979–1980, increasing to 6.2% between 1980–1981 and 1989–1990. But imports raised much more, from 4.5% to 9% for the same periods. The rise in oil price had a lot to do for explaining the increase in the imports, but there was also a marked rise in imports of capital and intermediate goods, especially during the Seventh Plan.

External debt/GDP ratio increased from 11.9% in 1980 to 27.1% in 1990, debt servicing went from 9.3% to 30.1% of exports, and interest grew from 4.2% to 18.2% of exports. Then, mainly, the collapse of the USSR and the first Gulf War detonated the balance of payment crises of 1989–1990. Imports were affected by skyrocketing prices of petroleum products, and there was a marked decline of exports to the Middle East, which had become a major market for Indian goods and services. On top of that, the remittances of Indians working in Iraq and other petroleum-producing countries went down drastically.

5.2.3.2 Redefining self-sufficiency

During the 1980s, India started to discuss the redefinition of self-reliance, mainly in the Sixth Five-Year Plan (1980–1985) and the Technology Policy Statement of 1983. As explicitly observed in the Sixth Plan: "[S]elf-reliance . . . does not necessarily mean self-sufficiency in all sections of the economy", adding that "self-reliance can no longer take the form of indiscriminate import-substitution . . . export promotion is as much a part of the drive for self-reliance as efficient import-substitution". Krishna (2013) comments:

> Having established technological capabilities in some high technology areas such as space, nuclear, pharmaceuticals and green revolution technologies, the government realized that a "watertight"

> compartmentalised framework on self-reliance and import-substitution of the previous phase was no more tenable for the 1980s . . . The old policy regime which was often referred to as "nationalist technological policies" of the 1960s was out of date in the 1980s as India had already initiated the indigenisation programmes from defence, space and military industrial projects to pharmaceuticals and the whole public sector enterprises in power, steel, fertiliser, railways, among others. There prevailed a serious concern of the increasing technological gap with industrialised countries and the need for "catching up" within a perspective of endogenous technological capability. As far as India could maintain the balance of her endogenous technological base, it was thought wise to liberalise import of technology and open up to export regimes. This was important as India's dependence on foreign technology increased as the era of the 1980s came into sharp policy focus over new technologies such as microelectronics, information technologies, and biotechnology.

There were three main discussions related to the achievements and challenges of the Indian STI policy during the 1980s: the "catch up" with the new techno-economic paradigm, the encouraging of the Indian corporate sector to acquire the means to industrial upgrading through technology imports and local R&D expenditures and the link between STI policy, and the Indian people's needs, particularly with respect to poverty alleviation (Joseph et al., 2008; Krishna, 2013; Lall, 1982).

The emergence of a new techno-economic paradigm including Information and Communications Technology (ICT), biotechnology, and nanotechnology prompted the authorities to make the decision to open the imports and allow the access of foreign enterprises to try to absorb and disseminate processes and knowledge in a local scale. As stated in the Technology Policy Statement of 1983, "[T]here shall be a firm commitment for absorption, adaptation and subsequent development of imported know-how through adequate investment in research and development to which importers of technology will be expected to contribute". There was an attempt to stimulate the training and upgrading of the local private sector via tax incentives, credits, subsidies, and so forth and through the incorporation of new technologies and R&D in-house activities (Joseph, 2008; Long, 1988). A new STI policy was started, and programmes were launched, such as the Programme Aimed at Technological Self Reliance (PASTER), the Technology Absorption and Adaptation Scheme, the National Register of Foreign Collaborations, the Technology Development Fund, and the Science and Technology Entrepreneurship Park (Joseph and Kakarlapudi, 2014). Also, the Ministry of Science and Technology was created in 1985, with the earlier DST and a new Department of Scientific and Industrial Research (DSIR) as its main departments.

A relevant sub-product of the Technology and Policy Statement of 1983 was the creation of the Technology Information and Forecasting Assessment Council (TIFAC), which prepared the first technology foresight study in India, the Technology Vision 2020 (Mani, 2001). This study focused on the future prospects of the following areas: food processing, civil aviation, electricity, agriculture, sea and road transport, health, life sciences and biotechnology, advanced sensors, industrial engineering, materials and processes, services, electronics and communication, processes and chemical industries, telecommunications, and strategic industries.

In "sectoral" terms, biotech, supercomputers, and energy received paramount attention. In biotech, a National Biotechnology Board was set up (Long, 1988). The Board issued a report in 1983 with a long-term plan for biotech: manpower development was identified as a priority, and strong incentives were given to speed up the development of industrial applications. A Centre for Cellular and Molecular Biology was created, and well-funded, increased resources were oriented to genetic engineering, and a new Department of Biotechnology was established. Regarding energy, the percentage of the total resources destined to power in the Sixth (1980–1984) and Seventh Plans (1985–1989) jumped to 28.3% and 30.5%, 10 percentual points more than during the 1970s (Chakravarty, 1987). Initial steps were taken in the development of supercomputers: the Centre for Development of Advanced Computing (C-DAC) was created in 1987, and in 1991, the first Indian supercomputer was presented, the PARAM 8000, with all of its hardware and most of its software produced in India.

Furthermore, the government implemented "Technology Missions" around the mid-1980s. They were time-bounded schemes for tackling the basic needs through redirection of S&T inputs in water, immunisation, oilseeds, telecommunications, leather, and literacy (Krishna, 1997). With these interministerial and collective efforts, they tried to shape the technology policy to face new global challenges and population needs. In fact, pro-poor innovation efforts and science for the people movements gained a wider space during Indira's second term as prime minister (Abrol, 2010, 2014).

All in all, around 90% of the public R&D expenditure in 1984–1985 continued focused on five large agencies: the DRDO, the DAE, the DOS, the CSIR, and the DST (Long, 1988). Petroleum, defence, heavy industry, communications, and irrigation concentrated almost 70% of the R&D efforts. Related to the R&D expenditure, public expenditure was markedly preponderant in electrical and electronics, defence, fuels, metallurgical industries, telecommunications, and fertilisers. Private-sector efforts predominated in chemicals, drugs and pharmaceutical, industrial machinery, transportation, and textiles.

Regarding higher education, 55 new universities were created, reaching 145 establishments in 1990. There was an impressive increase in the amount of technical and scientific manpower between 1980 and 1991. Degrees in engineering more than doubled, going from 221,400 to 546,700; graduates in science more than tripled, from 750,500 to 2,430,300; and the number of medical graduates also almost doubled, increasing from 165,400 to 310,300. Compared with China, India has achieved greater visibility in the world of scientific publications: in 1990, it recorded 10,103 publications in the Science Citation Index (SCI), while the current second economy in the world had 6,509.

Finally, the attitude towards FDI during the 1980s tended to be much more open, assigning a greater role to multinational corporations in the promotion of manufactured exports (Abrol, 2013). Higher foreign equity in the export-oriented unit was allowed, and procedures for remittance of royalties and technical fees were liberalised, mainly in the newer technology sectors such as molecular, biotechnology, IT, telecom, and so on. The main accent was on technological upgradation of Indian industries with a judicious mix of indigenous and imported technology, allowing imports with an emphasis on R&D indigenisation (Mani, 1992). However, many restrictions and pro-Indian firms' schemes still operated, such as the prohibition of foreign brand names, the authorisation to Indian companies to be free to manufacture patent products even after the expiry of the collaboration agreement, and so on. According to the World Development Indicators (2017), the average FDI inflows as percentage of the GDP was 0.04% between 1980 and 1989, a marginal contribution.

Table 5.9 Selected indicators, 1950–1989

Selected indicators	*Period*		
	Nehru	*Indira (mainly)*	*Indira–Rajiv*
	1950–1964	*1965–1979*	*1980–1989*
GDP average growth	4.1	3.2	5.8
GDP per capita average growth	2.0	1.5	3.4
Investment % of GDP	13.7	17.0	21.6
Public investment % of GDP	5.8	7.3	10.6
Private investment % of GDP	7.9	9.7	11.0
Sectoral composition of GDP	**1960**	**1980**	**1990**
Agriculture	48.7	36.1	29.6
Industry	20.5	25.9	27.7
Services	30.8	38.0	42.7
Exports as % of GDP	4.2	3.7	4.7
Imports as % of GDP	6.1	5.5	7.2
Commercial balance	–1.8	–1.8	–2.5
R&D as % of GDP	**1958**	**1968**	**1984**
	0.23	0.44	0.90
GINI	**1965**	**1973**	**1988**
	31.14	29.17	31.15
Poverty		**1973**	**1987**
		54%	39%

Source: Own elaboration based on Lall (1982, 1992), Joseph et al. (2008), Nagaraj (2006), Kapila (2014), and Panagariya (2008).

Notes

1 The debate about "decolonisation" is long, diverse, and still open (Bandyopadhyay, 2004; Prakash, 1999; Chandra et al., 1987; Chandra, 2008, 2016; Bhagwati and Desai, 1970; Habib, 2017; etc). In general terms, the broad discussion is oriented to understand the influence of the British rule or the local reaction in the dialectic process that resulted in the independence.

2 The Parsis constituted less than 0.03% of the Indian population but were a dominant business class in Bombay.

3 In Anderson's (1983) terms, it was significant to think the nation as the myth of origins, building a collective sense of belonging to an immemorial past.

4 It is out of our scope to explain the caste system; a deep analysis can be found in Raheja (1994). In general terms, the caste system is a quite unique form of social organisation hierarchy based on religion that gives a professional specialisation. In historical terms, the main groups have been the Brahmans or priests; the Kshatriyas or warriors; the Vaishyas or farmers, traders, or wealth producers; and the Sudras, who served these three others groups. The Dalits or untouchables are a fifth group, even lower in the social hierarchy. Members of each caste have a moral code of conduct (dharma), and their good or bad performance (karma) determines their position in the caste hierarchy in the next life. However, in modern India, these groups are not homogeneous between regions: there are more than 3,000 *jatis*, or "caste-clusters" (Bandyopadhyay, 2004).

5 For a deeper exploration in Nehru's ideas, see Nehru (1936, 1946), among many other works.

6 The debate on the Indian planning is very rich; the main works consulted for this section are the ones of Bhagwati and Desai (1970), Byres (1998), Patnaik (1998), Chaudhury (1998), Bardhan (1984), Chakravarty (1987), Panagariya (2008), Nagaraj (2013a), and Kapila (2003).

7 The National Planning Committee set up in 1938 by the National Congress Party had members of a broad spectrum of Indian capitalists, trade unions, intellectuals, professors, non-Congress provincial governments, and so on.

8 Mahalanobis' model was a variant of the models used in the Soviet planning, particularly the model developed by Feldman in 1928 and popularised by Domar in the mid-1950s (Chakravarty, 1987).

9 This discussion could be deepened in Appu (1995), Vaidyanathan (1994), Basu (1994), Chandra et al. (2008), Kapila (2003, 2014), Bardhan (1984), and Chakravarty (1987), among many others.

10 In this video, Indira Gandhi was interviewed by a BBC reporter on the Indian geopolitical and internal political situation during her first government: www.youtube.com/watch?v=q8aETK5pQR4.

11 The debate on Green Revolution is diverse, and there are many kinds of literature on it. In this section, we will deal only with some issues mainly based on the works of Rao and Storm (1998), Chandra et al. (2008), Chakravarty (1987), Bardhan (1984), Kapila (2003, 2014), and Panagariya (2008).

12 After the uprising of a local Sikh leader, Bhindranwale, and his supporters who took the Temple, the army used heavy artillery in the operation, destroying parts of the Temple, causing deaths of many Sikh fighters and innocent pilgrims.

13 According to Joseph et al. (2008), the proportion of people under the poverty line went down from 54% in 1973–1974 to 38% in 1987–1988, and the Gini index in consumption went from 47% in 1968 to 30% in 1990.

6

THE INDIAN STATEBUILDING AND A BROAD UNDERSTANDING OF ITS NATIONAL SYSTEM OF INNOVATION

> [I]t is surprising that most of the analyses about National Systems of Innovation (NSI) have neglected the discussion about the role of defence R&D expenditures . . . As noted by Richard Nelson in the conclusion of his well known work comparing National Systems of Innovation, "the concerns regarding national security have been an important element in the conformation of innovation systems" and that "military R&D will probably continue to be most of the government R&D expenditure in USA, France, United Kingdom and Israel" (Nelson, 1993, p. 508)
>
> Cassiolato et al. (2008, p. 8)

> Between 1950 and 1980, developmental states that made domestic industrialisation their main strategy for national development, included Indonesia and India. Five-year plans, a high percentage of state companies in strategic sectors of heavy industry and infrastructure, strict protection of the internal market and import substitution, were the core of this strategy. In India, its neutral position during the Cold War and the influence of Soviet planning led to the formation of an autonomous military strategy with a significant impact on the priority of heavy industry. In both countries, these strategies led to performances quite different to those of the Southeast Asian countries, and structurally more similar to that of Latin America. With an underdeveloped agricultural system, a vast majority of the population engaged in the struggle for survival, little intra-sectoral mobility and an insubstantial industry of handcrafted consumer goods, Indian developmentalism resulted in modest growth rates and income concentration (given the vast rural poverty), yet it has managed to internalise important segments of modern industry and its infrastructure.
>
> Medeiros (2011, p. 47)

DOI: 10.4324/9781003091752-9

> The Latin American "developmental debate" would not have any specificity if it had to be reduced to a macroeconomic discussion between neoclassical "orthodoxs" or liberals and keynesian "heterodoxs" or structuralists. In fact, the debate would not have existed if it had not been for the state and the discussion about the effectiveness or not of the state intervention oriented to accelerate economic growth above the "market laws". Above all because, in Latin America as well as in Asia, the developmental governments always used orthodox macroeconomic policies, depending on the occasion and the circumstances. The opposite can also be said of several European or North-American conservative governments or ultraliberals that used keynesian policies. In fact, the axis of all the discussion and the bone of contention has always been the State and the definition of its role in the process of economic development.
>
> Fiori (2020, p. 4)

In the previous chapter, we have mainly dealt with the period between the First World War and the fall of the Berlin Wall. In this part of the book, we would like to contribute by giving a better understanding of the Indian state and its National System of Innovation (NSI) emergence, and its main feature configuration during the Cold War. With this in mind, in the previous chapter, we have contextualised the emergence of the Indian state both in global and domestic terms, trying to give account of the geopolitical configuration of the period and adopting a broad – Latin American – understanding of the NSI conceptual device. In doing so, we integrated the Indian NSI co-evolution with the Indian statebuilding and, in more general terms, with different elements that influence innovation and competence building, such as geopolitics and inter-state competition, growth performance, colonial heritage, the external constrains, financing, social and political tensions, and so on (Cassiolato, 2008; Cassiolato and Lastres, 2005, 2017; Cassiolato and Gonzalo, 2015 etc.).

In broad terms, there are some common characteristics for the period between 1947 and 1989: a) in geopolitical terms, it was configured under the Cold War scenario, giving space to a Non-Alignment foreign policy stance; b) in domestic political terms, India was mainly ruled by Congress, heir of the anti-colonial struggle; c) planning in the form of Five-Year Plans was the main designing policy instrument, and state-owned enterprises and the licensing regime were the two main implementing instruments; d) it was a mixed economy, with space for capital accumulation mainly for the Indian national groups; e) Science, Technology, and Innovation (STI) policy was mainly conceived as science-driven, linear, and top-down, with a marked concentration of R&D in "big science" (around the triad composed by nuclear, space, and defence); and f) trade (both exports and imports) and foreign direct investment (FDI) were not relevant in terms of gross domestic product (GDP) participation.

As said, in our narrative, key importance was given to the conditions of emergence of the Indian state. Indeed, most of the frameworks and policies applied in the independent India were incubated mainly during the inter-war years (Gonzalo and Crespo, 2019). The two world wars gave a main impulse to the Indian industry, showing the relevance of the state purchasing power and making the initial development of the steel industry viable (favouring the Tata Group's main primitive capital accumulation linked to siderurgy). The wealth drain theory was presented by the Congress leaders and intellectuals as a main conceptual and political tool to question the British rule, demanding industrialisation and poverty reduction.

The Indian National Movement grew strong during the Gandhian phase, a phase of mass mobilisation which included the spreading of a decentralised idea of development, based on *Swaraj*. The Russian Revolution of 1917 bent the national movement framework to the Left, influencing Nehru's economic thinking, installing the idea of planning, and giving birth to the Communist Party of India and the Congress Socialist Party. The idea of Hindu Science gained strength, including a British-educated Indian upper-caste scientist elite and an embryonic scientific institutional development, the colonial science. In the last decades of the colonial rule, several religious and regional heterogeneities strengthened in parallel with the consolidation of a mainstream national movement, with the main critical situation taking place during the Partition Holocaust.

Given this background, the "Nehruvian statebuilding" is better understood. Without neglecting the key role of Nehru, many institutional initiatives and conceptual guidelines adopted during the post-independence years were preconfigured as a reaction to the last decades of colonial rule. Indeed, the main conceptual frameworks that emerged at the time of independence were the Nehruvian, the Gandhian, and the Left ones (Abrol, 2014; Patnaik, 1998). With Mahatma Gandhi's assassination, Nehru's ideas were the ones that moulded the Indian state. However, these three frameworks cohabit and still influence the Indian economic and political debate until today.

During the Nehruvian period, India managed to maintain its territorial unity, based on a formal secular democracy. This was not a minor achievement, given the size of the Indian territory, the stress of partition, and the regional and religious heterogeneities. From a Latin American perspective (a continent that has suffered several military coups, with the Armed Forces having main relevance in the political spheres until nowadays), it seems surprising that a country so influenced by geopolitical conflicts, military developments, and internal tensions, such as India, has not suffered any military coup during its history. No doubt, the rigid caste system, such as slavery in some Latin American countries, has functioned as a regulator of social tensions and distributive conflict. However, more elements related to the

Constitution of the Indian democracy and the control of the Armed Forces should exist, with the initial years of the Indian democracy seeming to be fundamental for this configuration. This issue deserves further research.

GDP growth performance during the Nehruvian period was of 4% with a GDP per capita growth of 2%, more than doubling the first half of the century growth rates. Among the main achievements of the Indian NSI, we can point out the industrial development and diversification, based on heavy industry and state-owned enterprises; the strengthening of public-sector capabilities, with planning and the Five-Year Plans as the main instruments; the irrigation works; the building of the main developmental financing institutions; the increase in the investment rates; and the progress in the power sector, social infrastructure, plus the mortality rates reduction (Nagaraj, 2013a). And, more related to our ends, a dense network of institutions and labs oriented to science and technology was developed (Gonzalo and Cassiolato, 2016, 2017).

Despite the relation between defence efforts and NSI developments having been clearly pointed out in the pioneer work of Nelson (1993) and, for instance, in the subsequent works of Mowery (2008) for the US, as stated by Cassiolato et al. (2008), in general terms, the NSI literature has not given enough attention to the central relevance that defence expenditures and technological efforts have had for the configuration of the NSIs. The Indian case is not the exception: the connection between geopolitics, defence R&D and technological efforts, and the Indian NSI profile has not been elaborated thoroughly. There are several elements to frame this relationship. India inherited some relevant military capabilities and features from its colonial period, when its territory and people played an important role for the Allies in Asia. The Cold War and Non-Alignment facilitated the development of military and technological collaboration with countries on both sides of the Iron Curtain, including the US and the USSR. The Chinese war of 1962 had several consequences in terms of defence expenditure and nuclear development. The tensions and conflicts with Pakistan also demanded relevant technological efforts. In sum, as we have shown in the previous chapter, the post-independence Indian technological path of development has been marked by several geopolitical tensions that have configured the Indian NSI institutional building and R&D efforts that still deserve further research efforts.

Planning, state-owned enterprises, and the different "inward-looking" frameworks were explained as a postcolonial national identity search anchored in the Cold War context. Indeed, the science-led, linear, and top-down STI policy framework was a consequence of the independence movement ideas, influenced by the Hindu Science movement, but they were also aligned with the most advanced international scientific institutional development experiences of the moment, such as the Manhattan Project. Then, in addition to the explicit policies, in Herrera's (1973) terms, Nehru's relationship with science and the scientific community, and the status that the upper-caste scientist elite occupied in the Indian society, was a key implicit policy backing the role of science in the Indian statebuilding.

Clearly, the role and place that science played, and the influence that the scientific community had in the Indian case, have been much stronger than in the Latin American countries (Krishna, 1997). First, the link between the upper castes, mainly Brahmans, and the access to knowledge, and second, the type of insertion of the Indian upper castes in the Raj, which allowed them to be educated in top British scientific institutions, are the main differences with the Latin American elite scientific education that influenced the different place that the scientific communities occupy in India and in Latin America.

All in all, despite our general positive evaluation of the Nehruvian period, the broad NSI framework also allows us to point out some important weaknesses: the limited (and heterogeneous) advance in the implementation of the land reform, the exogenous role attributed to exports, and the tendency to have an excessive focus on heavy industry, without sufficiently considering the forward and backward linkages and the agricultural and infrastructure bottlenecks.

Then, the period between 1966 and 1977 was characterised by several shocks, as well as by many technological and institutional efforts. In this sense, the economic critique of Indira's period, presented, for instance, by Delong (2003), related to the slowdown in GDP growth rates, seems not to take into account the extremely stressful external and internal contexts experienced by India: the draughts of 1965–1967 and 1971–1973, the Pakistan wars of 1965 and 1971, and the oil crisis of 1973, with its impact in terms of industrial costs, trade balance, and inflation. These events induced several efforts in the orbit of the Indian NSI: the Green Revolution, the channelling of resources to rural areas, the partial indigenisation of fertilisers and HYV seeds production capabilities, the creation of the National Commission of Science and the first Science and Technology Plan, the strengthening of the nuclear and defence sectors, the pharmaceutical and computer industry drive, the increase in investment rate and R&D expenditure, and the advances in the import-substitution process. And last but not least, an explicit pro-poor innovation agenda was also introduced.

The 1970s consolidated the main Indian economic development challenges: "food and fuel". With the need to strengthen the defence and rural development expenditure, the public resources destined to power stagnated during these years at around 18% (Chakravarty, 1987). Food problems were tackled with the Green Revolution, but the relation between land productivity and rural population density was still the main bottleneck for Indian development. The capital-intensive techniques that could be introduced in the Indian agriculture would make a huge amount of people redundant, and these would have to be employed in some other fields. This has not been an easy issue to solve, and it is still a problem for the Indian economy nowadays. Indeed, since the pioneer contributions of Prebisch and Lewis related to the dualist development models, the relevance of improving the productivity of the agrarian sector for developing economies has been pointed out by both Indian and Latin American scholars with different emphases and focuses (Nagaraj, 2013a, 2013b; Serrano and Medeiros, 2004; Medeiros, 2001; among many others). This is a key issue that still needs further cross-fertilisation and joint research among the Global South scholars.

In political terms, despite having long-term roots, three main groups of interest were consolidated in the Indian state structure during the 1970s, with clear objectives regarding public policy: big businesses, big farmers and the (Hindu-framed) professionals, and state bureaucracy (Bardhan, 2010). Big businesses, consolidated through the import-substitution policy, increasingly used the licensing regime as a source of rent-seeking and protection. Evolved from the zamindars, big farmers consolidated with the Green Revolution, acting as an influential lobby group in matters related to subsidies, price support, and institutional credit. The Hindu-framed professionals and bureaucracy used their privileged education and caste networks to reinforce their position in the Indian social structure, particularly in the state structure. Consequently, the introduction of uncoordinated regulations created a huge bureaucracy that resulted in coalitions between these three groups to capture the state resources avoiding taxation.

However, the worst aspect of this "class" arrangement was not their rent-seeking behaviour, which has been part both of capitalism and communism worldwide, but the fact that they did not consider the living conditions of the Indian people. In fact, although Indira explicitly introduced poverty alleviation and pro-poor innovation programmes, and significant achievements were reached; in 1987, around 40% of the Indian population was poor. This exclusion seems to be both caste- and class-based.

In this sense, Medeiros (2011) states that in countries where food productivity was low and internal structural heterogeneity was high, such as in Brazil, India, or Indonesia, the lower the peasant's income, the stronger the influence of the traditional oligarchy over the political power. As discussed by Kohli (2004, 2007a, 2007b), the "fragmented and multiclass" configuration of the Indian state leads to an industrialisation process accompanied by extensive social marginalisation, exclusion of rural masses, and growing suburban areas of modern consumption, with a large income concentration. The similarities between the Indian and the Brazilian experience, particularly related to income distribution (and exclusion), deserve more comparative research efforts.

The 1980s have also shown a different way of dealing with the globalisation between Asia and Latin America: while the 1980s was a "lost decade" for Latin American countries in terms of growth, with the external debt crises affecting most of them, they were a growth decade for Asia (Medeiros, 1997).

In India, the 1980s were a period of growth acceleration, with an average GDP growth rate of 5.8% and a GDP per capita growth of 3.4%. Despite the advance of some sort of domestic liberalisation, Indian growth during the 1980s has been mainly explained by the increase in government expenditure and personal transfers (Rakshit, 2009; Nell, 2012). In fact, state participation in the economy increased during these years, reaching a peak in terms of expenditure, public enterprises ownership, and public employment (Nagaraj, 2013a). Actually, public investment increased until it equated private investment with more than 10% each, with a jump in power investment of more than 10 percentual points in relation to Indira's first period.

But in addition to government expenditure, investment, and transferences, there was another key difference between the Latin American and the Indian 1980s: India entered this decade with almost no external debt and a low FDI penetration in the Indian economy. For Latin America, which started the 1980s with a greater level of external debt and FDI, Volker's shock of 1980 initiated a decade of external stress, inflation, stagnation, and conditionalities imposed by the multilateral organisations. On the contrary, the Indian "self-reliance" model allowed the country to enter the 1980s with a low external exposure and more freedom to increase both public and private external debt.

If the low participation of external trade was part of the import-substitution planning model in India, a main difference with the Latin American industrialisation experience is the low FDI participation in India until the end of the 1980s. The "commanding heights" of the Indian economy were in hands of the domestic state policymakers, the big businesses, and/or big farmers, with multinational enterprises having a limited role. Besides, although India received foreign aid and financial assistance from different countries and multilateral institutions (which conditioned the internal policymaking decisions, such as the case of the International Monetary Fund (IMF) loans of 1966 and 1980), it managed to maintain its Non-Alignment posture with respect to the main world powers, without having to accept any military base from the US or from the USSR in the Indian territory.

A common criticism for the whole period refers to the low levels of competition experienced by the industrial sector that affected the product design and technological advancement not having to compete with external markets. In microeconomic terms, this is a valid point. However, in macroeconomic terms, the main external restriction for the Indian economy was triggered by the dependence on oil and food imports, as seen in the external crises of 1954, 1965, 1980, and 1989. In this context, self-reliance initiated a redefinition in the 1980s, giving a stronger role to export promotion and the implementation of different initiatives focusing on R&D indigenisation efforts. Technology missions were introduced as a main organisational form to directly tackle people's needs, such as water, immunisation, oilseeds, telecommunications, literacy, and so on. Pro-poor initiatives gained visibility and volume, and the emergence of the new techno-economic paradigm resulted in the promotion of both biotech and supercomputers. All in all, despite these efforts, R&D remained concentrated around petroleum and fuels and the triad made up by defence, nuclear, and space.

The increasing weight of the external debt interests, the downfall of the USSR, and the increase in the oil prices after the Gulf War caused another external crisis in 1989–1990 that would mark a turning point in the Indian style of development. Both the external and the internal contexts were there for the weakening of the planning scheme and an increase in the liberalisation of the Indian economy during the global consolidation of the US during the 1990s, with the predominance of the Washington Consensus in the policymaking arena. We will discuss this in the next chapters.

Part III

DEMAND-LED GROWTH

7

THE INDIAN OCEAN SINCE THE 1990s

(Geo)political chessboard and demand-led growth

> There is nothing that many neo-liberal scholars would like more than to fit the story of India's economic rise as a successful example of their prescriptions. I have argued recently, however, that such an analysis of India is quite misleading . . . India's economic growth accelerated around 1980, well before India adopted some liberalizing reforms in 1991. Over the last twenty five years India has indeed liberalized its domestic economy and slowly opened it to the outside world. However, India is hardly a neo-liberal model. India brought down tariffs only slowly, limited foreign investment to certain sectors, continued to maintain fairly strict controls on capital movements, hardly undertook much privatization, and the size of government deficits have remained large, much too large by IMF's standards of what is prudent.
>
> Kohli (2007a, p. 13)

> A third perspective – a structuralist view – would hold that for a large, agrarian economy like India, a strategy for growth with equity would have to focus on improving agricultural productivity, which would call for considerable public infrastructure investment, and institutional reforms; rapid industrialization would depend on growing market surplus from agriculture and public investment in industrial infrastructure that would "crowd-in" private investment; and, to strategically integrate with the world economy, where export growth would serve as a lubricant for the engine of agriculture-led growth.
>
> Nagaraj (2013a, p. 202)

> India is set to contribute more than any other country to the projected rise in global energy demand, around one-quarter of the total: even so, energy demand per capita in 2040 is still 40% below the world average. India's total energy demand more than doubles in our main scenario, propelled higher by an economy that is more than five times larger in 2040 and

DOI: 10.4324/9781003091752-11

> a demographic expansion that makes India the world's most populous country. With energy use declining in many developed countries and China entering a much less energy-intensive phase in its development, India emerges as a major driving force in global trends, with all modern fuels and technologies playing a part.
>
> International Energy Agency (2015, p. 4)

> It goes without saying that much of contemporary India's tremendous dynamism is located in the urban sector. This is true in terms of services, trade and production. But it is also true in relation to politics, culture, the arts, civil society, and education, for example. If the word "development" means anything, it refers to what goes on in the towns. And it is the movement of societies from being predominantly rural to being predominantly urban – i.e. the process of urbanization – that underpins progress and development in our modern world. Therefore the issue arises as to how urbanization comes about.
>
> Dyson (2008, p. 4)

In this chapter, we will mainly discuss the period initiated in 1991 with the New Economic Policy (NEP) implementation. After more than 25 years of the NEP, the Indian path of growth and global insertion is still underdiscussed. First, we will broadly present the Indian political and geopolitical contexts since the 1990s, and then we will introduce a discussion on the interpretations of the growth process since the NEP. In general terms, this period is commonly described as one of liberalisation of the Indian economy. Some relevant contextual aspects that have not been explored by the mainstream literature growth drivers will be introduced in order to give a demand-led growth understanding.

7.1 From Congress to BJP, with the Indian Ocean geopolitical chessboard as a background

Three main relevant trends characterised the post-1990s Indian geopolitical and domestic landscapes: a) an increasing influence of a (neo)liberal framework, which, although neither dominant nor exempt from several difficulties and opposition to be implemented, had preconfigured the Indian political economy debate and policymaking in parallel with the global consolidation of the Washington Consensus; b) in political terms, even though it was the Congress that initiated the liberalisation, the novelty has been the emergence and consolidation of the BJP, based on Hindutva politics (Hindu identity based), with the contemporary Indian prime minister Narendra Modi as its main political leader; and c) with the downfall of the USSR, the consolidation of China as a global superpower, and the boom of the Indian

IT industry, the rapprochement of India with the US (and the North Atlantic Treaty Organization (NATO) countries) has gained force, in a context of increasing weaponisation of the Indian Ocean neighbourhood.

In chronological terms, in the three years after Rajiv Gandhi's death, every Indian government was formed by a coalition of parties or survived by the support of one party that did not integrate the coalition but backed it from the outside. In December 1989, V. P. Singh took over as the new prime minister with the support of a faction of the Congress, the Lok Dal, and one major faction of the Janata Party. In August 1990, the Iraq invasion to Kuwait directly affected the Indian external front through an increase in the oil price and a decrease of foreign remittances (Desai, 1999). In November 1990, the Parliament ended its support to Singh, and Chandra Shekhar was elected the prime minister. The economic situation was critical, as explained by Nayyar (2017, p. 42), who was chief economic adviser at the time:

> The external debt crisis and payments situation was the Achilles heel of the economy. It was particularly vulnerable for three reasons: short-term debt was about $6 billion, of which $2 billion was rolled-over every 24 hours with overnight borrowing in international capital markets; outstanding NRI deposits, more than $10 billion, were prone to capital flight, while foreign exchange reserves were a mere $1 billion that were not enough to finance imports even for a fortnight, let alone debt service payments . . . The prospect of default hung over our heads like the sword of Damocles.

The International Monetary Fund (IMF) helped raise US$1.8 billion; some debt service payments, mainly related to defence purchases, were differed; and almost 50 tons of gold were sold to the Bank of England and the Bank of Japan to raise around US$400 million. However, Prime Minister Chandra Shekhar could not keep the Parliament coalition together and fell in March 1991. New elections were called. On May 21 that same year, Rajiv Gandhi was killed during the election campaign. In political terms, the assassination resulted in a boost to Congress, which won enough seats in the Parliament to form a minority government with the support of the Left Front parties. P. Narasimha Rao was elected as prime minister in June 1991 and governed until 1996, appointing Manmohan Singh as finance minister. The NEP was being born.

There were different factors, both internal and external, conjunctural and structural, that pushed for a deepening of the liberalisation policies and framework of the Indian economy (Bhaduri and Nayyar, 1996; Desai, 1999; Ghosh, 1998). On the international stage, the downfall of the USSR and the Soviet bloc was a strong blow to the Left and state-led political economy frameworks all around the world, and India was not the exception, giving place to the spread of neoliberal ideas and economists sympathetic to the Washington Consensus of 1989. In Asia, since the 1980s, the Korean, Japanese, and other East Asian experiences were presented in the Indian economic debate as cases of successful transitions to "export-led" and/or "market-led" developing economies (Panagariya, 2008; Desai, 1999). In India, the balance of payments crisis did not leave any space for many financing choices but to knock at the doors of the multilateral organisations that pushed for classic structural adjustment programmes (Desai, 1999; Ghosh, 1998). On the political domestic side, after some years of prime minister changes, most of the political parties were willing to support a prime minister in order to maintain political stability (Nayyar, 2017). In ideological terms, there was an increasing mood among the political parties, bureaucracy, and some economists, backed by the IMF and the local business community, that efficiency and productivity were the main objectives for the Indian economy (Pedersen, 2000; Desai, 1999).

After Rao's government, the centre-right National Democratic Alliance (NDA) led by the BJP won the majority in Parliament, and Atal Bihari Vajpayee was elected prime minister in 1998. In 2004, Congress returned leading the United Progressive Alliance (UPA) a coalition of centre-left parties, with Manmohan Singh, Rao's former minister of finance, as prime minister. Then, after ten years of Congress-led government, in 2014, Narendra Modi, from the BJP, was elected as Indian prime minister. Modi was re-elected in 2019, consolidating as a relevant leader in the Indian twenty-first-century political arena.

The BJP's gradual rise was based on a reinvented Hindutva style of politics which reaffirms the Hindu identity from a state level. Despite the BJP having its main political base in the northern and western states, while the south and north-east remained less influenced, the BJP emergence means a paradigmatic shift in Indian politics. For the first time since the 1984 elections, a single political party, under the leadership of Narendra Modi, won absolute majority in the Lok Sabha in 2014, winning 281 of the 543 seats, thus being able to govern alone.[1] For our ends, broadly, BJP's main lines of government combine a nationalistic and Hindu-based discourse and practices in the domestic sphere, a (neo)liberal discourse for the international press and foreign investors, and an emphasis in infrastructure and defence expenditure orientated to consolidate and expand the Indian national groups and multinational enterprises, mainly from the US.

Clearly, the Indian military needs to exceed the BJP military doctrine and should be understood in the broader geopolitical pressures faced by India in the twenty-first century. According to Stockholm International Peace Research Institute (SIPRI), the Indian military expenditure as a percentage of gross domestic product (GDP) averaged 2.9% in the 1990s, 2.7% in the 2000s, and around 2.5% in the 2010 decade. Despite this slight reduction in its participation, with an economy growing around 6.5% per year average during this period, the military expenditure has constantly increased from around $10 billion in the 1990s to more than $50 billon in the last decade.[2] India was the largest importer of major arms in 2013–2017, accounting for 12% of the global total (SIPRI, 2018). The IHS Jane's Defence Budgets forecast (2015) projected that the Indian total military expenditure in US dollars would reach 60 billion in 2018, turning India into the third country in the world in terms of total military expenditure, after the US (around 800 billion) and China (around 240 billion).

There are several factors driving India's need to strengthen its military capabilities. Mainly we can point out the re-emergence of China as a main global economic and military superpower, with Indo-Chinese borders still a matter of dispute in areas such as Kashmir, and an increasing competition in terms of energy needs, water sources, and food; the growing relevance of the Indian Ocean in terms of trade flux (particularly China's oil imports) and its geopolitical relevance for military operations in South Asia and in the Middle East; the increasing nuclear weaponisation of India's neighbours; and the terrorist attacks suffered inside Indian borders,[3] mainly from Pakistani terrorist groups. In this context, India has embarked on a massive military modernisation programme primarily oriented to project power in the Indian Ocean and increase its presence and control over the Himalaya's borders.

In global terms, as stated by Kaplan (2010a, 2010b, 2013), the Indian Ocean is where the rivalry between the US and China in the Pacific interlocks with the regional rivalry between China and India, and with America's fight against Islamic terrorism in the Middle East, mainly to contain Iran. As shown in Figure 7.1, China has been building ports and re-refuelling stations (which could be converted in military bases) in Chittagong (Bangladesh), Sittwe (Myanmar), Hambantota (Sri Lanka), and Gwadar (Pakistan). India has naval bases in its own territory in Mumbai, Karwar, Kochi, Visakhapatnam, and the Andaman Islands and listening stations in Madagascar, Seychelles, and Mauritius. The US has a strategic military naval base in the Diego Garcia Island.

With the downfall of the USSR and the emergence of China, India has been getting closer to the US and the NATO countries. For the US, the Indian Ocean chessboard has achieved great relevance, in order to balance China's expansion and to have access and contention over the Middle East countries (Cliff, 2020). Indeed, the relevance of India for the US has been increasing since the Clinton administration up to Trump's, with no changes on the main emphasis between Republicans and Democrats. A broader context of relations between India and the US includes segments of the entrepreneurial community of both countries, with a key role played by the Indian Americans who were pioneers in the Silicon Valley boom and the public and private actors related to defence, nuclear energy, tourism, finance, and real estate (Scott, 2011; Cohen, 2001; Gonzalo and Kantis, 2017; Fair, 2009).

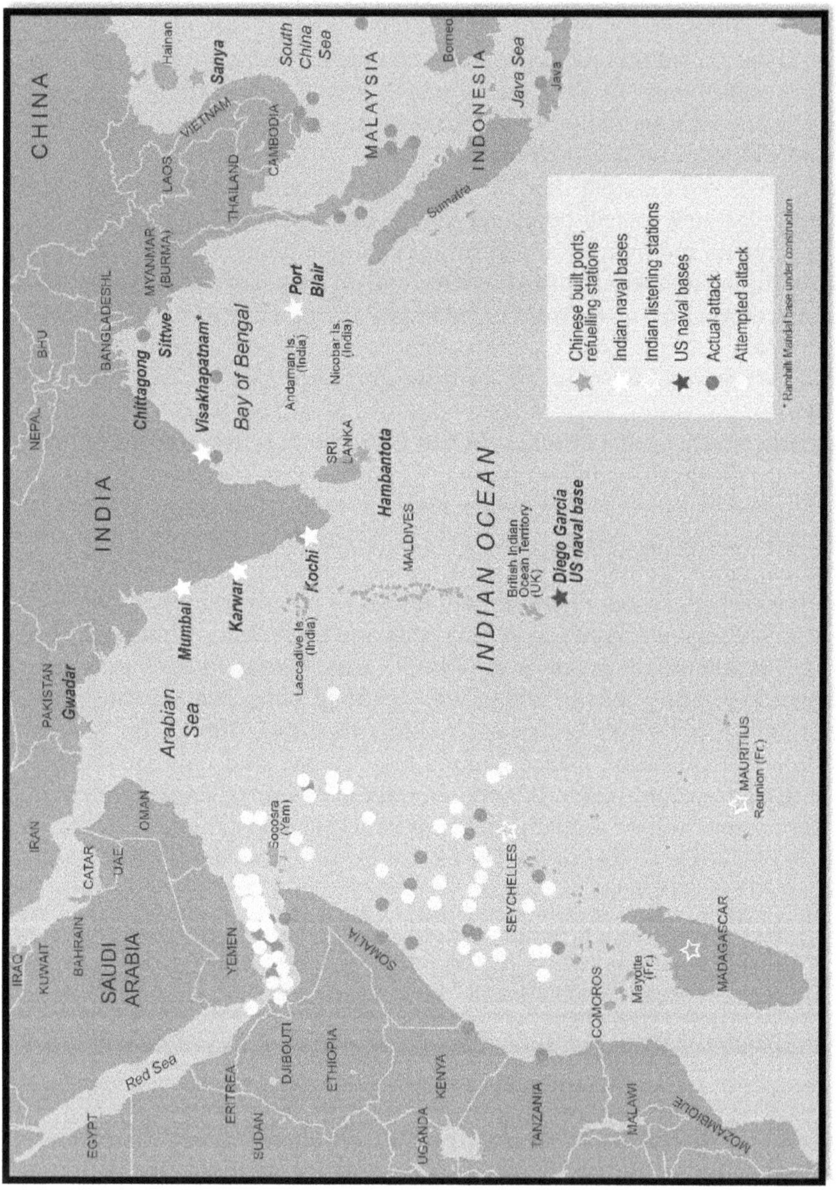

Figure 7.1 Indian, Chinese, and American presence in the twenty-first-century Indian Ocean.

Source: Elaborated by Rosaura Flynn

With 3.5 million people, Indian Americans comprise approximately 18% of the Asian American population of the United States, being the third-largest Asian ethnic group living in the US after the Chinese and Filipinos (Dubey, 2011; East-West Center, 2019). Indian Americans are among the wealthiest ethnic groups in the US. By 2000, about half of Silicon Valley's scientists and engineers were foreign-born, with Indian and Chinese immigrants alone accounting for over one-quarter of the region's scientists and engineers, approximately 20,000 Indian and 20,000 Chinese (Saxenian, 2005). Nowadays, with more than half a million Indian Americans living in California, this state concentrates almost 20% of them (Chakravorty et al., 2016).

The total value of US-India bilateral trade went from US$37 billion in 2005 to US$109 billion in 2015 (East-West Center, 2019). More than 2,000 US multinationals are operating in India today. The state of Karnataka, with Bengaluru as its capital, concentrated almost 1,000 US firms, showing a clear link between the US multinationals and the Indian ICT sector. Indeed, Indian Americans related to Silicon Valley are playing a key role in the development of the Indian IT entrepreneurial ecosystem, not just as managers of venture capital funds and angel investors but also as serial entrepreneurs (Mani, 2014a; Bala Subrahmanya, 2015, Gonzalo and Kantis, 2017). Indian students are the second-largest source of international students in the US, being the top destination for Indian students studying abroad. For instance, Sundar Pichai, who studied technology in the Indian Institute of Technology and did an MBA in Stanford, is Google's present CEO. US firms and government have been directly involved in several investments and innovation support programmes such as Startup India, Skill India, Digital India, Smart Cities Mission, Make in India, and Clean India.

According to the East-West Center (2017), the India-US defence trade increased to $15 billion in 2016, when India was named a "Major Defense Partner" of the US, a status which was created to facilitate technology sharing to a level at par with that of the US closest allies and partners. According to SIPRI (2018), between 2008–2012 and 2013–2017, arms imports from the US increased by 557%, making it India's second-largest arms supplier.[4] The Defense Framework Agreement, renewed in 2015, and the Defense Technology and Trade Initiative (DTTI) aim to strengthen defence cooperation through technology. The Logistics Exchange Memorandum Agreement (LEMOA) furthers cooperation by allowing for an exchange of logistic support, supplies, and services between the two countries' armed forces and opening access to each other's military bases. India has conducted more than 50 events with the US, including bilateral exercises and personnel exchanges. Israel and France have significantly grown as India's weapon.

Finally, a main challenge for the Indian foreign policy continues to be its relationship with Pakistan, mainly regarding Kashmir. With the militant insurgency growing since the 1980s, encouraged and financed

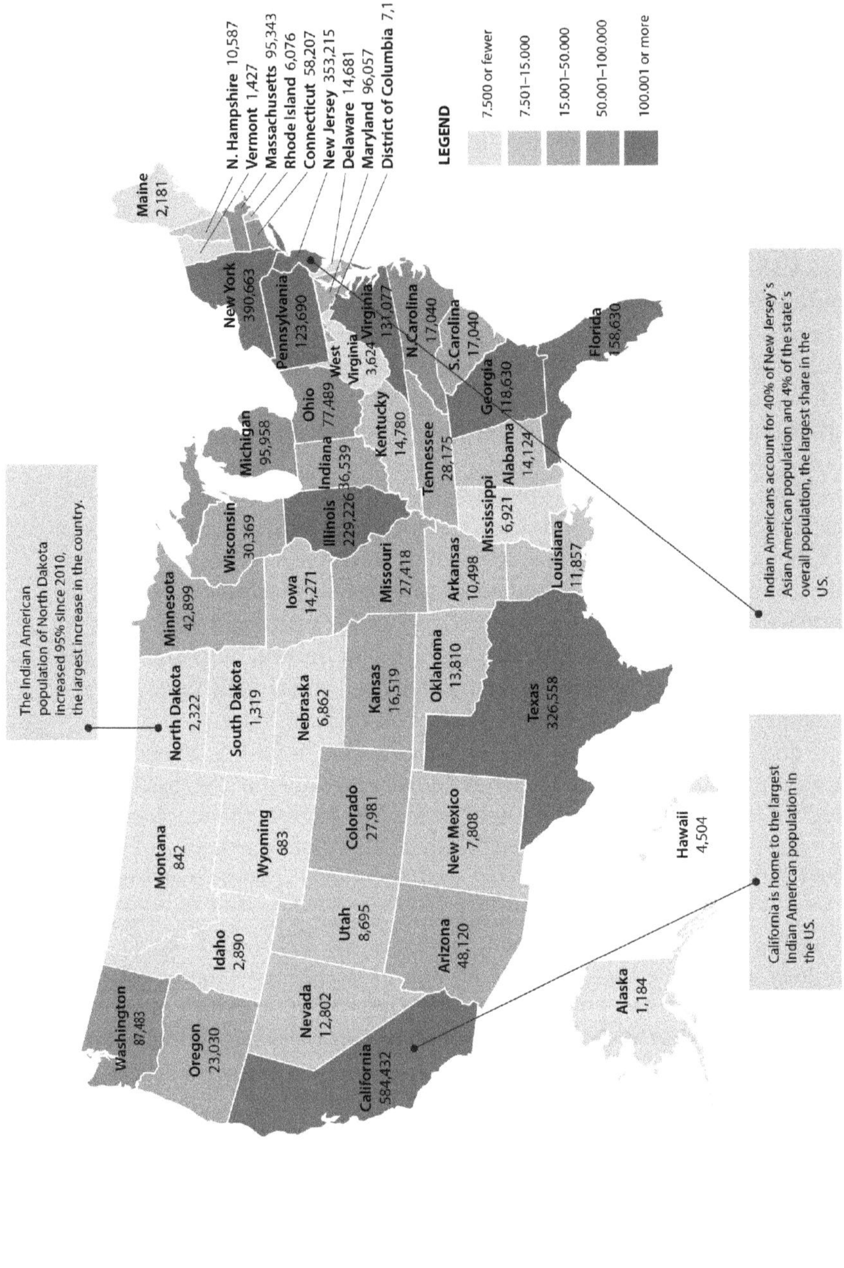

Figure 7.2 Indian American population by state, 2016.

Figure 7.3 President Donald J. Trump and Prime Minister Narendra Modi.
Source: Drawn by Rosaura Flynn.

by the Pakistani army, India got involved in a proxy war in Kashmir and a short war in Kargil in 1999. A main consequence of the conflict was the nuclearisation of the region with the BJP-led NDA government deciding to go nuclear, detonating three devices in May 1998 (Chandra et al., 2008). The tension caused by the Indian nuclear weaponising included economic and technological sanctions due to its persistent refusal to sign the restrictive Nuclear Non-proliferation Treaty and the Comprehensive Test Ban Treaty. However, in August 2008, the US-India Civil Nuclear Agreement was signed, ending India's nuclear isolation and allowing it to purchase nuclear fuel and technology from the US for civil nuclear installations.

7.2 The post-NEP growth interpretations

The NEP is often seen as the liberalisation programme that propelled the Indian growth since the 1990s. However, as said, the Indian growth drivers of the 1990s, 2000s, and 2010s are underdiscussed. The objective of this section is to briefly present some features of the NEP implementation, to cluster some main interpretations on the growth process since the NEP, and to introduce a first big picture of an alternative, demand-led understanding.

The macro-stabilisation programme implemented in 1991 consisted of a) a 20% devaluation of the rupee; b) a fiscal deficit reduction through expenditure compression, tax reforms, partial privatisation, and signs of adjustment in the Central Public Sector Enterprises (CPSE); c) a transition to a system of market-driven exchange rate with current account convertibility of the rupee; d) allowing selected Indian corporate firms to raise funds from the international capital markets; and e) encouraging capital inflows of foreign institutional investment (FII), FDI, or non-resident Indian (NRI) deposits (Nayyar, 2017; Rakshit, 2009). However, the degree of advance on the NEP objectives and initiatives has not been homogeneous. Next, we will summarise the main specific initiatives and their relative advance during the 1990s and 2000s:

- The investment and imports licensing and entry restrictions were abandoned in most of the sectors. However, some sectors remained "licensed": arms, munitions and defence equipment, aircrafts and warships, atomic substances, narcotics, psychotropic substances and hazardous chemicals, alcoholic drinks and cigarettes, and manufactured tobacco. Besides, consumer goods also remained under licensing until 2001, by request of the World Trade Organization (WTO). No antitrust legislation was introduced until the 2000s.
- Public-sector monopoly was abandoned gradually. However, the state still maintained a high participation in most of the sectors through the CPSEs. A process of privatisation of the CPSEs, also called "disinvestment process", was promoted. However, this process was slow and partial and with the central and state governments still maintaining a majority ownership in most of the CPSEs in energy, transport, and agricultural sectors, among others.
- The 40% maximum FDI shareholding was abandoned, and the concept of automatic approval was introduced, in which the Reserve Bank was empowered to approve equity investment of up to 51% in 34 priority industries. The FDI controls were gradually abandoned, although they have been maintained in retail sector, atomic energy, defence, lottery business, and FM, cable networks, and broadcasting.
- Imports of foreign technology were liberalised.

- Trade tariffs were gradually lowered. However, they still widely exist, and there are some sectors, such as the automobile, that have remained highly protected.
- Agriculture tariffs have been maintained and subsidies increased.
- The financial sector was subjected to deregulation, foreign competition, and partial privatisation of some public banks. Basel norms were adopted. However, public banks, both at the centre and the state levels, still maintained a considerable share of the Indian banking sector.
- Export restrictions were gradually eliminated, and export supporting programmes were implemented.
- Infrastructure sectors such as railways, electricity, oil, coal, telecommunications, ports, and airports remain under the state gravitation. Public Private Partnerships (PPP) schemes were developed and implemented during the 2000s as a second-best option to the privatisation process.
- Deficit reduction was postulated as a main objective. A Fiscal Responsibility and Budget Management Act (FRBMA) was signed in 2003, but it was suspended with the 2008 crisis. All in all, the state participation in GDP did not decrease compared between the beginning of the 1990s and the end of 2010s.

Next, different authors discussing the Indian growth path since the NEP are grouped in clusters. Although this is not an exhaustive list, it helps to capture some main groups of understanding.

a **Liberalisation and trade.** There is a mainstream interpretation of the post-1990s growth process which is represented by a group of authors clustered under the conceptual approach of liberalisation and trade, which mainly explains that the growth process is directly linked to the liberalisation process, mixing a supply-side view with some autonomous expenditure related to export. Jagdish Bhagwati is its main referent. In Bhagwati and Panagariya (2013), they underline the impacts of trade liberalisation on efficiency gains. In Panagariya (2008), market discipline is seen as the main growth driver. For Desai (1999), competition both at economic and social levels is the mechanism that has pushed growth, ending with a patrimonial state. Although the path from liberalisation and competition to growth is not so clearly defined, efficiency improvement and exports are explicitly postulated as the main growth drivers.

b **Business environment.** A subgroup of authors, such as Rodrik and Subramanian (2005) and Delong (2003), maintains that the main growth driver was the change in the governmental attitude towards the local business community, which began in the mid-1980s with Rajiv Gandhi and was then deepened in the 1990s. The change in the business environment, mainly the attitude towards the national business communities, resulted in an investment increment. The liberalisation oriented to the local business community during the 1980s, and broadened since the 1990s, would have also boosted exports.

c **(Neo)-Marxists.** This group of authors emphasises the financial-led and super-exploitation pattern of growth. Chandrasekhar (2008, 2016, 2017) points out that India has deepened a financial-led mode of growth since the 1990s. Capital inflows triggered a boom in domestic credit, mainly to finance elite and upper-middle-class/caste consumption in durable goods, real estate, automobiles, and so on. Household consumption and overfunded corporate investment have been the main drivers of growth. Ghosh (2016) stresses on the relevance of the finance, insurance, and real estate (FIRE) sectors. Bhaduri (2008a, 2008b) highlights the impressive productivity increase since the 1990s, without a similar increase in salaries, deepening the exploitation of the Indian working class.

d **"Demand-side".** Both Nell (2012) and Nabar-Bhaduri and Vernengo (2012) adopt a demand-led model with a balance of payments restriction. Nell (2012) maintains that service exports have been growing as an indirect result of the protectionist policies of the "planning era" and that they contributed to push the Indian external restrictions. Nabar-Bhaduri and Vernengo (2012) argue in the same line, stating limits of the service-led Indian growth (comparing it with the Mexican maquila pattern). Rakshit (2009) builds a mixed explanation, stressing that in the first half of the 1990s, the good monsoons impacted the rural expenditure, and then, mainly exports and government expenditure oriented to domestic services led the growth process. He points out the role of the forward and upward linkages of the different sectors and their impact on service growth. Exports, household expenditure, and government expenditure are the main drivers of growth for these authors.

e **Eclectics.** A fifth group of scholars uses different conceptual approaches and empirical elements. Nayyar (2017) adopts an institutional perspective, highlighting the role of the technological, educational, and productive capabilities that were developed during the planning period and, then, scaled up after liberalisation. The channel to growth is not clearly defined, but it could be inferred that it is mainly through exports. Azad et al. (2017) divide the growth process into different sub-periods (1990–2000, 2001–2008, and 2009–2016). Exports, credit, government expenditure, and PPPs propelled growth in each of them. Bardhan (2010) builds a narrative on both China's and India's growth process, accepting the relevance of the entrepreneurial and exports drive after liberalisation, although highlighting some nuances in the role of the state and the markets' contribution. Nagaraj (2013b, 2017a) analyses the 2003–2008 growth period mainly as a credit boom phase, with an increase in private investment, FDI, and real estate investment.

Table 7.1 Some main Indian growth interpretations since 1990s

Cluster	*Authors*	*Growth Explanation*	*Channel*
Liberalisation and trade	Panagariya (2008)	Opening the economy to the world markets and subjecting it to greater market discipline	Exports + Efficiency
	Desai (1999)	Ending with the "patrimonial state" and bringing both economic and social competition to India	Competition + Exports
	Bhagwati and Panagariya (2013)	Liberalisation causes an increase in trade and investment and a reduction in poverty	Exports + Investment
		Openness to current account trade played a significant role in India's growth. The main driver was the lowering of trade restrictions on a wide range of imported technologies and inputs and a spectacular acceleration in the export of commercial IT enabled services	Imports Efficiency Gains + Exports
Attitudinal shift and business environment	Rodrick and Subramanian (2005)	Attitudinal shift by the government in the 1980s: pro-business rather than pro-market	Investment
	Delong (2003)	Attitudinal shift and liberalisation	Investment + Exports
"Neo" Marxists	Chandrasekhar (2008, 2016, 2017)	Financial-led growth – the capital inflow triggered a boom in bank credit, focused largely on retail lending (housing, automobile and durable purchases, and personal expenditures) and on lending to investments in capital intensive industry and infrastructure	Consumption (push by credit) + Investment
	Ghosh (2016)	FIRE (finance, insurance, and real estate along with related professional services) led growth	Consumption + Construction + Real Estate
	Bhaduri (2008a, 2008b)	Productivity (relative and absolute plus labour) increase	Upper-Caste/Class Consumption + Exports

(*Continued*)

Table 7.1 (Continued)

Cluster	*Authors*	*Growth Explanation*	*Channel*
"Demand" Side	Nell (2012)	Faster export growth allowed government spending to remain at a high level. This is the indirect effect of export growth working through Hicks' super-multiplier. Faster export growth and hence faster output growth for a given income elasticity of demand for imports in the post-liberalisation period are therefore the endogenous outcomes of protectionist demand-side policy measures	Exports + Government Expenditure
	Nabar-Bhaduri and Vernengo (2012)	Service (both export and domestic market) led	Export + Consumption
	Rakshit (2009)	Mixed: goods monsoons in the years after the NEP, exports, government expenditure on domestic services	Domestic Private Consumption + Exports + Government Expenditure
"Eclectic" Approaches	Nayyar (2017)	The success is attributable to institutional capacities which existed at the time the reforms were introduced. The essential foundations were provided by the preceding four decades of economic development. Entrepreneurial abilities were created. A system of higher education was developed. The social institutions and the legal frameworks necessary for a market economy were in place	Not clearly defined, implicitly exports
	Azad et al. (2017)	Different growth momentums pushed by exports, state expenditure, public and private credit, and PPP	Exports + Consumption (credit) + Government Expenditure + PPP
	Bardhan (2010)	A mix of exports, entrepreneurial drive, and upper-caste/class consumption	Exports + Upper-caste/class Consumption + Investment
	Nagaraj (2013b)	The Indian economy boom from 2003–2004 to 2007–2008 was underpinned by a sharp rise in the investment rate, largely domestically financed, boosted by an unprecedented influx of foreign private capital	Exports + Investment + Foreign Investment + Credit + Real Estate

Source: Own elaboration

7.3 A demand-led big picture of the Indian growth

Next, we will present some evidence in order to build our own understanding on the growth process, mainly between the 1990s and 2015, after 25 years of the NEP implementation. Dealing with Indian statistics is not an easy issue. There are many studies that question them, particularly regarding the GDP growth rate, the size of formal private sector, and the poverty line measuring (Nagaraj, 2017b, 2016, 2015, 2014; Ghosh, 2017; Krishnaji, 2012; among others). Although these discussions are extremely important, they are out of the scope of this research. That said, three data sources are mainly used: Reserve Bank of India (RBI), Ministry of Statistics and Programme Implementation (MOSPI), and World Bank (WB).

7.3.1 The 1990s boom?

A first clarification that should be made regarding the Indian growth path is related to its periodisation. A snapshot on the Indian GDP growth rates since the 1980s looks impressive. The average growth rate for the 1980s was 5.6% for GDP and 3.3% for GDP per capita; for the 1990s, GDP growth was 5.8% and GDP per capita 3.7%, and for the 16 years between 2000 and 2015, GDP growth average was 7.1% and GDP per capita 5.4%.

This means, in a general context of high growth, that the main growth acceleration occurred since the 2000s and not immediately after the NEP implementation: GDP and GDP per capita growth averages increased 2pp for the 2000s. What is more, if we see Figure 7.4 with the average growth rate from 1990 to 2002, which includes 13 years after the NEP implementation, the average GDP growth rate was 5.5%, lower than the 5.6% of the 1980s and 7.7% from 2003 to 2015. This is not to say that the 5.5% average growth rate after the NEP was not significant but to contextualise it in the broader Indian growth acceleration. In line with Nagaraj (2013a), India is experiencing a growth process acceleration since the 1950s, with two main leap decades: the 1980s, as we have seen in the last chapters, and the 2000s (Nell, 2012; Kohli, 2007a, 2007b).

7.3.2 A glimpse of India's national accounts

Next, we will present a simple national account exercise based on the WB figures, in order to give a glimpse on the contribution of the main components of the aggregate demand to the GDP growth. This exercise is useful to give a basic idea of which have been the main aggregate demand components' behaviour and its impact on GDP. In methodological terms, we first calculate the weight of each component of the aggregated demand in 1990, and then we compute the growth of each one for the period under study and

Table 7.2 Indian average GDP and GDP per capita growth rates

Growth Rate Average	*GDP*	*GDP per Capita*
First half of twentieth century	0.5%	Negative
Nehru (1947–1964)	3.5	2.0
Indira (1966–1977)	3.2	1.5
1980s	5.6	3.3
1990s	5.8	3.7
2000–2015	7.1	5.4
2016–2020	6.5	5.0

Source: Own elaboration based on RBI

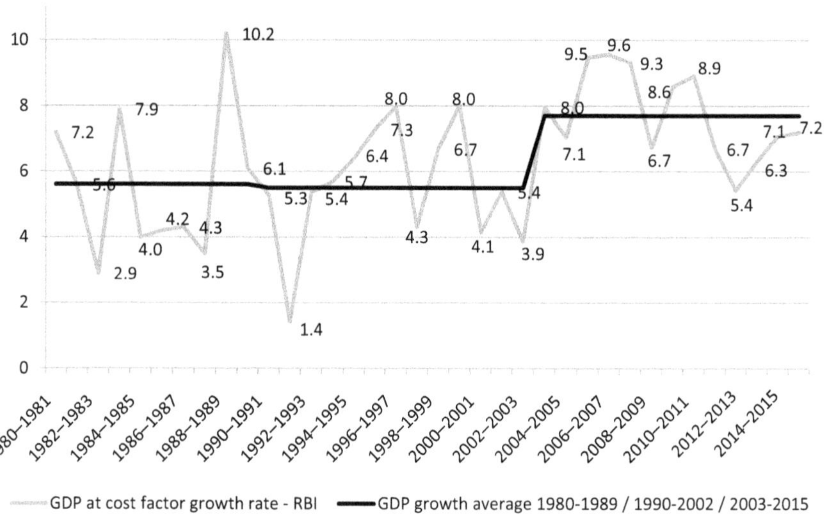

Figure 7.4 Indian GDP growth rate and growth average, 1980–2015.
Source: Own elaboration based on figures from RBI.

multiply it by the share of participation. Finally, we "normalise" them as a proportion of the GDP growth.

If we take the whole period from 1990 to 2015, exports contributed 20% to GDP growth, household final consumption expenditure 43%, government consumption 7%, and gross domestic capital formation (GDCF) 30%. If we divide this period in two sub-periods, the first one of around 5.5% GDP average growth rate, from 1990 to 2002, and the other one of 7.7% average growth rate, from 2003 to 2015, the shares are quite similar, although GDCF reduced its contribution for 1990–2002 to 23% and then increased it for the period between 2002 and 2015 to 32%. Thus, this

Table 7.3 Aggregate demand accounting exercise (at constant local currency)

Aggregate Demand Components	*Exports of Goods and Services*	*Household Final Consumption Expenditure*	*General Government Final Consumption Expenditure*	*Gross Domestic Capital Formation*
Demand composition (1990)	6%	60%	12%	22%
% increase **2015/1990**	1417%	322%	280%	613%
Weight increase (ex post)	88%	193%	32%	136%
Growth contribution (%)	**20%**	**43%**	**7%**	**30%**
% increase **2002/1990**	305%	72%	81%	97%
Weight increase (ex post)	19%	43%	9%	22%
Growth contribution (%)	**21%**	**46%**	**10%**	**23%**
Demand composition (2002)	13%	53%	11%	23%
% increase **2015/2002**	275%	145%	110%	262%
Weight increase (ex post)	36%	78%	12%	59%
Growth contribution (%)	**20%**	**42%**	**6%**	**32%**

Source: Own elaboration based on WB database

rough exercise suggests that private consumption, GDCF, and exports are the main contributors to the Indian growth process between the 1990s and mid-2010s.

It is interesting to see the evolution of the private consumption growth, which explains around 40% of the demand growth, vis-à-vis the GDP growth rate: both series show a close correlation. Indeed, the general picture described by several authors is one of an increase in private consumption, mainly driven by the urban upper-class/caste groups linked to the global economy, property, and the formal/corporate sector (Bhaduri, 2008a, 2009; Chandrasekhar and Ghosh, 2015; Nagaraj, 2013b, 2015; Chancel and Piketty, 2017; Patnaik, 2009; Nayyar, 2017; etc.).

As we will detail in the next chapter, Bhaduri (2008a, 2008b) points out that the pattern of household consumption led by upper-class/caste groups has created significant markets, from luxury and durable goods to leisure and education. Chandrasekhar and Ghosh (2015) point out that the national

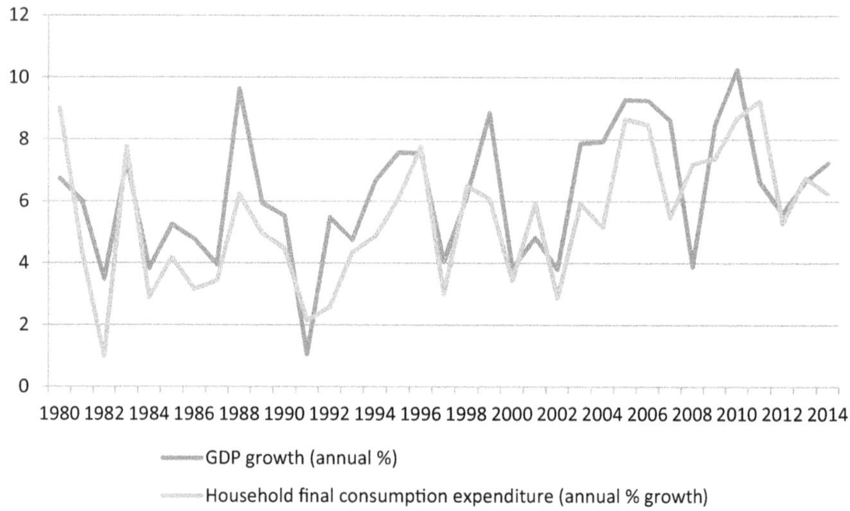

Figure 7.5 GDP and household final consumption expenditure growth rates, 1980–2015.

Source: Own elaboration based on WB database.

Gini coefficient for consumption increased from 0.31 in 1993 to 0.36 in 2009, and the ratio of urban to rural consumption went up from 1.62 to 1.96. To Chandrasekhar (2011), much of the Indian growth in income corresponds to urban residents, with the urban share of national income having risen from 46% in 1990 to close to 60% in the 2000s. In fact, the largest increase in consumption expenditure seems to be concentrated in the top decile of the urban population: between 1993–1994 and 2009–2010, the income of the top urban decile went from 7.1 to 10.3 times that of the bottom urban decile, and from 10.5 to 14.3 times that of the bottom rural decile (ILO, 2016a). According to Chancel and Piketty (2017), the share of the top 20% decile in total consumption has increased around 5 percentage points, rising from around 39% in 1990 to 44% in 2011.

Closely related with household consumption, a crucial aspect to understand the Indian economy performance, particularly since the 2000s, is the remarkable credit expansion (Azad et al., 2017; Chandrasekhar, 2017, 2016, 2008 and Nagaraj, 2013b, 2008). During the 2000s, the commercial banks' credits as percentage of GDP boomed, going from an average of about 20% during 1990s to reach more than 50% in the beginning of 2010s.[5]

Credit oriented to housing and real estate averaged around 20% of the total gross bank credits during the 2000s, and from the total of personal loans, housing represents around 50%. If we add the total personal loans (including consumer durables, education, credit card, advance consumption,

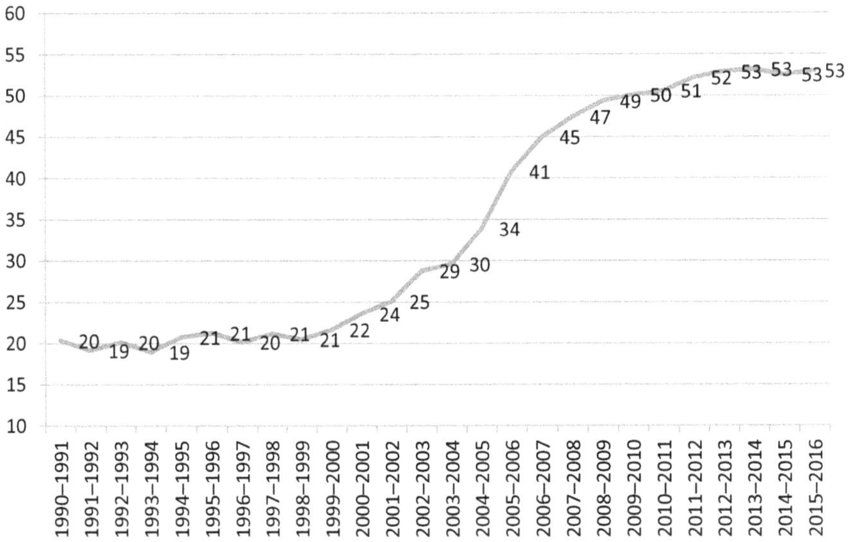

Figure 7.6 Private and public commercial banks' total credit as % of GDP, 1990–2016.
Source: Own elaboration based on RBI.

and vehicle loans) and the credit related to real estate and housing, they average around a third of the total gross bank credit. In other words, one-third of the total amount of credit, which has more than doubled in the 2000s. Nagaraj (2008), for instance, emphasises the role of personal loans to stimulate automobile and durable manufactures' consumption as well as construction industry in the 2000s. In this line, Chandrasekhar (2016) says:

> There were also significant changes in the sectoral distribution of credit. Overall there were two sets of sectors that gained in share. The first comprised of retail advances, covering housing loans, loans for automobile and consumer durable purchases, educational loans, and the like. The share of personal loans increased from slightly more than 9 per cent of total outstanding commercial bank credit at the end of March 1996 to close to a quarter of the total more recently (2015). The second area of change was the distribution of credit going to industry, which at around 40 per cent of total bank credit outstanding was still substantial. The share of infrastructural lending in the total advances of scheduled commercial banks to the industrial sector rose sharply, from less than 2 per cent at the end of March 1998 to 16.4 per cent at the end of March 2004 and as much as 35 per cent at the end of March 2015. That is, even as the volume (though not share) of lending to industry in the total

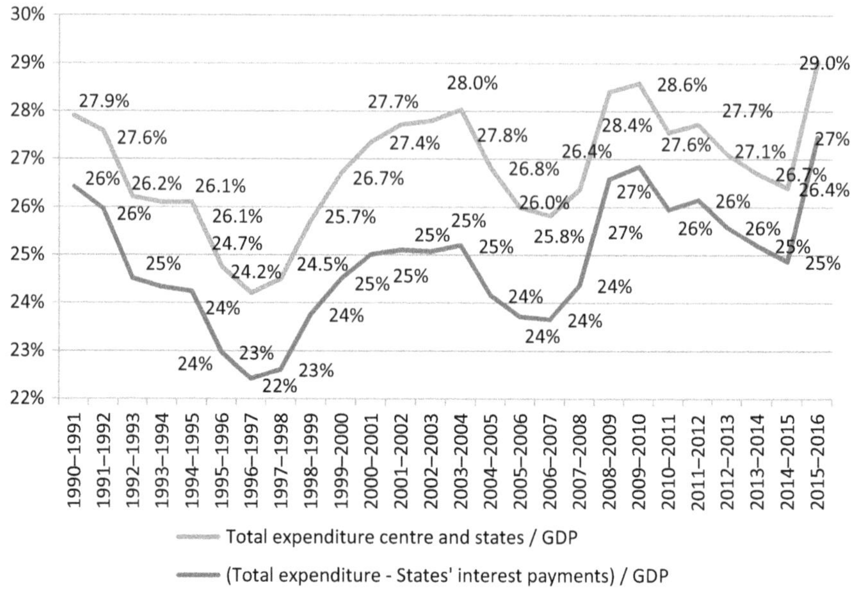

Figure 7.7 Government expenditure: centre and states as % of GDP, 1990–2016.
Source: Own elaboration based on RBI.

advances of the banking system has risen, the importance of lending to infrastructure within industry has increased hugely. Sectors like power, roads and ports, and telecommunications have been the most important beneficiaries.

Interestingly, government expenditure did not experience a permanent reduction as was postulated by the NEP objectives. In fact, it experienced periods of reduction, mainly after the first years of the NEP, but when the economy slowed down, government expenditure was used to stimulate growth, both at the end of 1990s and during the global crisis that started in 2007.

Indeed, after the NEP implementation, the centre plus the states expenditure, as a percentage of GDP, had decreased as a result of the adjustment policies and the effects of the recovery of growth between 1992 and 1997, which statistically reduced the state share as the GDP increased. However, in the second half of the 1990s, when the GDP growth rates turned more unstable, state participation in the economy returned in order to reach in 2003 the same levels as in 1990, at around 28% (25% excluding the states' interest payments). In other words, after a decade of NEP, the government expenditure as percentage of GDP was almost the same (with the interest paid by the states taking a bigger share, as can be seen in Figure 7.7).

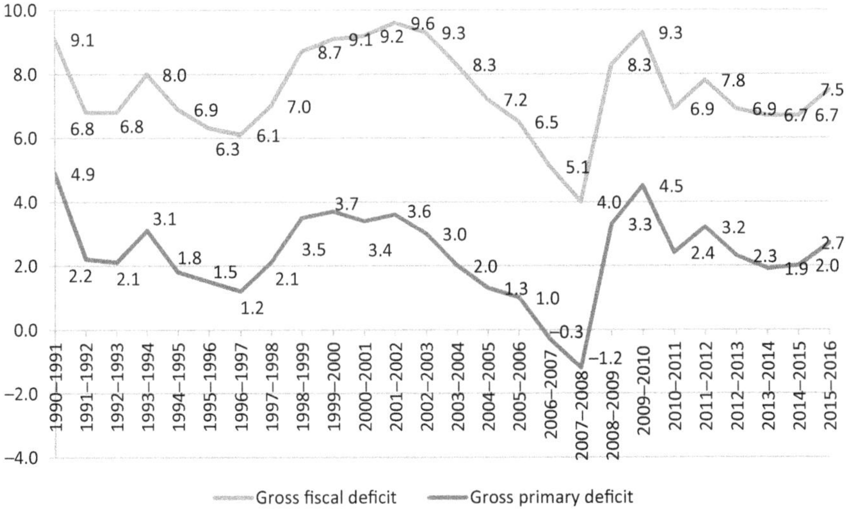

Figure 7.8 Gross fiscal deficit and gross primary deficit as % of GDP, 1990–2016.
Source: Own elaboration based on RBI.

In 2003, a Fiscal Responsibility and Budget Management Act (FRBMA) was passed, aiming to reduce fiscal deficit to 3% of GDP. Later, a new reduction in the government participation occurred with a new minimum of 26% (less than 24% excluding states' interest payments). However, in 2006, an ambitious government funded a rural employment guarantee scheme; the National Rural Employment Guarantee Scheme (later "Mahatma Gandhi" was added to its title, now known as MGNREGS) was passed by the Parliament, with the support of the Congress and the Left parties. Between 2007 and 2009, the state expenditure again increased in order to deal with the subprime global crisis that started in 2007, and the FRBMA fiscal deadlines were postponed (Nagaraj, 2015; Azad et al., 2017).

In 2009, the state participation reached a new peak of 28.5% of GDP. After that, we can see a new decrease in the state participation until 2016, when another peak was reached at 29% of GDP. In 2016, around 25 years after the NEP implementation, state expenditure was bigger in percentage of GDP! And the average gross fiscal deficit for the whole period between 1990 and 2015 has been higher than 5%, with peaks of 9% and an average of 7.5%. According to Rakshit (2009), for several years the successive budgets overestimated tax collections, with tax reduction, rural subsidies, and exemptions (instead of public investment expansion) contributing to the permanent fiscal deficit.

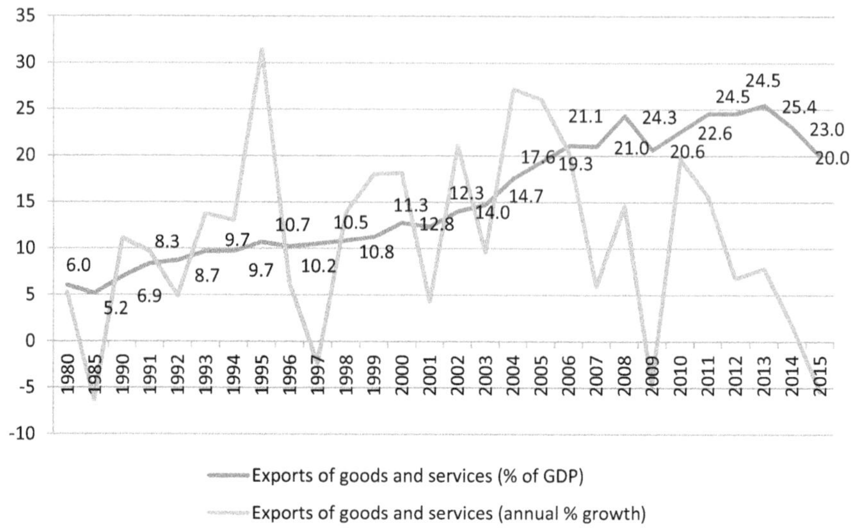

Figure 7.9 Exports of goods and services, 1980–2015, % of GDP and annual % growth.

Source: Own elaboration based on WB database.

All in all, in the midst of great pressure from the multilateral organisations and a policymaking framework influenced by the neoliberal times, the different attempts to reduce government expenditure in the Indian economy went back and forth. In contrast, government expenditure has been used as a clear anti-cyclical mechanism whenever the Indian economy was slowing down.

Exports, which explain around 20% of the growth in aggregate demand, went from around 5% of GDP in the 1980s to 10% during the 1990s. However, the main increase occurred during the 2000s, when they surpassed 20% of GDP participation. A main driver of exports growth were service exports, particularly ICT ones, pretty much destined to the US. Indeed, the emergence of foreign demand as a major source of services growth constitutes one of the most striking features of the Indian economy. We will particularly explore the role and peculiarities of the Indian service exports and the external sector evolution and sustainability since the 1990s in the next chapter.

If we analyse the sectoral composition of GDP for the period 1990–2013, there is a marked increase in the participation of trade, hotels, transport, and communication and finance, insurance, real estate, and business services, both registered as services, growing between 1990 and 2013 from 17.6% to 26.4% and from 11.5% to 20.6%, respectively. Both sectors

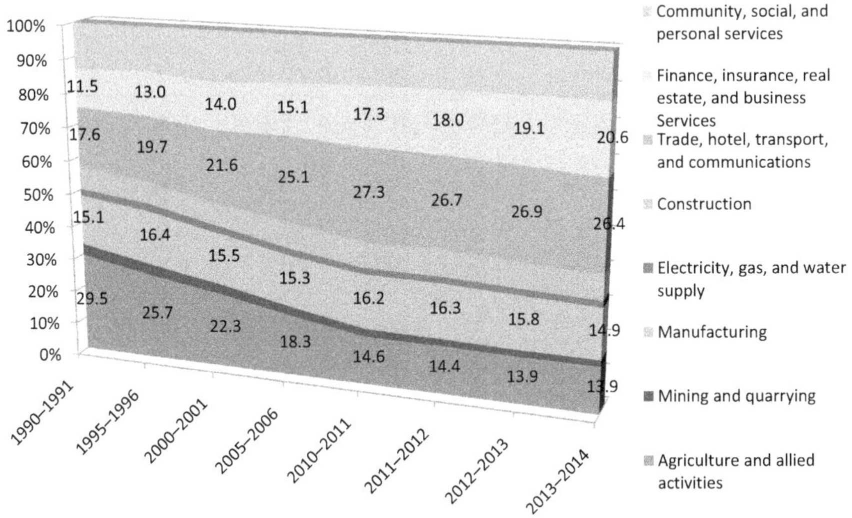

Figure 7.10 Sectoral composition of GDP (at factor costs), 1990–2014.

Source: Own elaboration based on RBI.

increased their share around 10 pp in 24 years in order to represent together almost 50% of GDP!

In contrast, agriculture participation decreased significantly, falling from 29.5% to 13.9%, while manufacturing remained stagnant at around 15%. These figures are in tune with the works of Ghosh (2016), Chandrasekhar (2017, 2016), Azad et al. (2017), and Nagaraj (2013b), who point out the impressive increase of the FIRE sector along with related professional services as the main characteristic of the Indian growth, particularly since the 2000s.

The evolution of the GDCF composition by sector shows some similar trends. Agriculture share decreased from 20% in 1980 to 7% in 2015. Real estate, ownership of dwelling, and professional services impressively increased, more than doubling, from 11% in 1990 to 26% in 2015. Construction rose from 1% in 1990 to 6% in 2007 and then dropped to 4% in 2015. Trade, repair, hotels, and restaurants also tripled, increasing from 4% in 1990 to 10% in 2015.

As will be detailed in the next chapter, the slow but constant urbanisation process contributed to put pressure on urban housing demand, particularly from the upper-class/caste groups. Construction performance was fuelled by the credit expansion, the different public housing and urban development programmes, and the rural impulse, mainly stimulated by the slight increase in rural incomes (Mahajan and Nagaraj, 2017). In addition, the information

Table 7.4 GDCF share by sector, 1980–2016

Activity	*1980–1981*	*1990–1991*	*2000–2001*	*2007–2008*	*2010–2011*	*2015–2016*
Agriculture, forestry, and fishing	**20%**	**14%**	**10%**	**7%**	**8%**	**7%**
Mining and quarrying	**3%**	**5%**	**2%**	**5%**	**4%**	**2%**
Manufacturing	**22%**	**27%**	**31%**	**35%**	**30%**	**18%**
Electricity, gas, water supply, and other utility services	**11%**	**12%**	**9%**	**6%**	**6%**	**9%**
Construction	**1%**	**1%**	**2%**	**6%**	**5%**	**4%**
Trade, repair, hotels, and restaurants	**4%**	**3%**	**3%**	**7%**	**9%**	**10%**
Transport, storage, communication, and broadcasting services	**11%**	**11%**	**16%**	**7%**	**8%**	**7%**
Railways	3%	2%	1%	1%	1%	2%
Communication and services related to broadcasting	1%	3%	5%	3%	3%	2%
Others	7%	6%	9%	3%	3%	0%
Financial services	1%	1%	1%	1%	1%	1%
Real estate, ownership of dwelling, and professional services	**10%**	**11%**	**16%**	**12%**	**13%**	**26%**
Public administration and defence	**15%**	**10%**	**8%**	**9%**	**10%**	**11%**
Other public services	**3%**	**3%**	**4%**	**7%**	**7%**	**6%**
Total GDCF % of GDP	**22%**	**24%**	**25%**	**37%**	**35%**	**33%**

Source: Nagaraj (2013b) and MOSPI Web page

technology outsourcing and services sector boom created a massive demand for high-quality commercial real estate, met by the private sector, mostly in the metropolitan areas.

Regarding the participation of private corporate sector, public sector, and households in GDCF, public sector reduced its share from 10% in 1990 to 6% in 2002 and then recovered to 8% from 2005[6] (Nagaraj, 2015). Since then, public-sector contribution stabilised at 8%. Private sector went from 5% in 1990 to 10% in 1995, decreased again to 5% in 2000, and since then

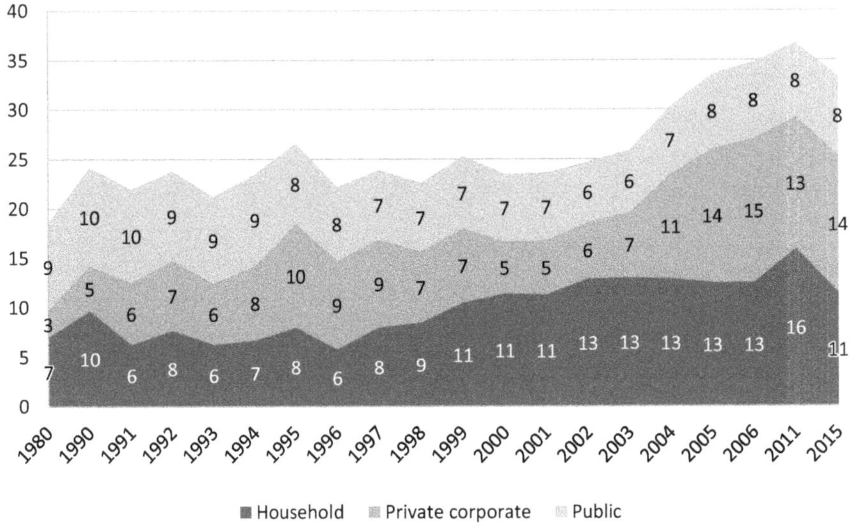

Figure 7.11 GDCF: participation of household, private corporate, and public, 1980–2015.

Source: Own elaboration based on the Report of the High Level Committee on Estimation of Saving and Investment (2009) and MOSPI.

increased to around 14%. In this sense, several studies show that private corporate investments, particularly in manufacturing, have responded to the accelerator mechanism (Nair, 2005; Rakshit, 2009; Bhattacharyya, 2008; Bhaduri, 2005; etc.).

The faster expansion of private investment in the 2000s occurred not only in manufacturing and services, where the private corporate sector had a traditional presence, but also in the infrastructure sector, where private investment was practically absent until the 1990s. According to the Twelfth Five-Year Plan (2012–2017), total investment in the infrastructure sector (defined as electricity, roads and bridges, telecommunications, railways, irrigation, water supply and sanitation, ports, airports, storage, and oil and gas pipelines) reached a peak of little more than 8% of GDP in 2010 with private-sector participation increasing from 1.4% of GDP in 2006 to 3.7% in 2010. Public investment in infrastructure was superior to 4% of GDP for all the years.

Traditional procurement, that is, public procurement, was the main form of infrastructure expenditure. However, the PPPs have played an increasing role to mobilise private investment in infrastructure, mainly since the 2007 global crisis (Azad et al., 2017).[7] According to the WB database, PPPs constantly increased their share of GDP since 2007,

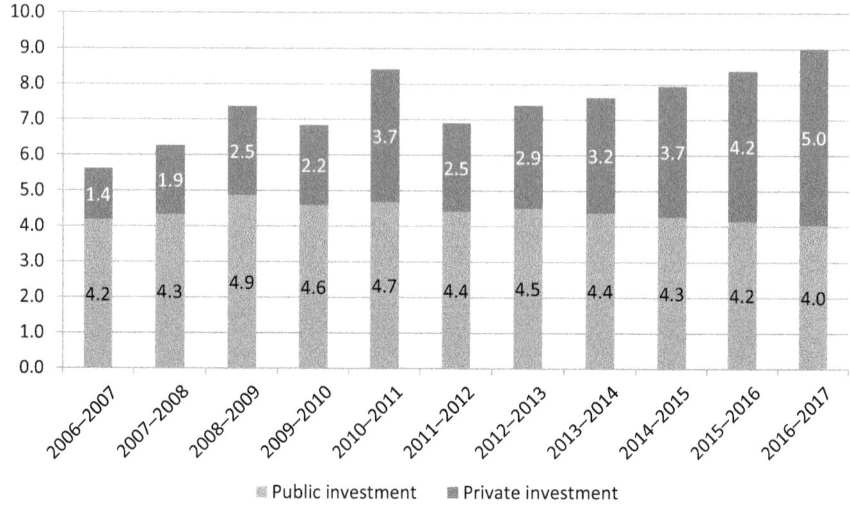

Figure 7.12 Total investment in infrastructure. Public and private sector, 2006–2017 (estimated for 2012–2017).

Source: Own elaboration based on the Twelve Five-Year Plan.

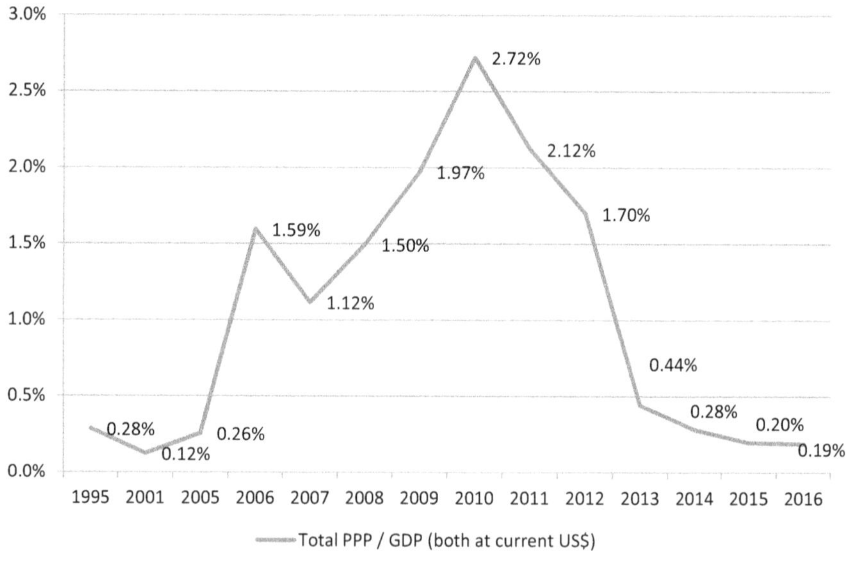

Figure 7.13 Public Private Partnerships (PPPs) as % of GDP, 1995–2016.

Source: Own elaboration based on WB database.

reaching a peak of 2.7% in 2010. Most of the PPPs were signed in energy and transport sectors, reaching peaks of US$30 billion in 2010 and US$22 billion in 2012. The role of public banks financing has been relevant in supporting PPPs and private investment in infrastructure since the 2000s (Azad et al., 2017; Chandrasekhar, 2016). We will discuss the role of public and private sectors regarding the energy sector in the next chapter.

Finally, the household share in GDCF went from a minimum of 6% in 1996 to a peak of 16% in 2011. The relevance of household share in GDCF, which surpassed both the private corporate sector and the public sector share in 2011, is closely related to the relevance of the informal sector in the Indian economy and the real estate and construction boom, driven by families, which is mainly categorised in the national accounts as household investment. In particular, the investment in housing and construction by channelling the remittances that come from the NRIs is not a minor phenomenon in some states, such as Kerala.

Summing up, our interpretation of the post-NEP growth, which integrates several Indian authors' contributions to a demand-led framework, points out that the main growth acceleration for the Indian economy occurred during the 1980s and from the 2000s on, but not in the 1990s. Broadly, from 1990 to 2015, private consumption has been the main growth driver, followed by public and private contributions to GDCF and exports. Upper-class/caste autonomous consumption, pushed by a credit boom and global capital inflows; government and private investment in infrastructure, pushed by energy and urbanisation pressures; and the export growth, mainly explained by the particular role of the Indian Diaspora in the US and the complementation between Indian capabilities and the US ICT outsourcing business opportunities, are of primary importance to understand the Indian growth process in the past three decades. Besides, government expenditure did not decrease after 25 years of the NEP.

Notes

1 Another significant political development of the 1990s was the higher participation of the "socially underprivileged" groups in the electoral politics. This included Dalits (Bahujan Samaj Party (BSP)), OBSs (Other Backward Class) (Samajwadi Party (SP)), Adivasis, Muslims, and other religious minorities and women, politically organised. Indeed, in 1995, a government was formed by a coalition between BJP and BSP.

2 It is important to highlight that the Indian military expenditure is composed by around 50% of salary and pension payments, with R&D activities representing around 5%.

3 In 2008, India suffered ten coordinated terrorist attacks in Mumbai, causing 173 deaths and 327 injured.

4 India's arms imports from Israel also increased by 285% between 2008–2012 and 2013–2017, making Israel the third-largest supplier to India.

5 The figures presented by Azad et al. (2017) about credit oriented to industry, services, and agriculture are much lower. However, we are using the data presented in the RBI *Handbook of the Indian Economy*. Our figures are in line with the ones presented in Chandrasekhar (2016).

6 These figures are particularly highly discussed (Nagaraj, 2015, 2008, etc.). Most of the critics suggest that there is an overestimation of the private corporate sector. However, as there is no other source or data, we decided to use them.

7 There are different types of PPP contracts and modalities, as we will explore in the next chapter. In each of them, the public and the private sectors divide their roles and involvement. In this sense, inside the category of PPP, there are both private and public investments. Regarding the aggregate numbers that we present here, which are taken from the WB database and the Department of Economic Affairs of India, it is not possible to disaggregate between the public and private investment proportion of the PPPs. However, in general terms, most of the investments are registered as private, despite it commonly receiving support from the public sector banks.

8

STRUCTURAL GROWTH DRIVERS, EXTERNAL SECTOR, AND STRUCTURAL HETEROGENEITY

In this chapter, we will introduce more evidence showing some key structural processes that are behind the Indian growth process that were partially presented in the previous chapter. To begin with, we will show some data and interpretations of the relationship between urbanisation, construction, and real estate, given the credit boom and their growing relevance to gross domestic product (GDP) and gross domestic capital formation (GDCF) growth. Then, we will discuss the role of infrastructure, particularly the case of energy and the correlation between public and private investments. Then, we will explore the main indicators of the Indian external sector, given the relevance of the Indian exports growth and remittances to finance the Indian trade deficit. Finally, we will briefly present some evidence on the Indian "structural heterogeneity", mainly related to salaries, employment and labour market, and some other social indicators.

8.1 Urbanisation, construction, and real estate boom

Construction and real estate have significantly boosted the Indian GDP growth. As a general background, the Indian demographic transition has been driving urbanisation up and, consequently, putting pressure on the development of real estate, construction, and housing programmes.

Public efforts to reduce mortality rates initiated after independence, particularly the vaccines campaigns during Nehru's period, resulted in the different rates of reduction of the Indian Crude Death Rate (CDR) and the Crude Birth Rate (CBR). This resulted in a significant increase in the Indian population (Dyson, 2008). Given the gap between CBR and CDR, according to Census data, India almost quadrupled its population between 1951 and 2011, going from 361 million to 1,210 million.[1] In 2020, the average Indian age was only 29 years old, compared with an average age of 37 in China and the US, 45 in Western Europe, and 48 in Japan (Chandrasekhar, 2011).

For Dyson (2008), the constant fall in mortality that occurred during the second half of the twentieth century transformed the situation regarding urbanisation, with India's urban sector benefiting much more from

DOI: 10.4324/9781003091752-12

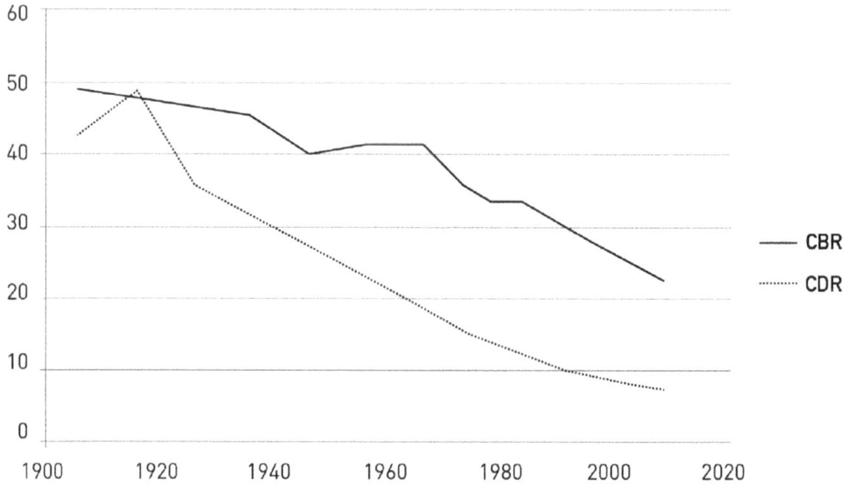

Figure 8.1 Crude Birth Rate (CBR) and Crude Death Rate (CDR), 1900–2020.
Source: Based on Kulkarni (2014).

mortality decline than the rural sector. By 1970–1975, life expectancy in urban India was 11 years higher than in the rural areas. In the 1990s, the gap was still of 6.9 years. Thus, despite internal migrations, produced both by push and pull factors that had also contributed to the slow but constant Indian urbanisation process, the sustained mortality decline in urban areas is the main driver.

According to Census data, urban population ratio has increased a little more than 10 percentage points between 1971 and 2011, going from 19.7% to 31.2%. Urban population more than tripled between 1971 and 2011, going from 108 million to 377 million. For the first time since independence, the increase in urban population of 91 million between 2001 and 2011 is larger than the increase in the rural population of 90.5 million. Besides, the annual growth rate of urban population was of 2.76% during 2001–2011, which is slightly above that experienced during 1991–2001.

India's urbanisation rate is still below the world's average. In 2015, India's urbanisation rate was of 32.7%, while the world's average was 54%. Particularly, India's urbanisation rate is lower than the African (40%) and the Asian (48%) average, mainly led by China, Pakistan, and Indonesia. However, in absolute terms, India concentrates more than 10% of the world's urban population. Among the 15 largest urban agglomerations ranked by population size in 2010, India had three cities: Delhi, with 22 million; Mumbai, with 19.4 million; and Kolkata, with 14.2 million.[2]

Table 8.1 Total, rural, and urban population (in millions), urban %, 1951–2011

Census Year	*Total Population*	*Rural*	*Urban*	*Urban Ratio*
1951	361	299	62	17.3%
1961	439	360	79	18.0%
1971	547	438	108	19.7%
1981	665	507	157	23.6%
1991	836	621	215	25.7%
2001	1.028	742	286	27.8%
2011	1.210	833	377	31.2%

Source: Own elaboration based on Census data

Table 8.2 Urbanisation evolution by continents, 2000–2015 (in hundred millions and %)

	India	*Asia*	*Africa*	*Europe*	*Latin America and Caribbean*	*North America*	*Oceania*	*World*
Annual urban population								
2000	288	1.393	279	517	396	250	22	2.856
2005	330	1.622	331	526	433	264	24	3.199
2010	373	1.865	395	538	468	280	26	3.571
2015	420	2.113	472	547	503	295	28	3.957
Percentage of population living in urban areas								
2000	27.7	37.5	34.5	70.9	75.3	79.1	70.5	46.6
2005	29.2	41.1	36.3	71,7	76.9	80,0	70.5	49.1
2010	30.9	44.8	38.3	72,7	78.4	80,8	70.7	51.6
2015	32.7	48.2	40.4	73,6	79.8	81,6	70.8	54.0
Average annual rate of change of urban population								
2000–2015	3,0	3,4	4,6	0,4	1,8	1,2	1,8	2,6

Source: Own elaboration based on MOSPI data

The urbanisation process has direct implications for the construction sector and the real estate sector. As can be observed in the Table 8.3, since the 2000s, construction has become the major source of incremental employment in India. Employment in construction increased by only 5.3 million between 1983 and 1993–1994 and by 13.9 million between 1993–1994 and 2004–2005, but it rose by 23.9 million during the seven years after 2004–2005. Between 2004–2005 and 2011–2012, the construction sector accounted for almost half, or 23.9 million out of 48 million, of the incremental non-agricultural employment generated in India, and almost all the new employment opportunities that emerged in the country's rural areas.

Table 8.3 Sector-wise distribution of India's GDP and employment

	Shares in GDP (%)		*Shares in Employment (%)*		*Employment in Millions*
	1982–1983	*2011–2012*	*1983*	*2011–2012*	*2011–2012*
Agriculture and allied sectors	34.3	14.1	68.2	47.5	224.4
Mining and quarrying	3.1	2.1	0.6	0.5	2.6
Manufacturing	14.3	15.7	10.6	13	61.3
Electricity, gas, and water	1.6	1.9	0.3	0.5	2.5
Services and construction	45.9	66.3	19.9	38.5	181.7
Construction	6.9	7.8	2.3	10.6	49.9
Trade, hotels, transport, and communication	17.3	27.5	8.8	16.5	77.9
Financing, real estate, and business services	8.9	18.1	0.7	2.9	13.5
Community, social, and personal services	12.9	12.8	8.1	8.6	40.4
GDP/Total employment	**100**	**100**	**100**	**100**	**472.5**

Source: Own elaboration based on Thomas (2015)

In fact, the construction boom was the main driver of the Indian urban employment since the 2000s (Chandrasekhar and Ghosh, 2015).

There are different real estate segments in India: residential spaces, contributing with more than 70% of the real estate expansion; commercial spaces, mainly office spaces; retail spaces; hospitality spaces, mainly hotels; and Special Economic Zones (SEZs), particularly related to IT sector.

According to MOSPI, the total number of housing units in 2001 was 193 million, of which 137.7 million were in rural areas and 55.8 million in urban areas. In 2011, the total number of occupied housing units had increased to 246.8 million, of which 167.9 million were in rural areas and 78.9 million in urban areas. The ratio of rural and urban households has evolved in the same line as the urbanisation process: in 1951, around 20% of the households were urban, but in 2011, this percentage increased to 32%. At the same time, it is also important to point out that the deficit in housing for the whole of India has increased between 2001 and 2011, reaching 10.7 million, mainly in rural areas. This fact put pressure on the housing demands, giving space to public housing programmes, private-sector developments, and credit-oriented programmes.

It is particularly interesting to see the evolution of the type of building: the proportion of pucca[3] houses in urban areas has increased from 57% to 93% between 1986 and 2012. This means a structural change in the type of house construction, mainly from wood and mud to bricks and cement.

All in all, India is still mostly a rural country, with more than 800 million people living in rural areas in 2011. Even though most of the research and private consultancy reports are focused on the Indian urban transformation, there is a marked increase in the rural construction employment dynamics (Mahajan and Nagaraj, 2017; Thomas, 2015). Mahajan and Nagaraj (2017) highlight that between 1999 and 2011, there has been a rising share of public work employment, from 6% in 1999 to 34% in 2011, as a proportion of total workforce in construction, mainly related to the Mahatma Gandhi National Rural Employment Guarantee Act (MGNREGA) rural employment programme. Thus, as can be seen next, an impressive reconversion from kutcha houses to pucca houses in rural India occurred, with the pucca houses share going from 17.2% in 1986 to 65.8% in 2012!

Table 8.4 Distribution of census households by type of household structure, urban, 1986–2012 (%)

Type of Structure	*1986*	*1991*	*1994*	*2000*	*2001*	*2002*	*2003*	*2004*	*2006*	*2009*	*2012*
Pucca	57.2	66.8	70.4	75.2	77.2	81.8	81.7	85.5	86.0	92.0	93.6
Semi-pucca	25.7	22.8	20.0	17.4	16.0	13.7	13.4	10.2	10.0	6.2	5.0
Kutcha	17.0	10.2	9.5	7.4	6.8	4.4	4.8	3.5	4.0	2.1	1.4

Source: Own elaboration based on MOSPI data

Table 8.5 Distribution of census households by type of household structure, rural, 1986–2012 (%)

Type of Structure	*1986*	*1991*	*1994*	*2000*	*2001*	*2002*	*2003*	*2004*	*2006*	*2009*	*2012*
Pucca	17.2	26.5	29.6	38.4	40.5	45.7	43.9	48.2	50.0	55.0	65.8
Semi-pucca	33.1	34.6	37.9	31.6	32.9	32.7	34.9	32.8	31.0	28.0	24.6
Kutcha	49.6	38.9	32.4	30.0	26.6	21.5	21.1	17.2	19.0	17.0	9.6

Source: Own elaboration based on MOSPI data

In this sense, Mahajan and Nagaraj (2017, p. 62) point out:

> If the foregoing reasoning is correct and evidence credible, then the argument that construction employment boom as mostly an urban phenomenon does not hold. In reality – invisible to urban eyes – the boom seems to consist of widespread minor (incremental) construction by farm households, such as converting mud walls to brick and cement walls, and thatched roofs replaced by concrete roofs, and cement lining of irrigation channels, etc.

The increase in rural income and the diminishing price of the construction materials such as cement have stimulated the rural construction. As can be seen next, between 1999 and 2016, cement production in India almost quadrupled, going from around 90 million tons to almost 290 million tons. What is more, cement production grew annually faster than the manufacturing sector growth rate of 6%, with cement's real price decreasing around 40% between 1991 and 2012.

The segment of the real estate sector related to commercial spaces and the SEZs is related to shopping malls, foreign direct investment (FDI), and corporate sector, particularly the IT industry. Real estate is the fourth-largest sector in terms of FDI inflows in India with a projected growth reaching US$25 billion by 2022 (IBEF, 2017). According to the figures on FDI of the Department of Industrial Policy and Promotion, FDI inflows to real estate reached a peak in 2011, with US$3.1 billion, mainly directed to Mumbai, Delhi, and Bengaluru, cities associated with the Information and Communications Technology (ICT) sector.

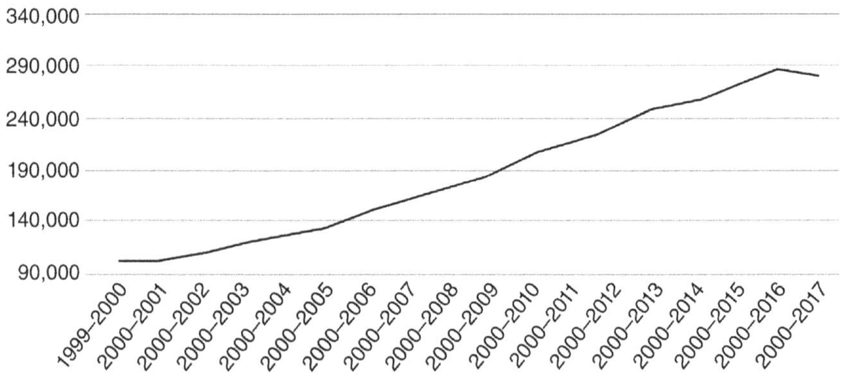

Figure 8.2 Cement production in India (thousand tons), 1999–2017.

Source: Based on Chandrasekhar and Ghosh (2017b).

The Indian government has implemented several policies to stimulate FDI, particularly in the SEZs, such as a 100% FDI permitted for developing townships with residential areas, markets, playgrounds, recreation centres, and so on. Retail and hospitality spaces are also increasing in terms of real estate development, mainly driven by the increase in the urban upper-caste/class consumption of foreign brands and global trends of mass consumption. For instance, there has been a relevant increase in the amount of malls during the 2010s in India. Furthermore, Delhi and Mumbai are by far the biggest hospitality markets in India, followed by Bengaluru, Hyderabad, and Chennai. In addition to hotels, the hospitality market comprises serviced apartments and convention centres. A mix of a growing domestic tourism industry, the increasingly global nature of Indian businesses, and fiscal incentives to hotels are boosting this segment.

Another important element that has been propelling the real estate and construction boom was the development of a housing finance industry and the implementation of several public-led housing and urban development programmes. According to Chandrasekhar (2011), in historical terms, the creation of the National Housing Bank (NHB) in 1988 was an attempt to make housing finance companies (HFCs) significant financial intermediaries, helping to create new HFCs and regulating them. Many new HFCs were set up, including several sponsored by banks and financial institutions and some with equity support from the NHB. Since the New Economic Policy (NEP), the emphasis shifted to encouraging banks to enter housing finance business.

In 2002, following the Basel Capital Accord of 1988 and the New Capital Adequacy Framework, the Reserve Bank of India (RBI) decided to liberalise the prudential requirement on risk weight for housing finance by banks and encourage investments by banks in mortgage-backed securities (MBS) of HFCs. The RBI allowed banks to extend housing loans to individuals, against mortgage on residential housing properties. In 2005, FDI was allowed in the real estate sector, pushing another transformation of instruments and funds developed for the Indian market. The Indian housing finance industry began to receive global real estate funds, private equity funds, and so on. Funds have been actively looking at residential projects due to their self-liquidating nature and commercial leased assets that provide attractive rental yields along with capital appreciation.

Finally, several massive public-financed urbanisation missions and programmes were launched since the mid-2000s. The main one was launched in December 2005, the Jawaharlal Nehru National Urban Renewal Mission (JNNURM), with several subsequent spin-off programmes related to urban development and housing. With an investment of around US$7 billion in a mission period of seven years, the JNNURM has been the single largest initiative of the Government of India for planned urban development. The mission had two components: basic services for the urban poor and an integrated housing and slum development programme, which aimed at integrating the development of slums through projects for the provision of shelter and basic services.

After the JNNURM, the Pradhan Mantri Awas Yojana (PMAY) – Housing for All was launched in 2015, to promote affordable housing for the weaker section through credit-linked subsidies and by providing affordable housing through public and private stakeholder collaborations. Sixty million houses are to be built, which include 40 million in rural areas and 20 million in urban areas by 2022. The mission has four components: i) slum redevelopment with private-sector participation using land as a resource, ii) affordable housing through credit-linked subsidies, iii) affordable housing in partnership with private and public sectors in the form of Public Private Partnerships (PPPs), and iv) beneficiary-led house construction. The houses given under this scheme are owned by women alone or jointly with men. A technology sub-mission was set up to facilitate the adoption of green technologies.

National missions connected to urban development

In addition to the Housing for All programme, several state-led missions related to urban development were launched in 2014 and 2015:

Atal Mission for Rejuvenation and Urban Transformation (AMRUT): launched in 2015 for the development of basic infrastructure in 500 cities. The objective was to ensure that every household has access to a tap with assured supply of water and a sewerage connection, to increase the amenity value of cities by developing greenery and well-maintained open spaces, and to reduce pollution by switching to public transport or constructing facilities for non-motorised transport.

Smart City Mission (SCM): launched in 2015 with the objective of promoting cities that provide core infrastructure, a clean and sustainable environment, and application of "Smart" Solutions. These include adequate water supply; assured electricity supply; sanitation, including solid waste management; efficient urban mobility and public transport; affordable housing, especially for the poor; robust Information Technology (IT) connectivity; and digitalisation and e-governance. The mission covers 100 cities for five years.

Swachh Bharat Mission (SBM): launched in 2014 with a broad funding pattern concentrated on i) household toilets, including conversion of insanitary latrines into pour-flush latrines; ii) community toilets; iii) public toilets; iv) solid waste management; v) information, education, and communication and public awareness; and vi) capacity building and administrative and office expenditure.

Source: Own elaboration based on the missions' websites.

8.2 The Indian energy challenge: public/private investment and state-led electrification

Both public and private investment directed to infrastructure, mainly to energy and transport, have been of central relevance for the Indian growth process since the 1990s. In this section, we will briefly explore two main connected issues: the main challenges and efforts related to the Indian energy sector and the main features of both public- and private-sector involvement in this segment.

In 2006, Prime Minister Manmohan Singh said in an interview with the *Financial Times* that "the quest for energy security is second only in our (India´s) scheme of things to food security"[4]. In fact, energy has always been a main issue for India. In the contemporary high-growth days, energy has turned into the main bottleneck for Indian growth, implying several geopolitical, technological, and institutional challenges. According to the Integrated Energy Policy (2006, p. xiii):

> To deliver a sustained growth rate of 8% through 2031–32 and to meet the lifeline energy needs of all citizens, India needs, at the very least, to increase its primary energy supply by 3 to 4 times and, its electricity generation capacity/supply by 5 to 6 times of their 2003–04 levels. With 2003–04 as the base, India's commercial energy supply would need to grow from 5.2% to 6.1% per annum while its total primary energy supply would need to grow at 4.3% to 5.1% annually. By 2031–32 power generation capacity must increase to nearly 8,00,000 MW from the current capacity of around 1,60,000 MW inclusive of all captive plants. Similarly, the requirement of coal, the dominant fuel in India's energy mix will need to expand to over 2 billion tonnes/annum based on the domestic quality of coal. Meeting the energy challenge is of fundamental importance to India's economic growth imperatives and its efforts to raise its level of human development.

GDP growth, urbanisation, and rural electrification are the main drivers of the energy demand in India. According to the International Energy Agency (2015),[5] although India uses only 6% of the world's primary energy, energy consumption has almost doubled in the 2000s, and it is projected that India will contribute more than any other country to the global rise of energy demand. A large expansion of coal output makes India the second-largest coal producer in the world, but at the same time, India became the world's largest coal importer too in 2019. India is the world's third-largest importer of crude oil, although a large refinery sector gives it a surplus of oil products, mainly transport fuels, for export. India's power system needs to almost quadruple in size by 2040 to catch up and keep pace with electricity demand, which, driven by rising incomes and new connections to the grid, increases almost 5% per year.

The Twelfth Five-Year Plan (2012–2017) called for several actions in order to deal with the energy challenge: a) to step up the domestic production of coal, oil, and gas and other energy sources, implementing energy efficiency technology and R&D efforts; b) to ensure substantial private investment, including foreign investment, in oil and natural gas blocks and new capacities for renewable energy; c) to emphasise investments in renewable energies; d) to invest in energy assets in foreign countries, especially in coal, oil, gas, and uranium; and e) to increase energy storage capacities.

Energy security has become a central aspect of the Indian foreign policy, in what is called "energy diplomacy" (Sachdeva, 2011a). The Indian energy security strategy includes a) to diversify suppliers and sources of energy, trying to harness hydroelectricity to reduce dependence on fossil fuels, developing joint power projects with its neighbouring countries: Bhutan, Nepal, Myanmar, and Afghanistan; b) to purchase equity in coal, oil, and gas abroad, both through the power Central Public Sector Enterprises (CPSEs) and national private companies, in countries such as Indonesia, Australia, Bangladesh, and South Africa; c) to promote investment in oil refining infrastructure and capabilities, in order to emerge as an "energy outsourcing hub" in the Indian Ocean; d) to increase its energy reserves; e) to promote cooperation with China oriented to reduce the competition for energy security, and with the US, to develop civil nuclear energy; and e) to boost military capabilities, mainly navy and air force, to enforce energy trade in the Indian Ocean (Pardesi and Ganguly, 2009).

Given this big picture, we will next present some data supporting the argument that, although the private sector has significantly increased its role in the infrastructure and energy sectors since the 2000s, the Indian central state still has a primary position, mainly through public procurement, CPSEs, the organisation and financing of PPPs, and its direct involvement in several infrastructure projects, mega projects and national missions, and massive electrification programmes.

According to the Twelfth Five-Year Plan (2012–2017), during the period between 2007 and 2012, the total average investment in infrastructure in India was 7.21% of GDP,[6] with the public sector contributing 4.57% (centre 2.5% and the states 2%) and the private sector 2.64%. Electricity, renewable energy, and oil and gas totalised investments for about 2.7% of the GDP, with electricity, by large, as the main sector, with 2.2% of the investment. Indeed, these three sectors concentrated more than one-third of the total investment in infrastructure in India. Public-sector investment was higher than the private-sector one in electricity, with 1.24% and 0.92% of GDP, respectively, and oil and gas, with 0.12% and 0.07%, respectively. Private sector was the main investor in renewable energy infrastructure, with 0.23% of GDP.[7]

To give an idea of the relevance of energy in the Indian public expenditure, in Figure 8.3, we will show the total outlay of the Eleventh Five-Year Plan (2007–2011), including centre, states, and CPSEs by major sectors. We can see that energy is the second main sector, encompassing around 19% of the outlay, only surpassed by social services. The third main sector of expenditure is transport, mainly related to highways and road construction.

Table 8.6 Investment in infrastructure: centre, states, total public, and private, 2007–2017[8] (%)

Sectors	*Eleventh Plan (2007–2012) % of GDP*	*Twelfth Plan (2012–2017) (Projection) % of GDP*
Grand Total	**7.21**	**8.18**
Centre	2.55	2.35
States	2.02	1.89
Total Public	4.57	4.24
Private	2.64	3.94
Electricity	**2.17**	**2.20**
Centre	0.69	0.65
States	0.55	0.51
Total Public	1.24	1.16
Private	0.92	1.05
Renewable Energy	**0.27**	**0.47**
Centre	0.03	0.05
States	0.00	0.01
Total Public	0.03	0.06
Private	0.23	0.41
Oil and Gas Pipelines	**0.19**	**0.22**
Centre	0.10	0.11
States	0.01	0.01
Total Public	0.12	0.12
Private	0.07	0.10

Source: Own elaboration based on the Twelve Five-Year Plan (2012–2017).

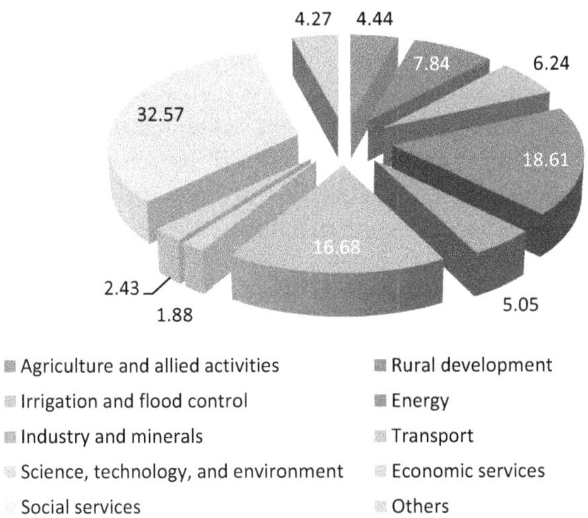

Figure 8.3 Total outlay (centre + states + CPSEs) by major sector. Accumulated outlay % of the Eleventh Five-Year Plan (2007–2011).

Source: Own elaboration based on the Twelfth Five-Year Plan (2012–2017).

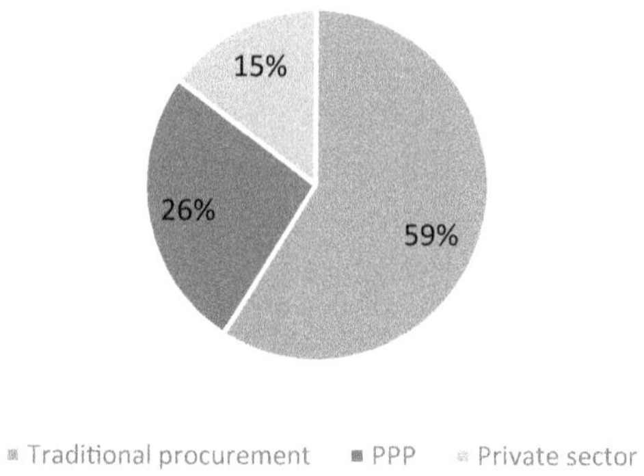

Figure 8.4 Total expenditure in infrastructure projects. Private, PPPs, and traditional (public) procurement, 1991–2016 (%).

Source: Own elaboration based on the Department of Economic Affairs database on infrastructure projects.

Since the 2000s, there were three main ways to mobilise infrastructure projects: PPPs, private investment, and traditional (public) procurement.[9] The Department of Economic Affairs database presented a total of 9,137 projects in infrastructure between 1991 and 2016. From the total amount of projects executed in this period, 6,131 (around two-thirds of the total amount) were contracted as traditional (public) procurement, and the rest were 1,678 of PPPs and 1,318 of private investment. Regarding the total expenditure, the ratios are similar: 59% of traditional procurement, 26% of PPPs, and 15% of private investment.

Energy is at the top of the expenditure in infrastructure, including public, private, and PPP projects, with 48.6% of the expenditure, while transport is the second one, with 36%. After them, water sanitation received 13% of the resources and social and commercial infrastructure and communication around 2.5%. Particularly, electricity transmission and renewable energy concentrated more than 90% of the total expenditure in energy between 2000 and 2016.

The Indian CPSEs' experience in dealing with the global privatisation agenda of the 1990s is an interesting one. CPSEs play a main role channelling public investment (Kapila, 2014). However, with the NEP, a privatisation or disinvestment agenda was launched.[10] As detailed in Nagaraj (2008) and Khanna (2015), the privatisation and disinvestment process has four phases:

1 **From 1992 to 1998**: The Congress Party–led government promoted a policy of disinvestment of up to 20% of its shares to mutual funds, the general public, and workers (since 1993, foreign investors were also included). However, only one CPSE was privatised: the automobile

company Maruti Udyog was sold to Suzuki (the petroleum marketing company IBP was sold to another CPSE, the Indian Oil Corporation).[11] In 1997, the Disinvestment Commission recommended restructuring the CPSEs before disinvestment, to strengthen the well-functioning CPSEs and to utilise the disinvestment proceeds to create a fund to restructure CPSEs. The well-functioning CPSEs were declared *Navaratnas* (jewels in the government crown) and were granted a greater managerial and financial autonomy.

2 **From 1998 to 2004:** A coalition led by the now BJP-led government pushed for privatisation and "strategic sales". Twelve CPSEs were privatised, including Indian Petrochemicals, VSNL (monopoly of long-distance communications and the largest provider of the internet at that moment), Bharat Aluminium, and several hotels that were run by the Indian Tourism Development Corporation. There were several allegations of corruption and malpractice in some of the deals.

3 **From 2004 to 2014:** The Congress-led government, in alliance with two communist parties, returned to power, and the disinvestment process was frozen. A Board for Reconstruction of Public Sector Enterprises was constituted with the objective of restructuring the ailing CPSEs. The Board recommended restructuring 60 CPSEs, to close 2 and to sell another 2.

4 **From 2014 to nowadays:** With the BJP back in power, the policy of disinvestment has been ambiguous. Several initiatives have gone in line with a strengthening of the privatisation process. For instance, Bharat Earth Movers Limited (BEML), one of the nine defence public-sector units; the Salem, Durgapur, and Bhadravati plants of Steel Authority of India Limited (SAIL); Bridge and Roof Company; Dredging Corporation of India; and Hindustan Fluorocarbons were identified for strategic sale. However, there have not been massive sales, and the role of the CPSEs in some sectors has been reinforced.

Less than 50 CPSEs were fully privatised between 1990 and 2019. In fact, the evolution in the number of CPSEs,[12] as seen next, shows they have increased! In 1992, there were 246 CPSEs, but in 2016, there were 320.[13] This means that new CPSEs were created during the post-NEP years. Although some of these new CPSEs have been created to establish PPPs with the private sector or to finance the private sector, it does not seem to be a process of reduction of the CPSEs' role.

According to Khanna (2015), there are some political-economic reasons that explain the low progress of the privatisation process: a) although most of the governments since the 1990s expressed their commitment to the privatisation process, the majority of the voters were against it; b) trade unions and middle-class groups have resisted the reforms; c) there were many government changes during this period, causing different readjustments in the

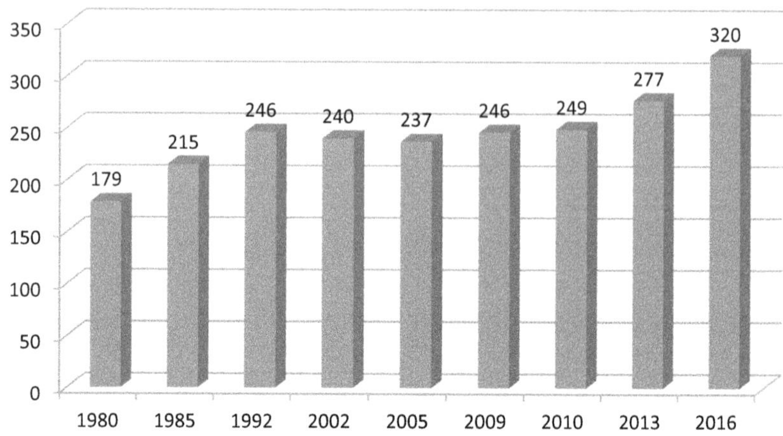

Figure 8.5 Number of CPSEs, 1985–2016, selected years.

Source: Public Enterprises Survey, various issues.

privatisation strategy; d) a number of privatisation cases received severe criticisms of corruption; and e) there are some strategic sectors where the government does not want to lose control.

As reported in the Public Enterprises Survey 2015–2016, while there were five CPSEs at the time of the First Five-Year Plan, there were 320 CPSEs (excluding seven insurance companies) as on 31 March 2016. Services and manufacturing, with 113 and 87, respectively, are the main CPSE sectors. However, in terms of investment, the 14 electricity CPSEs (11 of generation and 3 of transmission) totalised around 25% of the total CPSEs' investment between 2013 and 2015. Besides, there are 76 enterprises under construction, subsidiaries of existing CPSEs, which are going to operate in new sectors.

Several CPSEs are leading companies with significant market shares in sectors such as petroleum (ONGC, GAIL, HPCL, BPCL, and Indian Oil Corporation), mining (Coal India Ltd. and NMDC), power generation (NTPC and NHPC), power transmission (Power Grid Corporation of India Ltd.), nuclear energy (Nuclear Power Corporation of India Ltd.), heavy engineering (BHEL), aviation (Hindustan Aeronautics Ltd. and Air India Ltd.), storage and public distribution (Food Corporation of India and Central Warehousing Corporation), shipping and trading (Shipping Corporation of India Ltd. and State Trading Corporation of India Ltd.), steel (Steel Authority of India Ltd and Rashtriya Ispat Nigam Ltd.), and telecommunication (BSNL and MTNL).

Of the top ten CPSEs in terms of investment during 2015–2016, eight of them belong to the energy sector (five to oil and gas and three to power), one to steel, and one to telecommunications.

Table 8.7 Top ten CPSEs in terms of investment in 2015–2016 (% of total CPSEs' investment)

CPSE Name	*Sector*	*% of Total CPSEs' Investment*
Oil and Natural Gas Corporation Ltd.	Oil and Gas	12.7
NTPC Ltd.	Power – Generation (Thermal)	10.5
Power Grid Corporation of India Ltd.	Power – Transmission	9.6
Bharat Sanchar Nigam Ltd.	Telecommunications	8.6
Indian Oil Corporation Ltd.	Oil and Gas	8.5
ONGC Videsh Ltd.	Oil and Gas	6.1
Steel Authority of India Ltd.	Steel	5.0
Nuclear Power Corporation of India Ltd.	Power – Generation (Nuclear)	3.0
Bharat Petroleum Corporation Ltd.	Oil and Gas	2.9
Hindustan Petroleum Corporation Ltd.	Oil and Gas	2.8
Total		69.6
Grand Total		100.0

Source: Own elaboration based on the Public Enterprises Survey 2015–2016

In terms of R&D expenditure, Bharat Heavy Electricals Ltd. and Bharat Electronics Ltd. are the leaders. After them, five CPSEs related to energy form part of the top ten, including four from the oil and gas sector and one from power (generation). These figures are in line with the work of Mishra et al. (2013) that highlights the relevance of CPSEs' expenditure in R&D for India related to oil and gas, defence, heavy equipment, power, and electronics.

Regarding the disinvestment process up to the fiscal year 2015–2016 for the top ten CPSEs in terms of investment, we can see that in:

- Oil & Natural Gas Corporation, the Government of India (GoI) had 68.9% of the shares, with foreign investors owning 7.2% and the rest in hands of national private investors (23.9%);
- NTPC, the GoI had 63% of the shares, foreign investors 10.7%, and other investors 26.3%;
- Power Grid Corporation, GoI had 57.9%, foreign investors 26.3%, and the rest 15.8%;
- Bharat Sanchar Nigam and the Nuclear Power Corporation of India, GoI had 100% ownership, and ONGC Videsh is totally owned by another CPSE;

Table 8.8 Top ten CPSEs in terms of R&D expenditure in 2015–2016 (% of total CPSEs' expenditure)

CPSE Name	*Sector*	*% of Total CPSEs' Investment*
Bharat Heavy Electricals Ltd.	Heavy equipment	24.7
Bharat Electronics Ltd.	Electronics	19.5
Oil & Natural Gas Corporation Ltd.	Oil and Gas	14.9
Steel Authority Of India Ltd.	Steel	7.7
Indian Oil Corporation Ltd.	Oil and Gas	6.5
Hindustan Petroleum Corporation Ltd.	Oil and Gas	5.0
NTPC Ltd.	Power – Generation	3.6
Bharat Sanchar Nigam Ltd.	Telecommunications	2.2
Gail (India) Ltd.	Oil and Gas	2.1
BEML Ltd.	Heavy equipment	1.8
Total		88.1
Grand Total		100.0

Source: Own elaboration based on the Public Enterprises Survey 2015–2016

- the Indian Oil Corporation, 58.6% of the shares belonged to the GoI, 4.2% to foreign investors, and 37.2% to other investors;
- Bharat Petroleum Corporation, 55.8% belonged to the GoI, 21.1% to foreign investors, and 21.1% to the rest of local investors;
- Hindustan Petroleum Corporation, 51.1% of the shares belonged to the GoI, 19.3% to foreign investors, and 29.6% to other local investors.

This means the GoI still has around 60% of the shares of the top ten investing CPSEs, maintaining in some sectors, such as nuclear, 100% of the ownership. The participation of foreign investors, in general terms, is not superior to 20% of the shares. A little more of 20% of the shares are distributed among different types of national investors.

Finally, the electrification process has advanced significantly since the 1990s in India. According to the World Bank, in 1990, less than 45% of India's population had access to electricity, but in 2014, the electrification rate reached 80%. Rural electrification went from around 30% to 70% for the same period. Although the Indian electrification rate is still much lower than the other BRICS countries, the Indian increase is notable.

A strong impulse in the electrification process came in 2005 with the launch of the Rajiv Gandhi Grameen Vidyutikaran Yojana (RGGVY), a mainly central government–funded programme. The main aims of RGGVY

Table 8.9 Top ten CPSEs in terms of investment (shares ownership at 2015–2016 fiscal year)

CPSE Name	*Shareholders*					
	GoI	*Others*	*Mutual Funds*	*Financial Institutions*	*Insurance Companies*	*Foreign Investors*
Oil & Natural Gas Corporation Ltd.	68.9	13.5	0.9	1.2	8.3	7.2
NTPC Ltd.	63.0	3.3	6.4	16.1	0.6	10.7
Power Grid Corporation of India Ltd.	57.9	7.5	4.8	0.8	2.8	26.3
Bharat Sanchar Nigam Ltd.	100.0	0.0	0.0	0.0	0.0	0.0
Indian Oil Corporation Ltd.	58.6	24.9	1.6	0.5	10.2	4.2
ONGC Videsh Ltd.	Wholly owned by another CPSE					
Steel Authority of India Ltd.	-	-	-	-	-	-
Nuclear Power Corporation of India Ltd.	100.0	0.0	0.0	0.0	0.0	0.0
Bharat Petroleum Corporation Ltd.	55.8	14.6	5.7	0.1	2.7	21.1
Hindustan Petroleum Corporation Ltd.	51.1	15.6	9.9	4.1	0.0	19.3

Source: Own elaboration based on the Public Enterprise Survey 2015–2016 and the web page of each CPSE

were to electrify all villages, provide access to electricity to all rural households, and provide electrical connection to Below Poverty Line (BPL) families free of charge. In 2010–2011, there was a significant increase in the budgetary outlay for the RGGVY, with a marked increase in the number of electrified villages. With Narendra Modi as prime minister, the programme changed its name to Deendayal Upadhyaya Gram Jyoti Yojana (DDUGJY). The Rural Electrification Corporation, a CPSE, is the nodal agency for implementation of DDUGJY.

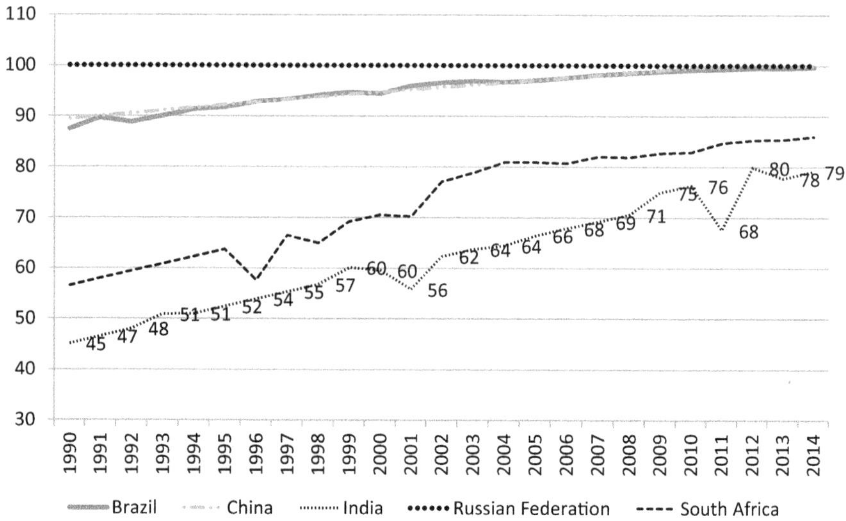

Figure 8.6 Access to electricity, % of population, BRICS countries, 1990–2014.
Source: Own elaboration based on World Bank database.

According to the DDUGJY web page, in January 2019, almost 100% of the Indian villages were electrified. However, village electrification does not mean that every household has access to electricity. Village electrification is defined as a) basic infrastructure such as a distribution transformer and distribution lines provided in the inhabited locality as well as the Dalit basti/hamlet where it exists; b) electricity is provided to public places like schools, health centres, community centres, and so on; and c) the number of electrified households is at least 10% of the total number of households in the village. Besides, this requires only the provision of the electricity line, not actual continuous access to electricity. Even if a few houses in a village receive only a couple of hours of electricity a day for a few days in the year, the village is still deemed to be electrified.

Despite the mentioned heterogeneities, there is no doubt that the electrification process has advanced significantly since the 1990s in India, and this process has been driven by huge state-financed programmes. The progress in the electrification process implies several changes in the household consumption and a wide range of new business opportunities for the power sector, the Indian entrepreneurs, and the informal sector, and it is a potential booster for Indian productivity. At the same time, it implies a huge challenge that is still not resolved, in order to ensure the provision of continued energy to all Indian villages and households.

The Ultra Mega Power Projects (UMPPs) Programme and the national missions in power

With the Twelfth Five-Year Plan (2012–2017), the Ultra Mega Power Projects (UMPPs) Programme was also launched, which integrates private investment into power generation. Nine UMPPs have been launched with an initial capacity of 4,000 MW, to attract $160–200 billion of private investment. At the same time, different national missions were launched oriented to the power sector:

National Mission for Enhanced Energy Efficiency (NMEEE): one of the eight missions under the National Action Plan on Climate Change. NMEEE aims to strengthen the market for energy efficiency. The mission will help achieve a total capacity addition of 19,598 MW, fuel savings of around 23 million tons per year, and greenhouse gas emission reduction of 98.55 million tons per year.

Jawaharlal Nehru National Solar Mission (JNNSM): launched in 2010, the mission has set the ambitious target of deploying 20,000 MW of grid-connected solar power by 2022.

Indian Electrical Equipment Industry Mission Plan: the aim of this mission plan is to make India the country of choice for production of electrical equipment and reach an output of US$100 billion by balancing exports and imports.

National Smart Grid Mission (NSGM): the NSGM is the institutional mechanism for planning, monitoring, and implementing the policies and programmes related to Smart Grid activities.

Source: Own elaboration based on the Twelfth Five-Year Plan (2012–2017).

8.3 External sector: trade deficit, capital inflows, IT exports, and remittances

Next, we will analyse some main Indian external sector indicators. Both exports and imports increased their share of GDP since 1990. Exports of goods and services passed from 4.5% of GDP in 1980–1981 to a peak of 17.2% in 2013–2014. Between 1990 and 2015, exports grew at an average rate of 10.4%. Imports increased even higher, going from 8.8% of GDP in 1980–1981 to a maximum of 27.5% in 2012–2013. The import of goods and services growth rate between 1990 and 2015 was 11.7%. External trade participation in GDP more than doubled, going from 14.6% in 1990–1991 to an average of 38.3% between 2010–2011 and 2018–2019. Trade deficit increased sharply from the mid-2000s, reaching a peak of US$166 billion in 2012.

In fact, since the 1990s, the Indian external trade balance has been deteriorating. As shown next, broadly, petroleum-related imports represented 30% of imports, being the most relevant item between 2010 and 2016. The Indian petroleum dependency has been the main characteristic of the Indian development path that has clearly increased with the growth acceleration. After petroleum, electronic goods, machinery, and transport equipment totalised 19% of imports, reflecting a poor performance of Indian capital goods. Fertilisers, mining and steel, and chemicals complete the main import segments in terms of importance.

Table 8.10 Main Indian balance of payments indicators, 1980–1981/2018–2019

Year	Trade		Invisibles			Current Account			Capital Account		Important Cover of Reserves (in months)	Total Foreign Exchange Reserves US$ Thousands
	Exports/ GDP	Imports/ GDP	Receipts/ GDP	Payments/ GDP	Net/GDP	Current Receipts/ GDP	Current Receipts/ Current Payments	Current Account Balance/ GDP	Foreign Investment/ Exports	Foreign Investment/ GDP		
2018–2019	12,4	19,1	11,3	6,8	4,5	23,7	91,8	–2,1	1,1	8,9	9,6	412.871
2017–2018	11,6	17,7	10,7	6,5	4,2	22,3	92,4	–1,8	17,0	2,0	10,9	424.545
2016–2017	12,2	17,1	10,5	6,3	4,3	22,8	97,3	–0,6	15,4	1,9	11,3	369.955
2015–2016	12,7	18,8	11,2	6,0	5,1	23,8	95,8	–1,1	12,0	1,5	10,9	360.176
2014–2015	15,5	22,6	11,9	6,1	5,8	27,4	95,4	–1,3	23,2	3,6	8,9	341.638
2013–2014	17,2	25,1	12,6	6,4	6,2	29,7	94,5	–1,7	8,3	1,4	7,8	304.223
2012–2013	16,8	27,5	12,3	6,4	5,9	29,0	85,8	–4,8	15,2	2,6	7,0	292.046
2011–2012	17,0	27,4	12,0	5,9	6,1	29,0	87,1	–4,3	12,7	2,2	7,1	294.398
2010–2011	15,3	22,9	11,4	6,6	4,7	26,7	90,3	–2,9	16,4	2,5	9,5	304.818
2009–2010	13,6	22,4	12,2	6,2	6,0	25,8	90,1	–2,8	27,6	3,8	11,1	279.057
2008–2009	15,8	25,7	14,0	6,4	7,6	29,8	92,7	–2,3	4,4	0,7	9,8	251.985
2007–2008	13,7	21,2	12,2	6,0	6,2	25,9	95,2	–1,3	26,1	3,6	14,4	309.723
2006–2007	13,7	20,3	12,2	6,6	5,6	25,9	96,2	–1,0	11,4	1,6	12,5	199.179
2005–2006	12,8	19,1	10,9	5,8	5,1	23,7	95,2	–1,2	14,8	1,9	11,6	151.622
2004–2005	12,0	16,8	9,8	5,4	4,4	21,8	98,4	–0,3	15,3	1,8	14,3	141.514
2003–2004	10,9	13,2	8,8	4,2	4,6	19,7	113,3	2,3	20,7	2,3	16,9	112.959
2002–2003	10,4	12,5	8,1	4,8	3,3	18,6	107,1	1,2	7,7	0,8	14,2	76.100
2001–2002	9,2	11,6	7,6	4,5	3,1	16,8	104,4	0,7	15,0	1,4	11,5	54.106
2000–2001	9,7	12,4	6,9	4,8	2,1	16,6	96,7	–0,6	12,9	1,3	8,8	42.281
1999–2000	8,2	12,1	6,6	3,7	2,9	14,8	93,5	–1,0	13,6	1,1	8,2	38.036
1998–1999	8,1	11,3	6,1	3,9	2,2	14,3	93,7	–1,0	6,7	0,5	8,2	32.490
1997–1998	8,6	12,3	5,6	3,2	2,4	14,2	91,5	–1,3	15,0	1,3	6,9	29.367
1996–1997	8,7	12,5	5,4	2,9	2,6	14,1	92,3	–1,2	18,0	1,6	6,5	26.423
1995–1996	9,0	12,1	4,9	3,4	1,5	13,9	89,4	–1,6	14,3	1,3	6,0	21.687
1994–1995	8,2	11,0	4,8	3,0	1,7	13,0	92,6	–1,0	17,9	1,5	8,4	25.186
1993–1994	8,1	9,6	4,1	3,0	1,0	12,2	96,7	–0,4	18,7	1,5	8,6	19.254
1992–1993	7,6	9,8	3,8	3,0	0,8	11,4	88,9	–1,4	3,0	0,2	4,9	9.832
1991–1992	6,8	7,8	3,5	2,9	0,6	10,3	95,9	–0,4	0,7	0,0	5,3	9.220
1990–1991	5,8	8,7	2,3	2,4	–0,1	8,1	72,8	–3,0	0,6	0,0	2,5	5.834
1980–1981	4,5	8,8	3,9	1,1	2,7	8,4	84,8	–1,5	0,0	0,0	5,0	6.823

Source: Own elaboration based on the *Handbook of Statistics on Indian Economy* (RBI)

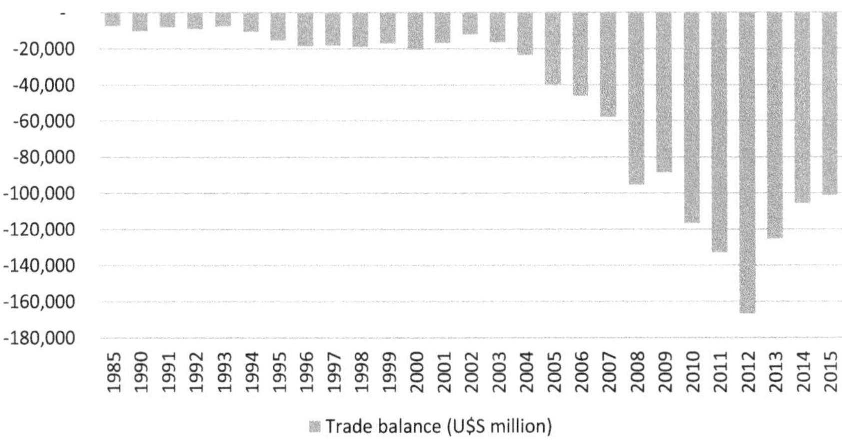

Figure 8.7 Trade balance, 1985–2015.

Source: World Bank database.

Indeed, Goldar et al. (2017) highlight that the import content in exports increased steadily in India from about 11% to about 22% between 1995 and 2011. The rise in import content was greater for merchandise exports, going from about 11% to 26% for the same period (in services exports, the foreign value-added content has been relatively low). At the domestic level, based on input-output classification, between 2003 and 2011, there has been an increase in foreign value-added share for a majority of the commodities, particularly for the case of communication equipment, electrical industry machinery, electronic equipment, motor vehicles, electrical wires and cables, other electrical equipment, and so on. These figures show that the global insertion post NEP has increased the penetration of foreign goods and equipment in the Indian productive structure, reducing the domestic content.

However, trade deficit has been more than compensated by net invisibles and capital inflows. Net invisibles reflect both a services exports boom and NRI remittances, as we will see later. International capital inflows have been a relevant and new feature of the Indian economy post 1990. According to United Nations Conference on Trade and Development (UNCTAD), FDI net inflows experienced a significant increase, going from $236 million in 1990 to a peak of almost $50 billion in 2008. In terms of GDP, FDI net inflows reached a maximum of almost 4% in 2008 (and around 10% of GDCF), but it averaged at 1.6% between 1990 and 2016. Thus, although they have been extremely relevant to the Indian external sector, FDI has not been a main driver of GDP and GDCF growth.

Table 8.11 Indian imports, 2010–2016 (millions US dollars)

Commodity/Year	*2010–2011*	*2011–2012*	*2012–2013*	*2013–2014*	*2014–2015*	*2015–2016*	*2016–2017*	*Average 2010–2016/ Total Imports*
Petroleum, crude and products	105.964	154.968	164.041	164.770	138.326	82.944	86.866	30%
Electronic goods	27.939	34.081	32.906	32.378	36.871	40.032	41.941	8%
Machinery, electrical and non-electrical	26.129	33.099	30.765	27.091	28.002	29.483	28.663	7%
Gold	40.547	56.320	53.695	27.477	34.453	31.693	27.490	9%
Pearls, precious and stones	33.830	28.040	22.637	23.849	22.565	20.066	23.849	6%
Transport equipment	14.901	18.725	21.289	19.324	18.403	18.251	21.224	4%
Organic and inorganic chemicals	13.464	16.718	16.787	17.464	18.562	16.549	16.578	4%
Coal, Coke and briquettes, etc.	9.804	17.444	17.008	16.385	17.812	13.641	15.715	4%
Artificial resins, plastic materials, etc.	7.855	8.835	9.990	10.456	12.057	11.772	11.961	2%
Iron and steel	14.599	18.255	17.701	12.659	16.314	14.963	11.690	4%
Vegetable oil	5.689	8.119	9.844	9.395	10.613	10.490	10.891	2%
Non-ferrous metals	6.539	8.407	9.038	8.857	10.748	9.713	9.872	2%
Metalliferous ores & other minerals	6.473	8.113	9.144	8.395	9.305	7.267	6.168	2%
Chemical materials and products	3.823	4.549	4.862	4.878	5.303	5.151	5.367	1%
Fertilisers, crude and manufactured	6.921	11.124	8.771	6.307	7.408	8.019	5.028	2%

Source: Own elaboration based on RBI

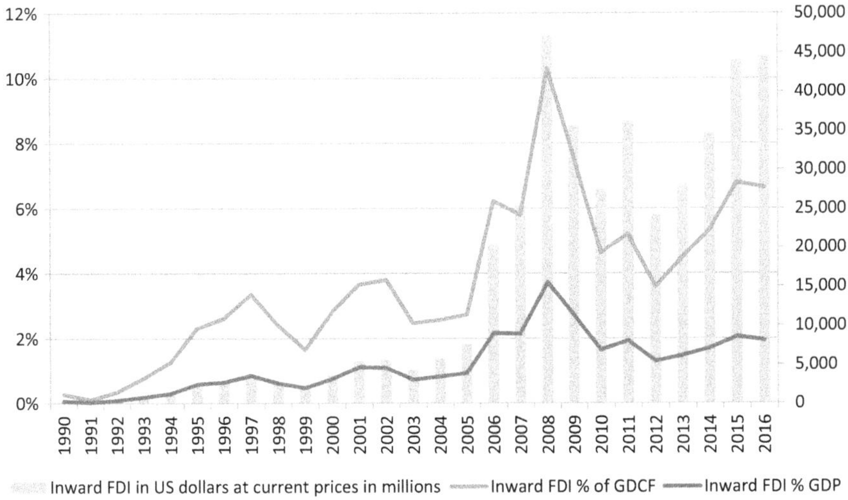

Figure 8.8 Inward direct investment flows, 1990–2016 (% of GDP, % of GDCF in millions US dollars).

Source: Own elaboration based on UNCTAD database.

In addition to an active intervention in the foreign exchange market to stabilise the rupee, there has been a clear hierarchy in the liberalisation of capital flows in India, with non-debt flows or equity flows preferred over debt flows. Gupta and Sengupta (2016, p. 106) say:

> Within equity flows, direct investments have been the preferred choice compared to portfolio investments, while within debt flows longer term and domestic currency denominated flows have been preferred over short-term and foreign currency denominated flows. This hierarchy has resulted in significantly modifying India's composition of external liabilities. While in the 1990s, almost 95% of India's foreign liabilities took the form of debt liabilities, by 2014 the share of debt liabilities had dropped to less than 50% . . . While many other economies such as China, Brazil, and South Korea have also experienced similar changes in the composition of external liabilities, the extent of reduction of debt liabilities in India, is significantly higher than the comparators . . . it is evident that the policymakers have been successful in altering the composition of flows.

Consequently, reserves show an impressive increase, going from $5 billion during the 1991 crisis to $369 billion in 2017. Thus, although the

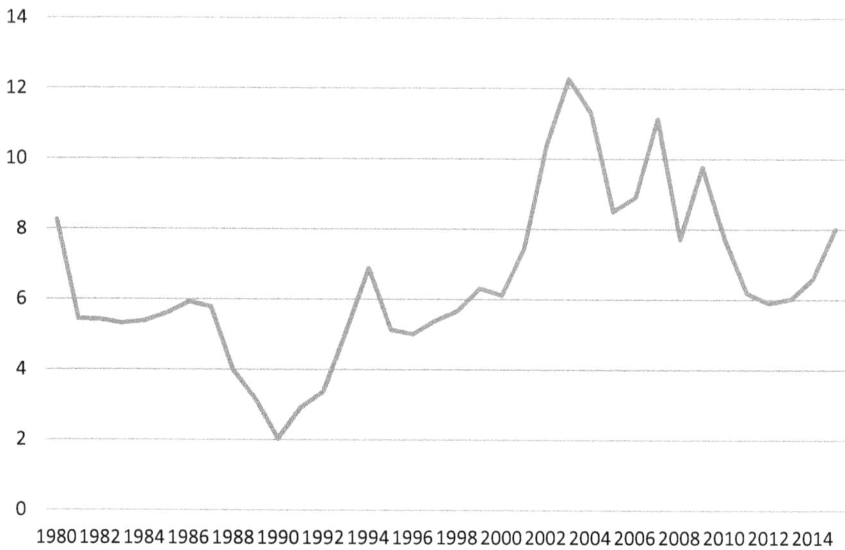

Figure 8.9 Indian reserves in months of imports, 1980–2014.

Source: World Bank database.

imports also increased, the total reserves in months of imports, after reaching a minimum of two months in 1990, recovered to a maximum of 12 months in 2013 and fell to 8 months in 2015.

Regarding the central government's external sustainability, most of the indicators have improved. External debt stock as the percentage of exports of goods and services has significantly reduced, going from more than 350% in 1991 to less than 100% since 2003. Debt service with the International Monetary Fund (IMF) as a percentage of exports of goods and services has also decreased from around 30% at the beginning of the 1990s to 3% since 2005.

We will now zoom in to two of the "new" and extremely relevant components of the Indian external sector, registered in the balance of payments as invisibles: remittances and service exports. Service exports have surpassed US$140 billion since 2010, remittances exceeded 60 billion, and FDI was estimated between 20 billion and 40 billion. Services and remittances are, by large, the two main components in terms of contribution to the external balance.

There is quite a unique and structural aspect of the Indian development path with relevant implications regarding the external sector sustainability: the Indian Diaspora, mainly in the US, UK, and the Middle East countries.

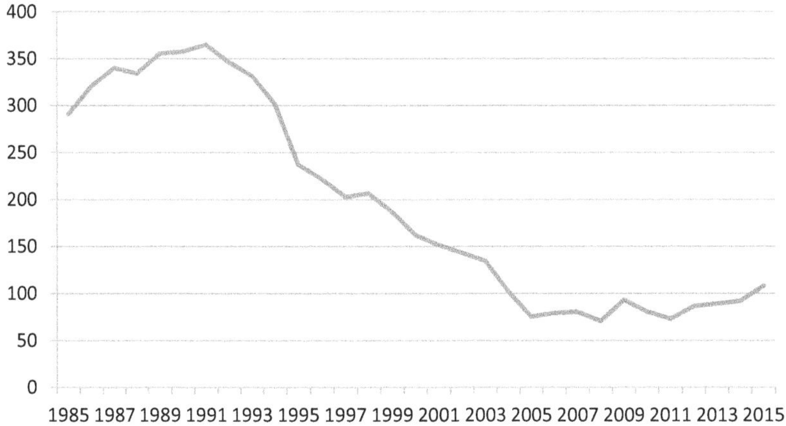

Figure 8.10 External debt stock of centre, % of exports of goods and services, 1985–2015.

Source: Own elaboration based on World Bank database.

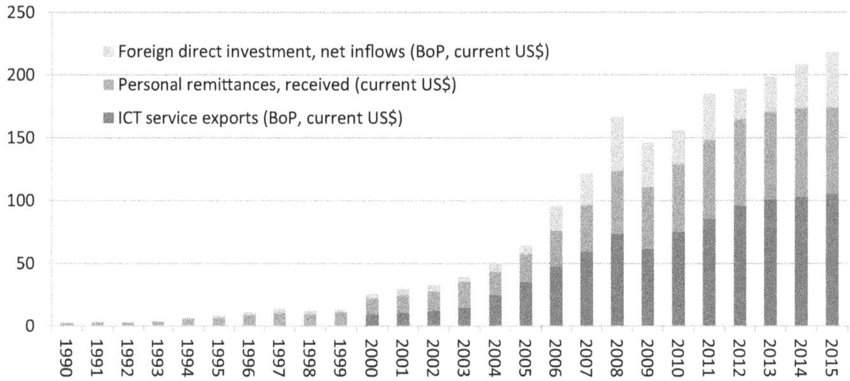

Figure 8.11 FDI, service exports, and personal remittances, 1990–2015 (billion US dollars).

Source: Own elaboration based on World Banka database. BoP, Balance of Payment.

In fact, both remittances and services exports are closely related to the NRI community. As can be seen next, since 2010, India is the first country in the world in terms of remittances inflows, reaching US$69 billion in 2016, surpassing China, Philippines, Mexico, and France, which were the top five countries. The Indian remittances have multiplied by 30 since 1990. In terms of GDP, they have passed from less than 1% at the end of the 1980s

Table 8.12 Top ten remittances countries, 1985–2016 (millions US dollars)

Migrant Remittance Inflows	*1985*	*1990*	*1995*	*2000*	*2005*	*2010*	*2015*	*2016*
India	2,472	2,382	6,224	12,845	22,125	53,480	68,910	62,744
China	271	124	350	758	23,626	52,460	63,938	61,000
Philippines	806	1,462	5,362	6,957	13,733	20,563	29,799	31,145
Mexico	1,619	3,096	4,365	7,522	22,742	22,080	26,233	28,670
France	1,391	4,034	4,636	8,610	14,212	19,903	23,766	24,373
Nigeria	10	10	804	1,390	14,640	19,745	21,060	20,112
Pakistan	2,540	2,010	1,710	1,080	4,280	9,690	19,306	19,761
Egypt, Arab Rep.	3,210	4,280	3,230	2,850	5,017	12,453	18,325	16,590
Germany	2,018	4,878	4,526	3,640	6,867	12,792	16,133	16,683
Vietnam	–	–	–	1,340	3,150	8,260	13,200	11,880

Source: World Bank Migration and Remittances data

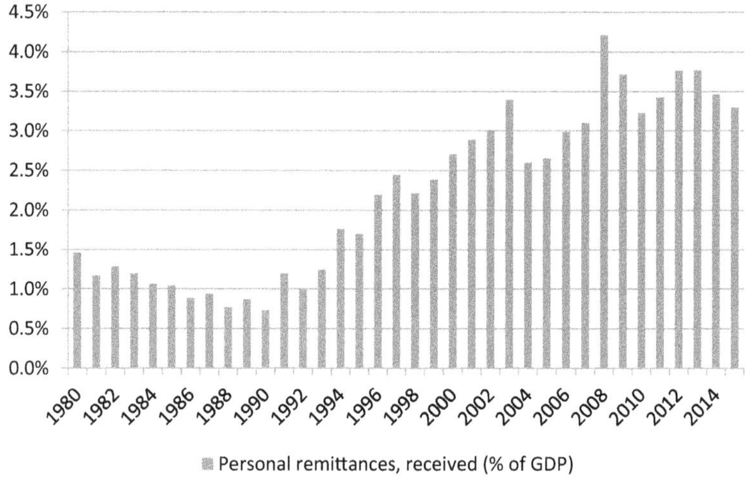

Figure 8.12 Personal remittances, 1980–2015.

Source: Own elaboration based on World Bank database.

and the beginning of 1990s to an average of 3.5% in the 2010s. Thus, they almost doubled the average of US dollars that entered India as FDI during the 2000s.

Remittances have two main regional origins: the Anglo-Saxon countries, mainly the US, the UK, and Canada; and the Middle East ones. The US represented 17% of the 2016 remittances, the UK 6%, and Canada 4%. The NRIs living in the oil-rich countries contributed with more than 60% of the remittances, led by the United Arab Emirates with 26% and Saudi Arabia with 16%.

Regarding the oil-rich countries' remittances, they are mainly related to the historical relationship between the West Indian coast, mainly the Malabar Coast, and the Middle East, which has strengthened since the 1970s. Indian workers have inserted themselves in the petroleum, construction, nursing, and intermediate qualification jobs. In fact, in some South Indian states such as Kerala, the Middle East remittances represent around a quarter of the state GDP, and, with a significant proportion invested in construction, it has functioned as an autonomous expenditure.

There have been some specific post-1990s initiatives that have stimulated the remittances inflows, such as removing the ten-year lock-in restriction to NRI deposits, the easing of the process of sending money for investment, some incentives to NRIs to invest in real estate, and so on (Jayaraman et al., 2012). In more general terms, by the late 1980s, the NRIs caught the attention of the Indian policymakers, and they gradually were reconceptualised as a potential source of knowledge, connections, and wealth (Gonzalo and Kantis, 2017; Dossani and Kenney, 2001).

Service exports are a main outstanding feature of the Indian economy in the past three decades. According to the World Bank data, service exports as a percentage of the total exports of goods and services went from 20% in 1990 to 36% in 2015, growing at an average annual rate of 15%. Particularly, ICT exports increased from 15% of total exports in 2000 to 25%

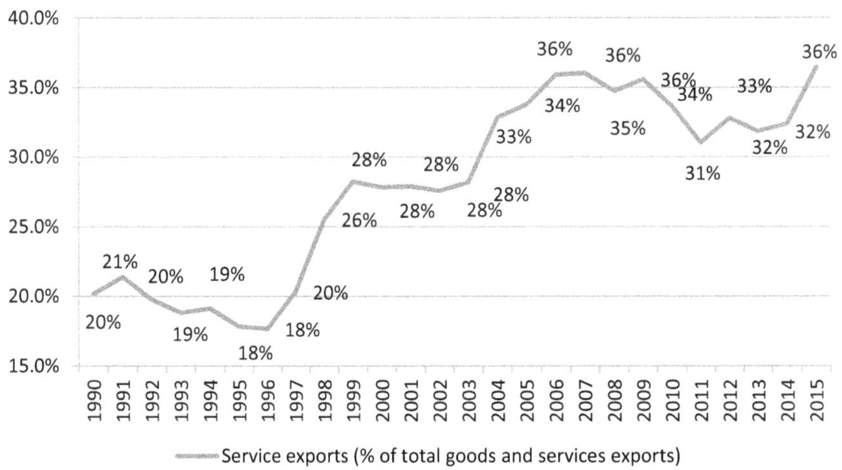

Figure 8.13 Services exports as % of total Indian exports, 1990–2015.

Source: Own elaboration based on World Bank.

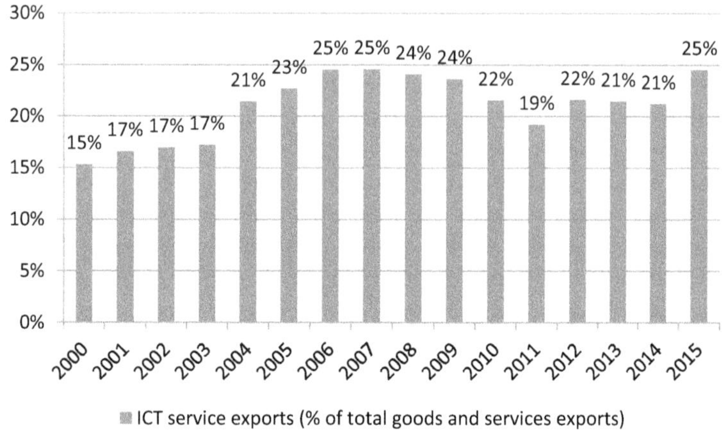

Figure 8.14 ICT exports as % of total exports, 2000–2015.

Source: Own elaboration based on World Bank.

in 2015, averaging an annual growth rate of almost 18%. In 2006, India surpassed Ireland as the first country in terms of Computer and Information Services (CIS) exports, with around 17% of the world market (Mani, 2014b).

Among the main reasons that explain the Indian ICT boom, we can enumerate[14] a) the process of outsourcing which deepened in the US since the 1980s and the role of the Indian Diaspora located in Silicon Valley in order to connect opportunities, wealth, and networks with India; b) the qualification and quantity of the Indian manpower, its timeline complementation with the US, its mastery of the English language, and its relative lower cost; c) the public policy oriented to support the ICT exports: different education programmes, fiscal incentives, the establishment of SEZs, and the financing of physical infrastructure through the development of software technology parks and telecommunication connections; d) the active involvement of the Indian industry association (NASSCOM) and of a new generation of entrepreneurs; e) Bengaluru's R&D and manpower accumulation based on the Indian Space Research Organisation (ISRO; space), Defence Research and Development Organisation (DRDO; defence), and several state-owned enterprises labs; and f) the establishing of the R&D centres and labs of various global firms such as HP, Oracle, IBM, Apple, Google, Microsoft, Intel, and so on.

The ICT sector has made some relevant contributions to the Indian economy. It generates US dollars, helping to diversify Indian profiled exports. More than half of the ICT revenues are generated by national firms, and, with almost 4 million jobs in 2017, it is the largest private-sector (formal) employer of India (NASSCOM, 2017).

At the same time, there are some limitations in the development path of the ICT sector. Its contribution has been much more relevant to exports than to GDP: in 2016, it contributed with 25% of the Indian exports and between 5% and 3%[15] of the Indian GDP. It is extremely concentrated in terms of sales, with around two-thirds of the exports going to the US, and in regional terms, mainly related to some specific cities of India, such as Bengaluru (D´Acosta, 2003; Joseph, 2014). Furthermore, although there are cases of success, explored, for instance, in Lee et al. (2013), the passage from outsourcing and service firms to the development of products and the construction of their own regional and global value chains is still a challenge. Finally, in parallel with the ICT exports growth, there has been an impressive increase of hardware imports, in line with the deterioration of the trade balance in goods of the Indian economy since 1990 (Chandrasekhar and Ghosh, 2017a, 2017b).

8.4 The "Indian" structural heterogeneity

In this last section, we will highlight some elements to give a general idea of the structural heterogeneity that still persists in India.[16] First, the Indian labour market. Of the total employment of India in 2011–2012, 52.2% were self-employed, 18% were regular workers, and 30% casual workers (Papola and Kannan, 2017). In 1993, self-employment was 55%, regular 13.1%, and casual 32%. For an economy that has grown about 6.5% per year in the last 20 years, to pass from 13% of regular workers to 18% is almost insignificant. Furthermore, in the rural areas, self-employment is even greater, representing 56% in 2011–2012, with only 9% of regular workers and 35.4% casual workers. Urban areas registered the major share of regular workers: 43.3%.

According to Chandrasekhar and Ghosh (2015), in 2004–2005, informal employment represented almost 85% of the total employment. In 2015, at an all India level, just 20.6% of workers, except self-employed, received paid leave, and only 21.6% availed of social security benefits, with 71.2% of workers not eligible for social security benefits (Unemployment Survey, 2015–2016). Besides, 64.9% of the regular wage workers, 67.8% of the contract workers, and 95.3% of the casual workers do not have a written job contract (only 27% of the regular wage workers and 11.5% of the contract workers had written job contracts of more than three years).

According to the Global Wage Report 2016/2017 (ILO, 2016a, 2016b), as we can observe in Figure 8.16, since 2006, average real wages increased by about 60% in India, more than double in China.

However, the wage share of the organised sector in gross value added has constantly declined in India since the 1980s. According to Abraham and Sasikumar (2017), the figures show that the wage share was 28.5% in 1980, 21.4% in 1990, 15.5% in 2000, and 11% in 2012. Kannan (2014) states

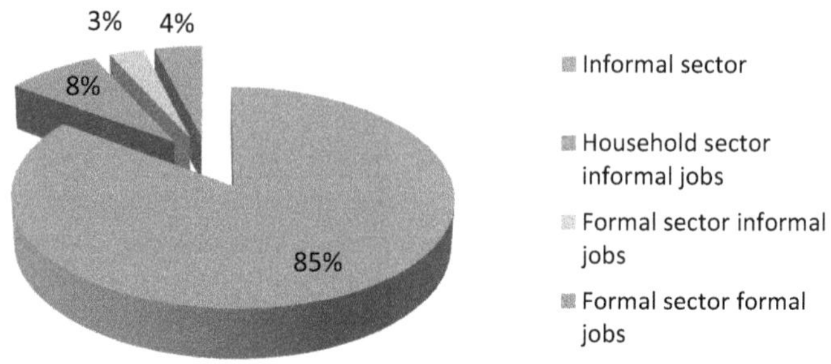

Figure 8.15 Distribution of employment, 2004–2005 (%).

Source: Own elaboration based on Chandrasekhar and Ghosh (2015).

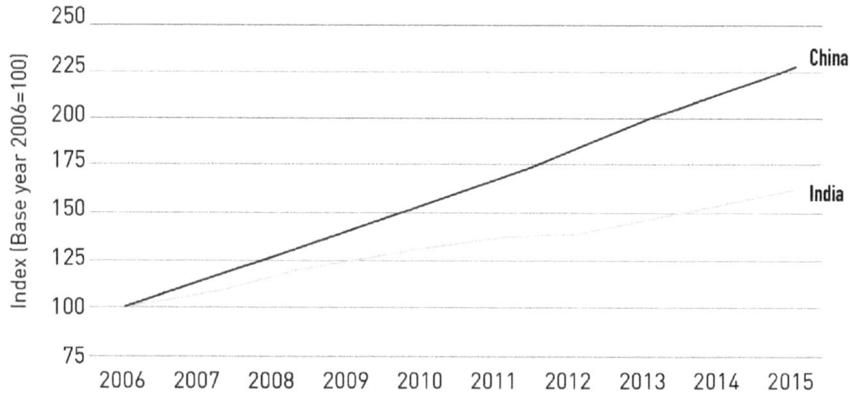

Figure 8.16 Average real wage index for emerging G20 countries, 2006–2015.

Source: Based on Global Wage Report 2016/2017 of the ILO (2016a, 2016b).

Note: Figures for 2015 are preliminary estimates as national estimates are not yet available for all countries.

that the wage share was 32% in 1981, 28.7% in 1993, dropping to 21% in 2004–2005. Chandrasekhar and Ghosh (2015) show a reduction of the share of compensation to employees from around 40% in the 1980s to 34% in the 2000s. Furthermore, Papola and Kannan (2017) claim that the post-NEP period witnessed a decline in the power of trade unions. In fact, the intervention of the state in the labour market, particularly in wage setting, except in government public sector, has been virtually absent.

Wage inequalities are also highlighted by the Global Wage Report 2016/2017 (ILO, 2016a, 2016b). The lowest-paid 50% receives 17.1% of all wages paid, and the top 1% earns about 33 times as much as the bottom 10%. Regarding gender, the ratio of women in the bottom two deciles is similar to that of Europe (about 60%) but plummets thereafter, and in the upper half of the distribution, women represent no more than 10–15% of wage earners. What is more, wage inequality measured as a Gini coefficient presented no changes between 1993 and 2011, with no equity improvements (Papola and Kannan, 2017).

Household consumption follows a similar trend. As we said in the previous chapter, the general picture described by many authors is one of an increase driven mainly by the urban upper-class/caste groups linked to the global economy, property, and the formal sector (Bhaduri, 2008a, 2008b, 2009; Chandrasekhar and Ghosh, 2015; Nagaraj, 2013b, 2015; Chancel and Piketty, 2017; Patnaik, 2009; Nayyar, 2017). Indeed, most of the figures related to income inequality show a trend of increasing concentration favouring the top segments of the Indian society.

For instance, in the Forbes India Rich Lists, the wealth of the richest Indians amounted to less than 2% of national income in the 1990s but increased substantially throughout the 2000s, reaching 10% in 2015 and a peak of 27% before the 2008–2009 financial crisis. According to Chancel and Piketty (2017), India recorded the highest increase in the share of the top 1% in national income over the past three decades, going from 6.2% in 1982–1983 to 21.7% in 2013–2014. Incomes of the top 10%, the top 1%, and the top 0.001% grew at rates of 394%, 750%, and 2,726%, respectively. Furthermore, India recorded the highest gap between the income growth of the top 1% and the growth rate of incomes of the full adult population, with the participation of the bottom 50% in total income decreasing from around 22% to around 15%.

All in all, despite the state having had a minor role in the determination of salary in urban India, the relevance of the state interventions was relevant to explain the increase in rural wages since the mid-2000s, as Papola and Kannan (2017, p. 46) explain:

> [G]rowth in wages during the second period (2000s) is seen as faster than during the first period. This is especially so for rural areas, primary sector and socially most disadvantaged groups. This is especially so for casual workers. Here it would be in order to record several national level state interventions in the form of programmes and schemes to improve the livelihood security of the rural poor . . . These are the National Rural Employment Scheme (NREGS) under the National Rural Employment Guarantee Act (NREGA), the National Rural Health Mission, the Sarva Shiksha Abhiyan (SSA) for improving the elementary education and the rural housing schemes of the central government (e.g. Indira Awas Yojana) and schemes by the state governments. All these put together must have helped in raising the consumption level as well as establishing a measure of social security that could have helped in raising

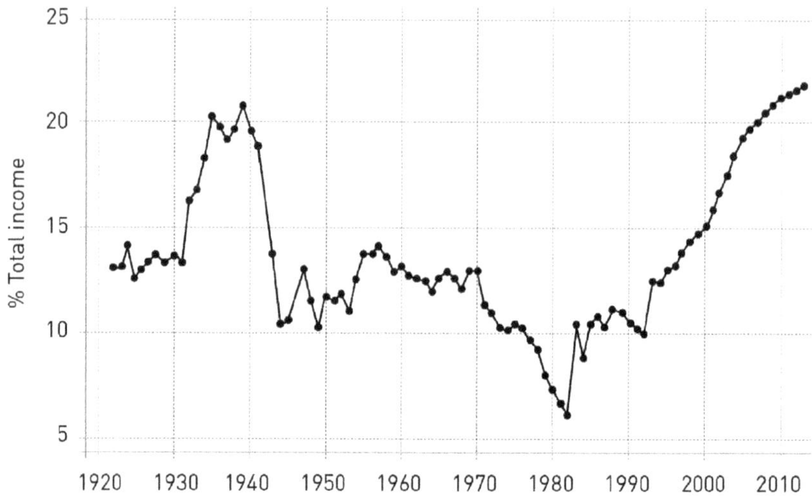

Figure 8.17 Top 1% income share in India, 1922–2014.

Source: Based on Chancel and Piketty (2017).

> the reserve price of labour. In addition, the accelerated growth in the economy increased the demand for labour in the construction sector in urban areas leading to increased migration of labour from the primary sector of the economy . . . the higher growth rate in the wages of rural casual workers could be interpreted as a result of the public intervention and expenditure in rural areas as well as the increased demand for unskilled casual workers leading to a higher reserve price of labour.

Major Employment Generation Schemes functioning in the mid-2010s in India

MGNREGA: enacted in 2005 to enhance livelihood security of households in rural areas of the country by providing at least 100 days of wage employment in a year to every household whose adult members volunteer to do unskilled manual work.

Prime Minister Employment Generation Programme (PMEGP): launched in 2008 to generate employment opportunities in rural as well as urban areas, by providing credit-linked subsidy for setting up of micro enterprises.

Swarnajayanti Gram Swarozgar Yojana (SGSY): came in to effect in 1999 to bring the rural BPL families above poverty line by organising them in to self-help groups (SHGs) to allow their training and capacity building by credit provision, technology inputs, and so on in order to enable them to be self-employed and take up some income-generating activity.

Major Employment Generation Schemes functioning in the mid-2010s in India
Swarna Jayanti Shahari Rozgar Yojana (SJSRY): implemented in 1997 for urban areas, it's a holistic scheme aiming to provide employment to the urban unemployed and underemployed poor population and to help them set up self-employment ventures, and also by providing wage employment using their labour for construction of useful public assets.

Source: Own elaboration.

According to Ghosh (2015), the MGNREGA was a historic legislation based on two goals: to ensure livelihood security to rural residents by providing at least 100 days of guaranteed wage employment in a year to every household whose adult members volunteer to do unskilled manual work and to use the programme to mobilise existing surplus labour in the countryside. The total spending on the programme amounted to 0.8% of GDP in 2009, which means almost 1% GDP of autonomous expenditure directed to the bottom layer of the Indian social structure (Ghosh, 2015). About a quarter of all Indian households benefited from employment-generating schemes like MGNREGA, PMEGP, SGSY, and SJSRY, with three poor north-eastern States, Tripura, Manipur, and Mizoram, accumulating more than 70% of the households benefited from MGNREGA (Report on Fifth Annual Employment – Unemployment Survey, 2015–2016).

Consequently, the daily wage in agriculture has more than tripled since 2006, both for women and men. In this sense, the MGNREGA, the main policy initiative of the United Progressive Alliance (UPA), produced a

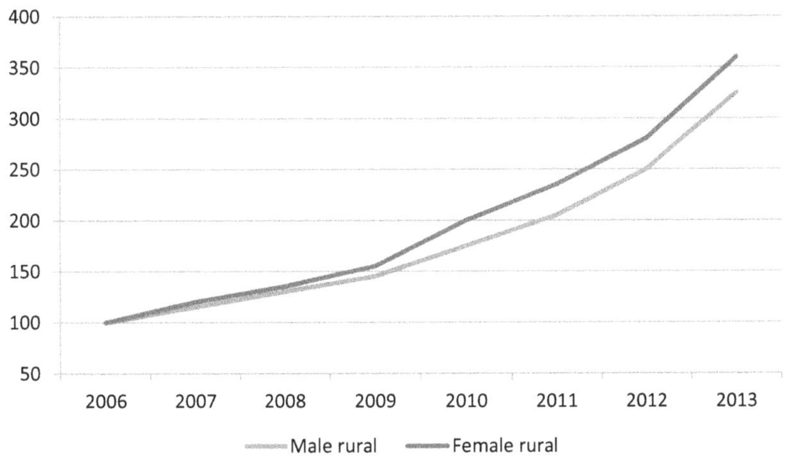

Figure 8.18 Average daily wage rates of male and female workers in agriculture, 2006–2013, Index 2006 = 100.

Source: India Labour Market Update (ILO, 2016a, 2016b).

Table 8.13 Rural-urban distribution of drinking water facilities (Census data 2011)

Drinking Water Characteristics	*Total*	*Rural*	*Urban*
Within the premises	46.6	35.0	71.2
Near the premises	35.8	42.9	20.7
Away	17.6	22.1	8.1
Total	100.0	100.0	100.0
Tap water	43.5	30.8	70.6
Tap water from treated source	32.0	17.9	62.0
Tap water from un-treated source	11.6	13.0	8.6
Well	11.0	13.3	6.2
Covered well	1.6	1.5	1.7
Uncovered well	9.4	11.8	4.5
Tube well/Borehole	8.5	8.3	8.9
Hand pump	33.5	43.6	11.9
Spring	0.5	0.7	0.2
Tank/Pond/Lake	0.8	1.1	0.4
Other sources	2.2	2.2	1.8
Total	100.0	100.0	100.0

Source: Own elaboration based on MOSPI.

substantial impact on rural employment and rural wages, stabilising the rural wage floor and providing a better bargaining situation for rural workers (Thomas, 2015; Papola and Kannan, 2017; Chandrasekhar and Ghosh, 2015; Nagaraj, 2017a; Ghosh, 2015).

All in all, the urban-rural gap is another main source of inequalities in India. For instance, according to the Census of 2011 (the most recent one), while 71.2% of urban India's population had access to drinking water within their premises, only 35% of rural people had the same. And even worse, 22% of rural population had to travel a significant distance to have access to drinking water.

Only 30% of rural India had access to a latrine facility within premises in 2011, with 67.3% of rural India using open spaces as a toilet.[17] In international terms, according to World Bank data, although India has evolved from a rate of around 6% of rural people using basic sanitation in 1991 to 29% in 2011, it still shows the worst indicators compared with the other BRICS countries.

At the same time, the Indian urbanisation process is not exempt from urban bottlenecks. Between 2001 and 2011, urban population living in slums grew from 55.8 million to 80.8 million, meaning an increase of 45%.

In regional terms, there are still significant asymmetries between the Indian states. For example, regarding the population living below the poverty line,[18] southern states such as Goa, Kerala, Tamil Nadu, and Puducherry (Union Territory) have the best figures, being below 7%, but the poorest states such as Bihar, Uttar Pradesh, and Jharkhand, among others, are above 25%.

Table 8.14 Rural-urban distribution of toilet facilities in India (Census data 2011)

Type of Toilet	*Total*	*Rural*	*Urban*
Latrine facility within premises	**46.9**	**30.7**	**81.4**
Water closet	36.4	19.4	72.6
Piped sewer system	11.9	2.2	32.7
Septic tank	22.2	14.7	38.2
Other systems	2.3	2.5	1.7
Pit latrine	9.4	10.5	7.1
Other latrines	1.1	0.8	1.7
No latrine within the premises	**53.1**	**69.3**	**18.6**
Public latrine	3.2	1.9	6.0
Open	49.8	67.3	12.6
Total	**100.0**	**100.0**	**100.0**

Source: Own elaboration based on MOSPI.

Table 8.15 People living in urban slums (Census data 2001–2011)

Urban Slum All Towns	*2001*	*2011*	*Absolute Change*	*%*
	55,832,570	80,888,766	25,056,196	44.9

Source: Own elaboration based on MOSPI.

Table 8.16 Life expectancy at birth. India, the continents, and the world, 2000–2015

Life Expectancy at Birth	*India*	*Asia*	*Africa*	*Europe*	*Latin American and Caribbean*	*North America*	*Oceania*	*World*
2000–2005	63.1	68.8	52.9	73.8	72.1	77.4	75.3	67.1
2005–2010	64.9	70.3	55.6	75.3	73.5	78.4	76.8	68.7
2010–2015	66.3	71.4	58.2	76.1	74.7	79.1	77.6	70.0

Source: Own elaboration based on MOSPI.

Finally, regarding human development indicators, we can observe that life expectancy (male, female, or both?) has improved, going from 63.1 years for 2000–2005 to 66.3 years for 2010–2015. However, it is still below the Asian average and of all the other continents' indicators, with the only exception of Africa. In particular, the figures of infant mortality (less than one year), although improving in the last decades, are still huge in India. In 1985, infant mortality totalised more than 2.5 million, and in 2016, it dropped to around 900,000, being, by large, the highest in comparison with the BRICS countries, Indonesia and South Korea.

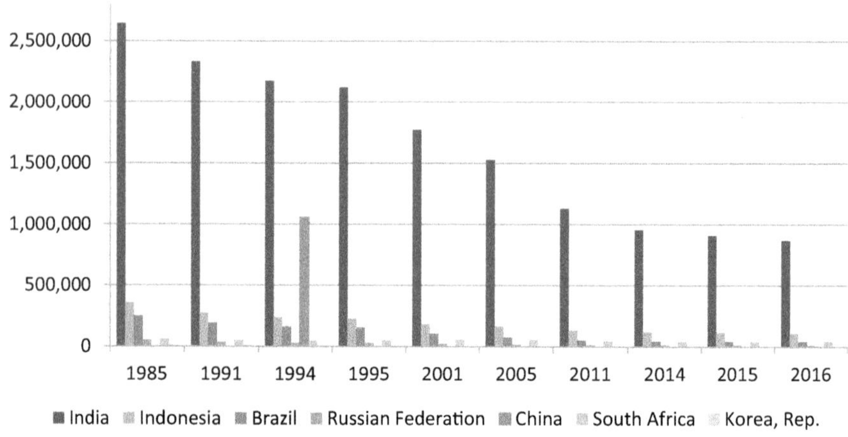

Figure 8.19 Number of infants dying before reaching one year of age, 1985–2016, India, Indonesia, China, Russia, Brazil, South Africa, and South Korea.

Source: Own elaboration based on MOSPI.

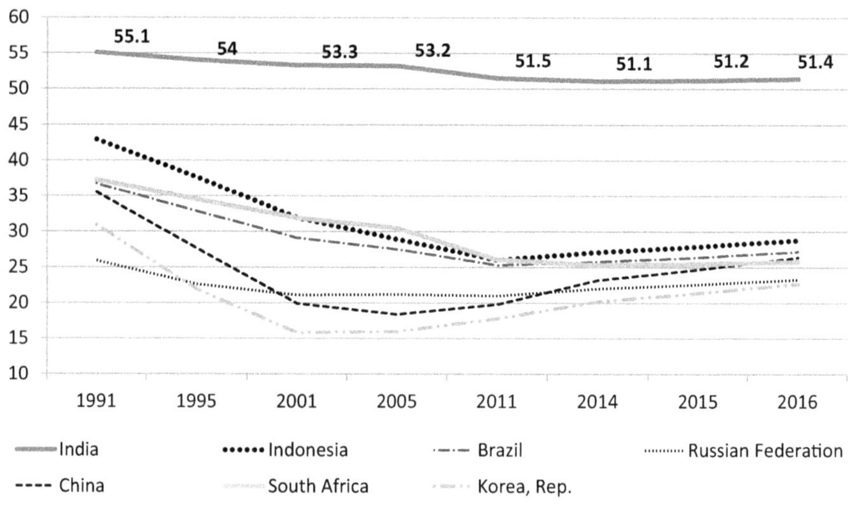

Figure 8.20 Anaemia in women of reproductive age (15–49), India, Indonesia, China, Brazil, South Africa, Russia, and Korea (%).

Source: Own elaboration based on World Bank database.

There are strong asymmetries related to Indian women indicators too. For instance, if we compare the rate of anaemia in women between 15 and 49 years old, India, with around 50%, doubles the indicators of the rest of the BRICS countries, South Korea, and Indonesia.

Notes

1 It is estimated that India will overtake China and will become the most populated country before 2030 (Kulkarni, 2014). Some regions, lagging in demographic transition, mainly the north-central states, would double their populations during the next 50 years, creating huge regional growth imbalances with varied sociopolitical consequences.

2 There are marked internal heterogeneities between the Indian states. For instance, according to the Ministry of Statistics and Programme Implementation's (MOSPI) data, in 2001, Delhi presented an urbanisation ratio of 97.5% and Chandigarh 97.25%, but Meghalaya, Uttar Pradesh, and Rajasthan registered ratios of only 20%, 22%, and 25%, respectively.

3 A pucca construction includes a varying combinations of cement, concrete, oven-burnt bricks and/or hollow cement/ash bricks, stone and/or stone blocks, jack boards, iron, zinc, or other metal sheets, timber, tiles, corrugated iron, asbestos cement sheet, plywood, artificial wood of synthetic material, and PVC material. A kutcha house is made up of wood, mud, straw, and dry leaves. A hut is a kutcha house. A semi-pucca house is one in which at least one basic component, either roof or walls, is made with pucca materials.

4 Quoted in Pardesi and Ganguly (2009).

5 Several studies discussed the Indian energy transition. Among them, we could mention the works of Mishra and Kumar (2012) and Tranum (2013).

6 Infrastructure figures include electricity (including renewable energy), roads and bridges, telecommunications, railways, irrigation, water supply, ports, airports, storage, and oil and gas pipelines.

7 See the Report on India's Renewable Electricity Roadmap 2030 (2015) for further details.

8 The figures for 2007 to 2012 are confirmed; the ones for 2012–2017 are estimated in the Twelfth Five-Year Plan (2012–2017).

9 According to the official web page of the Department of Economic Affairs on PPPs (www.pppinindia.gov.in/), PPPs are defined as infrastructure projects owned, developed, and implemented jointly by the government and private sector, through a partnership arrangement. PPP means an arrangement between government or statutory entity or government-owned entity, on one side, and a private-sector entity, on the other, for the provision of public assets and/or related services for public benefit, through investments being made by and/or management undertaken by the private-sector entity for a specified period of time. Government infrastructure projects (traditional procurement) are defined as infrastructure projects owned, developed, and implemented by the government. Private-sector infrastructure projects are infrastructure projects implemented by the private sector.

10 The privatisation framework for the Indian case can be read in the World Bank reports (1990), Bhagwati and Srinivasan (1993), and Bhandari and Goswami (2000), among others.

11 According to Nagaraj (2008), a corruption scandal with the stockbroker Harshad Mehta led to a slowdown in the Indian stock market, which remained depressed until the mid-1990s, critically discouraging the CPSEs' sales in the stock market.

12 A government company is defined as any company in which not less than 51% of the share capital is held by the central government, or by any state government or governments, or partly by the central government and partly by one or more state governments, and includes a company which is a subsidiary company of such a government company. The Public Enterprises Survey covers those

government companies wherein more than 50% equity is held by the central government. The survey does not cover departmentally run public enterprises, banking institutions, and insurance companies. Finally, there are several public-sector enterprises that belong to the state level. Although quite relevant, these enterprises are not included here given the data restrictions.

13 These numbers include the CPSEs under construction which are being launched but still not in the market.

14 Several authors studied the Indian ICT boom and its causes. Among others, we can highlight the works of Mani (2009, 2014a, 2014b), Joseph and Harilal (2001), Joseph (2002, 2011, 2014), Parthasarathy (2004a, 2004b), Lee et al. (2013), Krishnan et al. (2009), Chandrasekhar and Ghosh (2017a), D'Acosta (2003), and Bala Subrahmanya (2016, 2015). In Gonzalo and Cassiolato (2017, 2016) and Gonzalo and Kantis (2017), we have also pointed out some main elements.

15 There are different discussions around the software contribution to the GDP. We adopted Joseph (2014) and NASSCOM data.

16 This is not an exhaustive study of the Indian structural heterogeneity but a snapshot on some aspects. For a deeper discussion and facts, see, for instance, Drèze and Sen (2013).

17 As stressed by Joseph and Abrol (2009), the digital divide in terms of the use of internet and mobiles between rural and urban population is another strong asymmetry of the recent times.

18 This poverty line indicator is the one provided by the GoI, published by RBI.

9

BELINDIA'S GROWTH ACCELERATION

An important consequence of the acceptance of the secular stagnation thesis is the damage it brings to the understanding of the current dynamics of capitalism in the largest economies in the region (Latin America). The certainty that capitalism does not advance or that, very soon, will stop doing so, leads to the lack of interest in the analysis about how it operates and expands, which would be essential as a starting point for all those who propose to promote or accelerate its replacement.

Tavares and Serra (1971, p. 594)

The root of the whole matter lies in the anomalies previously identified, mainly disproportionate metropolisation and spurious tertiarization. In the last analysis, these interrelated phenomena nurture structural heterogeneity, which is associated with, and reinforced by, disproportions of equal or greater depth in social production relations (including the ownership of assets) and the power system . . . Ultimately, income distribution is determined by these conditions, which in turn are reproduced and sustained by income distribution itself, in a vicious circle of reciprocal and cumulative interactions.

Pinto (1984, p. 23)

We will argue that the developmental economy only managed to free itself from this type of vision when the economists who founded the UNICAMP school started to analyse the developing economies as a certain type of capitalist economy, using the theory with which Kalecki analysed the developed economies, instead of thinking of peripheral economies as if they were planned economies. Only then was it possible to realise the importance that the expansion of unproductive spending as a stimulus (and not as impediment) to accumulation has in fact had on capitalism in general and historically on the expansion of the domestic market in developing countries with unequal income distribution like Brazil.

Serrano (2001, p. 4)

DOI: 10.4324/9781003091752-13

During the last three decades, India has been experiencing deep transformations. A huge rural/urban migration and increasing housing and real estate expenditure have been happening. Meanwhile, a small but dynamic segment of the Indian society is deepening its global insertion and adopting cosmopolitan lifestyles and consumption trends. The Indian Diaspora, well inserted in Silicon Valley, is having a unique role mediating its relationship with the US. Infrastructure demands (mainly in the energy and transport sectors) are being prioritised over the past industrial preferences. Global capital flows are entering India. An important military modernisation effort has been undertaken given the Indian Ocean geopolitical context and so on. In the last two chapters, we have mainly presented the Indian geopolitical and political contexts from the 1990s to mid-2010s, focusing on the growth process, its main structural growth drivers, and some main socio-economic indicators introduced under the concept of structural heterogeneity.

In general terms, any analysis of the Indian path of development since the 1990s should be framed in the context of the downfall to the USSR, the re-emergence of China as a global economic superpower, and the external and internal pro-liberalisation pressures. The Indian external crisis of 1990 was the event that gave space to the gravitation of a much more market-led, export-led, and pro-efficiency agenda in the country, in parallel to the consolidation of the US global hegemony during the 1990s, materialised in the spread of the Washington Consensus framework all around the world. In the domestic front, the "liberalisation consensus" has been growing since the 1980s, including a broad spectrum of actors such as the national business community, liberal economists, policymakers, and political groups, both in the Congress and BJP parties. Clearly, the multilateral organisations have also made their contribution to the liberalising agenda.

Among the post-1990s new features, it is a fact that external trade has had much more relevance in India. Despite several sectors of the Indian economy such as agriculture, automotive, defence, and so on that are still under different types of protections-restrictions, the country has gradually opened to foreign trade: the ratio of exports plus imports over gross domestic product (GDP) has gone from 15% in 1990 to more than 40% in the 2010s, with imports growing more than exports. Imports have been mainly of energy products, capital goods, and other intermediate goods and supplies. China has increased its participation in the Indian imports. Exports have risen predominantly in the service-led sector, with the US and the UK as main markets. In this context, the increasing trade deficit, particularly in the case of manufactured goods with China, in addition to a reduction of the supermultiplier, could represent a potential economic and geopolitical vulnerability to India.

Another important new feature of the Indian economy is the relevance of the capital account to finance trade deficits, articulating capital inflows with an active policy of reserve accumulation led by the Reserve Bank of India

(RBI), improving most of the external sustainability indicators.[1] "Invisibles", mainly services exports and remittances, have significantly contributed to finance trade deficits. These flows are related to a foreign policy approximation and unique economic complementation between India and the US and some other Western economies than to an abstract idea of liberalisation.

The downfall of the USSR and China's re-emergence have driven India to look for a closer alignment with the US and the North Atlantic Treaty Organization (NATO) countries (Israel is another post-1990s emergent military and technological partner), in order to balance China's power. India's relationship with the US has mainly been fostered by mutual defence and nuclear cooperation and by the business community related to defence, IT, real estate, and finance, with a relevant and increasing role of the Indian Americans and the Indian Diaspora in the Indian domestic politics. In this context, the economic and political relevance of the Indian private sector, mainly the Indian national business groups, has grown, including joint ventures with foreign business groups, showing the relevant entrepreneurial and productive capabilities accumulated during the past decades in industries such as software, automotive, biotech, pharma, telecommunications, defence, steel, and so on (Nayyar, 2017). Thus, in parallel with the Indian business community, multinational firms, mainly, but not only, from the US, have also gained visible presence in India since the 1990s.

That said, the liberalisation agenda has had several nuances, intermediate agreements, and political restrictions, preventing us from saying that the neoliberal agenda has fully spread in India. In Herrera's (1973) terms, we could say that despite the formal implementation of some explicit neoliberal policies, the Indian implicit policies have tended to act as a barrier that still preserve the role of the Indian state in the Indian economy. For instance, although government expenditure was not the main growth driver during the period under analysis, we cannot say that after more than 25 years of the New Economic Policy (NEP) implementation, government expenditure has declined. On the contrary, it reached a peak of almost 30% of GDP in 2015 and functioned as an anti-cyclical instrument whenever the Indian economy was slowing down, such as in the events of 1996 and 2007.

Instead of a reduction of the state participation in the Indian economy, there has been a change in its role. Mainly, the state has shifted from focusing on the direct industrial production towards a greater involvement in infrastructure development and financing and social transfer programmes. Still, Central Public Sector Enterprises (CPSEs) are fundamental players in the Indian growth dynamic and capability building. The disinvestment process and the emergence of Public Private Partnerships (PPPs) in the energy sector are a good example. The improvements in the process of privatisations have been limited, with the Indian business groups as the main beneficiaries. PPPs have emerged as a second-best option to privatisation in order to mobilise private investment in infrastructure, assuring minimum levels of profitability and demand. Even more, public procurement is still the main instrument to mobilise infrastructure.

The role of massive state programmes in India has been central in several areas, and, since the 1980s, government-led technology missions have been the main instruments to achieve collective objectives and to confront technological and productive challenges. A transference programme, the Mahatma Gandhi National Rural Employment Guarantee Act (MGNREGA), the main rural employment programme in India (and in the world), has been the primary cause of the increase in rural wages since the mid-2000s, working as an authentic autonomous expenditure in rural India, impacting not only employment but also consumption patterns, construction and housing techniques, and so on. The electrification programmes, despite their heterogeneity and implementation issues, also meant the arrival of modern capitalism to rural India (around 800 million people!), with close links and benefits for the private sector in terms of new consumers for durable goods, home appliances, and so on. The electrification of rural India necessarily implies an increase in the productivity levels for the whole country through improvements in agriculture yields. Finally, regarding the housing programmes, it is needless to mention the impact they have had in terms of GDP multiplier effect, employment, indirect industrial demand, and so on.

Focusing on the Indian GDP growth acceleration, we have seen that the 1990s average growth rate was not dissimilar to the 1980s one, pointing out that the main growth acceleration occurred since the 2000s (and in the 1980s).[2] With growth acceleration arriving a decade after the NEP's implementation, this casts some doubts on the relationship between the NEP policymaking and the Indian spectacular growth process. In our demand-led insight, to explain growth acceleration mainly since the 2000s, we have to emphasise that autonomous private consumption has had a main role, being driven by the upper-class/caste autonomous consumption, the slow but steady salary increases, and the credit boom (oriented both to upper-class/caste "sumptuous consumption" and to the financial inclusion of rural population). In this sense, despite the deteriorating general context of the labour market indicators, as said, the MGNREGA has functioned as a main autonomous expenditure during the 2000s with about 1% of the GDP determining a minimum level for rural real wages.[3]

Gross domestic capital formation (GDCF) has also shown a spectacular performance, going from an average of 25% of GDP during the 1990s to 35% since the 2000s. Private investment, particularly in manufacturing, has been mainly an answer to the growing final demand stimulus through the accelerator mechanism. But mainly, the role of semi-autonomous investments, such as household investment in housing, construction and real estate, PPPs (mostly financed by public credit), and autonomous public investment, has significantly contributed to the GDCF increase. The urbanisation process and the energy challenge, fuelled by the credit boom and global capital inflows, have worked as a main growth driver for real estate, construction, and infrastructure expenditure, both private and public (the Indian government have assured a minimum of 8% contribution to GDCF and 4% in infrastructure, creating, in addition, the financing conditions to PPPs).[4] At the same time, rural construction has also fuelled growth, including a structural change in the type of houses and building techniques, going from kutcha to pucca houses (from wood and mud to brick and cement).

The particular Indian global insertion, based on services exports mainly to the US and the UK, and the opening of the growing domestic market to multinational firms and private equity funds have contributed in terms of exports growth and access to capital inflows to finance the deficit of the Indian current account, dislocating the Indian economy external restriction. As highlighted by Serrano and Medeiros (2004), the key to understand the capital accumulation process in developing countries is the study of the complex interaction, in each historical period, between international trade and the economic financial environment, the associated geopolitical situation (crucial to understand access to markets and finance), and the development policies of each state. In the Indian case, the geopolitical approximation and economic complementation with the West, particularly with the US, have been of main relevance to overcome the balance of payments growth bottleneck.

However, the Indian spectacular growth process does not mean that inequality has been reduced. On the contrary, it has increased significantly. As has been correctly pointed out by some (neo)Marxist authors such as Ghosh, Chandrasekhar, and Patnaik, among others, the wage share of the Indian economy has significantly decreased since the 1990s (implying a reduction in the size of the supermultiplier). The different indicators introduced in the last chapter reveals that the "Latin American" structural heterogeneity concept totally fits with the contemporary Indian social and productive landscapes (Pinto, 1970, 1972). Indeed, despite the improvement in some socio-economic indicators in the past decades, India is still an underdeveloped country with marked productive, social, and infrastructural deficits. This means a growing income concentration, informality and uberisation of the labour market, urban-rural gaps, digital divide, slum growth, disparity between rich and poor states, blatant gender issues, and so on. These facts show that, first, although growth is a necessary condition for development, it is not enough on its own, and second, that neither state nor market could resolve some basic concerns for the Indian people.

In the mid-1970s, the Brazilian economist Bacha (1974) published a paper titled "The Economist and the King of Belindia: A Fable for Technocrats" describing a hypothetical kingdom called Belindia situated between the West and the East. This name had to do with the original colonisation nature of the kingdom, where the people brought from India admired aromatic essences that were sold in foreign markets by Belgian merchants. This hypothetical kingdom was later used to illustrate the cohabitation in Brazil of both a dynamic segment of the society, similar in wealth, lifestyle, and productivity levels to Belgium, and a vast subsistence segment of the Brazilian society, living in similar conditions to India's poorest population.[5]

The post-1990s Indian growth acceleration has similar features to the Brazilian high-growth process during the so-called miracle, mainly during the 1970s. In this respect, the debate between Tavares and Serra (1971) (originating the subsequent Kaleckian contributions of the Brazilian University of Campinas (UNICAMP) scholars) and Furtado's (1966) stagnationist models of the 1960s is extremely useful to give an insight into the Indian post-1990s growth understanding.

In short, Furtado (1966) affirmed that in peripheral economies such as the Latin American ones, but particularly in Brazil, between the 1930s and the 1960s, the industrialisation by import substitution model based on the domestic market was limited by an increasing regressive income distribution, given that the abundance of labour limited the increase in wages. This structural regressive income distribution (which, in turn, generates a regressive demand profile) was reinforced by the incorporation of labour-saving technical changes originated in foreign countries (with a totally different labour market to the abundant-in-labour Latin American one) ending in a stagnant growth model, given the saturation of the high-income (upper-class) markets and consumptions. Indeed, the Latin American upper-class import-intensive conspicuous consumption, replicating global elite's consumption patterns, competed for resources for investment, increasing the capital-to-output ratio, reducing profits, savings, and, finally, growth (Scherer, 2007).

Tavares and Serra (1971, p. 593) began their paper highlighting that in some neoclassical and Marxist stagnation approaches, "the size of the market depended more on the number of people who are part of it than on the magnitude of the economic interchangeable surplus". Then, without neglecting the Latin American Brazilian regressive growth model described by Furtado (1966), they criticised the relevance given by him to the capital-to-output ratio as a limit to growth. For Tavares and Serra, the capital-to-output ratio was an endogenous result of the accumulation process but not an independent variable or a technical or a fix relation. To them, to understand the capital-to-output relation as the main limit to growth dressed Furtado in the straitjacket of a neoclassical model.[6]

Instead, from a "fully" demand-side perspective, to Tavares and Serra, the main limit to growth was not related to the profit-saving-investment relation but to the conditions of realisation of the capitalist investment (and its financing). In Brazil, the limits to the industrialisation by import substitution growth model were more related to the reduction of the investment rate than to the capital-to-output relation. And this limit could be removed, not only by a reduction of the elite conspicuous consumption or an increase in salaries but also by an increase in government expenditure/investment, for instance, in infrastructure.

This debate around the Brazilian stagnation between Furtado and Tavares and Serra was of key relevance to the Latin American economic thinking related to development, growth, and income distribution (Scherer, 2007; Serrano, 2016; Bastos and D'Avila, 2007; among others). On one hand, implicitly assuming Say's law (savings determining investments), Furtado understood, in a similar line to Lewis (1969, 1972) but with different results, that a change in income distribution, meaning a relative increase in salaries, was necessary to overcome the Latin American stagnation. On the other hand, Tavares and Serra were opening the door to an autonomous expenditure, the government one (but also the upper-class autonomous consumption), as a source for the "realisation" of the production. In this sense, it was not savings that limited the Brazilian growth but expenditure (and, we could add, US dollars!). Thus, Serra and Tavares were disconnecting growth from income distribution in the Latin American growth modelling – a theoretical path that was later further explored in the Latin American Sraffian growth models (Serrano, 1995; Serrano and Freitas, 2017).

In historical terms, the Brazilian stagnation was "solved" by the military governments, by reinforcing wages repression to finance capitalist investments (and contain inflation) and by securing the realisation of the conglomerate private-sector investments by government expenditure, mainly in infrastructure, and by stimulating the upper-class consumption of intermediate and durable goods by credit. In political terms, the Brazilian 1970s high-growth model was based on the "triple alliance": an implicit arrangement between the military government (with the state-owned enterprises as its main economic arm), the multinational corporations, and the domestic national groups (Cardoso and Faletto, 1967; Evans, 1979, 1982; Vernengo, 2006). This concentrated and exclusive growth model was fuelled, as said, by the government's autonomous expenditure and public-sector financing of the national and multinational big businesses and upper-class autonomous expenditure (Rodríguez, 2006; Serrano, 2001; Bastos and D'Avila, 2007).

In India, after more than 25 years of the NEP implementation, the high-growth model has been fuelled by a regressive income distribution that has stimulated upper-caste/class autonomous consumption, direct government expenditure and financing of PPPs and private investment in infrastructure, and exports (a unique service-led aspect of the Indian economy). The Indian business groups, the multinational firms, and the government (upper segments of the bureaucracy and the main political parties) are the main components of the post-1990s Indian "triplé". Thus, GDP has boomed, inequality has soared, and the US has contributed to finance the external sector, such as in the Brazilian miracle but in (Bel)India.

Notes

1 As we have seen in the previous chapter, foreign exchange reserves experienced an impressive increase, reaching 370 billion in 2016–2017. The external liabilities of the centre as a percentage of GDP, the external debt stock as a percentage of exports of goods and services, and debt service with the International Monetary Fund (IMF) as a percentage of exports of goods and services have improved.
2 In line with Rakshit (2009) and Nell (2012), further research should be conducted to understand the Indian growth acceleration with the 1980s and the 2000s as key decades.
3 Further research should be conducted on the role of government expenditure, particularly transferences, in the Indian growth acceleration (we had data limitations to build long-term series of transferences).
4 This is another evidence that, despite the neoliberal rhetoric, the explicit and implicit arrangements between the Indian bureaucracy and the Indian national business groups have functioned as a way to mobilise autonomous and semi-autonomous investments.
5 This metaphor was latter formalised as a growth model in Taylor and Bacha (1976) and Taylor (1979).
6 Tavares and Serra (1971, p. 600) say:

> [W]hen considering that profit rates for different industries would tend to equalize in the same way as wages, by separating the intensified use of capital of the penetration of technical progress and, moreover, not considering its effects on investment productivity or the effects of different types of external economies, Furtado seems to have dressed – even inadvertently – "the straitjacket" of a neoclassical model, elegant but ineffective to explain the dynamics of a capitalist economy.

FINAL REMARKS

The main objective of this book has been to present a long-term narrative of the Indian path of development from a Latin American perspective, paying special attention to the (geo)political, technological, financial, and institutional aspects related to the specific geographical and demographical features of the Indian subcontinent. In this sense, we understand that the main contributions of the book are a) to present a long-term narrative of the Indian path of development introducing some novel insights and reflections based on the Latin American experience and authors; b) to systematise a substantial amount of authors, literature, and data regarding the Indian economic, productive, technological, and social structures; and c) to discuss the Indian development path integrating the work of several Indian and South Asian scholars, establishing an initial dialogue on economic development with some relevant Latin American counterparts. Indeed, we hope to contribute towards the development of a common economics development research agenda oriented to the Global South needs and economic development potentialities and challenges.

In methodological terms, inspired by long-term perspectives and authors, following the Economic Commission for Latin America's (ECLAC) historical-structuralism, and in line with Chaudhury's Braudelian masterpiece, we have explicitly avoided the so-called methodological nationalism. This means we have defined the Indian Ocean and the Indian subcontinent as our main research objects. In the same line, our analyses on the Indian National System of Innovation (NSI) and the Indian growth path since the 1990s have given main relevance to the Indian Ocean and the Indian subcontinent's geopolitical and geoeconomic dynamics. In fact, this book is a plea for the integration of long-term/structural approaches (with geography, history, and demography in a central place) to our "Latin American", heterodox, development economics conceptual toolbox.

In this Latin American conceptual toolbox, we have tried to combine a heterodox political economy approach based on Latin American structuralism, Latin American contributions on inter-state competition and the broad understanding of NSI, and the Keynesian-Kaleckian-Sraffian principle of

DOI: 10.4324/9781003091752-14

effective demand, understood in the "Brazilian way", giving special attention to the autonomous expenditures as long-run growth drivers. This research agenda is still open, deserving much more research efforts aimed both to the analyses of other development experiences and to the integration of the different conceptual elements.

That said, we do not stand for any Latin American conceptual chauvinism. We have done a significant research and narrative effort in order to understand the Indian Ocean ecosystem "on its own" instead of "applying" a Latin American framework. This has not been a minor effort for a non-Indian author. In this sense, we understand that Latin American scholars should (and do) read, study, and interact with "global" authors and development economics traditions. Consequently, the conceptual toolbox described in the previous paragraphs is formulated mainly with the contributions of the Latin American author's knowledge on global lines of thinking and schools of political economy.

Next, some final remarks related to our Latin American insight and conceptual tools are pointed out. First, following our historical-structuralist approach in the first part of the book, and after describing the unique place of the Indian Ocean as a main centre of gravitation based on textile production, we have dealt with the Indian subcontinent peripherisation. Prebisch's centre-periphery framework and the relevance that Latin American scholars such as Furtado, Caio Prado, and the subsequent ECLAC-related authors have given to the Latin American external insertion into global capitalism proved to be extremely useful to interpret the Indian subcontinent engagement and the role in the emergent global capitalism. For the British, the Indian peripherisation contributed to the sustainability of the pound sterling, by controlling trade triangulations with Europe and China, resetting the Indian agriculture to fulfil the British food needs and through the "wealth drain". This is not a minor process in the emergence of global capitalism.

On the other hand, the peripherisation, particularly through the structural change experienced by the Indian subcontinent from being the main textile producer of the world to a primary goods producer oriented to the British needs, has configured the long-term Indian external sector dynamics, and it has significantly influenced the internal ones. Indeed, both in India and Latin America, the articulation between the agriculture performance and the external restrictions has been the main cause of economic (and political) stress during the "planning period". In India, this can be seen in the external crises of 1954, 1965, 1980, and 1989.

This issue has been further discussed in Latin America in relation to the industrialisation-by-import-substitution period under the so-called stop-and-go growth model (Diamand, 1973). This model refers mainly to the different productivity levels of the industrial and agriculture sectors as the main cause for the insufficient amount of US dollars to finance import needs. Thus, when a growth process is initiated, the different productivities (different coefficients of imports and exports) cause an overshooting of the exchange rate that reduce domestic consumption to "balance" the external sector (through an adjustment of the exchange rate and the domestic private consumption). Deeper comparative research efforts and discussions should be conducted among the Global South scholars on the connection between the agriculture sector (and actors), the industrial heterogeneity, and the external sector and the way to deal with the "stop-and-go" crises. Indeed, in addition to this "productive" issue, nowadays, we must add the relevance and implications of a financialised global economy.

As discussed in the last part of this book, with the downfall of the USSR, the global re-emergence of China, and the economic and geopolitical complementation with the US, the Indian external restriction has been shifted. Remittances, invisible exports, and capital inflows have more than compensated the Indian trade deficit. The potentiality and limits of this type of insertion into global capitalism are correctly discussed mainly by the South Asian neo-Marxist scholars. However, by now, there is no doubt that this external complementation, in addition to the long-term caste system as a moderator of the income distribution pressures, has contributed to avoid the classical stop-and-go crisis of the "planning" period. Unfortunately, for Latin America, most of its countries do not have this type of economic complementation with the US economy, such a big and well-inserted Diaspora, or the geopolitical relevance that India has in the twenty-first century.

The peripherisation process is also of primal importance to understand the arising of the Indian National Movement and the frameworks, groups, and political and institutional arrangements that configured the emergence of the Indian state, the Indian "national project" (in terms of Amilcar Herrera), and its correlation with the NSI configuration. Following the "wealth drain" theory of the moderate nationalists, after Gandhi's assassination, the Congress Party, led by Nehru, consolidated the idea of state intervention in the economy by planning, industrialisation, and science development. Both the Russian Revolution and the effects of the Second World War in the Indian domestic industry made the need of public procurement and state intervention for development evident. Simultaneously, the emergence of the idea of Hindu Science and the consolidation of the relationship between the Indian political and scientific elites laid the foundation for the post-independence NSI main actors and lines of development even up to the 1990s. As seen, it was a linear, top-down, and science-driven conception of the Science, Technology, and Innovation (STI) policy based on a triad comprised by nuclear, space, and defence fields.

In the second part of this book, we have adopted a broad approach to NSI. From this broad Latin American perspective, the interrelation between the industrial and STI policies and the infrastructure, energy, and agriculture bottlenecks and technological challenges are of main relevance. India is a clear example that R&D, by itself, does not solve development issues.

In fact, India is a case of Nelson's *Moon and the Ghetto* paradox in the Global South: the coexistence of the biggest nuclear and space programme ever developed in a developing country and the fact that around one-third of the Indian population has no access to drinking water and toilets. At this point, both the Indian and the Latin American experiences show how the scientific and technological institutions related to the elite's national project of a country can neglect the lower castes' and classes' needs.

Some significant contemporary challenges will configure the Indian NSI research and policymaking agenda during this century. In broader terms, food, fuel, defence, digitalisation, housing, and urban/rural challenges should receive central attention. Despite the Indian significant scientific and technological capabilities, the links between these and the social, productive, and environmental needs are still weak. Fundamental organisational and budget efforts should be put in place in order to connect with these needs. Besides, trade deficit, especially in manufactured and capital goods, reveals an external vulnerability of the Indian economy. The Make in India programme, for instance, should be encouraged in order to deal with the magnitude of the Indian manufacturing and employment challenges. Finally, some structural issues should receive a crucial budget increase: the urban-rural challenges (housing, urban mobility, health, rural electrification, etc.); the energy efficiency efforts and the green agenda; public investment in agriculture; the indigenisation of defence capabilities related to the Indian Ocean geopolitics; and so on.

In the third part of the book, we have mainly discussed the Indian growth acceleration, contextualising it with the emergence of the BJP and the Indian Ocean's geopolitical tensions at the beginning of the twenty-first century. Even though more than 25 years have passed since the NEP implementation, the understanding of the Indian GDP boom is still open to discussion. In order to contribute to this issue, we presented a demand-led narrative highlighting the role of some main autonomous (or semi-autonomous[1]) expenditures: the upper castes/classes' autonomous consumption, construction, and real estate investments fuelled by credit and capital inflows and public and private investment in infrastructure and exports. Next, we introduced some data briefly displaying the Indian structural heterogeneity. And finally, we reinterpreted this process under the Belindia metaphor, mainly based on the Brazilian debate between Furtado and Tavares and Serra, and the subsequent Brazilian contributions on demand-led growth.

From our perspective, there are some key processes and facts that contribute to qualify the Indian growth debate and its salient limits: a) a main new trend in the Indian political economy since the 1980s is the relevance given to infrastructure, showing a changing role in the state intervention: partially moving from its direct involvement in production to increasing its role as infrastructure purchaser, developer, and financier; b) the alignment and complementation with the US economy and the main geopolitical relevance of India in the twenty-first century have contributed to the financing of the Indian trade deficit, clearing the Indian external restriction; c) with a stagnant manufacturing sector and the agriculture expelling employment (i.e., rural population), services and, largely, construction have been the main employment and sectorial growth drivers; and d) the stagnant industrial sector and the low agriculture productivity profits are a main vulnerability to the Indian economy, given the advance of the Chinese manufacture exports and multinational firms' penetration.

Despite growth acceleration, Pinto's structural heterogeneity seems to be coined for the Indian context. India is one of the most heterogeneous countries in the world (if not the most). And this can be appreciated by anyone who has travelled around the country. High-tech/globally inserted sectors and segments of the society coexist with rural tribal forms of living. Leading achievements in big science coexist with the biggest informal sector in the world. There are huge territorial and religious heterogeneities: from the Hindustan to the tropical south and from the Muslim Sufis to the Dalai Lama. This structural heterogeneity, combined with its scale, makes the understanding of the Indian society extremely interesting and challenging, explaining why so many Western intellectuals including Hegel, Adam Smith, Marx, Kalecki, Joan Robinson, and others have in some moment of their life reflected on the Indian experience. The main contemporary difference with the time and reflections of these Western intellectuals is that Asia and India are recovering their central position in global capitalism. Consequently, the Indo-Pacific dynamic and tensions should return to the centre of the analyses.

We have ended the writing of these paragraphs during the conjunctural time of the COVID-19 global crisis. After the virus emerged in China with a strong impact in Europe and the US, South Asia, particularly India, and Latin America, particularly Mexico and Brazil, have been among the most affected regions and countries in the world. The Western world is full of distress. Donald Trump tested positive from COVID-19, while the US transited the 2020 presidential election, engaged in a racist escalation that included several black people murdered both in hands of the police and by right-white-wing militias. China, on the other hand, is leading the world economic recovery after the initial COVID-19 shock, with some analysts (finally) asserting that 2020 is the beginning of the "Asian century".

Interestingly enough, some main trends highlighted in this book have deepened during the pandemic. With the forced increase of the digitalisation, the US IT multinational firms have reinforced their involvement in the Indian IT sector with the 5G dispute between the US and China as a background (Gonzalo and Harfuch, 2020). Facebook, in April 2020, and Intel, in July 2020, capitalised Reliance Jio, one of the main Indian national groups, to foster their consolidation in the telecommunication sector (the Indian market is the biggest in the world after the Chinese one). In June 2020, the Indian government officially banned TikTok and other 58 Chinese apps alleging security issues, and the pressure to ban Huawei operations in India is increasing. That same month, a confrontation between Indian and Chinese troops in the Galwan Valley, in the Kashmir area, resulted in a military clash that included the death of at least 20 Indian soldiers, in what has been described by the media as one of the most relevant military escalations in this area since the 1962 Sino-Indian war. All these events reaffirm our insight about the closer alignment and complementation between India and the US, vis-à-vis an increasing tension with China.

The long-term methodological approach adopted in this research can help to transcend the conjunctural time of the pandemic. Despite the uncertain (and dystopic) context in the West in the twenty-first century, with the Indo-Pacific turning to be the gravitation centre of the capitalist dynamic, once again, the Indian Ocean is taking a central geopolitical and geoeconomic relevance. For the US, the Indian Ocean is of main relevance to contain the Chinese economic and military expansion. For the Arab countries, the Indian Ocean is a central petroleum corridor, with China and India as main clients. But altogether, South Asia, with India in its centre, and the global dispute between the US and China as a background, will be one of the most dynamic regions in the world in terms of GDP growth, infrastructure development, urbanisation, energy consumption, middle-class emergence, weaponisation and military expenditure, and so on. The analyses and data presented in this book give account of the type of processes that we are talking about and, at the same time, of the Indian structural heterogeneity.

Note

1 It would be interesting that the contemporary autonomous expenditures growth-led research agenda, although assuming induced investment, zoomed in on the public-private explicit and implicit relationships oriented to muster private investment in infrastructure and residential segment, such as Tavares and Serra, given that it seems to have much more "autonomous" logic than the manufacturing one.

REFERENCES

Abraham, V. and Sasikumar, S.K. (2017), 'Declining wage share in India's organized manufacturing sector: Trends, patterns and determinants'. *ILO Asia-Pacific Working Paper Series*, December 2017.

Abrol, D. (2010), 'Policies for self-reliant development lessons from India'. *History and Sociology of South Asia*, v. 4, n. 1, pp. 41–73.

Abrol, D. (2013), 'Foreign direct investment and national innovation system: Evidence from India'. In Cassiolato, J., Zucoloto, G., Abrol, D. and Xielin, L. (eds.), *Transnational corporations and local innovation*. Routledge.

Abrol, D. (2014), 'Pro-poor innovation making, knowledge production, and technology implementation for rural areas'. In Ramani, S. (ed.), *Innovation in India: Combining economic growth with inclusive development*. Cambridge University Press.

Aggarwal, A. (2015), 'Promoting SEZs as a strategy of industrialization and lessons learnt'. In Goyal, A. (ed.), *A concise Handbook of the Indian economy in the 21st century*. Oxford University Press.

Amsdem, A. (2001), *The rise of "the rest": Challenges to the west from late-industrializing economies*. Oxford University Press.

Anderson, B. (1983/1991), *Imagined communities: Reflections on the origin and spread of nationalism*. Verso.

Appu, P. (1995), *Land reforms in India: A survey of policy, legislation and implementation*. Land Reform Unit, Lal Bahadur Shastri National Academy of Administration.

Arnold, D. (2013 June), Nehruvian science and postcolonial India. *Isis*, v. 104, n. 2, pp. 360–370.

Azad, R., Bose, P. and Dasgupta, Z. (2017 August 5), "Riskless capitalism' in India Bank credit and economic activity'. *Economic & Political Weekly*, v. LII, n. 31.

Baber, Z. (1996), *The science of empire: Scientific knowledge, civilization, and colonial rule in India*. State University of New York Press.

Bacha, E. (1974), 'El Economista y el Rey de Belindia: Una Fábula para Tecnócratas'. *Latin American Journal of Economics (formerly Cuadernos de Economía)*, v. 11, n. 33, pp. 60–64.

Bagchi, A. (1972), *Private investment in India 1900–39*. Cambridge.

Bagchi, A. (1976), 'Deindustrialization in Gangetic Bihar 1809–1901'. In De, B. et al. (eds.), *Essays in Honour of Prof. S.C. Sarkar*. People's Publishing House.

Bagchi, A. (2003), *The developmental state in history and in the twentieth century*. Regency Publications.

Bairoch, P. (1982 Fall), 'International Industrialization Levels from 1750 to 1980'. *Journal of European Economic History*, v. 11, pp. 269–333.

Bala Subrahmanya, M.H. (2015 March), 'New generation start-ups in India what lessons can we learn from the past?'. *Economic and Political Weekly*, v. 50, n. 12, pp. 56–63.

Bala Subrahmanya, M.H. (2016), *Entrepreneurial ecosystem for technology based start-ups in Bangalore: An empirical perspective*. Indian Institute of Science.

Bandyopadhyay, S. (2004), *From Plassey to partition and after. A history of modern India*. Second edition. Orient BlackSwan.

Barbosa, A., Cacciamali, M. and Rodgers, G. (2017), *Growth and inequality: The contrasting trajectories of India and Brazil*. Cambridge University Press.

Bardhan, P. (1984), *The political economy of development in India*. Oxford University Press.

Bardhan, P. (2010), *Awakening giants. Feet of clay. Assessing the economic rise of China and India*. Princeton University Press.

Bastos, C. and D'Avila, J. (2007), 'O Debate do Desenvolvimento na Tradição Heterodoxa Brasileira: da Cepal à Escola da Unicamp'. *VII Congresso Brasileiro de História Econômica*. Aracaju, Brazil, 2007.

Basu, K. (1994), *Agrarian questions*. Oxford University Press.

Beckert, S. (2014), *The empire of cotton. A global history*. Penguin Books.

Berg, M. (2009), 'Quality, cotton and the global luxury trade'. In Riello, G. and Roy, T. (eds.), *How India clothed the world. The world of South Asian textiles, 1500–1850*. BRILL.

Bhaduri, A. (2008a), 'Growth and employment in the era of globalization: Some lessons from the Indian experience'. *ILO Asia-Pacific Working Paper Series*, January 2008.

Bhaduri, A. (2008b), 'Predatory growth'. *Economic & Political Weekly*, April 19, 2008.

Bhaduri, A. (2009), *The face you were afraid to see. Essays on the Indian economy*. Penguin Books.

Bhaduri, A. and Nayyar, D. (1996), *The intelligent person´s guide to liberalization*. Penguin Books.

Bhaduri, S. (2005), 'Investment, financial constraints and financial liberalization: Some stylized facts from a developing economy, India'. *Journal of Asian Economics*, v. 16, pp. 704–718.

Bhagwati, J. and Desai, P. (1970), *India: Planning for industrialization. Industrialization and trade policies since 1951*. Oxford University Press.

Bhagwati, J. and Panagariya, A. (2013), *Why growth matters: How economic growth in India reduced poverty and the lessons for other developing countries*. PublicAffairs.

Bhagwati, J. and Srinivasan, T. (1993), *India´s economic reforms*. Ministry of Finance.

Bhandari, L. and Goswani, O. (2000), *So many lost years: The public sector before and after reforms*. NCAER.

Bhattacharyya, S. (2008), 'Determinants of corporate investment: Post liberalization panel data evidence from Indian firms'. *Munich Personal RePEc Archive*, Paper No. 6702, 2008.

Bielschowsky, R. (1998), 'Evolución de las ideas de la CEPAL'. *Revista de la CEPAL*, Santiago de Chile, Número extraordinario.

Bielschowsky, R. (2016), 'Fifty years of ECLAC thought: A review'. In *ECLAC Thinking: Selected Texts (1948–1998)*. ECLAC.

Bielschowsky, R. (2020 Jan./Abr), 'Do "Manifesto latino-americano" de Raúl Prebisch aos dias de hoje: 70 anos de estruturalismo na CEPAL'. *Revista de Economia Contemporanea*, v. 24, n. 1.

Boianovsky, M. (2015), 'Between Lévi-Strauss and Braudel: Furtado and the historical-structural method in Latin American political economy'. *Journal of Economic Methodology*. doi: 10.1080/1350178X.2015.1024879

Braudel, F. (1949/2001), *El Mediterráneo y el mundo mediterráneo en la época de Felipe II*. Fondo de Cultura Económica de España.

Broadberry, S. and Gupta, B. (2005 June), 'Cotton textiles and the great divergence: Lancashire, India and shifting competitive advantage, 1600–1850'. *The Rise, Organization, and Institutional Framework of Factor Markets*, pp. 23–25.

Brown, J. (1972), *Gandhi´s rise to power: Indian politics, 1915–1922*. Cambridge University Press.

Byres, T. (1998), *The Indian economy. Major debates since independence*. Oxford University Press.

Caio Prado Jr. (1942/2011), *Formação do Brasil contemporâneo*. Companhia das Letras.

Cardoso, F.H. and Faletto, E. (1967/1970), *Dependência e Desenvolvimento na América Latina*. Zahar.

Cardoso de Mello, J. and Novais, F. (1998), 'Capitalismo tardio e sociabilidade moderna'. In Schwarcz, L.M. (ed.), *Historia da vida privada no Brasil*, v. 4. Companhia das Letras.

Cassiolato, J. (2008), *As vantagens e desafios da visão sistêmica como instrumento analítico e político normativo*. Nota técnica 04–2008. RedeSist.

Cassiolato, J., Britto, J. and Bittencourt, P. (2008), *Sistemas de defesa e esforços inovativos no âmbito dos BRICS: uma análise exploratória*. Research Report 26/08, RedeSist -IE-UFRJ.

Cassiolato, J. and Gonzalo, M. (2015), *O papel do Estado no desenvolvimento dos sistemas de inovação dos BRICS*. Texto para Discussão – RedeSist Desenvolvimento, Inovação e Território, TD DIT – N° 01/2015.

Cassiolato, J. and Lastres, H. (1999), *Inovação, globalização e as novas políticas de desenvolvimento industrial e tecnológico*. Research Report 21/98. RedeSist -IE-UFRJ.

Cassiolato, J. and Lastres, H. (2005 jan./mar), 'Sistemas de Inovação e Desenvolvimento: as implicações de política'. *São Paulo em Perspectiva*, v. 19, n. 1, pp. 34–45.

Cassiolato, J. and Lastres, H. (2017), 'Políticas de inovação e desenvolvimento'. In Coutinho, D.R. and Foss, M.C. (eds.), *Mouallem and Pedro Salomon B*. Inovação no Brasil: avanços e desafios jurídicos e institucionais.

Cassiolato, J., Szapiro, M., Maxnuck, E., Podcameni, M., Hausmann, J., Pessoa de Matos, M. and Fontaine, P. (2013), *Dimensões estratégicas do desenvolvimento brasileiro: as fronteiras do conhecimento e da inovação: oportunidades, restrições e alternativas estratégicas para o Brasil*, v. 2. Centro de Gestão e Estudos Estratégicos.

Cesaratto, S., Serrano, F. and Stirati, A. (2013/2003), 'Technical change, effective demand and employment'. *Review of Political Economy*, v. 15, n. 1.

Chadra, B., Mukherjee, M., Mukherjee, A., Mahajan, S. and Panikkar, K. (1988), *India's struggle for independence*. Penguin Books.

Chakravarty, S. (1987), *Development planning. The Indian experience*. Clarendon Press.

Chakravorty, S., Kapur, D and Singh, N. (2016), *The other one percent: Indian in America*. OUP.

Chancel, L. and Piketty, T. (2017), 'Indian income inequality, 1922–2015: From British Raj to Billionaire Raj?'. *World Inequality Lab, Working Paper Series*, N° 2017/11.

Chandavarkar, R. (1994), *The origins of industrial capitalism in India: Business strategies and the working classes in Bombay, 1900–1940*. Cambridge University Press.

Chandra, B. (2008), *Indian national movement. The long-term dynamics*. Har-Anand Publications.

Chandra, B. (2016), *The rise and growth of economic nationalism in India*. Anamika Publishers and Distributors.

Chandra, B., Mukherjee, M. and Mukherjee, A. (2008), *India since independence*. Penguin.

Chandra, B., Mukherjee, M., Mukherjee, A., Mahajan, S. y Panikkar, N. (1988/2016), *India´s struggle for independence*. Penguin Books.

Chandrasekhar, C. (2008), 'Financial liberalization and the new dynamics of growth in India'. *Third World Network Global Economy Series*, v. 13.

Chandrasekhar, C. (2011), 'The housing market and housing finance under liberalization in India'. *Global Housing Markets: Crises, Policies, and Institutions*, pp. 343–356.

Chandrasekhar, C. (2016), 'Finance capital and the nature of capitalism in India Today'. *IDEAS Articles*, November 25, 2016. www.networkideas.org/featured-articles/2016/11/finance-capital-and-the-nature-of-capitalism-in-india-today/

Chandrasekhar, C. (2017), 'The Economy: 70 years after Independence'. *IDEAs*, August 30, 2017.

Chandrasekhar, C. and Ghosh, J. (2015), 'Growth, employment patterns and inequality in Asia: A case study of India'. *ILO Asia-Pacific Working Paper Series*, January 2015.

Chandrasekhar, C. and Ghosh, J. (2017a), 'ICT: Implications of imbalanced growth'. *IDEAS*.

Chandrasekhar, C. and Ghosh, J. (2017b), 'Spreading light: Are the Modi government's electricity promises being fulfilled?' *IDEAs*, January, 2017.

Chang, H. (2005), 'Kicking away the ladder – "good policies" and "good institutions" in historical perspective'. In Gallagher, K. (ed.), *Putting development first – the importance of policy space in the WTO and IFIs*. Zed Press.

Chatterjee, P. (1997), 'Introduction: A political history of independent India'. In Chatterjee, P. (ed.), *State and politics in India*, 1–40. Oxford University Press.

Chaudhury, K.N. (1978), *The trading world of Asia and the English East India Company, 1660–1760*. Cambridge University Press.

Chaudhury, K.N. (1983), 'Foreign trade and balance of payments (1757–1947)'. In Kumar, D. and Raychaudhuri, T. (eds.), *The Cambridge Economic History of India*, v. 2: c.1757-c.1970. Cambridge Press.

Chaudhury, K.N. (1985), *Trade and civilization in the Indian Ocean. An economic history from the rise of Islam to 1750*. Cambridge University Press.
Chaudhury, K.N. (2008), European trade with India. In Raychaudhuri, T. and Habib, I. (eds.), *The Cambridge history of India*, v. I: 1200–1750. Cambridge University Press.
Chaudhury, S. (1998), Debates on industrialization. In Byres, T.J. (ed.), *The Indian economy. Major debates since independence*. Oxford University Press.
Chaulia, S. (2011), 'India´s 'power' attributes'. In Scott, D. (ed.), *Handbook of India's international relations*. Routledge.
Chibber, V. (2003), *Locked in place. State building and late industrialization in India*. Princeton University Press.
Ciccone, R. (1995), 'Accumulation and capacity utilization: Some critical considerations on Joan Robinson´s theory of distribution'. *Conference on Sraffa´s production of commodities by means of commodities after 25 years*. Florence, 1985.
Cliff, R. (2020), *A new U.S. strategy for the Indo-Pacific*. NBR Special Report #86, The National Bureau of Asian Research.
Clingingsmith, D. and Williamson, J.G. (2008 July), 'De-Industrialization in 18th and 19th Century India: Mughal Decline, Climate Shocks and British Industrial Ascent'. *Explorations in Economic History*, v. 45, pp. 209–234.
Cohen, S. (2001), *India: Emerging power*. Brookings Institution Press.
Crespo, E. (2016 Primavera), 'La demanda efectiva en la historia económica. Una omisión de 80 años'. *Céfiro. Revista de Economía y gestión*, Año 3, n. 2.
Crespo, E. and Muñiz, M. (2017 Mayo-Septiembre), 'Una aproximación a las condiciones globales de Desarrollo Económico'. *Revista Estado y Políticas Públicas*, n. 8, pp. 21–39.
Cuenca Esteban, J. (2001), 'The British balance of payments, 1772–1820: India transfers and war finance'. *Economic History Review*, v. LIV, n. 1, pp. 58–86.
D´Acosta, A. (2003), Uneven and combined development: Understanding India´s software exports. *World Development*, v. 31, n. 1, pp. 211–226.
Dalrymple, W. (2015), 'The East India company: The original corporate raiders'. *The Guardian*, March 04, 2015.
Dasgupta, A. (1967), *Malabar in Asian trade, 1740–1800*. Cambridge University Press.
Dasgupta, A. (2008), 'Indian merchants and the trade in the Indian Ocean'. In Raychaudhuri, T. and Habib, I. (eds.), *The Cambridge history of India*, v. I: 1200–1750. Cambridge University Press.
Davis, M. (2001), *Late Victorian Holocausts. El Niño famines and the making of the third world*. New Left Books.
De Cecco, M. (1975), *Money and empire: The international gold standard, 1890–1914*. Rowman and Littlefield.
Deleidi, M. and Mazzucato, M. (2019), 'Putting austerity to bed: Technical progress, aggregate demand and the supermultiplier'. *Review of Political Economy*, v. 31, n. 3, pp. 315–335. doi: 10.1080/09538259.2019.1687146
Delong, J.B. (2003), 'India since independence. An analytic growth narrative'. In Rodrick, D. (ed.), *In search of prosperity. Analytic narratives on economic growth*. Princeton University Press.
Desai, A. (1999), 'The economics and politics of transition to an open market economy: India'. *Working Paper*, n. 155, OECD Development Centre.

De Vries, J. (1973), 'On the modernity of the Dutch Republic'. *Journal of Economic History*, v. 33, n. 1, pp. 191–202.
Diamand, M. (1973), *Doctrinas económicas, desarrollo e independencia*. Paidós.
Diamond, J. (1997), *Guns, germs and steels: The fate of human societies*. W. W. Norton.
Dossani, R. and Kenney, M. (2001), *Creating an environment: Developing venture capital in India*. Berkeley Roundtable on the International Economy (BRIE), n. 143.
Drèze, J. and Sen, A. (2013), *Glória incerta. A Índia e suas contradições*. Companhia das Letras.
Dubey, A. (2011), 'India and the Indian diáspora'. In Scott, D. (ed.), *Handbook of India´s international relations*. Routledge.
Dutt, R. (1901), *The economic history of India, Under early British rule*, v. I. (Second edition, London, 1906, repr., Delhi, 1990). Kegan Paul, Trench, Trubner.
Dyson, T. (2008), 'India's demographic transition and its consequences for development'. *Golden Jubilee Lecture Series of the Institute of Economic Growth Delivered at IEG*, on March 24, 2008.
East-West Center. (2017), *India Matters for America*. East-West Center.
East-West Center. (2019), *EAST-WEST CENTER ANNUAL REPORT 2017–18*. East-West Center.
Ellison, T. (1968), *The Cotton Trade of Great Britain*. Kelley.
Evans, P. (1979), *Dependent development. The alliance of multinationals, state, and local capital in Brazil*. Princeton Paperbacks.
Evans, P. (1982), *A Tríplice Aliaca. As multinacionais, as estatais e o capital nacional no desenvolvimento dependente brasileiro*. Zahar editores.
Evans, P.B. (1995), *Embedded autonomy: States and industrial transformation*. Princeton University Press.
Fair, C. (2009), 'India and the US: Embracing a new paradigm'. In Pant, H. (ed.), *Indian foreign policy in a unipolar world*. Routledge India Paperbacks.
Famine Commission. (1880), *Report of the Indian Famine Commission*, Part I, Calcutta.
Ferrer, A. (1963/2004), *La economia Argentina*. Fondo de cultura Económica.
Findlay, R. and O'Rourke, K. (2007), *Power and plenty. Trade, war and the world economy in the second millennium*. Princeton University Press.
Fiori, J. (1999), 'De volta à questão da riqueza de algumas nações'. In Fiori, J. (ed.), *Estados e moedas no desenvolvimento das nações*. editora Vozes Ltda.
Fiori, J. (2007), *O poder global*. Boitempo Editorial.
Fiori, J. (2014), *No princípio era Portugal. In História, Estratégia e desenvolvimento para uma geopolítica do capitalismo*. Boitempo.
Fiori, J. (2020), 'Estado e desenvolvimento na América Latina'. *Revista de Economia Contemporânea*, v. 24, n. 1, pp. 1–23. ISSN 1980–5527.
Freeman, C. (1982), *Technical infrastructure and international competitiveness*. Draft paper submitted to the OECD Ad hoc-group on Science, technology and competitiveness, august 1982, mimeo.
Freeman, C. (1987), *Technology and economic performance: Lessons from Japan*. Pinter Publishers.
Freeman, C. (1995), 'The 'national system of innovation' in historical perspective'. *Cambridge Journal of Economics*, v. 19, pp. 5–24.

Freeman, C. and Louçã, F. (2001), *As time goes by. From the industrial revolution to the information revolution*. Oxford University Press.
Furtado, C. (1959), *Formação econômica do Brasil*. Fundo de Cultura.
Furtado, C. (1966), *Subdesenvolvimento e estagnação na América Latina*. Civilização Brasileira.
Furtado, C. (1969/2007), *Formação econômica de América Latina*. Companhia das Letras.
Furtado, C. (1971), *Development and underdevelopment*. University of California Press.
Gallagher, J. and Robinson, R. (1953), 'The imperialism of free trade'. *The Economic History Review*. New Series, v. 6, n. 1, pp. 1–15.
Garegnani, P. (1962/2015), 'The problem of effective demand in Italian economic development: On the factors that determine the volume of investment'. *Review of Political Economy*, v. 27, n. 2, pp. 111–123.
Garegnani, P. and Palumbo, A. (1998), 'Accumulation of capital'. In Kurz, H.D. y Salvadori, N. (eds.), *The Elgar companion to classical economics*. Edward Elgar.
Ghose, A.K. (1982 July), 'Food supply and starvation: A study of famines with references to the Indian sub-continent'. *Oxford Economic Papers*, New Series, v. 34, n. 2, pp. 368–389.
Ghosh, J. (1998), 'Liberalization debates'. In Byres, T.J. (ed.), *The Indian economy. Major debates since independence*. Oxford University Press.
Ghosh, J. (2015), 'India's rural employment programme is dying a death of funding cuts'. *IDEAs*, February 6, 2015.
Ghosh, J. (2016), 'Recent growth in the Indian Economy'. *IDEAs*, September 12, 2016.
Ghosh, J. (2017), 'The GDP elephant'. *IDEAs*, June 6, 2017.
Godbole, M. (2006), *The holocaust of Indian partition: An inquest*. Rupa.
Goldar, B., Kusum Das, D., Sengupta, S. and Chandra Das, P. (2017), 'Domestic value addition and foreign content: An analysis of India's exports from 1995 to 2011'. *Working Paper 332*, ICRIER, January 2017.
Gonzalo, M. and Cassiolato, J. (2016), 'Evolução do Sistema Nacional de Inovação da Índia e seus Desafios Atuais: uma primeira leitura a partir do pensamento latino-americano'. *BRICS Policy Center – BPC Papers*, v. 4, n. 4.
Gonzalo, M. and Cassiolato, J.E. (2017 Octubre), 'Trayectoria histórica de desarrollo del Sistema Nacional de Innovación de India (1947–2017)'. *Márgenes Revista de Economía Política*, Año III, n. 3.
Gonzalo, M. and Crespo, E. (2019), 'Indian nationalism. Asian context, interwar years and Nehruvian state-building'. In Trincado, E., Lazarini, A. and Melnik, D. (eds.), *Ideas in the history of economic development. The case of peripheral countries*. Routledge.
Gonzalo, M. and Harfuch, M. (2020), 'Economía política de la emergencia del 5G en la India, entre Huawei y los Estados Unidos de América'. *Revista Márgenes, UNGS*, Noviembre de 2020.
Gonzalo, M. and Kantis, H. (2017), 'Venture capital in India: A critical view from an evolutionary and systemic perspective'. *Globelics Conference*, Atenas.
Gore, C. (1996 June), 'Methodological nationalism and the misunderstanding of East Asian Industrialization'. *European Journal of Development Research*, v. 8, n. 1.
Government of India. (2006), *Integrated energy policy*. Government of India.

Government of India. (2015), 'Report on India's Renewable Electricity Roadmap 2030: Towards Accelerated Renewable Electricity Deployment'. *NITI AAyog*, 2015.

Gupta, A. and Sengupta, R. (2016 March 19), Capital account management in India. *Economic & Political Weekly*, v. LI, no. 12.

Gurrieri, A. (2011), 'A economia política de Raúl Prebisch'. In *O Manifiesto Latino-americano e outros ensaios/Raul Prebisch*. Centro Internacional Celso Furtado.

Habib, I. (1963), *The agrarian system of Mughal India*. Asia Publishing House.

Habib, I. (1982), *Population*. In Raychaudhuri, T. and Habib, I. (eds.), *The Cambridge economic history of India*, v. 1: c.1200-c.1750. Cambridge University Press.

Habib, I. (1995a), *Essays in Indian history. Towards a Marxist interpretation*. Tulika Books.

Habib, I. (1995b), Potentialities of capitalistic development in the economy of Mughal India. In *Essays in Indian history. Towards a Marxist interpretation*. Tulika.

Habib, I. (2017), 'Seventy years on, India cannot allow the divisive forces to Triumph again'. *The Wire*. https://thewire.in/168806/bjps-fascist-character-grave-danger-democracy-civil-rights-india/ (accessed 22 August 2017).

Hazari, R.K. (1966), *Structure of the corporate private sector*, Asia Publishing House.

Headrick, D. (1988), *The tentacles of progress. Technology transfer in the age of imperialism, 1850–1940*. Oxford University Press.

Hejeebu, S. (2015), 'The colonial transition and the decline of the East India Company, c1746–1784'. In Roy, T., Gupta, B., Swamy, A. and Chaudhury L. (eds.), *A new economic history of colonial India*. Routledge Press.

Herrera, A. (1973), 'Los determinantes sociales de la política científica en América Latina. Política científica explícita y política científica explicita'. *Revista REDES*, n. 5, 1995.

Herrera, A. (2015), 'Ciencia y política en América Latina'. *Colección PLACTED. Biblioteca Nacional.*

Herzog, W. (2016), 'Into the inferno'. *Netflix*.

Hicks, J. (1950), *A contribution to the theory of the trade cycle*. Oxford.

Hobsbawm, E. (1999), *Industry and empire. The birth of the industrial revolution*. The New Press.

Hoffman, P.T. (2015), *Why did Europe conquer the world?* Princeton University Press.

Hurd, J. (1983), Railways. In Kumar, D. and Raychaudhuri, T. (eds.), *The Cambridge economic history of India*. Cambridge Press.

IHS. (2015), *HIS Jane´s Navigating the Emerging Markets*. IHS.

India Brand Equity Foundation. (2017), *Real estate. Department of Commerce*, Ministry of Commerce and Industry, Government of India.

International Energy Agency. (2015), *India Energy Outlook*. International Energy Agency.

International Labour Organization. (2016a), Global Wage Report 2016/7. Wage inequality in the workplace. IOL.

International Labour Organization. (2016b), *India labour market update*. ILO Country Office for India, July 2016.

Israel, J. (1989), *Dutch primacy in world trade*, 1585–1740. Clarendon Press.

Jayaraman, T., Choong, C. and Kumar, R. (2012), Role of remittances in India´s economic growth. *Global Business and Economic Review*, v. 14, n. 3.

Joseph, K. (2002), *Growth of ICT and ICT for development: Realities of the myths of Indian Experience*. Discussion paper n. 2002/78, Helsinki, ONU/WIDER.

Joseph, K. (2011), 'Sectoral innovation systems in developing countries: The case of ICT in India'. In Lundvall, B.Å., Joseph, K.J., Chaminade, C. and Vang, J. (eds.), *Handbook of innovation systems and developing countries: Building domestic capabilities in a global setting*. Edward Elgar Publishing.

Joseph, K. (2014 January–March), 'India´s software industry in transition: Lessons for other developing countries and implications for South-South cooperation'. *Productivity*, v. 54, n. 4.

Joseph, K. and Abrol, D. (2009), Science, technology and innovation policy in India: Achievements and limits. In Cassiolato, J. and Vitorino, V. (eds.), *BRICS and development alternatives. Innovation Systems and Policies*, Anthem Press.

Joseph, K. and Harilal, K. (2001 August 25), Structure and growth of India's IT exports: Implications of an export-oriented growth strategy. *Economic and Political Weekly*, v. 36, n. 34, pp. 3263–3270.

Joseph, K. and Kakarlapudi, K. (2014), 'Innovation and development in India. Changing paradigms and trajectories'. In Goyal, A. (ed.), *The Orford Handbook of the Indian economy in the 21st century. Understanding the inherent dynamism*. Oxford University Press.

Joseph, K., Sarma, M. and Abraham, V. (2008), *National system of innovation: India*. Research Report 27/08. RedeSist -IE-UFRJ.

Kabra, K.N. (1989), *Nationalizations in India. Political economy of policy options*. Eastern Books.

Kaldor, N. (1978), *Further essays on economic theory*. Holmes & Meier.

Kalecki, M. (1933), 'Outline of a theory of the business cycle'. In *Selected essays on the dynamics of the capitalist economy 1933–1970*. Cambridge University Press.

Kalecki, M. (1968), 'Trend and business cycle'. In *Selected essays on the dynamics of the capitalist economy 1933–1970*. Cambridge University Press.

Kalecki, M. (1971), *Selected essays on the dynamics of the capitalist economy 1933–1970*. Cambridge University Press.

Kannan, K.P. (2014), *Interrogating inclusive growth: Poverty and inequality in India*. Routledge.

Kapila, U. (2003), *Understanding the problems of Indian economy*. Academic Foundation.

Kapila, U. (2014), *Indian economy since independence*. Twenty fourth edition. Academic Foundation.

Kaplan, R. (2010a), *Monsoon: The Indian Ocean and the future of American power*. Random House.

Kaplan, R. (2010b), *South Asia's geography of conflict*. Center for New American Security.

Kaplan, R. (2013), 'Next geopolitical power play will be all at sea'. *The Australian*, 13 de Novembro de 2010.

Karnad, Bharat. (2015), *Why India is not a great power (yet)*. Oxford University Press, 564 pp.

Kaul, H. (1991), *K D Malviya and the Evolution of Indian Oil*. Allied Publishers.
Keynes, J. (1936), *The general theory of employment, interest and money*. McMillan.
Khanna, S. (2015 January 31), 'The transformation of India's public sector' political economy of growth and change. *Economic & Political Weekly*, v. L, n. 5.
Kohli, A. (2004), *State directed-development: Political power and industrialization in the global periphery*. Cambridge University Press.
Kohli, A. (2007a), *State and redistributive development in India*. United Nations Research Institute for Social Development (UNRISD).
Kohli, A. (2007b June), 'State, business, and growth in India'. *Studies in Comparative International Development*, v. 42, pp. 87–114. https://doi.org/10.1007/s12116-007-9001-9
Kolff, D. (1990), *Naukar, Rajput and Sepoy: The Ethnohistory of the military labour market in Hindustan*. Cambridge University Press.
Kreimer, P., Thomas, H., Rossini, P. and Lalouf, A. (eds.) (2004), *Producción y uso social de conocimientos*. Universidad Nacional de Quilmes Editorial, Estudios de sociología de la ciencia y la tecnología en América Latina.
Krishna, V. (1997), 'A portrait of the scientific community in India: Historical growth and contemporary problems'. In Gaillard, J., Krishna, V.V. and Waast, R. (eds.), *Scientific communities in the developing world*, 236–280. Sage Publications.
Krishna, V. (2013), 'India'. In Scerri, M. and Lastres, H. (eds.), *The role of the state, BRICS – National systems of innovation*. Routledge.
Krishnaji, N. (2012 April 14), Abolish the poverty line. *Economic & Political Weekly*, v. XLVII, n. 15.
Krishnan, M.S., Ramasubbu, N. and Subramanian, R. (2009), Evolution of the Indian software industry: The emerging model of mobilizing global talent. In Swaminathan, J.M. (ed.), *Indian Economic Superpower Fiction or Future?* Chapter 5, 59–74. *World Scientific Series*.
Kulkarni, P.M. (2014), Demographic transition in India. CSRD, SSS, J.N., University December 4, 2014, Office of Registrar General of India.
Kumar, D. (1982), *The Cambridge economic history of India*, v. II: 1957–2003. Cambridge University Press.
Kumar, R. (1971), *Introduction to essays in Gandhian politics: The Rowlatt Satyagraha of 1919*. Clarendon Press.
Lall, S. (1982), *Developing countries as exporters of technology. A first look at the Indian experience*. McMillan Press.
Lall, S. (1992), 'Technological capabilities and industrialization'. *World Development*, v. 20, n. 2, pp. 165–186.
Lastres, M.H. and Cassiolato, J.E. (2017), 'Development and innovation: Learning from the legacies of Freeman and Furtado'. *Innovation and Development*, v. 7, n. 2, pp. 271–286. doi: 10.1080/2157930X.2017.1361057
Lavoie, M. (1992), *Foundations of post-Keynesian economic analysis*. Edward Elgar.
Lee, K., Park, T. and Krishnan, R. (2013), 'Catching-up or leapfrogging in the Indian CIS sector: Windows of opportunity, path-creating, and moving up the value chain'. *Development Policy Review*, forthcoming.
Lemire, B. (2009), 'Fashioning global trade: Indian textiles, gender meanings and European consumers, 1500–1800'. In Riello, G. and Roy, T. (eds.), *How India clothed the world. The world of South Asian textiles, 1500–1850*. BRILL.

Lewis, A. (1973 December), 'Maritime skills in the Indian Ocean 1368–1500'. *Journal of the Economic and Social History of the Orient*, v. 16, n. 2/3, pp. 238–264.
Lewis, A. and Runyan, T. (1985), *European naval and maritime history, 300–1500*. Midland Book Edition.
Lewis, W.A. (1969), 'Desenvolvimento Econômico com Oferta Ilimitada de Mão de Obra'. In Agarwala, A.N. e Singh, S.P. (orgs.), *A Economia doSubdesenvolvimento*. Forense.
Lewis, W.A. (1972), 'Reflections on Unlimited Labour'. In diMarco, L.E. (ed.), *International Economics and Development*. Academic Press.
List, F. (1841), *The national system of political economy*. English edition (1904). Longman.
Long, F.A. (1988), 'Science technology and industrial development in India'. *Technology in Society*, v. 10, pp. 395–416.
Lundvall, B. (1985), *Product innovation and user-producer interaction*, Aalborg University Press.
Lundvall, B. (1992), *National systems of innovation: Towards a theory of innovation and interactive learning*. Pinter Publishers.
Lundvall, B. (2015), 'The origins of the national innovation system concept and its usefulness in the era of the globalizing economy'. *13th Globelics Conference 2015*, Havana, September 23–26.
Lundvall, B.Å., Vang, J., Joseph, K.J. and Chaminade, C. (2009), 'Bridging innovation system research and development studies: Challenges and research opportunities'. Paper presented at *GLOBELICS 2009, 7th International Conference 2009*, Dakar, Senegal.
Machado, P. (2009), 'Cloths of a new fashion: Indian Ocean networks of exchange and cloth zones of contact in Africa and India in the eighteenth and nineteenth centuries'. In Riello, G. and Roy, T. (eds.), *How India clothed the world. The world of South Asian textiles, 1500–1850*. BRILL.
Mahajan, K. and Nagaraj, R. (2017 December 30), 'Rural construction employment boom during 2000–12. Evidence from NSSO Surveys'. *Economic and Political Weekly*, v. LII, n. 52.
Mancini, M. and Lavarello, P. (2013), 'Heterogeneidad estructural: origen y evolución del concepto frente a los nuevos desafíos en el contexto de la mundialización del capital'. *Entrelíneas de la Política Económica*, n. 37 – Año 6/Diciembre de 2013.
Mani, S. (1992), *Foreign technology in public enterprises*. Oxford and IBH Publishing CO, PVT, LTD.
Mani, S. (2001), 'Role of government in promoting innovation in the enterprise sector: An analysis of the Indian experience'. *Discussion Paper Series*. INTECH, The United Nations University.
Mani, S. (2009), 'The growth of knowledge-intensive entrepreneurship in India, 1991–2007'. *UNUWIDER, Research Paper* n. 2009/49. November 2009.
Mani, S. (2014a), 'Financing innovation: India'. In Kahn, M., Martins de Melo, L. and Matos, M. (eds.), *Financing innovation*. Routledge.
Mani, S. (2014b December 6), 'Emergence of Indian as the world leader in computer and information services'. *Economic and Political weekly*, v. XLIX, n. 49.
Mann, M. (1986), *The sources of social power*, v. 1. *A history of power from the beginning to AD 1760*. Cambridge University Press.

Mann, M. (1993), *The sources of social power*, v.2. *The rise of classes and nation states, 1760–1914*. Cambridge University Press.
Mann, M. (2012a), *The sources of social power*, v. 3. *Global empires and revolution, 1890–1945*. Cambridge University Press.
Mann, M. (2012b), *The sources of social power*, v. 4. *Global Globalizations, 1945–2011*. Cambridge University Press.
Margariti, R. (2008), 'Mercantile networks, port cities, and "pirate" states: Conflict and competition in the Indian Ocean World of trade before the sixteenth century'. *Journal of the Economic and Social History of the Orient*, v. 51, pp. 543–577.
Marks, R. (2007), *The origins of the modern world: A global and ecological narrative from the fifteenth to the twenty-first century*. Rowman & Littlefield Publishers, Inc.
Marx, K. (1853), La dominación británica en la India. C. Marx and F. Engels, Obras Escogidas, en tres tomos, Editorial Progreso, Moscú, 1974; t. I.
Mazzucato, M. (2013), *O estado empreendedor* (E. Serapicos, Trans.). Portfolio Penguin.
Medeiros, C. (1997), 'Globalização e inserção internacional diferenciada na Ásia e A. Latina'. em Tavares, M.C. e Fiori, J.L. (eds.), *Poder e Dinheiro*. Vozes.
Medeiros, C. (2001), 'Rivalidade estatal, instituições e desenvolvimento econômico'. em Fiori, J. e Medeiros, C. (eds.), *Polarização Mundial e Crescimento*, Vozes.
Medeiros, C. (2003), 'The post-war American technological development as a military enterprise'. *Contributions to Political Economy*, v. 22, n. 1, pp. 41–62.
Medeiros, C. (2010 December), 'Instituições e desenvolvimento econômico: uma nota crítica ao "nacionalismo metodológico" '. *Economia e Sociedade, Campinas*, v. 19, n. 3 (40), pp. 637–645.
Medeiros, C. (2011), 'The political economy of the rise and decline of developmental states'. *Panoeconomics*, v. 1, pp. 43–56.
Medeiros, C. (2013), 'Estratégias nacionais de desenvolvimento'. In Santos, M. (ed.), *Padrões de Desenvolvimento Econômico (1950–2008): América Latina, Ásia e Rússia'*, v. 2. CGEE.
Medeiros, C. (2020 Jan./Abr.), '70 anos do Manifesto da CEPAL: Ontem e hoje'. *Revista de Economia Contemporanea*, v. 24, n. 1.
Metcalf, B. and Metcalf, T. (2013), *História concisa da Índia moderna*. Edipro.
Ministry of Statistics and Programme Implementation (MOSPI). https://www.mospi.gov.in/; https://training.niip.gov.in/web/mospi/annual-reports
Mishra, R., Kolluru, S. and Raveendran, J. (2013), *Technology mapping in Indian Central Public Sector Enterprises. Challenges of heightened competition*. Academic Foundation.
Mishra, R. and Kumar, V. (2012), *India´s energy transition. Possibilities and prospects*. Academic Foundation.
Morris, M. (1963), 'Towards a reinterpretation of nineteenth century Indian economic history'. *Journal of Economic History*, v. 23, n. 4, pp. 662–684.
Mowery, D. (2008), 'National security and national innovation systems'. *Journal of Technoly Transference*, v. 34, pp. 455–473. doi: 10.1007/s10961-008-9100-4
Mukherjee, A. (1986), 'The Indian capitalist class: Aspects of its economic, political and ideological development in the colonial period, 1927–1947'. In Bhattacharya, S. and Thapar, R. (eds.), *Situating Indian history for Sarvepalli Gopal*, 239–287. Oxford University Press.

Nabar-Bhaduri, S. and Vernengo, M. (2012), 'Service-led growth and the balance of payments constraint in India: An unsustainable strategy'. *Working Paper*, n. 2012–06, June 2012, University of Utah, Department of Economics.

Nagaraj, R. (2006), 'Public Sector Performance since 1950'. *A Fresh Look. Economic and Political Weekly*. June 24, 2006.

Nagaraj, R. (2008), *Disinvestment and privatization in India: Assessment and options. Trade policy, industrial performance and private sector development in India*. OUP.

Nagaraj, R. (2013a), 'India's economic development'. In Kohli, A. and Singh, P. (eds.), *Routledge Handbook of Indian Politics*. Routledge.

Nagaraj, R. (2013b May 18), 'India's dream run, 2003–08 understanding the boom and its aftermath'. *Economic & Political Weekly*, v. XLVIII, n. 2.

Nagaraj, R. (2014/2015 November 7), 'Size and structure of India's private corporate sector implications for the new GDP series'. *Economic & Political Weekly*, v. L, n. 45.

Nagaraj, R. (2015 March 28), 'Seeds of doubt on new GDP numbers'. *Economic and Political Weekly*, v. 50, n. 13.

Nagaraj, R. (2016 April 02), 'Unorganized sector output in the new GDP series'. *Economic and Political Weekly*, v. 51, n. 14.

Nagaraj, R. (2017a January 14), 'Economic reforms and manufacturing sector growth'. *EPW*, v. 52, n. 2.

Nagaraj, R. (2017b March 11), 'Quarterly GDP estimation'. *Economic and Political Weekly*, v. 52, n. 10.

Nah, J.W. and Lavoie, M. (2016), 'Convergence in a neo-Kaleckian model with endogenous technical progress and autonomous demand growth'. *Working Paper*.

Nair, V. (2005), 'Determinants of fixed investment: A study of Indian private corporate manufacturing sector'. *Working Paper 369*, Center for Development Studies.

Namboodiripad, E.M.S. (1973), 'Chile and the parliamentary road to socialism'. *Social Scientist*, v. 2, n. 5, pp. 3–14.

Naoroji, D. (1901), *Poverty and un-British rule in India*. Swan Sonnenschein.

NASSCOM. (2017 May), *Jobs and skills: The imperative to reinvent and disrupt*. NASSCOM.

Nayyar, D. (2013), *A corrida pelo crescimento. Países em desenvolvimento na economia mundial*. Contraponto.

Nayyar, D. (2015 August 15), Birth, life and death of development finance institutions in India. *Economic and Political Weekly*, v. L, n. 33.

Nayyar, D. (2017 January 14), 'Economic liberalization in India. Then and now'. *Economic and Political Weekly*, v. LII, n. 2.

Nehru, J. (1936/2017), *An autobiography. Toward freedom*. Penguin Books India.

Nehru, J. (1946), *The discovery of India*. Penguin Books India.

Nehru, J. (1963), 'Changing India'. *Foreign Affairs*, v. 41, n. 3, pp. 453–465.

Nell, K. (2012/2013), 'An alternative explanation of India's growth transition: A demand-side hypothesis'. *Cambridge Journal of Economics*, v. 37, pp. 113–141.

Nelson, R. (1977), *The moon and the Ghetto: An essay on policy analysis*. W.W. Norton.

Nelson, R. (1993), *National innovation systems: A comparative analysis*. Oxford University Press.

Niosi, J., Saviotti, P., Bellon, B. and Crow, M. (1993), 'National systems of innovations: In search of a workable concept'. *Technology in Society*, v. 15, pp. 207–227.

Ogden, C. (2011), 'India and nuclear weapons. India´s relations with the USA'. In Scott, D. (ed.), *Handbook of India's international relations*. Routledge.

Panagariya, A. (2008), *India: The emerging giant*. Oxford University Press.

Panikkar, K. (1953), *Asia and western dominance*. George Allen & Unwin.

Pant, H. (2011), 'Indian strategic culture: The debate and its consequences'. In Scott, D. (ed.), *Handbook of India's international relations*. Routledge.

Papola, T. and Kannan, K. (2017), 'Towards an India wage report'. *ILO Asia-Pacific Working Paper Series*, October 2017.

Pardesi, M. and Ganguly, S. (2009), 'Indian and energy security: A foreign policy priority'. In Pant, H. (ed.), *Indian foreign policy in a unipolar world*. Routledge India Paperbacks.

Parthasarathi, P. (2011), 'Why Europe grew rich and Asia did not'. Cambridge University Press.

Parthasarathy, B. (2004a), *Globalizing information technology: The domestic policy context for India's software production and exports*. The Charles Babbage Institute for the History of Information Technology.

Parthasarathy, B. (2004b September), 'India's silicon valley or silicon valley's India? Socially embedding the computer software industry in Bangalore'. *International Journal of Urban and Regional Research*, v. 28, n. 3, pp. 664–685.

Patel, S. (1993), *Technological self-reliance in India*. Ashish Publications.

Patnaik, P. (1998), 'Some Indian debates on planning'. In Byres, T.J. (ed.), *The Indian economy. Major debates since independence*, Oxford University Press.

Patnaik, P. (2009), 'A Perspective on the growth process in India and China', *The IDEAs Working Paper Series*, 05/2009.

Patnaik, U. (2017), 'Revisiting the 'drain', or transfers from India to Britain in the context of global diffusion of capitalism'. In Chakrabarti, S. and Patnaik, U. (eds.), *Agrarian and other histories essays for Binay Bhushan Chaudhuri*, Tulika Books.

Pedersen, J. (2000), 'Explaining economic liberalization in India: State and society perspectives'. *World Development*, v. 28, n 2, pp. 265–282.

Pedersen, J. (2008), *Globalization, development and the state: The performance of India and Brazil since 1990*. Palgrave Macmillan.

Pérez, C. (2001), 'Cambio tecnológico y oportunidades de desarrollo como blanco móvil'. *Revista de la CEPAL*, v. 75, pp. 115–136.

Pérez, C. (2010), 'Technological revolutions and techno-economic paradigms'. *Cambridge Journal of Economics*, v. 34, n. 1, pp. 185–202.

Pérez Candeltey, E. and Vernengo, M. (2016 April), 'Raúl Prebisch and economic dynamics: Cyclical growth and centre-periphery interaction'. *Revista de la CEPAL*, v. 118.

Pérez Candeltey, E. and Vernengo, M. (2018), 'Heterodox central banking in the periphery'. In *Including a Symposium on Latin American Monetary thought: Two centuries in search of originality*. Published online: November 06, 2018; 81–100.

Pérez Candeltey, E., Vernengo, M. and Torres, M. (2019), 'Raúl Prebisch y su faceta de banquero central y doctor monetario (textos publicados e inéditos de la década de 1940)'. In *Revista CEPAL*, suplemento especial (LC/PUB.2019/28-P), Comisión Económica para América Latina y el Caribe (CEPAL).

Pinto, A. (1970 janeiro-março), 'Naturaleza e implicancias de la 'heterogeneidad estructural' en América Latina'. *El Trimestre Económico, México, Fondo de Cultura Económica*, v. 37, n. 145.
Pinto, A. (1972), 'La "heterogeneidad estructural": aspecto fundamental del desarrollo latinoamericano'. *Documentos de la CEPAL*, 1972.
Pinto, A. (1984), 'Metropolization and tertiarization: Structural distortions in Latin American development'. *CEPAL Review*, n. 24, pp. 17–38.
Pinto, A. and Di Filippo, A. (1982), 'Desarrollo y pobreza en América Latina: un enfoque histórico estructural'. *Pobreza, necesidades básicas y desarrollo* – E/ICEF/TACRO/G.1006–1982 – pp. 133–155.
Polanyi, K. (1944), *The great transformation*. Beacon Press.
Pomeranz, K. (2000), *The great divergence. China, Europe and the making of the modern world economy*. Princeton University Press.
Possas, M. (1987), *Dinâmica da economia capitalista: uma abordagem teórica*. Brasiliense.
Possas, M. and Baltar, P. (1983), 'O modelo de ciclo econômico de Kalecki'. *Revista de Econometria*, April 1983.
Prakash, G. (1999), *Another reason: Science and the imagination of modern India*. Princeton University Press.
Prakash, O. (1990), 'The transfer of science and technology between Asia and Europe'. *Itinerario*, v. 14, n. 2, pp. 15–21.
Prakash, O. (2008), *The New Cambridge history of India. European commercial enterprise in pre-colonial India*. Cambridge University Press.
Prakash, O. (2009), 'From market-determined to coercion-based: Textile manufacturing in eighteenth-century Bengal'. In Riello, G. and Roy, T. (eds.), *How India clothed the world. The world of South Asian textiles, 1500–1850*. BRILL.
Prebisch, R. (1949/1962 fevereiro de), 'El desarrollo económico de América Latina y algunos de sus principales problemas'. *Bolletín Económico de la Amércia Latina*, v. VII, n. 1, pp. 1–24.
Prebisch, R. (1950), 'Estudio económico de América Latina, 1949'. *Serie conmemorativa del XXV aniversario da CEPAL*, Santiago de Chile 1973.
Prebisch, R. (1951), 'Problemas teóricos y prácticos Del crecimiento económico'. *Serie conmemorativa del XXV aniversario da CEPAL*, Santiago de Chile 1973.
Qaisar, A.J. (1982), *The Indian Response to European Technology and Culture (a.d. 1498–1707)*. Oxford University Press.
Raheja, G. (1994), 'Caste system'. In Stearns, P.N. (ed.), *Encyclopedia of social History*. Garland Publishing.
Rajamaram, V. (2012), *History of computing in India (1955–2010)*. Indian Institute of Science, Bangalore.
Rakshit, M. (2009), *Macroeconomics of post reform India*. Oxford University Press.
Rangel, I. (2012), *Obras reunidas*, v. 1. Contraponto editora Limitada.
Rao, C. (2008), 'Science and technology policies: The case of India'. *Technology in Society*, v. 30, n. 3, pp. 242–247.
Rao, M. and Storm, S. (1998), 'Distribution and growth in Indian agriculture'. In Byres, T.J. (ed.), *The Indian economy. Major debates since independence*, Oxford University Press.
Ray, I. (2016), 'The myth and reality of deindustrialization in early modern India'. In Chaudhary, L., Gupta, B., Roy, T. and Swamy, A. (eds.), *A new economic history of colonial India*. Routledge, New York.

Ray, R. (1984), *Social conflict and political unrest in Bengal, 1875–1927*. Oxford University Press.

Ray, S.K. (2014), 'Reforms in land system in post-independent India'. In Kapila, U. (ed.), *Indian economy since independence*. Twenty fourth edition. Academic Foundation.

Raychaudhuri, T. (1982a), 'Non-agricultural production'. In Raychaudhuri, T. and Habib, I. (eds.), *The Cambridge economic history of India*. v. 1: c.1200-c.1750. Cambridge University Press.

Raychaudhuri, T. (1982b), 'The Mughal Empire'. In Raychaudhuri, T. and Habib, I. (eds.), *The Cambridge economic history of India*. v. 1: C.1200-C.1750. Cambridge University Press.

Raychaudhuri, T. (1983), 'The mid-eighteenth-century background'. In Kumar, D. and Raychaudhuri, T. (eds.), *The Cambridge economic history of India*. v. 2: c. 1757-c. 1970. Cambridge Press.

Reddy, S.V. (2011), 'India and outer space'. In Scott, D. (ed.), *Handbook of India's international relations*. Routledge.

Reinert, E. (1999), 'The role of the state in economic growth'. *Journal of Economic Studies*, v. 26, n. 4/5, pp. 268–326.

Rekhade, R. (2017), 'Will India ever be a great power? Here's what Bharat Karnad has to say about it'. *Swarajya's Interview*. https://swarajyamag.com/defence/will-india-ever-be-a-great-power-heres-what-bharat-karnad-has-to-say-about-it (accessed 31 March 2018).

Richards, J. (1993), 'The Mughal Empire'. In *The New Cambridge history of India*, v. 1.5. Cambridge University Press.

Ricupero, B. (1999), 'Caio Prado Jr.: o primeiro marxista brasileiro'. *Revista USP*, n. 38, pp. 64–77. https://doi.org/10.11606/issn.2316-9036.v0i38p64-77

Riello, G. and Roy, T. (2009), 'How India clothed the world'. In *The World of South Asian Textiles, 1500–1850*. BRILL.

Rodríguez, O. (2006), *O estruturalismo latino-americano*. CEPAL.

Rodrik, D. and Subramanian, A. (2005), 'From 'Hindu growth' to productivity surge: The mystery of the Indian growth transition'. *IMF Staff Papers*, v. 52, n. 2, pp. 193–228.

Rodrik, D. and Subramanian, A. (2008), 'Le mystère de la transition de l'Inde: de la "croissance hindoue" au boom de la productivité'. In Rodrik, D. (eds.), *Nations et mondialisation: les stratégies nationales de développement dans un monde globalicé*, 95–134. Éditions la Découverte.

Rothermund, D. (1988), *An economic history of India. From pre-colonial times to 1991*. Routledge.

Roy, T. (2000), 'De-industrialization: Alternative view'. *Economic and Political Weekly*, v. 35, n. 17, pp. 507–523.

Roy, T. (2012a), *India in the world economy: From antiquity to the present*. Cambridge University Press.

Roy, T. (2012b), *The East India company: The world's most powerful corporation*. Allen Lane.

Sachdeva, G. (2011a), 'Geoeconomics and energy for India'. In Scott, D. (ed.), *Handbook of India's international relations*. Routledge.

Sachdeva, G. (2011b), 'India´s relations with Russia'. In Scott, D. (ed.), *Handbook of India's international relations*. Routledge.

Saxenian, A. (2005 Summer), 'From brain drain to brain circulation: Transnational communities and regional upgrading in India and China'. *Studies in Comparative International Development*, v. 40, n. 2, pp. 35–61.

Scerri, M. and Lastres, H. (2013), *The role of the state. BRICS, national systems of innovation*. Routledge.

Scherer, M. (2007), *A relação entre crescimento e distribuição de renda na economia do desenvolvimento: do modelo de Lewis a Belindia*. Master Thesis, PPGE-IE-UFRJ.

Schvarzer, J. (1996), *La industria que supimos conseguir. Uma historia político social de La industria argentina*. Planeta.

Scott, D. (2011), 'India´s relations with the USA'. In Scott, D. (ed.), *Handbook of India's international relations*. Routledge.

Sen, A. (1977), 'Starvation and exchange entitlements: A general approach and its application to the Great Bengal famine'. *Cambridge Journal of Economics*, v. I.

Sen, A. (1980), 'Famines'. *World Development*, v. 8, n. 9, pp. 613–621.

Serra, A. (1613), *Breve trattato delle cause che possono far abbondare l'oro el'argento dove non sono miniere*. Lazzaro Scorriggio.

Serrano, F. (1995), *The Sraffian supermultiplier*. PhD Dissertation. University of Cambridge.

Serrano, F. (2001), *A Acumulação e o Gasto Improdutivo na Economia do Desenvolvimento*. IE-UFRJ.

Serrano, F. (2016), 'Garegnani´s Svimez Report, development economics and the role of government spending in long run growth. Il ruolo della domanda nello sviluppo: il Mezzogiorno italiano, i Sud del mondo e la crisi dell'Europa', *Centro Sraffa, UniRomaTre*, venerdì ottobre 14, 2016.

Serrano, F. and Freitas, F. (2017), 'The Sraffian supermultiplier as an alternative closure for heterodox growth theory'. *European Journal of Economics and Economic Policies*, v. 14, n. 1, pp. 70–91.

Serrano, F. and Medeiros, C. (2004 abril-junho), 'O Desenvolvimento Econômico e a Retomada da Abordagem Clássica do Excedente'. *Revista de Economia Política*, v. 24, n. 2 (94), pp. 244–263.

Seth, V. (1986 October), 'State and spatial aspects of industrialization in post-independence India'. *Political Geography Quarterly*, v. 5, n. 4, pp. 331–350.

Sharif, N. (2006), 'Emergence and development of the National innovation systems concept'. *Research Policy*, v. 35, n. 5, pp. 745–766.

Sharma, M. (2019), *Allahu Akbar. Understanding the great Mughal in today's India*. Bloomsbury India.

Shiva, V. (1991), *The violence of the green revolution: Third world agriculture, ecology and politics*. The Other India Press.

Sikka, P. (2008), *Science policy. New strategies for India´s modernization*. Uppal Publishing House.

SIPRI. (2018), 'Trends in international arms transfers, 2017'. *SIPRI Fact Sheet*, 2018.

Sirohi, R.A. (2019), *From developmentalism to neoliberalism: A comparative analysis of Brazil and India*. Palgrave Macmillan.

Skocpol, T. (1985), 'Bringing the state back in: Strategies of analyses in current research'. In Evans, P., Rueschemeyer, D. and Skocpol, T. (eds.), *Bringing the state back in*. Cambridge University Press.

Subrahmanyam, S. (1988), 'A note on Narsapur Peta: A 'syncretic' shipbuilding center in South India, 1570–1700'. *Journal of the Economic and Social History of the Orient*, v. 31, n. 3, pp. 305–311.

Subrahmanyam, S. (1990), *The political economy of commerce: southern India, 1500–1650*. Cambridge University Press.

Subrahmanyam, S. (2012), *The Portuguese empire in Asia, 1500–1700: A political and economic history*. John Wiley & Sons Ltd.

Subrahmanyam, S. and Thomaz, L.F. (1991), 'Evolution of empire: The Portuguese in the Indian Ocean during the sixteenth century'. In Tracy, J.D. (ed.), *The political economy of merchant empires, state power and world trade 1350–1750*, 304. Cambridge.

Sweeney, S. (2011), *Financing India´s imperial railway, 1875–1914*. Pickering and Chatto.

Sztulwark, S. (2003), *El estructuralismo latinoamericano. Fundamentos y transformaciones del pensamiento económico de la periferia*. UNGS-Prometeo.

Tavares, M.C. (1973), *Da Substituição da Importações ao Capitalismo Financeiro*. 3ª Edição. Zahar.

Tavares, M.C. (1976/1986), *Acumulação de capital e industrialização no Brasil*. Instituto de Economia da INICAMP, Editora Unicamp.

Tavares, M.C. (1978/1986), *Ciclo e crise*. Instituto de Economia da INICAMP, Editora Unicamp.

Tavares, M.C. (1999), 'Imperio, territorio e dinheiro'. In Fiori, L. (ed.), *Estados e moedas no desenvolvimento das Nações*, Ed. Vozes.

Tavares, M.C. and Serra, J. (1971), 'Más allá del estancamento: una discusión sobre el estilo de desarrollo reciente'. *El Trimestre Económico, México*, v. 38, n. 152 (4), pp. 905–950, 1971 reproduced in Bielschowsky, R. (ed.), *Cinquenta anos de pensamento da CEPAL*, v. 1. CEPAL, 2000.

Taylor, L. (1979), 'Luxury as the fruit of misery in the modern sector'. In *Macro Models For Developing Countries*. McGraw-Hill.

Taylor, L. and Bacha, L. (1976 maio), 'The unequalizing spiral: A first growth model for Belindia'. *Quarterly Journal of Economics*, v. 90, n. 2, pp. 197–218.

Thomas, J. (2015), 'India´s labour market during the 2000s: An overview'. In Ramaswamy, K.V. (ed.), *Labour, Employment and Economic Growth in India*, 21–56. Cambridge University Press.

Tomlinson, B.R. (1979), *The political economy of the Raj, 1914–1947: The economics of decolonization in India*. Palgrave Macmillan London.

Tranum, S. (2013), *Powerless: India's energy shortage and its impact*. Sage Publications India.

Tyabji, N. (1989), *The small industries policy in India*. Oxford University Press.

Vaidyanathan, A. (1994), 'Performance of Indian agriculture since independence'. In Basu, K. (ed.), *Agrarian questions*. Oxford University Press.

Vernengo, M. (2006), 'Technology, finance, and dependency: Latin American radical political economy in retrospect'. *Review of Radical Political Economics*, v. 38, n. 4, pp. 551–568.

Vernengo, M. (2020), 'From developmentalism to neoliberalism in Latin America'. In Trincado, E., Lazzarini, A. and Melnik, D. (eds.), *Ideas in the history of economic development. The case of peripheral countries*. Routledge Studies in the History of Economics. Routledge.

Vidal, C. e Marí, M. (2002), 'La Escuela Latinoamericana de Pensamiento en Ciencia, Tecnología y Desarrollo. Notas de un Proyecto de Investigación'. *Revista Iberoamericana de Ciencia Tecnología e Innovación*, n. 4. Septiembre-Diciembre 2002.

Visara, L. and Visara, P. (1983), 'Population (1757–1947)'. In Kumar, D. and Raychaudhuri, T. (eds.), *The Cambridge economic history of India*. Cambridge Press.

Vries, P. (2016), *What we do and do not know about the great divergence at the beginning of 2016*. Researchgate.

Wade, R. (1990), *Governing the market: Economic theory and the role of government in East Asian industrialization*. Princeton University Press.

Wallerstein, I. (1986), 'Incorporation of Indian Subcontinent into capitalist world-economy'. *Economic and Political Weekly*, v. 21, n. 4, pp. 28–39.

Williamson, J. (2008), 'Globalization and great divergence: Terms of trade booms, volatility and the poor periphery, 1782–1913'. *European Review of Economic History*, v. 12, n. 3, pp. 355–391.

Wilson, P. (2003), *Wars, proxy-wars and terrorism: Post independent India*. Mittal Publications.

World Bank. (1990), *India: Strategy for trade reform*. Report No 8998-IN, v. 3.

Zelliot, E. (1988), 'Congress and untouchables, 1917–1950'. In Sisson, R. and Wolpert, S. (eds.), *Congress and Indian nationalism*, 182–197. Oxford University Press.

INDEX

For Product Safety Concerns and Information please contact our EU representative GPSR@taylorandfrancis.com
Taylor & Francis Verlag GmbH, Kaufingerstraße 24, 80331 München, Germany

www.ingramcontent.com/pod-product-compliance
Ingram Content Group UK Ltd.
Pitfield, Milton Keynes, MK11 3LW, UK
UKHW020151200926
475702UK00016B/2649
* 9 7 8 1 0 3 2 3 6 7 3 0 9 *